The Migration Conference 2021
2021
Programme

Organised with support of:

The Migration Conference 2021 Book of Abstracts

compiled by
TMC2021 Team

TRANSNATIONAL PRESS LONDON
2021

Chair's Welcome

Dear colleagues,

We're pleased to welcome you to the 9th Migration Conference. The Migration Conference series attracted a few thousand colleagues over the last 10 years and surely become one of the largest continuous events on migration and the largest scholarly gathering with a global scope.

The conference covers all areas of social sciences, humanities, economics, business and management. More popular areas so far included work, employment, integration, refugees and asylum, migration policy and law, spatial patterns, culture, arts and legal and political aspects which are key areas in the current migration debates and research.

Throughout the program of the Migration Conference you will find various key thematic areas covered in over 300 presentations by about 500 contributors coming from all around the world, from Australia to Canada, China to Ecuador, Brazil to Japan, and South Africa to Norway. We are proud to bring together experts from universities, independent research organisations, governments, NGOs and the media.

Like TMC 2020, we are forced to organize the conference online due to ongoing COVID-19 related travel restrictions. Hopefully, the next TMC will be again a face to face event.

We are also proud to bring you opportunities to meet with some of the leading scholars in the field. This year invited speakers include Theresa Alfaro-Velcamp, Dr Élise Féron, Ruth Gomberg-Muñoz, James F. Hollifield, Camilla Orjuela, Pia M. Orrenius, Dr Rodolfo Cruz Piñeiro, and Hna. Leticia Gutiérrez Valderrama.

Although the main language of the conference is English, every year we host a good number of sessions in other languages. This year is not an exception as we will have sessions in English, French, Spanish, and Turkish.

The Migration Conference, as known to regulars, is an event marked by its frank and friendly environment where constructive criticism foster scholarship, while being nice improves networks and quality of the event. We hope to continue with this tradition.

We thank all participants, invited speakers and conference committees for their efforts and contribution. We also thank many colleagues who were interested in and submitted abstracts but could not make it this year. We are particularly grateful to colleagues who served as reviewers and helped us in the selection process.

We are grateful to the host organisations, International British Business School and Ming-Ai (London) Institute.

Please do not hesitate to get in touch with us through the conference email (migrationscholar@gmail.com).

Ibrahim **Sirkeci**, Chair

On behalf of The Migration Conference Committee

The Migration Conference 2021

The Migration Conference is a global venue for academics, policy makers, practitioners, students and everybody who is interested in intelligent debate and research informed discussions on human mobility and its impacts around the world. The Migration Conference 2021 is the 9th conference in the series and hosted online and organised by Migration Letters journal. The Migration Conferences were launched at the Regent's Centre for Transnational Studies in 2012 when the first large scale well attended international peer-reviewed conference with a focus on Turkish migration in Europe in Regent's Park campus of Regent's University London. The migration conferences have been attended by thousands of participants coming from all around the world in London (2012), London (2014), Prague (2015), Vienna (2016), Athens (2017), Lisbon (2018), Bari (2019), Tetovo - Online (2020).

The Migration Conference 2021 is organised with funding raised by registration fees.

Supporters of The Migration Conference 2021 include:

- Ming-Ai (London) Institute, United Kingdom (TMC2021 Host)
- Association Marocaine d'Etudes & de Recherches sur les Migrations (AMERM), Morocco
- Centre for Development Evaluation and Social Science Research (CREDI), Sarajevo, Bosnia and Herzegovina
- Global Migration Research Centre, Social Sciences University of Ankara, Turkey
- Institut de Recherche, Formation et Action sur les Migrations, Belgium
- Migration Institute, Finland
- Migration Policies Research Centre, Istanbul Ayvansaray University, Turkey
- Research Centre in Economic and Organizational Sociology (SOCIUS), Universidade de Lisboa, Portugal
- Ruhr-Universität Bochum, Centre for Mediterranean Studies, Germany
- Sino-German Economic Development and Innovation Research Centre, Hefei University, P.R. China
- The Global Mobility Project, The Ohio State University, USA
- Unidad Académica en Estudios del Desarrollo, Mexico
- Universidad de Burgos, Spain
- Universidad Latina de México, Mexico
- Universidad Tecnica Partocular de Loja, Ecuador
- Universität Hamburg, Germany
- University of California, Davis, Gifford Center for Population Studies, USA
- University of Nottingham, Faculty of Humanities and Social Sciences, China
- Urban Development and Social Research Association, Turkey
- Western Balkans Migration Network (WB-MIGNET), Bosnia and Herzegovina
- Yaşar University Jean Monnet Migration Chair, Turkey
- Association Marocaine d'Etudes & de Recherches sur les Migrations, Morocco

- Remittances Review
- Migration Letters
- Journal of Posthumanism
- International Journal of Religion
- Yeiya
- Göç Dergisi
- Journal of Gypsy Studies
- Border Crossing
- Kurdish Studies
- Transnational Press London, UK

Past Supporters of The Migration Conferences included:

- Faculty of Contemporary Social Sciences, South East European University
- University of Bari Aldo Moro, Italy
- Dipartimento di Scienze Politiche, University of Bari, Italy
- Puglia Regional Administration, Italy
- Municipality of Bari, Italy
- Regent's University London Centre for Transnational Business and Management, UK
- ISTAT (Italian National Statistics Office)
- Red Cross, Italy
- International Organisation for Migration, Italy
- Association Marocaine d'Etudes & de Recherches sur les Migrations, Morocco
- Ordine Assistenti Sociali Regione Puglia, Italy
- Tourism Office of Lisbon
- ISEG and IGOT, University of Lisbon
- University of California Gifford Center for Population Studies
- Universität Hamburg, Germany
- Ohio State University, Department of Anthropology
- Harokopio University, Athens
- Danube University Krems, Austria
- Albrecht Mendelssohn Bartholdy Graduate School of Law, Germany
- Institut de Recherche, Formation et Action sur les Migrations, Belgium
- EKKE – The National Center of Social Research, Greece
- Hellenic Sociological Society
- Charles University Prague Faculty of Humanities, Czech Republic
- Regent's University Centre for Transnational Studies, UK
- Danube University Krems, Austria
- University of Vienna, Austria
- Manisa Celal Bayar University Faculty of Economics and Administrative Sciences, Turkey
- Celal Bayar University Population and Migration Research Center, Turkey
- Ria Money Transfers
- Global Policy and Strategy, Ankara, Turkey
- J. Hornig Coffee
- Vienna Convention Bureau
- Remittances Review

- Migration Letters
- Journal of Posthumanism
- International Journal of Religion
- Yeiya
- Göç Dergisi
- Journal of Gypsy Studies
- Border Crossing
- Kurdish Studies
- Transnational Press London, UK
- RGS Population Studies Group, United Kingdom
- IUSSP International Migration Expert Panel
- Univerziti Servis Prague, Czech Republic
- Austrian Air – Official Carrier for TMC 2016

migrationconference.net

@migrationevent

fb.me/MigrationConference

Email: migrationscholar@gmail.com

CONTENT and TIMETABLE

People
The Migration Conference Executive Committee
Prof Ibrahim Sirkeci, International British Business School, UK (Chair)
Prof Jeffrey H. Cohen, Ohio State University, USA
Prof Philip L Martin, University of California Davis, USA

The Migration Conference Transnational Advisory Committee
Prof Deborah Anker, Harvard University, United States
Prof Gudrun Biffl, Krems, Austria
Prof Lucinda Fonseca, University of Lisbon, Portugal
Prof Elli Heikkila, Migration Institute of Finland, Finland
Prof Mohamed Khachani, AMERM & University of Rabat, Morocco
Prof Beatrice Knerr, Kassell University, Germany and Hefei University, China
Prof Markus Kotzur, Universität Hamburg, Germany
Prof Jonathan Liu, Global Banking School, UK
Prof Apostolos G Papadopoulos, Harokopio University of Athens, Greece
Prof João Peixoto, University of Lisbon, Portugal
Prof Michela C. Pellicani, University of Bari "Aldo Moro", Italy
Prof Giuseppe Sciortino, University of Trento, Italy

The Migration Conference Scientific Committee
Africa
Agnes Igoye, Ministry of Interior Affairs, Uganda
Prof Mohamed Khachani, AMERM & University of Rabat, Morocco
Dr Rania Rafik Khalil, The British University in Egypt, Egypt
Dr Sadhana Manik, University of KwaZulu-Natal, South Africa
Prof Claude Sumata, National Pedagogical University, DR Congo
Dr Ayman Zohry, Egyptian Society for Migration Studies, Egypt

Americas
Dr Bharati Basu, Central Michigan University, USA
Prof Jeffrey H. Cohen, Ohio State University, USA
Dr José Salvador Cueto-Calderón, Universidad Autónoma de Sinaloa, Mexico
Dr Ana Vila Freyer, Universidad Latina de México, Mexico
Dr Pascual Gerardo García-Macías, Universidad Técnica Particular de Loja, Ecuador
Dr Torunn Haaland, Gonzaga University, USA
Prof Liliana Jubilut, Universidade Católica de Santos, Brazil
Prof Philip L Martin, University of California Davis, USA
Dr Eric M. Trinka, James Madison University, USA
Karla Angélica Valenzuela-Moreno, Universidad Iberoamericana, Mexico
Dr Hassan Vatanparast, Saskatchewan University, Canada
Prof Rodolfo García Zamora, Autonomous University of Zacatecas, Mexico
Dr Monette Zard, Columbia University, USA

Asia-Pacific
Prof Ram Bhagat, International Institute for Population Sciences, India

Dr Amira Halperin, University of Nottingham Ningbo, P.R. China
Dr Sadaf Mahmood, Government College University, Pakistan
Dr Shweta Sinha Deshpande, Symbiosis School for Liberal Arts, India
Prof Nicholas Procter, University of South Australia, Australia
Dr Ruchi Singh, Prin.L.N.Welingkar Institute of Management Development &
Research, India
Dr AKM Ahsan Ullah, University Brunei Darussalam, Brunei
Dr Zhongwei Xing, University of Technology Brunei, Brunei
Dr Xi Zhao, Hefei University, P.R. China

Eastern Europe
Dr Merita Zulfiu-Alili, South East European University, N. Macedonia
Dr Olga R. Gulina, RUSMPI- Institute on Migration Policy, Russian Federation
Dr Tuncay Bilecen, Kocaeli University, Turkey, UK
Prof Dilek Cindoglu, Kadir Has University, Turkey
Dr Yaprak Civelek, Anadolu University, Turkey
Dr Z. Banu Dalaman, Istanbul Ayvansaray University, Turkey
Dr Sevim Atilla Demir, Sakarya University, Turkey
Prof Vladimir Iontsev, Moscow State University, Russian Federation
Dr İnci Aksu Kargın, Uşak University, Turkey
Prof Sebnem Koser Akcapar, Ankara Social Sciences University, Turkey
Dr Oksana Koshulko, Alfred Nobel University, Ukraine
Dr Murat Lehimler, Urban Development and Social Research Association,
Turkey
Dr Armagan Teke Lloyd, Abdullah Gul University, Turkey
Dr Vildan Mahmutoğlu, Galatasaray University, Turkey
Dr Nermin Oruc, Centre for Development Evaluation and Social Science
Research (CREDI), Sarajevo, Bosnia and Herzegovina
Dr Gökay Özerim, Yaşar University, Turkey
Prof Irina Savchenko, Linguistics University of Nizhny Novgorod, Russian
Federation
Prof Ali Tilbe, Tekirdag Namik Kemal University, Turkey
Dr Fethiye Tilbe, Namik Kemal University, Turkey
Dr Onur Unutulmaz, Ankara Social Sciences University, Turkey
Dr Deniz Eroglu Utku, Trakya University, Turkey
Dr Pınar Yazgan, Sakarya University, Turkey
Dr Sinan Zeyneloglu, Kent University, Turkey

Europe
Dr Nirmala Devi Arunasalam, Oxford Brookes University, United Kingdom
Dr Bahar Baser, Coventry University, United Kingdom
Dr Gülseli Baysu, Queen's University Belfast, United Kingdom
Prof Petra Bendel, Friedrich-Alexander University of Erlangen-Nuremberg,
Germany
Dr Gul Ince Beqo, University of Bari, Italy
Prof Aron Anselem Cohen, University of Granada, Spain
Dr Martina Cvajner, University of Trento, Italy
Dr Carla de Tona, Independent Researcher, Italy

Dr Sureya Sonmez Efe, University of Lincoln, United Kingdom
Dr Deniz Cosan Eke, University of Vienna, Austria
Dr Alina Esteves, Universidade de Lisboa, Portugal
Dr Sarah E. Hackett, Bath Spa University, United Kingdom
Dr Serena Hussain, Coventry University, United Kingdom
Prof Monica Ibáñez-Angulo, University of Burgos, Spain
Prof Markus Koller, Ruhr University Bochum, Germany
Dr Emre Eren Korkmaz, University of Oxford, United Kingdom
Prof Jonathan Liu, Ming-Ai (London) Institute, United Kingdom
Dr Altay Manço, Institut de Recherche, Formation et Action sur les Migrations, Belgium
Dr A. Erdi Öztürk, London Metropolitan University, United Kingdom
Isabella Piracci, Avvocatura Generale dello Stato, Rome, Italy
Dr Sahizer Samuk-Carignani, University of Pisa, Italy
Prof Giuseppe Sciortino, University of Trento, Italy
Dr Selma Akay Sert, University College London, UK
Dr Caner Tekin, Ruhr-Universität Bochum, Germany
Irene Tuzi, Sapienza University of Rome, Italy
Dr Emilia Lana de Freitas Castro, Berlin, Germany
Dr Ülkü Sezgi Sözen, University of Hamburg, Germany

Near East
Dr Rania M Rafik Khalil, The British University in Egypt, Egypt
Dr Simeon Magliveras, King Fahd University of Petroleum and Minerals, Saudi Arabia
Dr Bradley Saunders, American University of Bahrain, Bahrain
Dr Paulette K. Schuster, Hebrew University Jerusalem, Israel
Dr Omar Al Serhan, Higher Colleges of Technology, United Arab Emirates
Dr Md Mizanur Rahman, Qatar University, Qatar
Dr Liat Yaknich, Beit Berl College, Israel

The Migration Conference Local Organisation Committee
Prof Ibrahim Sirkeci, International British Business School, UK (Chair)
Dr Nirmala Devi Arunasalam, Oxford Brookes University, United Kingdom
Dr A. Erdi Öztürk, London Metropolitan University, United Kingdom
Dr Aytac Yerden, Gedik University, Turkey (IT)
Ege Cakir, Middle East Technical University, Turkey (Admin)
Cagdas Torbacioglu, Transnational Press London, UK (Admin)
Nihal Yazgan, Transnational Press London, UK (Admin)

Keynote speakers at TMC 2021
The Migration Conferences team are proud to have leading scholars in the field as keynote speakers whose details are listed below.

Theresa Alfaro-Velcamp, Emeritus Professor, Sonoma State University, USA
Dr **Élise Féron**, Tampere Peace Research Institute, Tampere University, Finland
Ruth Gomberg-Muñoz, Associate Professor, Department of Anthropology, Loyola University Chicago, USA
James F. Hollifield, Director of the Tower Center for Public Policy and International Affairs at Southern Methodist University, Dallas, USA
Camilla Orjuela, Professor, School of Global Studies, University of Gothenburg, Sweden
Pia M. Orrenius, Vice President and Senior Economist Federal Reserve Bank of Dallas, USA
Dr **Rodolfo Cruz Piñeiro**, Director, Departamento de Estudios de Población, El Colegio de la Frontera Norte, Mexico
Hna. **Leticia Gutiérrez Valderrama**, Scalabrinian Missionary, founder of SMR and Sergio Mendez Arceo National Human Rights Prize in Mexico; Diocesan Delegate for Migration – Diocese of Sigüenza-Guadalajara-Spain

---

In previous years, The Migration Conferences entertained distinguished scholars delivering keynote speeches including:

Martina Cvajner, University of Trento, Italy [2020], Jelena Dzankic, European University Institute, Italy [2020], Nissa Finney, University of St Andrews, UK [2020], Elli Heikkilä, Migration Institute of Finland, Finland [2020], Agnes Igoye, Ministry of Internal Affairs, Uganda [2020], Helén Nilsson, Nordic Council of Ministers Office in Lithuania [2020], Giuseppe Brescia, MP, Parliamento Italiano, Italy [2020], Markus Kotzur, Universität Hamburg, Germany [2019], Karsten Paerregaard, Gothenburg University, Sweden [2019], Martin Ruhs, European University Institute, Italy [2019], Carlos Vargas Silva, University of Oxford, UK [2019], Sasskia Sassen, Columbia University, USA [2017], Oded Stark, U of Bonn, Germany [2017], Giuseppe Sciortino, University of Trento, Italy [2017], Joaquin Arango, Complutense University of Madrid, Spain [2018], Ruba Salih, SOAS, University of London, UK [2018], Fiona B. Adamson, SOAS, University of London, UK [2019], Pedro Calado, The High Commissioner for Migration, Lisbon, Portugal [2018], Ferruccio Pastore, FIERI – Forum of International and European Research on Immigration, Italy [2019], Michelle Leighton, International Labour Organization, Genève, Switzerland [2018], Yuksel Pazarkaya, Novelist, Turkey [2017], Caroline Brettell, Southern Methodist University, USA [2015], Barry Chiswick, George Washington University, USA [2014], Karen Phalet, KU Leuven, Belgium [2016], Douglas S. Massey, Princeton University, USA [2015], Ibrahim Sirkeci, Regent's University London, UK [2014, 2016], Jeffrey H. Cohen, Ohio State University, USA [2012, 2015, 2018, 2019, 2020], Samim Akgonul, Strasbourg University,

France [2016], Kemal Kirisci, Bogazici University, Turkey [2012], Nedim Gürsel, CNRS, CETOBaC & INALCO, France, Turkey [2015], Philip L. Martin, University of California, Davis, USA [2014, 2015, 2018, 2019, 2020], Tariq Modood, University of Bristol, United Kingdom [2012].

6 July 2021, Tuesday | DAY 1
11:45-12:30 – Welcome Reception and Opening Panel [Click here to Join]
– Welcoming Speeches:
- **Ibrahim Sirkeci**, IBBS, UK (Chair)
- **Chungwen Li**, Ming Ai (London) Institute, UK (Hosting Chair)
- **Jeffrey H. Cohen**, Ohio State University, USA (Executive Committee)
12:30-12:45 – Break
12:45-14:15 – Parallel Sessions I
14:15-14:30 – Break
14:30-16:00 – Parallel Sessions II
16:00-16:15 – Break

16:15-18:00 – Plenary Session I [Click here to Join]
Moderator: Jeffrey H. Cohen, Professor of Anthropology, Ohio State University, USA
Keynote Speakers:
- **Ruth Gomberg-Muñoz**, Associate Professor, Department of Anthropology, Loyola University Chicago, USA:
  "Alienating Citizenship: Insights from Mexico's Deported and Returned Community"
- **Theresa Alfaro-Velcamp**, Emeritus Professor, Sonoma State University, USA:
  "Commodification and Recalibration in Migration: Reflections from the Global South"

---

7 July 2021, Wednesday | DAY 2
10:45-12:15 – Parallel Sessions III
12:15-12:45 – Break
12:45-14:15 – Parallel Sessions IV
14:15-14:30 – Break
14:30-16:00 – Parallel Sessions V
16:00-16:15 – Break

16:15-18:00 – Plenary Session II [Click here to Join]
Moderator: Philip L. Martin, Emeritus Professor, University of California, Davis, USA
Keynote Speakers:
- **James F. Hollifield**, Director of the Tower Center for Public Policy and International Affairs at Southern Methodist University, Dallas, USA
- **Pia M. Orrenius**, Vice President and Senior Economist Federal Reserve Bank of Dallas, USA

---

8 July 2021, Thursday | DAY 3
10:45-12:15 – Parallel Sessions VI
12:15-12:45 – Break

12:45-14:30 – Institute for Mobile Studies Special Roundtable [Click here to Join]
Moderator: Eugene Ch'ng, Professor of Cultural Computing, School of International Communications, University of Nottingham Ningbo China
Panellists:
- **Antonio Lam**, Managing Director of Shores and Legal, London, UK: **"How technology has transformed my job as an immigration practitioner"**
- **Dr Xiaoge Xu**, Associate Professor in Media and Communication Studies, UNNC: **"Mapping, measuring and modelling mobility: initial thoughts for global collaboration"**
- **Amira Halperin**, Deputy Director of Institute for Mobile Studies, UNNC: **"Mobile Phones and Forced Migration"**
- **Lei Hao**, Teaching Fellow at School of International Communications; Research Fellow at Institute of Asia and Pacific Studies; Research Fellow at Institute for Mobile Studies, UNNC: **"The Concretisation of Blockchain Technology in Chinese Technoliberalist Crypto Space"**
- **Troy Chen** Director of Teaching, Assistant Professor in Media, Communication and Cultural Studies, UNNC: **"Mobile Self-portrayal of Chinese maid A reflection of the social tensions between female domestic workers and the rising middle class in China"**

12:45-14:15 – Parallel Sessions VII
14:15-14:45 – Break
14:45-16:15 – Parallel Sessions VIII
16:15-16:30 – Break

16:30-18:00 – Plenary Session III [Click here to Join] [This session is in Spanish]
Moderator: Dr **Ana Vila Freyer**, Universidad Latina de México, Mexico
Keynote Speakers:
- Dr **Rodolfo Cruz Piñeiro**, Director, Departamento de Estudios de Población, El Colegio de la Frontera Norte, Mexico
- Hna. **Leticia Gutiérrez Valderrama**, General Director of Scalabrinianas Misión para Migrantes y Refugiados (SMR) sección México, México

---

9 July 2021, Friday | DAY 4
10:45-12:15 – Parallel Sessions IX
12:15-12:45 – Break

12:45-14:45 – Plenary Session IV [Click here to Join]
Moderator: Dr **Bahar Baser Ozturk**, Coventry University, UK
Keynote Speakers:
- Dr **Élise Féron**, Tampere Peace Research Institute, Tampere University, Finland: "**Diasporas, new generations, and homeland conflicts: between transmission and rearticulation of the conflict heritage**"
- **Camilla Orjuela**, Professor, School of Global Studies, University of Gothenburg, Sweden: "**Diaspora struggles for memory and justice: opportunities and limitations**"

14:45-15:00 – Break
15:00-16:30 – Parallel Sessions X
16:30-16:45 – Break

16:45-18:30 – Special Panel: Syrian refugees in Canada, safe but worry about food [Click here to Join]
Moderator: Ginny Lane, Adjunct Professor, School of Public Health, University of Saskatchewan, Canada
Panellists:
- **Hassanali Vatanparast**, Professor of Nutrition, University of Saskatchewan, Canada
- **Mustafa Koc**, Professor of Sociology, Ryerson University, Canada

---

10 July 2021, Saturday | DAY 5
10:45-12:15 – Parallel Sessions XI

Day Five 10 July 2021
14:30-16:00

Special Panel: Türkiye Sınırötesi Kentlerde Göç Hareketliliği ve Kentsel Yaşanabilirlik: Afrin ve İdlib [Click here to Join] [Turkish]
Chair: Prof. Dr. M. Murat Erdoğan, Türk-Alman Üniversitesi, Turkey
- Doç. Dr. Serhat Erkmen (Jandarma ve Sahil Güvenlik Akademisi, Uluslararası Güvenlik ve Terörizm Ana Bilim Dalı Öğretim Üyesi): "**Güvenlik Perspektifinden İdlib'te Toplumsal Sorunlar**"
- Dr. Öğr. Üyesi Zeynep Banu Dalaman (İstanbul Ayvansaray Üniversitesi Göç Politikaları Araştırma ve Uygulama Merkezi Başkanı): "**Göç Kaynak Ülkesinde IDP (yerinden edilmiş kişiler) Hareketliliği ve Geri Dönüş Koşulları: Afrin**"
- H. Murat Lehimler (Kentsel Gelişim ve Sosyal Araştırmalar Derneği Başkan Yardımcısı, Rumeli Üniversitesi Küresel Politikalar Uygulama

ve Araştırma Merkezi Koordinatörü): **"Suriye İç Savaşının Kitlesel Göç Hareketlilikleri Kaynağı Alan Analizi: Kuzey Suriye Analizi"**

- Dr. Gökçe Ok (T.C. İç İşleri Bakanlığı Göç İdaresi Genel Müdür Yardımcısı): **"Göç İdaresi Genel Müdürlüğü'nün Gönüllü Geri Dönüş Politikaları ve Süreçlerine Katkısı"**

16:00 END OF THE PROGRAMME

Please note this programme is subject to change without notice.

Day One 6 July 2021 Tuesday

794   Performing diaspora: food, music and social integration among the South Asian diaspora in Hong Kong

Terence Shum

Hong Kong accommodates migrants of various nationalities and cultural backgrounds. South Asians (Indian, Pakistani, and Nepalese) form a dominant ethnic minority group in this city. Although the Hong Kong government has implemented various integration policies in the city, the policies largely neglect how to preserve cultural diversity among ethnic minorities, which is the most important element in building an inclusive and multicultural society. Integration is a key concern in policy discussions regarding the adaptation and settlement of migrants in host societies (Castle *et al.*, 2003). There are two main approaches in academic debate: normative and multidimensional. The normative approach of integration conceptualises "integration as insertion of a group or individual into an existing entity" (Favell, 2010:372). The multidimensional approach, on the other hand, conceptualises integration as a complex process of participation as well as personal and social change that involves not only the migrants, but also the host population (Ager and Strang, 2004). Underlying these discussions on migrant integration is the unexplored question of how migrants integrate into host societies. This research aims to explore the role of cultural practices in the social integration processes of South Asians in Hong Kong.

Food and music are key components of South Asian diasporic culture. These are expressive practices through which the South Asians reconstruct their identity in the host society. Food and music cultures are defined as practices, attitudes, beliefs, networks, and institutions related to the production, distribution, and consumption of food and music. These embodied practices can

17

help maintain and create new sociocultural relations both within and across borders. Drawing from individual interviews and participant observation with South Asians in Hong Kong, this research examines the dynamic relationships between food and music cultures, while also exploring identity and cross-cultural contact formation in diasporic conditions. Diaspora is a category of practice, and such practices as defining migrant's identity (Brubaker, 2005). This research proposes the concept of 'performing diaspora' to examine the embodied performativity and performance of traditional cultures in the South Asian diaspora in Hong Kong. 'Performing diaspora' refers to a diasporic sphere that is materialised through a collective affective experience in practicing material cultures and articulated in encounters with the local population in a 'multicultural' society. This research argues that the South Asian diaspora is a 'social imagination' (Dueck, 2011: 23) in which migrants, through the practices of traditional cultures, extend their respective homelands across borders, where identities are reconstituted, and where belonging and otherness is appropriated and contested (Brah, 1996). South Asian food and music cultural practices not only make this minority group visible in Hong Kong, but as foreign cultures of a marginalized minority in a Chinese community, it is also a marker of difference that triggers cultural curiosity among Hong Kong Chinese. This diasporic sphere demonstrates a series of negotiated authenticity in food and music cultures across time and space, which serves as an integral connecting site to explore the intercultural encounters between South Asians and Hong Kong Chinese.

References

Ager A and Strang A. (2004). *Indicators of integration: final report*. Home Office Development and Practice Report No. 28. London: Home Office.

Brah, A. (1996) *Cartographies of diaspora*. London: Routledge.

Brukbaker, R. (2005) The "diaspora" diaspora. *Ethnic and Racial Studies*, 28(1), 14-25.

Castles. S., Korac, M., Vasta, E. and Vertovec, S. (2001) Integration: mapping the field I (Research Report 28/03) and II (Research Report 29/03), London and Oxford: Home Office/Compas.

Dueck, B. (2011) 'Part 1: Migrants-Introduction'. In Toynbee J., & Dueck, B. (Eds.) *Migrating music* (pp. 21-27). London: Routledge.

Favell, A. (2010) 'Integration and nations: the nation-state and research on immigrants in Western Europe'. In Martiniello, M. & Rath, J. (Eds.) *Selected studies in international migration and immigrant incorporation*. Amsterdam: Amsterdam University Press.

808   Migration Narratives in First Person: Life Stories of Brazilian Immigrants in Portugal

Patricia Posch and Rosa Cabecinhas

Understanding migration as a result of multi-dimensioned processes, it is not a surprise that the Brazilian currently figures as the biggest immigrant community in Portugal. In 2019, Brazilian citizens residing in the country represented 25,6% of the total immigrant population (SEF, 2020). Historically, when it comes to this flow, two major waves can be characterized and distinguished from each other. The first one started in the 1980s with the remigration of Portuguese and their Brazilian relatives, but also Brazilian highly qualified professionals and exiled politicians, following a more favourable economic scenario in Portugal in face of the deceleration of Brazilian economy.

The second wave began to take shape in mid-1990s with the migration of individuals with lower education levels oriented to least qualified positions in specific areas of Portuguese growing service market due to its adherence to Schengen Agreement. This last wave lasted until the first years of the second decade of 2000s, when, as a consequence of a global economic recession panorama, statistics show a decline in the number of Brazilians living in Portugal, which can be associated to remigration and migration to other European countries. From 2015 on, the number that attest to the inflow of documented Brazilian immigrants to Portugal began to grow significantly, reaching its peak of a 143,74% increase in 2018 when compared to the previous year (SEF, 2018; 2019). This growth can be associated to a new wave of this migration flow – a wave that is still being shaped in contemporary times. In order to find out more about these newcomers Brazilians and their migration experience – given the scarcity of literature regarding the referred phenomenon when it comes to understanding their motivations and migration strategies, as well as their own thoughts about their migration experience - we conducted Life Story interviews with Brazilian immigrants who migrated between 2015 and 2020 to the North of Portugal, as statistical data have point out that this region has been gaining a significant prominence as their destination choice. In these interviews, Brazilian immigrants narrated their experience and expressed themselves on several topics related to their migration, like their motivations, life in Portugal, social dynamics in the new country and plans for the future.

Based on these enriching stories, we've made several findings related to different dimensions of newcomers Brazilian immigrants' life in Portugal, some that reassure characteristics of the previous waves and others that shed light on a whole new spectrum of sociocultural challenges faced by them, as, for example, the changes in the social status of the immigrants that lead to the necessity to adopt new strategies to insert themselves in the labour market in the new country and the discrepancies between the experience and the its consequences for women and men.

References

SEF.   (2018).   *Relatório   de   Imigração,   Fronteiras   e   Asilo   2017.*
         https://sefstat.sef.pt/Docs/Rifa2017.pdf

SEF.   (2019).   *Relatório   de   Imigração,   Fronteiras   e   Asilo   2018.*
         https://sefstat.sef.pt/Docs/Rifa2018.pdf

SEF.   (2020).   *Relatório   de   Imigração,   Fronteiras   e   Asilo   2019.*
         https://sefstat.sef.pt/Docs/Rifa2019.pdf

1062 Syrian Refugee Labor Market Integration in Austria: Field Reflections

Osama Hazzi

Since 2015 — when Austria has experienced asylum applications from different nationalities most peaked of 88,340 (Asylstatistik 2020), of which 24,547 were Syrian applications (Asylstatistik 2015) — the Syrian refugee labor market integration scene in Austria has not much changed. This especially holds true for Syrian women refugees — exhibiting the highest unemployment rate in 2019: 70.5% (The Expert Council for Integration 2020).

On the other hand, the Syrian scene (where the author's cultural background originally comes from) shows that Syrians work, and that Syrian women's role has become more noticeable in the Syrian labor market during the wartime Syria has experienced.

The labor market integration gap between the Austrian and Syrian scenes makes it critical to further research on Syrian refugees — numbering thousands a year since 2014 until 2020 (on this statistic, see Bundesministerium Für Inneres, n.d.).

The paper sheds light on highly qualified Syrian refugees — grounding in a firsthand experience with them — and offers an own perspective on Syrian women refugees to understand the shortcoming to the Syrian refugee labor market integration in Austria.

The paper analyzes the problem with an own insight (that is often missing in academic forums) — not to mention novel approaches to fieldwork this paper contemplates so that Syrian refugees could consider to their labor market integration as the paper also reflects on successful non-refugee (including the author) firsthand labor market integration experiences in Austria.

Syrian refugees and the host society in Austria (foremost, policymakers) needs to have what one might call a cognitive paradigm of coexistence. Both-side calls, whose their way is wisdom and fair exhortation, and who reason in the better way, could well revive the paradigm objectives of how Syrian women refugees could realize their integration into a foreign labor market, how highly qualified Syrian refugees could adapt to working in occupations the Austrian labor market demands, and how the host society and Syrian refugees in Austria should not treat each other as a stereotype. This is crucial to fulfill the Syrian refugee economic independence and the public interest.

This result could answer the question of why the Syrian refugee labor market integration in Austria is not up to optimistic expectations one thought would be the case and might also hold true for other non-Syrian refugee (or even Syrian refugees) labor market integration experiences in other territories; however, the own perspective here perhaps be wrong for others.

References

Bundesministerium für Inneres. (2015). *Asylstatistik 2015*. Republik Österreich, Bundesministerium für Inneres, Sektion III – Recht. https://www.bmi.gv.at/

301/Statistiken/files/Jahresstatistiken/Asyl_Jahresstatistik_2015.pdf

Bundesministerium für Inneres. (2020). *Asylstatistik 2020*. Bundesministerium Inneres. https://www.bmi.gv.at/301/Statistiken/files/Jahresstatistiken/Asyl_Jahressta tistik_2020.pdf

Bundesministerium für Inneres. (n.d.). *Statistiken*, ASYL, Startseite. https://www.bmi. gv.at/301/Statistiken/

The Expert Council for Integration. (2020). *Integration Report: 10 years Expert Council for Integration – 10 years Integration Report*. Federal Chancellery Republic of Austria. https://www.bundeskanzleramt.gv.at/dam/jcr:869a29f6-8745-4be0-b077-1fb27a6e1408/IB2020_EN_printversion.pdf

981   From Temporary Guests to Protracted Rival Invaders: Attitudes toward Syrian Refugees in Turkey

Ayşegül Kayaoğlu

The UNHCR survey on return intentions demonstrates that an overwhelming majority of Syrian refugees (75.2 percent) hope to return to their homeland one day but only a fraction (5.9 per cent) intends to do that in the next 12 months (UNHCR, 2019). Not returning - despite their best intentions - is driven by well-grounded concerns about security, access to livelihoods, amnesty from military service, access to the property and basic services opportunities inside Syria (RPIS, 2019:6). Moreover, the poor living conditions, problems in access to public services, precarious temporary status and highly selective integration policies that put Syrians in limbo are the main challenges for Syrian refugees in Turkey (Akcapar and Simsek 2018; Baban et al. 2017; Aras & Duman 2019). Permanent nature of refugees' residency in urban areas contrary to their legal 'temporary' status, and increasing social tensions between local populations and Syrian refugees particularly after 2017 makes it particularly important to understand the best policy options to improve social integration between local and refugee population groups. Moreover, according to the UNHCR (2019) statistics, 85 percent of the world's refugee population live in developing countries. Still, there is a scarcity of causal evidence about the impact of refugees on native attitudes in a developing country context although majority of refugees are settled in those countries. As the world's top refugee-hosting country where 3,655,067 Syrians live under temporary protection status as of February 2021 (DGMM, 2021), Turkey's case is crucial to understand in terms of how attitudes of the local population towards Syrian refugees are shaped. Using a natural experiment setting in Turkey and benefiting from a data on spatial distribution of Syrian refugees, this paper unveils the causal effect of being exposed to refugees on native's attitudes toward Syrian refugees and preferences for migration policies. Using a randomly collected representative survey of 2,601 residents in Turkey, estimates from the instrumental variables method show that refugee exposure of natives has significant impacts on the perceptions of economic burden, insecurity, social distance and migration governance. More importantly, it provides evidence that these negative attitudes are mainly due to relative deprivation of natives, which even cause biased perceptions for cultural alienation. That said, a negative attitude towards refugees is related more with the rivalry between refugees and natives in the labor market or in access to public services than ethnicity. In addition to these theoretical mechanisms, the paper also demonstrates that political identities and religiosity of individuals matter not for their attitudes but their beliefs. Finally, related with the integration paradox hypothesis, spending more time with refugees is found to result in cultural conflicts between refugees and natives with refugees being considered as a threat to the majority's culture in Turkey. There are three main contributions of this study to the literature. First, it provides an important causal evidence on this issue from a developing country context that hosts the world's largest refugee population within any national borders. Second, majority of refugees in Turkish provinces have a non-transitory stay, which increases the chances or occasions of interaction between natives and refugees. Thus, the variation of interaction among native population allows testing the role of interaction levels and exposure on the hospitality or hostility towards refugees. Third, the paper's attitude measurement is not downward biased due to a higher hospitality level in the early years of the Syrian crisis since the studied survey was conducted in 2017. This means that the current analysis is providing a long-term analysis of attitude formation instead of a contemporaneous one.

776   EMPATHY "Empowering Migrants Promoting Inclusion via Capacity Building and Communities Engagement"

Amira Bieber and Benedikt Pötz

What is it like to be a homosexual in today's EU capitals? Or to have spent years in prison after being accused of terrorism? Or to be a child from Niger growing up in Africa and trying to travel to Europe with your family? Or being a Jewish-Muslim couple? The Empathy Community will help you find out. Driven by these questions and motivated by the London Empathy Museum, a European project was born: EMPATHY: "Empowering Migrants Promoting Inclusion via Capacity Building and Communities Engagement".

The project is dedicated to helping EU citizens see the world through other people's eyes. Through a series of participatory arts and educational projects with a focus on storytelling and dialogue, the project aims to explore how empathy can not only transform our personal relationships, but also help address global challenges such as prejudice, conflict and inequality. In addition, the project aims to develop, test, validate, evaluate and scale a new methodology for integrating migrant youth into local communities based on the direct participation and engagement of local youth. Both groups participate together in a capacity-building programme: young migrants through the usage of integration and inclusion services, while local youth act as impetus and role models, helping them to navigate, integrate and be included.

The project is divided into three phases:

1.   **Orientation**. Activities contributing to acquire a thorough understanding of the effectiveness of **existing practices** to prevent intolerance.

2. **Integration**. Each project partners organizes open workshops where partners staff and external experts are invited. These workshops focus on controversial themes (migration, interculturality, integration and social cohesion, globalization, gender-related issues, LGBT rights, fighting racism and intolerance, political polarization etc.). During the capacity building programme, participants will be given the opportunity to specialize in the following pillars: **Hate Speech** and **Fake News/Misinformation**.

3. **Inclusion**. Activities where the trainees will become ambassadors of the project at local level and will deploy citizens' engagement activities aimed to spread the concept of EMPATHY. Supported by partners, groups will work for developing an action plan, starting from the definition of a vision to the specific actions to deliver as well as identifying partners and defining audience and media to use for channelling messages.

The project does not aim to propose a one-size-fits-all solution, but rather to design the framework for the provision of flexible and dynamic orientation, integration and inclusion programmes that take into account the different social, geographical and organisational contexts of each partner, city and country.

5 partners from Germany, Italy and Spain are implementing this ambitious and highly topical project, which has been funded by ERASMUS PLUS *(EACEA/34/2019, Social inclusion and common values: the contribution in the field of education and training)* since January 2021. The session at the Migration Conference will showcase the latest results of the project and its challenges.

1B   Education and Skilled Migration

Chair Sahizer Samuk Carignani, University of Pisa, Italy

910   Erasmus as a Perpetuator, not a Cause: Return to the Erasmus Ideals and Cities in the case of Highly Skilled Italians
Sahizer Samuk Carignani and Sandra Burchi

911   Education as a crucial key for integration of forced migrant new generation in Iran
Saeede Mokhtarzade

912   Conceptual Understandings of Mobility, Migration and Brain Drain: The Case of Highly Skilled Italians Abroad
Sahizer Samuk Carignani and Sandra Burchi

832   Highly skilled Syrian refugees moving to the West: 5 Case Studies
Dua'a Al-Namas

910   Erasmus as a Perpetuator, not a Cause: Return to the Erasmus Ideals and Cities in the case of Highly Skilled Italians

Sahizer Samuk Carignani and Sandra Burchi

How does Erasmus affect future mobility and emigration decisions of the highly skilled Italians? After having conducted 40 semi-structured and in-depth online interviews with highly skilled, spatially mobile and emigrant Italians, we have used grounded theory (Charmaz 2006) to examine the results. Along with the memo writing process, we used Atlas.ti to figure out each phrase, word and context in which Erasmus was used. The definition of the "highly skilled" in our research project, means that they are university graduates and the sample is restricted to four universities in Tuscan Region (UNIFI, UNISI, UNISTRASI and UNIPI). Amongst 40 interviewees more than two thirds have had Erasmus before. Furthermore, in our sample, there were also ones who benefited from different Erasmus programmes such as Erasmus exchange, Erasmus plus Master Loans and Erasmus traineeship. A major number of our interviewees who had Erasmus experience wanted to work in international environments (Samuk et al. 2021, forthcoming) and a few of them went back to the city or country in which they had had their Erasmus experience.

Our research also draws attention to the negative sides of Erasmus which are mentioned in the literature such as the low budget that is provided to the young mobile students and the fact that not everyone can afford to do their Erasmus experience considering the macroeconomic context (Cairns 2017; Van Mol and Timmerman 2013). With our research findings, we contribute to the literature on Erasmus, by using grounded theory to examine the case of highly skilled Italians answering this question: how does Erasmus mobility interact with contextual factors? Stickiness as a metaphor (Burchi 2020, Costas 2013) fits very well to Erasmus and further urge to be mobile. Moreover, we also find that all of the interviewees talked about their Erasmus context differently and with grounded theory we reach three categories and reasons for return abroad: sustainable cities, language acquisition, and different approaches in higher education.

We also argue, within this context that the reason for the highly skilled Italians to live and work abroad does not only emanate from the fact that Erasmus leads the way to such a life style, but it is also because of their discontent with the undergraduate system and the fact that they can combine their strong theoretical background of undergraduate degrees with more practical approaches outside of Italy. Another commonality between those who went abroad with Erasmus and who did not, was that most of them said: "I always wanted to go abroad". Hence, it seems that Erasmus might be a further motivation for this thought, not necessarily causing further mobility per se. Therefore, we argue that Erasmus is a perpetuator but not a reason, combined with other contextual factors: discontent with universities and structure of the labour market as well as finding the Italian higher education outdated, not offering all the innovative possibilities.

Bibliography

Burchi, S. (2020) Il lato vischioso della mobilità. In Arel 1985-2020

Cairns, D. (2017). The Erasmus undergraduate exchange programme: a highly qualified success story?. Children's Geographies, 15(6), 728-740.

Charmaz, K. (2006). Constructing grounded theory: A practical guide through qualitative analysis. sage.

Costas, J. (2013). Problematizing mobility: A metaphor of stickiness, non-places and the kinetic elite. Organization Studies, 34(10), 1467-1485.

Samuk, S., Nienaber, B., Kmiotek, E. A., Vysotskaya, V., Skrobanek, J., Ardic, T., Marinescu, D. & Muresan, L. Learning in transition: Erasmus+ as an opportunity for internationalization. The Palgrave Handbook of Youth Mobility, forthcoming in April 2021.

Van Mol, C., & Timmerman, C. (2014). Should I stay or should I go? An analysis of the determinants of intra-European student mobility. Population, Space and Place, 20(5), 465-479.

Education as a crucial key for integration of forced migrant new generation in Iran

(911)   Saeede Mokhtarzade

Education is one of the refugee children rights and their priorities which not only protect them from risks and vulnerability, but also is an empowering tool to achieve any of durable solution. Iran is one of the main host countries of refugees in protracted refugee situation in the world. With 979,400 refugees, Iran was ranked sixth in 2019. Moreover, according to the public available statistics, Iran hosts near two million undocumented migrants, mainly Afghans who are living in rural and urban areas around the country. Overviewing Iran refugee education policy during the past four decades is complex due to the diversity of forced migrants' population and fluctuated migration policy of Iranian government. Documented refugee children have been granted to study at public school in the last four decades, however the condition for large number of undocumented children was not the same and fluctuated policy about undocumented migrants caused difficulties to their education as well as access to other social services until recent policy change in May 2015.

This article argues the policy framework to respond refugee and undocumented children rights to education in the host countries, particularly in Iran. Afterward, the necessity and barriers of access to education for forced migrants especially in a procrastinated situation in Iran will be reviewed. It also looks for answering the question that to what extends education will affect integration and long-term policies.

912   Conceptual Understandings of Mobility, Migration and Brain Drain: The Case of Highly Skilled Italians Abroad

Sahizer Samuk Carignani and Sandra Burchi

How can the brain drain, mobility and migration be better conceptualised with the case of highly skilled Italians abroad? In our research project, we conducted 40 semi-structured and in-depth online interviews with highly skilled Italians abroad. Our sample is restricted to the graduates of four universities: UNIPI, UNISI, UNISTRASI and UNIFI. After having examined the data with grounded theory, we have found mixed categories regarding mobility, migration and brain drain. The commonality between the interviewees though was the fact that they had been spatially mobile at some point at the university or after the university for further studies, traineeship or work experiences. Out of forty interviewees only four were interested in return as they found jobs back in Italy or they could not move due to Covid-19. When we asked them "what are your plans for the future?", most of them responded that they want to be further (spatially) mobile going to another country for work and postdoctoral positions, or continue in the country they are residing. More than ninety percent of the interviewees added "I will return one day" except those who have been living abroad for more than ten years.

We argue in this paper that mobility can further turn into migration and migration can turn into brain drain if the stay becomes permanent and the effects of losing contacts with home country both emotionally and professionally would be experienced more significantly after four to five years of stay abroad. Most of the highly skilled Italians leave Italy keeping their connections and thinking about return. After four to five years, this idea leaves its place to further mobility, currriculum building and career development. Once they find a job abroad that provides secure salaries, possibility to save money, ensure that unemployment benefits will be covered and once they get accustomed to a well functioning labour market and favourable welfare conditions they do not want to return to insecurity. Those who left more than ten years ago finding immediately permanent contracts and establishing families do not plan to return as they are already acculturated to the country they have lived till now. Hence, if a large part of the life course is spent abroad including the turning points such as a permanent job, having kids, moving to a more permanent house, settling with language and culture, the migration turns into brain drain.

We argue in this paper that not every mobility is migration, not every migration is brain drain and yet, we need to be clear about these terms as they are quite nuanced despite the fact that the link between them can be chronological, preparatory and transversal. Therefore, this paper, contributes to the literature, drawing attention to the lack of clarifications regarding mobility, migration and brain drain, and proposing a more systematic and empirical approach to these definitions and categories by building a new theory. Our research shows that there is a need to do further research with follow up interviews to understand the longitudinal perspective and define these terms better with more functional and philosophical conceptualisations.

Acknowledgement

This research is funded by Regione Toscana.

832   Highly skilled Syrian refugees moving to the West: 5 Case Studies

Dua'a Al-Namas

The movement of highly-skilled people internally and internationally has noticed a higher attention recently. Migration policies of nation-states plays main role as it favours those with human and social capital over those who lack these skills and connections. This has been highly observed through some Western countries sending their representatives at the beginning of the Syrian conflict between 2011 and 2015 looking for and providing asylum to many skilled Syrian refugees from Syria's neighbouring countries. Turkey and Arab Countries were relatively late in taking advantage of many Syrian skilled refugees at the

26

beginning of the conflict, when Syrians were overflowing to these countries seeking safety and shelter away from Asad's brutal regime between 2011 and 2015. Neighbouring governments provided initially safety and shelter for those seeking refuge and assuming the situation is a temporary one. Jordan hosted 1.3Million Syrians, and Lebanon hosted 1.5Million, by 2020, with Turkey hosting the highest number of Syrians in the World today, 3.6Million. Turkey only took serious action towards the flowing of Syrian refugees in and out of Turkey in 2016, with the "EU-Turkey deal".

On another aspect, employment and access to a decent job is an important factor for refugees integration into the host society. From the skilled Syrian refugee's perspective, being dependent on charity of the host community was very heavy on their chests. Finding an acceptable job in the public or private sector outside the camps whether in Turkey, Jordan, or Lebanon, was a necessity for many skilled Syrian refugees, besides advancing their education and skills.

This paper looks into the reasons of out-migration of skilled Syrian refugees who initially went to neighbouring countries after 2011, and later to the West on another journey in hope of finding better opportunities. In order to better understand the reasons from the refugees themselves, qualitative interviews were conducted, to explore the push and pull factors in these migration flows and the methods of entry into Europe and Canada. Other policies, other than having high social and human capital, which played a role in facilitating these flows were also analysed.

From the interviews and literature available, it can be seen that human and social capitals can play a great role in the integration process for some of the Syrian refugees, those who managed to get to Europe. Flexibility, courage and hope played the major part in the process of integration and adapting to new life. It was also seen that language is a huge obstacle for many of the Syrian, particularly for the highly-skilled one, which was a factor in moving mainly to countries with an easier language to learn. On the issue of finding an adequate job or education advancement this was another obstacles faced. It is argued in this study that governmental policies were taken rather late, had these policies been put in place earlier it would've resulted in better and quicker integration of Syrian refugees, especially skilled ones, and might have had a different impact on their decision to move to Europe.

1C   Turkiye'nin Goc Deneyimi
Chair: H. Yaprak Civelek, Anadolu University, Turkey
1060 Ortadoğulu Göçmenler ve Uluslar İlişkisinde Sürdürülebilir Kalkınma
       İdealinin Eleştirelliği
       H. Yaprak Civelek
791   "Türkiye-Yunanistan Sınırında Yaşanan Kitlesel Göç Hareketinin ve
       Gelen Göçmenlerin Edirne Yerel Basınında Temsiliyeti"
       Jale Avyüzen Zobar
921   Türkiye'deki Nitelikli Suriyelilerin Sosyo-Ekonomik Entegrasyonunun
       Sosyal ve Beşerî Sermaye Yönünden Analizi

1060 Ortadoğulu Göçmenler ve Uluslar İlişkisinde Sürdürülebilir Kalkınma İdealinin Eleştirelliği

H. Yaprak Civelek

Sürdürülebilirlik imgesi altında ekonomik, ekolojik, toplumsal ve hijyenik-medikal alanlarda insanların bencil eylemlerinin, umarsız tüketim alışkanlıkları ile bir arada işleyerek gelecek kuşakların yaşam kaliteleri adına yarattıkları endişe yatmaktadır. Bu endişenin bilinç düzeyinde bir pozitif eyleme dönüşmesi ise yaşam kalitesinin arttırılması yönünde topyekûn bir kalkınmanın hedeflenmesine tekabül etmektedir. Her alanda bilinçli tüketime gidiş başlıca çağrıdır. Hızlı kentleşmeden, sanayiye dayalı kalkınmaya, eğitimden ve sosyal hizmetlere ve hatta toplumsal cinsiyetten ekolojiye kadar değişmeyen yoksunluklar ve kavrayışlar, sosyal kurumlarda eşitsizliklerle yüz yüze geliş, tamamı kapitalizmin kendini yeniden üretme telaşının birer sonucudur. Bu nedenle aslında bir küresel hareket olarak sürdürülebilir kalkınma idealini ve içerdiği ilkeleri bilinçli, büyük ve umut verici ele almak lazımdır.

Ancak demografik açıdan bakıldığında burada bir "ulusallık" vardır. Lesthaeghe, John Caldwell, Ansley Coale gibi önemli demograflar, her ülkenin demografik geçiş süreçlerini tarihsel, politik, ideolojik, kültürel ve ekonomik gelişmişlik düzeylerine göre özgünlükle tecrübe eder. Modernizasyon öncesi, doğurganlığı destekleyen dini ve kültürel destek alanları mevcuttur. Kadın, erkek ve doğurganlık arasındaki rol bağlamı bunlara dayalı olarak kurulmuştur. Bu durumda geniş ailenin, bir anlamda doğurganlığın ideolojiye katkısı olarak tarif edilmiştir. Bacci'nin İspanya, İtalya ve Portekiz nüfuslarını demografik geçiş teorisi açısından ele alan çalışması bir nüfusun hayatı apartman dairelerinde teknolojik aletlerden faydalanarak geçiyorsa çift başına asla ortalama sekiz çocuğa sahip olunamayacaktır. Bir başka deyişle hızla işleyen modernizasyon ile azalan doğurganlık arasında "kapılmışlıkla" vuku bulan bir negatif ilişki vardır. Geçiş teorisi elbette göçü dikkate almadığı için oldukça eleştirilmiştir. Ancak bu teorinin laboratuvarı olan Avrupa nüfuslarında özgün kültürel ve ideolojik "varoluşsal" hedefler, doğurganlık üzerine kurulan politikalar ve çağrılar üzerinden analiz edildiklerinde, bunun üzerine bugün özellikle Ortadoğulu göçmenlerin karşılaştıkları "bertaraf" edişler de eklendiğinde "ulusallık" meselesi karşısında küresel sürdürülebilir kalkınma kapsamında ele alınan insan hakları, yaşam kalitesi, yoksulluk gibi pek çok tema odaklı o koruyucu, kuşatıcı ve iyileştirici ilkeleri bir masaya yatırmak gerektiği açıktır.

Özellikle Avrupa ve Amerika nüfuslarının doğurganlık ve ulusallık arasındaki ilişkiye dayanarak, ulusun süreğenliğini ele alışları; "yüksek doğurganlık hızları" ile mimlenmiş Ortadoğulu farklı bir din ve kültür mensubu kitlesel bir akışa tabi zorunlu göçmenlere karşı politikaları değerlendirilmektedir bu makalede.

Sürdürülebilir kalkına hedefleri ve amaçları otağına bu ulusallık kavrayışları ve doğurganlık ilişkisi yerleştirildiğinde küresel idealin geldiği nokta da tam da eleştirelliğin kurulduğu noktadır. Bu çalışma var olan yazınsal kaynaklar, raporlar ve veriler üzerinden bu nokta üzerine bir argüman geliştirmektedir.

791 "Türkiye-Yunanistan Sınırında Yaşanan Kitlesel Göç Hareketinin ve Gelen Göçmenlerin Edirne Yerel Basınında Temsiliyeti"

Jale Avyüzen Zobar

Bu çalışma, Türkiye'nin açık kapı politikasını uygulamaya geçirmesinin ardından Yunanistan sınırına gelen kitlesel göç akınında göçmenlerin yaşadığı problemlere odaklanmaktadır. Çalışmada, Türkiye-Yunanistan sınırında neler olduğuna dair yaşananların ve göçmenlerin karşılaştığı problemlerin Edirne yerel basınında nasıl yer aldığı ortaya konulacaktır. Birinci yılı dolan kitlesel göç hareketinde kentte bulunan vasıflı yerel gazetelerin haberlerinde göçmenlerin temsiline ve yaşanan hak ihlallerinin nasıl ele alındığına ışık tutulacaktır. Çalışmanın amacı, göç konusunda medyanın rolünü anlamak ve göçmenlerin insan hakları açısından yaşadıkları sorunların medyada nasıl temsil edildiğini göstermektir. 2020 yılında yaklaşık bir ay süren kitlesel göç akını sırasında Edirne'ye gelen göçmenlerin deneyimlerini, pratiklerini ve hak kayıplarını içermesi açısından bu çalışma, sınırlı bir alanda üretilen haberlerin içeriğine odaklanacaktır.

921 Türkiye'deki Nitelikli Suriyelilerin Sosyo-Ekonomik Entegrasyonunun Sosyal ve Beşerî Sermaye Yönünden Analizi

Mustafa Kemal Şan ve Pınar Yazgan

2011 yılında Suriye'de ortaya çıkan iç savaş sadece Suriye'yi etkilememiş, son yılların en büyük siyasal nitelikli kitlesel göç akınına sebep olması nedeniyle bölgenin ötesinde küresel derin etkilere sebep olmuştur. 2011 yılının Nisan ayında 252 Suriyelinin Türkiye'ye gelmesiyle başlayan sınır geçişleri, iç savaşın şiddetlenmesiyle kitlesel göçe dönüşmüştür. Türkiye'nin bu sayı ile dünyada en fazla mülteci barındıran ülke konumuna gelmesi dikkatleri mültecilere ve mülteci politikalarına çekti. Mültecilerin büyük bir kısmının kalıcı olacağı gerçeğinin kabul edilmesiyle birlikte bu gruplara yönelik sosyal politikalara ihtiyacı da daha çok belirginleşmektedir. Sosyo-ekonomik entegrasyon sosyal politikaların temel sütunlarındandır. Bu kapsamda nitelikli işgücü özellikle üzerinde durulması gereken meseleler arasındadır. Nitelik-altı çalışma ise hem ev sahibi ülke açısından hem de mülteciler açısından önemli bir beşerî sermaye kaybıdır. Güven, aidiyet ve olumlu grup çıktılarına dayanan köprü kuran sosyal sermayenin artırılması ve beşerî sermaye arasında pozitif bir ilişki söz konusudur. Tersi anlamda bağlayıcı sosyal sermaye de, grupları kendi içerisinde kapalı ağlara sahip bütünde güven ve aidiyet anlamında negatif nitelikte çıktıları karşımıza çıkarma potansiyelini taşımaktadır.

Bu çalışma Türkiye'deki Suriyeli mültecilerin sosyal ve beşerî sermaye düzeyleri ve nitelik altı koşullarda istihdamına odaklanan sosyal-politika yaklaşımlarına öncül olabilecek kuramsal ve uygulama modelleri oluşturmayı amaç edinmiştir.

Çalışmanın yöntemi, nitel araştırma yaklaşımlarından gömülü kuram yaklaşımları içerisinde Charmaz'ın yapılandırmacı gömülü kuram anlayışıdır. Çalışmanın örneklemini Göç İdaresi'nin Aralık 2017 verilerine göre Türkiye'de geçici koruma altındaki Suriyelilerin oranının en yüksek olduğu 10 il oluşturmaktadır. Bu aşamada veri doygunluğuna ulaşma ve teorik örneklem adı verilen, mülakatların analizi aşamasında elde edilen kategorileri daha iyi anlamaya yönelik örneklem kullanıldı. Suriyeli mültecilerle ilgili ulaşılacak sonuçlar ile akademik literatüre katkı sağlamak ve politika yapıcılar/üreticiler ile yerel yöneticilere kaynak oluşturmak amaç edinildi. Sonuç olarak çalışmada sosyal sermayesi yatay ve yapısal nitelikte güçlü bir grup olarak tespit edilen toplulukta nitelik altı çalışan önemli bir kesimin varlığı sözkonusudur.

1022   Mülteci Krizi ve Türkiye Avrupa Birliği İlişkileri

İrfan Gümüşlü

2010 yılından itibaren Arap Baharı adında Kuzey Afrika ülkelerinden başlayarak Orta doğu ülkelerine yayılan rejim karşıtı toplumsal hareketlerin demokrasi, özgürlük, insan hakları ve reform çağrılarına karşılık sert askeri güçlerin kullanılmasından sonra gelişen iç savaşla milyonlarca insan göç etmek zorunda kaldı. Suriye'de iç savaşın etkisiyle artan kitlesel göç ve insani kriz karşısında Türkiye açık kapı politikasını uygulayarak Suriyeli sığınmacıları sınırdan içeri almaya başladı. Savaşın uzun sürmesiyle birlikte misafir statüsünde bulunan sığınmacılara Türkiye egemenlik haklarına dayanarak ve 1951 Cenevre Sözleşmesinde yapılan mülteci tanımından farklı olarak gelenlere "Geçici Koruma Statüsü" adında yasal bir statü hakkı verdi. Söz konusu ülkelerde misafir konumunda bulunan sığınmacılara duyarsız kalan Avrupa Birliği ancak 2015 yılının yaz aylarında Ege ve Akdeniz de yaşanan can kayıplarından sonra uluslararası kamuoyunun baskısı ve kendine yönelik kitlesel göç hareketlerinin artmasından sonra ilgilenmeye başladı. Mülteci krizi başladıktan sonra birlik içerisinde koordinasyonu sağlamada ve krizi yönetmede yetersiz kalan Avrupa Birliği sorunun çözümünü menşei ve transit ülkelerle yapılacak olan antlaşmalar ile çözüm bulmaya çalıştı. Mültecilerin transit ülke olarak kullandıkları ülkelerinden başında gelen Türkiye ile Avrupa Birliği arasında birtakım antlaşmalar imzalandı. Bu antlaşmalarla birlikte Avrupa Birliği sorunları erteleme ve üçüncü ülkelere havale etme gibi çözümden uzak bir takım politikalar uyguladı.

Bu çalışma da literatür taramasının yanı sıra 2011-2017 yılları arasında Türkiye Cumhuriyeti İçişleri Bakanlığı Göç İdaresi Genel Müdürlüğü, Frontex ve Birleşmiş Milletler Mülteciler Yüksek Komiserliğinin sayısal verilerinden de yararlanılmıştır. Çalışma ilk olarak tarihsel süreçte Türkiye'ye yönelik göç akınları, Türkiye'nin göç politikaları, Suriye Mülteci krizi ve Türkiye, Suriyeli Mültecilerin Türkiye'deki yasal statüleri, Avrupa Birliği'nin göç politikaları, Suriyeli mülteci krizi ve Avrupa Birliği ile Türkiye ve Avrupa Birliği arasında imzalanan antlaşmaların analiz ve değerlendirmeleri yapılmaktadır. Çalışmanın temel amacı Türkiye ile Avrupa Birliği arasında Mülteci krizinin karşılıklı çıkar ilişkisiyle pazarlık konusu haline getirilip getirilmediği sorusuna yanıt aramaktır.

759 **Mülteciler ve Göçmenler Üzerinde Covid-19 Hastaliğinin Değerlendirilmesi**

Sibel Terzioğlu

Geçmişten bu yana salgın hastalıklar toplumları derinden etkilemiş ve ağır tahribatlar bırakmıştır. Çin 31 Aralık tarihinde nedeni belirlenemeyen bir pnömönü vakasıyla karşı karşıya kalmış ve derhal Dünya Sağlık Örgütüne bildirmiştir. Artan vaka sayıları ve sonuçlarından etkilenen kitlenin yaygınlığı nedeniyle 11 Mart 2020'de pandemi ilan edildi. Dünya genelinde 2 Eylül 2020 tarihi itibariyle laboratuvar teyitli 25.602.665 vaka ve 852.758 ölüm bildirilmiştir. Göçmen kesim nüfus hareketliliğinin en önemli noktası olarak farklı birçok bulaşıcı hastalıktan etkilenmiş olup gelecekteki salgınlardan da etkilenme potansiyeli en yüksek gruplar arasında sayılmaktadır.

Pandemi süreci tüm dünyayı etkisi altına alıp kasıp kavururken göç hareketliliğine maruz kalan insanlar ekonomik, sosyal ve psikolojik olarak farklı bir değişim ve dönüşüm sürecine girmişlerdir. Neticede sağlıklı ekonomiler ve toplumların göç hareketliliğine dayanma kanısını kuvvetlendirmiş dolayısıyla göçmen kesim üzerinde bir çalışma yapılması faydalı görülmüştür. Hali hazırda var olan bulaşıcı hastalığa yakalanma endişesiyle zaten yerinden yurdundan edilme endişesi taşıyan bu kesim seyahat kısıtlamalarının olmasıyla da bir belirsizlik girdabına girmiştir. Bu süreçte sevdiklerinden ve günlük hayatlarından feragat edip pandeminin olumsuzluklarından en çok etkilenen kesim olmuşlardır. Dolayısıyla (COVID-19) salgınına yönelik tehdit unsuru oluşturan bu durum ikamet edecekleri metropol veya yerlerde hayatını sürdürmeye çalışan mülteciler yerel halk ile kıyaslandığında benzer durumlar yaşadıkları sonucuna varılmıştır. İlaveten insan hareketliliğinin doğurduğu göç sorunsalı yeni yerleşim yerine uyum süreci ve bu kesimlerde hayat koşulları yukarıda da değindiğimiz gibi toplumun en kırılgan noktalarından biri olan göçmen kesiminin yaşam koşullarının ve hayati durumlarını tehlikeye atabilmektedir. Bu kırılgan kesim özel gereksinimli gruplar tasnifine alınarak tekrar gözden geçirilmelidir. Sosyal hizmet birimlerinde ve toplumun sağlık uygulama ve politikalarına detaylı bir şekilde entegre edilmemiş bu kesim salgın ile savaşırken ciddi problem teşkil eden bir grup olarak yine karşımıza çıkmaktadır. Salgın ile mücadelede ihtiyaç duyulan gerekli bilgi birikimine vaka tesplt ve değerlendirme çalışmalarına, test edilebilir olma imkânına, yetkili birim ve görevlilerle takip kontrol durumlarından faydalanamayan bu kesim salgın vaka oranlarının artması ile karşı karşıya kalmıştır. Ülkeler mültecilerin COVID-19 hastalığına yanıt olacak durumları göz önünde bulundurmalı dolayısıyla hedeflenen çalışmalar; evrensel mücadele amaçlarına, insan haklarına ve uluslararası standartlar ile paralel olması gerekir.

1D   Gender, Sexuality and Migration
Chair: Marta Lemos, Universidade de Lisboa, Portugal
552   Gendered experiences of educational migrant returnees in Covid-19 times
Chiedza Mutsaka Skyum

552   Gendered experiences of educational migrant returnees in Covid-19 times

Chiedza Mutsaka Skyum

An African University with students from over 40 countries had no choice but to encourage students to return to their home countries when Covid-19 hit. They feared having the students 'stuck' in lockdown far away from their families. Flights were scheduled and students flew home. It was declared that there would be no interruption to the students' learning as classes would continue online. However, in the students' home countries, societal barriers existed that hindered some students from being able to continue with their classes. In many societies, girls and women are responsible for doing the majority of childcare tasks and domestic work in a household. Teachers began to receive emails from female students who could not dedicate the needed time for their classes. One had multiple siblings that were not in school and needed homeschooling and care, another's father was forced out of his job so her mother became a vendor and she in turn did the cooking and cleaning, and another was caring for her ill grandmother who needed palliative care. The family expectations and the de-prioritisation of their education by their families has affected their educational journeys. Without Covid-19, they would have continued as resident students whose time was fully committed fully to their studies. This article will share the experiences of a few of these students, examine some gendered migration theory and consider the Institutional response - it will also detail some techniques for differentiation used by teachers to ensure that when these students did find the time, they were able to catch up and still achieve the learning outcomes.

556   Identities put to the test of migration: the case of Russian homosexuals in France and in Canada

Ekaterina Koksharova

Migration is a journey that extends over time, with consequences which profoundly affect the identity of the people who experience it and who are affected by it. Arriving in the foreign country is a moment of culture shock. Their identity being wounded by the violence endured in Russia, the men and women concerned are first of all led to reject their culture of origin altogether. After an initial period of acculturation, they try, among other things, to rebuild a militant identity adapted to their new conditions.

However, the time of euphoria may not last and be followed by an identity crisis: feeling of being intruder into the LGBT movement of the host society, confrontation with ambient stereotypes about Russians, administrative difficulties, difficulties related to migrant status, psychological problems especially for women. In the longer term, the people concerned engage in a process of acculturation which allows them to articulate their belonging to the Russian community and integration in a new country. Finally, having settled in, LGBT migrants can consider returning to Russia, with attitudes differentiated by gender: gay men do not return to Russia, while women make temporary returns. It will then be a question of understanding the reasons for these returns and their consequences in order to provide an overview and its consequences.

575   Life Stories of Three Syrian Migrant Women in Turkey: Rights and Gender Equality Experiences

Hulya Şahin-Erbektaş

This paper, which is based on my master's thesis, includes the life stories of three women who migrated to Turkey from Syria through forced migration. Thoughts of Syrian women, who participated in the research, related to the gender roles and gender equality; and their gains in rights and new freedom fields provided by these civil rights after coming to Turkey are discussed over the participants' standpoints. This research using one of the qualitative data collection techniques "life story" has three main goals. To convey thoughts and experiences of the participant Syrian women on gender equality and women's right in Syria prior to migration; to investigate whether these women have experienced any change in their thoughts on gender equality and women's rights in their new life after immigrating to Turkey, and to present what aspect these changes lay on if there is any change; lastly, to reveal what the future expectations of these forced migrants women are. In the conclusion of the study, it was observed that after immigrating to Turkey, the Syrian women have had some questioning regarding gender equality considering their experiences in their life back in Syria; however, they do not have a strong belief in the fact that women and men can be equal. Although it seems to be effective to have information on civil rights and women rights in Turkey on their questioning of gender equality after living in Turkey, it was observed that they have had difficulties transforming the patriarchal codes they had adopted during their life in Syria. Lastly, it was observed that the expectations of the participating women for the future are not the ones locating themselves in the center; on the contrary, the expectations that coincide with the gender roles in patriarchal societies.

References

Atkinson, R. (2001). The life story interview. In Gubrium, J. F., ve Holstein, J. A. Handbook of interview research (pp. 120-140): SAGE Publications, Inc. doi: 10.4135/9781412973588

Baklacıoğlu ve Kıvılcım (2015). "Sürgünde Toplumsal Cinsiyet: İstanbul'da Suriyeli Kadın ve LGBTİ Mülteciler. İstanbul: Derin Yayınları.

Berger, M. S. (1997). "The Legal System of Family Law in Syria". Institut Fancais du Proche- Orient.

Castles, S. ve Miller, M.J. (2008). Göçler Çağı Modern Dünyada Uluslararası Göç Hareketleri, (1. Baskı), Çev. Bülent Uğur Bal ve İbrahim Akbulut. İstanbul: İstanbul Bilgi Üniversitesi Yayınları.

Connell, R. W. (2019). "Toplumsal Cinsiyet ve İktidar". Cem Soydemir (Çev.). İstanbul: Ayrıntı Yayınları.

Düzkaya, H. ve Yazıcı, E. (2017). Misafirlikten Vatandaşlığa Türkiye'deki Suriyelilerin Hukuki Statüsü: Türkiye ve Avrupa Birliği Mevzuatı Ekseninde Karşılaştırmalı Bir Değerlendirme. Hak İş Uluslararası Emek ve Toplum Dergisi, 6.16:419-456.

Donato, K. M., Gabaccia, D., Holdaway, J., Manalansan IV, M. ve Pessar, P. R. (2006) "A glass half full? Gender in migration studies", International Migration Review, 40(1), 3-26.

Ehrenreich B., English D., Cadılar, Büyücüler ve Hemşireler. (Ed. B. Ehrenreich, D. English, Çev. E. Uğur), İstanbul: Kavram Yayınları.

Eijik, E. (2013). "Family Law in Syria A Plurality of Laws, Norms, and Legal Practices". de graad van Doctor aan de Universiteit Leiden http://hdl.handle.net/1887/21765

Erbektaş- Şahin, Hülya "Türkiye'ye Zorunlu Göçle Gelen Suriyeli Kadınların Haklar ve Toplumsal Cinsiyet Eşitliği Bağlamındaki Deneyimleri", Yüksek Lisans Tezi, Hacettepe Universitesi. Ankara, 2020.

Erdogan, M. (2014). Perceptions of Syrians in Turkey. Insight Turkey, 16(4), 65-75.

Etherington, K. (2006). Understanding Drug Misuse and Changing Identities: A Life Story Approach. Drugs, Education, Prevention and Policy, 13:3, p.233-245.

Giddens, A. (2006). Sosyoloji. Ayraç: İstanbul.

Haraway, D. J. (2004). "The Haraway Reader". New York: Routledge.

Harding, R. (2004). "Social Enterprise: The New Economic Engine?". https://doi.org/10.1111/j.0955-6419.2004.00338.x

Kakuru, D. M. ve Paradza, G. G. (2007). Reflections on the use of the life history method in researching rural African women: field experiences from Uganda and Zimbabwe. Gender ve Development, 15 (2), 287-297.

Kandiyoti, D. (2019). "Cariyeler, Bacılar, Yurttaşlar: Kimlikler ve Toplumsal Dönüşümler". İstanbul: Metis Yayınları.

McAdams, D. P. (1985). Power, intimacy, and the life story: Personological inquiries into identity. New York: Guilford Press.

Mousa, D. (2018). "Syrian Personal Status Laws". Friedrich Ebert Stiftung.

Radin, P. (1920). "The Autobiography of a Winnebago Indian". Kessinger Publishing.

Ramazanoğlu ve Holland (2002). "Feminist Methodology: Challenges and Choices". Sage Publications.

Rose, H. (1994). "Love, Power and Knowledge. Towards a Feminist Transformation of the Sciences". Cambridge: Polity Press.

Tanesini, A. (2012). "Feminist Epistemolojilere Giriş". Gülhan Demiriz, Berivan Binay, Ümit Tatlıcan (çev.), 1. Basım. İstanbul: Sentez Yayınları.

Thompson, E. (2000). "Colonial Citizens: Republican Rights, Paternal Privilege, and

Gender in French Syria and Lebanon." New York: Columbia University Press.

Yıldız, Ö. (2013). "Türkiye Kamplarında Suriyeli Sığınmacılar: Sorunlar, Beklentiler, Türkiye ve Gelecek Algısı." Sosyoloji Araştırmaları Dergisi, 16:1.

890   Intimacy and Emotions in A Refugee Reception Centre in Portugal

Marta Lemos

The universes shared by refugees tend to create practices and strategies to succeed their escape and consequent survival. Crossing the concept of De Genova et al. (2018) of "autonomy of migration" and in the light of Papadopoulos & Tsianos (2013) these daily practices which the late authors call "mobile commons" can create informal economies, share crucial information during the trip, connectivity structures, access to entities that promote their rights and a policy of caring for the other. These practices are recreated and reconfigured so that they idealize their mobility. Looking into this reinvented mobility, I believe that, and in the context of a refugee reception centre and after ethnographic fieldwork for nine months, I assume that the digital space mediated by the smartphone is reconfigured not only in the sense of fitting into the "mobile commons" that Papadopoulos & Tsianos (2013) refer to, but also to meet and express refugee's affective and emotional needs. Identity forms are shared and promoted. These situations reveal the digital space as a stage for transgression of symbolic power, capable of creating private and safe spaces where "momentary intimacies" (MacLaren 2014:60), emotions and personal and identity issues are shared and expressed free of great risks leading to a reduction of the feeling of loneliness in an hostile environment. In this way, I understand the way refugees express their different emotions as a language created by them that allows the analysis of the meanings and strategies they imprint on their lives in mobility.

PAPADOPOULOS, Dimitris & Vassilis S. TSIANOS, 2013, "After citizenship: autonomy of migration, organisational ontology and mobile commons", Citizenship Studies, 17:2, 178-196.

MACLAREN, Kym, 2014, "Intimacy and embodiment: An introduction", Emotion, Space and Society, 13, 55-64.

DE GENOVA, N. et al., 2018, "Autonomy of Asylum?: The Autonomy of Migration Undoing the Refugee Crisis Script", South Atlantic Quarterly, 117 (2): 239–265.

1E   Migration Governance

Chair Ülkü Sezgi Sözen, University of Hamburg, Germany

494   Can the UN's Statelessness Global Action Plan Succeed? A Case Study of Myanmar
Katherine J Pratt

506   Administrative capacity vs. political will: the precarious existence of refugees and asylum seekers in South Africa
Meron Andemichael Okbandrias

494   Can the UN's Statelessness Global Action Plan Succeed? A Case Study of Myanmar

Katherine J Pratt

There are an estimated ten million stateless persons worldwide. These individuals are not recognized in the eyes of law; thus, are not granted fundamental rights. There are causes for statelessness, including state succession, gaps in laws pertaining to nationality and displacements and discrimination due to conflict. One of the most prominent groups in the world that experiences statelessness are the Rohingyas from Myanmar. With more than a million stateless Rohingya still within Myanmar and 2.5 million around the world, the group has experienced widespread persecution and discrimination. The United Nations (UN), recognizing the plight of millions of people who are unprotected by any domestic law, adopted the 1954 Convention relating to the Status of Stateless Persons and the 1961 Convention on the Reduction of Statelessness in order to protect stateless persons and reduce the global number. Acknowledging that statelessness did not end with these conventions, the UN created a framework through the Global Action Plan to End Statelessness: 2014 – 2024 (Global Action Plan) to resolve current situations of statelessness, prevent new cases from emerging and better protect stateless persons. This thesis analyzes whether the UN will succeed in eradicating statelessness by 2024 through asking the question: "Can the UN's Stateless Global Action Plan Succeed? A Case Study of Myanmar." Using two opposing theoretical frameworks, a traditional view of sovereignty advocated by Philip Cunliffe and a responsible view of sovereignty advocated by Amitai Etzioni, the research analyzes each individual action plan and its successes and failures in Myanmar. By looking at a specific state, this research will assess the efficacy of the UN when confronted with contradictory domestic policies. The analysis of the ten stateless action plans in Myanmar provides evidence that the Global Action Plan, representing responsible sovereignty, may not be as powerful as the traditional form of sovereignty that defines Myanmar. The implications of this research solidify the charge that a supranational organization such as the UN is only as powerful as the individual state allows it to be, and that in order for statelessness to be eradicated, it must fall onto the local people and government for implementation.

References

Chan, Aye. 2005. "The Development of a Muslim enclave in Arakan (Rakhine) state of Burma (Myanmar)." *SOAS Bulletin of Burma Research* 3, no 2 (Autumn): 396-420.

Cunliffe, Philip. 2010. "Introduction: Critical perspectives on R2P." *Journal of Intervention and Statebuilding* 4, no 1: 35-37. doi: 10.1080/17502970903541655.

Etzioni, Amitai. 1996. "The Responsive community: A Communitarian perspective." *American Sociological Review* 61, no 1 (February): 1–11.

"Myanmar laws and CEDAW. The Case for anti-violence against women laws." *Gender Equality Network* (January): 1-45. https://www.burmalibrary.org/docs20/Myanmar_Law+CEDAW-en-red.pdf

United Nations High Commissioner for Refugees. 2014. "Global action plan to end stateless." (November): 1-32. https://www.unhcr.org/statelesscampaign2014/Global-Action-Plan-eng.pdf

506 Administrative capacity vs. political will: the precarious existence of refugees and asylum seekers in South Africa

Meron Andemichael Okbandrias

Refugees and asylum seekers enjoy substantial rights according to the constitution and the refugee act. However, accessing these rights either in accessing documentation or public services is a challenge. Two significant issues negatively affect the way the refugee regime is managed in South Africa. One is the overburdened Department of Home Affairs (DHA) that determines asylum seekers' status and provides documentation. The asylum determination process, as well as the renewal of documentation is riddled with problems. Besides, refugees and asylum seekers battle to access certain public and private services. On the other hand, there is a lack of recognition of the difficulty that the asylum seekers and refugees are going through or their contribution. The question arises whether this problem arises from lack of administrative capacity due to resources constraint or lack of political will from the political class. The researcher has interviewed 117 asylum seekers and refugees from three nationalities and three local NGOs active in this area. The basis of the theoretical discussion in this article is Liberal Rights Theory and the concept of 'the right to have rights' as the basis of theoretical discussion. The research found that there is a significant lack of capacity that is structural. Most importantly, there doesn't seem to be the political will to address the particular challenges refugees and asylum seekers face. The path of citizenship is torturous, and there seems to be a deliberate effort to thwart refugees to access that right. Instead, they are seen as undesirable elements by the political elite of different parties and used as a scapegoat during local government elections.

515   Recentring the Political Figure - On Migration and Its Impact on Cosmopolitanism, State Identity, and Global Governance

Islam Ahmed

This paper discusses the relation between motion and migration, analysing migration from a kinopolitical perspective. If motion is an encompassing term for all sorts of movement, migration is its social manifestation. Yet, people move not only physically. Juridical, economic, and political expulsions are also sorts of motion between legal statuses, economic classes, and political memberships. These sorts of motion produce immense sociopolitical, economic, and cultural repercussions; if understood as central to social interactions, rather than being marginal or exceptional. Such kinesis at the centre of political theory ensures that it addresses the structural inequalities that otherwise arise.

As such, kinopolitics also works as a framework for changing our perspective of global politics. It helps us understand better, and also reverse, the logic that governs state sovereignty that had dominated the modern nation-state system and produced thematic and structural inequalities that are severe and oppressive for a great percentage of world population. Placing the migrant, rather than the status-citizen, at the centre of political analysis helps resolve the current troubles of biopolitics, connecting two important works in the field: Giorgio Agamben's *Homo Sacer* and Thomas Nail's *Figure of the Migrant*.

544   EU-Turkey Readmission Agreement In the Context of International Governance of Migration

Emrah Cengiz

This paper aims to examine one of the most crucial and controversial agreements have been signed recently, namely the EU-Turkey Readmission Agreement which has a significant role on easing the 2015-16 EU Migration Crisis from International Governance of Migration perspective. Migration has been one of the most important topics (if not the most important one) in the agenda of many countries and supranational organizations and it is still a subject in need of a global, sustainable, lawful and effective solution. EU-Turkey Readmission Agreement, on the other hand, is aaccepted by many as a critical step which eased the EU Migration Crisis and yet the doubts about its adherence to the International Law and Refugee rights remain. Therefore, it is important to analyze the mentioned agreement in the frame of Global Governance of Migration to give it the right place.

My study will begin with a literature review of history of international governance of migration, and potential steps to be made in future to have an efficient international governance of migration. Following that, study will focus on the EU-Turkey Readmission Agreement in the scope of international governance of migration. Within this framework, the deal with its much-debated articles will be examined. Consequently, the study will bring out what kind of changes and improvements could be applied to the agreement to eliminate the controversies.

1F   Health and Migration

560   The access to public medical services of young Central American migrants in Mexico, before and after the 211 Migration Law

Ken Nishikata and Liliana Meza Gonzalez

Using data from the 2010 Census and the 2015 Intercensal Survey, this paper tries to understand how the enactment of the 2011 Migration Law in Mexico affected the access of young migrants of NTCA origin to the public health system, to medical services through the job and to a formal job. Through the estimation of probit equations, this article finds that the enactment of the new Migration Law not only did not increase the migrant's access to health services but that, for other reasons, it decreased. We conclude that the change in government in 2012 meant a different approach to Central American migrants, and that xenophobia in the Mexican society is impeding the full implementation of the law. Finally, we argue that Mexico is not a country where the rule of law is applied. This means that many factors could explain our results. However, evidence suggests that the new migration legislation has not implied benefits for Central American migrants in a topic so close to human rights like health is.

600   Barriers to Sexual and Reproductive Healthcare for Documented Hispanic Migrant Women in the US: A Qualitative Study

Jessica Merone and Rossella De Facto

Several studies have analysed the challenges undocumented migrant women face when accessing sexual and reproductive health care in the US (Center for Reproductive Rights, 2006; Khanlou, Haque, Skinner, Matini, & Landy, 2017). A major barrier is their inability to access health insurance coverage, since undocumented immigrants in the US are not eligible to enrol in Medicare, Medicaid, or Children Health Insurance Program (CHIP). Likewise, they are unable to purchase health insurance through the Affordable Care Act (ACA) marketplace (Fortuny & Chaudry, 2011). In addition to this, evidence has shown that undocumented migrant women face other barriers when accessing sexual and reproductive health care, which include language difficulties, limited cultural sensitivity from health care practitioners, lack of familiarity with healthcare systems, discrimination, and fear of deportation. Despite extensive research on this topic, scholars have stressed the necessity for better understanding on how individual and contextual factors influence migrant health care access, decisions, and outcomes, and how they could better inform health care policies. Legal scholars Hasstedt, Desai, and Ansari-Thomas (2018) have called upon researchers to explore further the differences in accessing sexual and reproductive health care services among various groups of immigrant women. Therefore, this research project aims at responding to this call by examining the barriers documented migrant women face when accessing sexual and productive health care in Philadelphia, Pennsylvania (US). In this qualitative study, eight in-depth semi-structured interviews were conducted with women belonging to the following three migration status: i) US-born citizens with immigrant parents; ii) legal permanent residents (LPRs) (also known as green card holders); and iii) naturalized US citizens. All interviews were conducted with migrant women with origins from Central or South America, between the ages of 18-50. Participants were recruited by snowball sampling. Subsequently, interviews were coded and thematically analysed through the software NVivo. This exploratory case study concluded that, despite their immigration status, documented immigrant women experience similar barriers as undocumented migrant women in accessing sexual and reproductive health care. These similar barriers include their experiences with stigma and discrimination, as well as cultural, language, financial, and information barriers. This raises questions on the appropriateness of US health polices when it comes to respect, protect, and fulfil the sexual and reproductive rights of migrant women, in line with international human rights law. Henceforth, the final section of the paper undertakes a rightsbased policy analysis based on the empirical findings (International Organization for Migration (IOM), 2006).

References

Center for Reproductive Rights. (2006). Women's Reproductive Rights in the United States New York, NY. Retrieved from https://www2.ohchr.org/english/bodies/hrc/docs/ngos/CRR.pdf

Fortuny, K., & Chaudry, A. (2011). A Comprehensive Review of Immigrant Access to Health and Human Services. Urban Institute Retrieved from https://www.researchgate.net/profile/Ajay_Chaudry/publication/268400321_A_Com prehensive_Review_of_Immigrant_Access_to_Health_and_Human_Services/links/ 55d 68d1208aec156b9a86548.pdf

Hasstedt, K., Desai, S., & Ansari-Thomas, Z. (2018). Immigrant Women's Access to Sexual and Reproductive Health Coverage and Care in the United States. The Commonwealth Fund. Retrieved from https://www.commonwealthfund.org/publications/issue- briefs/2018/nov/immigrantwomens-access-sexual-reproductive-health-coverage

International Organization for Migration (IOM). (2006). Migration: A Social Determinant of the Health of Migrants. IOM MIgration Health Department. Geneva, Switzerland.

Khanlou, N., Haque, N., Skinner, A., Matini, A., & Landy, K. C. (2017). Scoping Reivew on Maternal Health among Immigrant and Refugee Women in Canada: Prenatal, Intrapartum, and Postnatal Care. Journal Of Pregnancy, 2017.

doi:10.1155/2017/8783294

777 The other side of the coin: The role of operators and intercultural mediators in asylum reception system and health care access

Alda Kushi, Gul Ince-Beqo, Michela Camilla Pellicani

The aim of this study is to understand the challenges these professionals face in providing services in the reception centers in the Apulia region of Italy, one of the main Mediterranean routes for asylum seekers heading for Europe. To this end, we exploit the data collected as part of the AMIF "Prevention 4.0" project, funded by the European Commission and the Italian Ministry of the Interior. This project is designed to create an integrated system of prevention, diagnosis, treatment and rehabilitation of asylum seekers and holders of international protection on the regional territory. We reinforce quantitative data with in-depth interviews with professionals, both employees and volunteers working in the field. Data shows that cultural mediators assist asylum seekers during the outpatient visits, especially in the first reception while in the second reception, the presence of the cultural mediator undergoes a slight decline. Data also points out that both the first and second reception centers consider it useful to have an ethno-clinical mediator with specialized professional health training.

779 Understanding the Enablers and Barriers in Health Service Access among COVID-19-Infected Refugees in Turkey

Seyda Eruyar

COVID-19 pandemic has been resulting in unprecedented economic and social consequences across the World. Where measures to prevent the disease and health service provision fell short in many countries during the pandemic, refugees became among the most vulnerable groups as they have preexisting adverse living conditions such as crowded households, poor living conditions, limited access to services and economic hardships (Brickhill-Atkinson, M., & Hauck, F. R., 2021). Yet, little is known about the constituents of health service access among refugees resettled in the Majority World Countries. Thus, this study aimed to understand the experiences of refugees in accessing health services in Turkey. Semi-structured interviews were conducted online with 17 adult refugees who were diagnosed with COVID-19 from three distinct of Turkey, i.e. İstanbul, Kahramanmaras, and Konya. Data were analysed through a thematic approach and results revealed two themes. The first theme, "the enablers in accessing health services" included high awareness of disease and transmission. Good level of knowledge about the disease and related symptoms, and having preexisting chronic disease prompted participants to apply to the hospitals. Most participants highlighted that they have no difficulty accessing health services, including having tests, medication, and in-patient care. They also reported that family practitioners made calls to check their health status after diagnosis. Moreover, participants with high awareness of transmission took precautionary measures before applying to hospitals, including wearing masks, applying hygiene practices and self-quarantine. Social media was reported as a source of knowledge, although the misinformation spread through the media regarding the disease caused anxiety in some participants. The second theme, 'the barriers', identify the difficulties in accessing health services. Fewer participants had difficulty in accessing health services because of registration issues. A participant stated that he had to apply private hospital as he was registered in another city. The language was another barrier for some participants as it causes communication problems with health workers and made it difficult for them to express related symptoms. Lastly, limited knowledge about service utilisation prevented some participants to apply hospitals. Understanding the refugees' experiences is essential in establishing their needs and increasing health service access. These findings suggest that the refugee population needs to be informed about the COVID-19, transmission and service usage, and language support should be provided by having interpreters presented at hospitals to increase the health service access.

References

Brickhill-Atkinson, M., & Hauck, F. R. (2021). Impact of COVID-19 on resettled refugees. *Primary Care: Clinics in Office Practice, 48*(1), 57-66. https://doi.org/10.1016/j.pop.2020.10.001

1G   Return Migration

Chair Sinan Zeyneloğlu, Istanbul Kent University, Turkey

563   "Oh my home, oh my home, when shall I see my home?" Initial findings of return migration intentions of professionals
Mohammed Abdullahi and Ngozi Louis Uzomah

649   Why do Lithuanian Migrant Families Return Home?
Ieva Ivinskyte and Vilmante Kumpikaite-Valiuniene

589   Re-emigration of Moldovan migrant communities: trends and consequences
Dorin Dusciac and Olga Coptu

492   Return migration intentions among Turks and Kurds in London
Ibrahim Sirkeci and Sinan Zeyneloğlu

563   "Oh my home, oh my home, when shall I see my home?" Initial findings of return migration intentions of professionals

Mohammed Abdullahi and Ngozi Louis Uzomah

– Initial findings of return migration intentions of professionals.

The migration of African doctors to high-income countries is set in the context of a debate about the net costs or benefits to the countries of origin (Arnold and Lewinsohn 2010; Azose and Raftery 2019).   Theories of migration, such as Neoclassical, New Economics of Labour Migration and the Structural Approach have been mainly Western-focussed (Stark 1991; Cassorino 2004; Mamattah 2006). My research will test the applicability of established theories to a non-Western context and assess the extent to which the theories can account for the migration decisions of highly mobile professionals.

Literature on return migration has largely addressed managed end-to-end migration-for-development policies (Kļave and Supule 2019). Much less is known about the potential for governments to intervene in hitherto unmanaged processes, particularly in a non-Western context (Debnath 2016). Specifically, there is a gap in current literature relating to the potential efficacy of such interventions to promote the return of mobile, highly skilled and globally in-demand groups, such as doctors. This paper will present and analyse the initial findings from my primary research conducted on the lived experiences of Nigerian doctors working in the UK, how they fare in the labour market and their return migration intentions.

The study adopts a mixed methods approach, recognised to address the lapses of different individual methods (Bryman and Bell 2015). With the involvement of Nigerian doctors working in the UK, the three stages employed are: an online survey, online focus groups, and semi-structured interviews. There will be three discrete categories of participants: those participants who have the definite intention of returning to Nigeria; those who do not have the intention of returning; and those who are undecided on their return intentions. These different groups will help in building a holistic picture of the return propensities of Nigerian doctors in the UK. The data collected will be analysed using a combination of descriptive analysis and thematic analysis to support the identification of factors affecting migration decisions of highly skilled professionals.

The research will add to the understanding of return migration to countries within a global economy that do not have managed migration policies. In presenting different participants' personal experiences of migration and their return intentions, the paper will contribute to the knowledge of how highly skilled professional migrants fare when working in a different regulatory framework. By understanding the professional migrants' perspectives and their return propensities, territorial governments and professional bodies can better develop policies to retain expertise and to influence migrants' return intentions.

References

Arnold, P. and Lewinsohn, D. (2010) Motives for Migration of South African Doctors to Australia since 1948. Medical Journal of Australia 192: 288-290.

Azose, J. and Raftery, A. (2019) Estimation of Emigration, Return Migration, and Transit Migration between All Pairs of Countries. PNAS 116: 116-122.

Bryman, A., and Bell, E., (2007) Business Research Methods. (2nd edn). Oxford University Press, Oxford.

Cassarino, J. P. (2004) Theorising Return Migration: the Conceptual Approach to Return Migrants Revisited, in International Journal on Multicultural Societies (IJMS), 6:2, pp. 253-279.

Debnath, P. (2016) Leveraging return migration for development: the role of countries of origin: a literature review. KNOMAD Working Paper No. 17. Washington DC: World Bank.

Kļave, E. and Supule I. (2019) Return Migration Process in Policy and Practice. In: Kasa R., Mieriņa I. (eds) The Emigrant Communities of Latvia. IMISCOE Research Series. Springer, Cham.

Mamattah, S. (2006) Migration and transnationalism: The complete picture? A case study of Russians living in Scotland. eSharp, Issue 6.2

Stark, O. (1991) The Migration of Labor. Cambridge: Basil Blackwell.

649 Why do Lithuanian Migrant Families Return Home?

Ieva Ivinskyte and Vilmante Kumpikaite-Valiuniene

Although return migration is still a relatively understudied field, it requires attention, as its impact to the home state's economic and social spheres can foster development (Debnath, 2016). Migrant's return and consequent investment can significantly improve life in home state communities and influence state-level economic growth (Abainza & Calfat, 2018). At the time of return, return migrants have accumulated not only financial, but also social resources: experience, knowledge and skills, bringing innovation and change to the home state (Coniglio & Brzozowski, 2016). On the individual level, return migration can significantly improve the social and psychological aspects of one's life. Emigration often includes separation from family and social circle, thus, return migration can bring a sense of belonging.

In fact, even though financial freedom is known for facilitating emigration, literature suggests that social factors are the key driver of return migration (Constant & Massey, 2003). Return migration, especially when it comes to family units, can be understood as an entirely social affair (Faist, 2000). Thus, *the purpose of this study is to investigate the main factors driving Lithuanian migrant families to return to their home state.*

The lack of existing comparable research determines the qualitative nature of this study. In order to investigate the subject, 15 semi-structured interviews were conducted with Lithuanian family unit representatives. All interviewees hold Lithuanian citizenship, have previously spent at least three years in emigration, and have been residing in Lithuania for at least a year after their return.

All participants indicated that they have made the decision to return collectively as a household, often for the benefit for children. Achievement of financial goals set out for emigration encouraged return, while disappointment with the host state did not have a significant effect. After reaching a certain tipping point, which could be defined as establishing financial safety, social factors appear to become more important. Interestingly, although the difference in volume of social ties between the home and host states did not have a significant effect. The strength of social ties to those left behind in the home state encouraged migrants to return.

Based on the results of this qualitative study, Lithuanian family return migration is based primarily on social factors: family and children's welfare. Financial factors appear to be playing a secondary role. The lack of policy awareness suggests that their potential is not maximized. However, overall, the positive attitudes of the participants in this study may indicate that Lithuania has the potential to attract those who had previously chosen to emigrate in a search for a better life.

References

Abainza, L., & Calfat, G. (2018). Home Sweet Home: Embracing the Return to Returnees' migration. *Migration and Development, 7*(3), 366-387. doi:10.1080/21632324.2018.1451247

Coniglio, N. D., & Brzozowski, J. (2016). Migration and Development at Home: Bitter or Sweet Return? Evidence from Poland. *European Urban and Regional Studies, 1*-21. doi:10.1177/0969776416681625

Constant, A., & Massey, D. S. (2003). Self-Selection, Earnings, and Out-Migration: A longitudinal study of immigrants to Germany. *Journal of Population Economics, 16*(4), 631-653. doi:10.1007/s00148-003-0168-8

Debnath, P. (2016). Leveraging Return Migration for Development: The Role of Countries of Origin. KNOMAD working paper 17. Retrieved from https://www.knomad.org/sites/default/files/2017-04/WP%20Leveraging%20Return%20Migration%20for%20Development%20-%20The%20Role%20of%20Countries%20of%20Origin.pdf

Faist, T. (2000). The Crucial Meso Link: Social Capital in Social and Symbolic Ties. *The Volume and Dynamics of International Migration and Transnational Social Spaces,* 96–123. doi:10.1093/acprof:oso/9780198293910.003.0004

589   Re-emigration of Moldovan migrant communities: trends and consequences

Dorin Dusciac and Olga Coptu

Eastern Europe experienced a strong wave of emigration after the collapse of the USSR, in early 1990's. Republic of Moldova is no exception but rather confirms the rule. A decade after having gained its independence, massive emigration originating from the Republic of Moldova retained two main destinations: the Russian Federation and the European Union member states. These routes have changed in the next decade, due to political developments in the destination countries. For instance, significant legislative changes were in place in the Russian Federation regarding residence and work permits for migrants. The tightening of residence legislation has raised the price of so-called "patents". At the same time, the introduction of entry ban lists on the territory of the Federation led to a temporary return of migrants from this country towards their countries of origin, including the Republic of Moldova. Subsequently was registered a re-emigration of some of the returning countries to EU countries, where they already had relatives (members of the westwards tide of emigrants). In the meantime, the political situation in Moldova changed, along with emigrants' preferences for destination countries and regions. The latest data show that Moldovan emigrants' preferred destination countries are: EU member states (72.7%) and CIS countries (14.7%)[1].

---

[1] Reintegration program for the citizens of the Republic of Moldova, returning from abroad 2021-2026, BRD.

Accordingly, to a recent survey conducted by OIM's mission to Moldova[2], 83% of respondents say they are directly affected by the COVID-19 pandemic, 50% of those most affected are from the Russian Federation and Italy, and 49% are from Portugal. Moldovan citizens' extended migration profile shows various trends and characteristics of the migrant community, depending on the country of destination. For example, a significant proportion of Moldovan migrants to the Russian Federation are involved in a circular migration trend, whilst many of the Moldovan migrants to Southern European countries (ex: Italy and Portugal) are near the retirement age. Economic and social crisis in destination countries, rapidly evolving demographic characteristics of the migrant community (ageing, for example) are examples of *push factors* that motivate migrants from certain countries (Russian Federation and Southern Europe) to leave for other destination countries or to the home country (in a lesser proportion). On the other hand, growing economies in need for qualified workforce, better wages and working conditions and more robust welfare systems in Northern European countries are *pull factors* that attract re-emigrating Moldovans.

In this work we will analyze re-emigration of the Moldovan migrant communities over the past decade. Our methodological approach is grounded on a thorough description of *push* and *pull factors*, as well as of their impact on the migration vectors. The quantification challenge will be confronted through the prism of surprisingly high participation rate in recent presidential elections (November 2020) in countries such as Germany, the United Kingdom and Ireland.

492   Return migration intentions among Turks and Kurds in London

Ibrahim Sirkeci and Sinan Zeyneloğlu

Migration is a relatively rare incident and yet a widely recognised strategic option for large segments of populations around the world. This is evident in the discrepancy between the number of international migrants around the world and the number of people who desire to migrate to another country. The latter is often three- or four-fold larger than the former as suggested by the Gallup World Poll (Esipova, Pugliese, Ray, 2018). In other words, as our good friend and one of the doayens of migration scholarship Philip L. Martin often says "migration is not a norm but exception". Sure, it is also arguable that people have been moving around the world since day one.

Migration itself is also a space of conflict and insecurity. It is not easy as it is costly both in material and non-material terms. Hence our understanding of human mobility revolves around this dynamic nature of perceived insecurities. Space of enactment for human mobility also revolves around the nexus of internal and international migration while perceiving the negotiating actors on a nexus of movers and non-movers (in other words, migrants and non-migrants) embedded in (multidimensional and multifaceted) structures. This makes all migrations, including return movements, in a sense a "forced" move where

---

[2] Impact of the COVID-19 pandemic on migration: mobility, number and profile of returned migrants, specific vulnerabilities of groups affected by declining remittances, SOCIOLOGICAL STUDY, IOM 2020.

voluntariness is about how strongly individuals and groups feel about insecurities and how these insecurities and responses to them are ingrained in their migratory reactions and eventually building up cultures (of migration).

Cultures of migration emerge over time becomes part and parcel of the space people move, re-settle, and return. A culture of migration offers an easy reference point when the conflicts intensify and heighten the perception of insecurity. Insecurity as a notional driver of human mobility allows us to capture the true dynamic nature of movement which is an open ended process. That means people move and continue considering the risks and benefits in their new homes. These considerations may lead to return migrations and remigrations.

Until the penultimate return, i.e. death, many people consider migrating, returning, re-migrating and so on. In this era of ubiquitous connectedness, moving to another place has become a more obvious option than ever. In this paper, we discuss the role of insecurities in return migration decisions and intentions embedded in emerging or established cultures of migration.

Reference

Esipova, N., Anita Pugliese and Julie Ray (2018, December 10). More Than 750 Million Worldwide Would Migrate If They Could. Gallup. Available: https://news.gallup.com/poll/245255/750-million-worldwide-migrate.aspx Accessed: 1/10/2020.

14:15-14:30 BREAK

Day One 6 July 2021 Tuesday

Day One 6 July 2021 - 14:30-16:00
2A   Migration and Integration
Chair Süreyya Sönmez Efe, University of Lincoln, United Kingdom
585   Exploring the Experiences of Kurdish Refugees in Finland
       Afrouz Zibaei
654   The Role of the Italian Civic Organizations in the Integration Process of
       Migrants and Refugees
       Mariann Domos
663   Potential Diaspora Direct Investment in Wales
       Sarah Louisa Birchley
743   Asylum policy and labour exploitation among asylum seekers and
       refugees in Italy. First research results
       Natalia Maria Szulc

585   Exploring the Experiences of Kurdish Refugees in Finland

Afrouz Zibaei

Background: There is a lack of knowledge and information about the Kurdish refugee process and impact on their mental health in Finland even though Kurds started to migrate to Finland at the beginning since the 1970s. The purpose of this qualitative life story study is to explore understanding mental health issues reported by 15 Kurdish refugee men and women through their life stories approach during the whole refugee process. The whole Kurdish refugee process is known in three portions of time, pre refugee, initial refugee and post refugee. The analysis was based on the listening guide methodology. The arrangement was for Kurdish refugee in Finland. The Kurdish population has been noticeable for many years. Kurdish refugee in European countries often has personal experiences of violence and persecution in their home countries, which increase their vulnerability to desirable mental health and psychological distress. Kurds are an ethnic group with a population of about 36.4–45.6 million which they are living in areas of Iran, Iraq, Turkey and Syria, they have been forced to migrate or refugee because of political and social turmoil. It is estimated that more than 2 million Kurds currently live in Europe. The number of Kurds in Finland is estimated to be around 14,054. Aims; The purpose of this study was to discover and describe the experiences of Kurdish refugee during three periods of migration to Finland with the investigation to mental health issues. knowledge of the Kurdish refugee process impact on mental health based on the life story approach. Method; Qualitative research methods based on life story interview are used in the study. The life story approach has come to dominate the contemporary understanding of the Kurdish refugee theme. Taking a life story approach and drawing on mental health perspectives, the main aim of this research was to explore the stories told by Kurdish refugee men and women. Placing the life stories of women and men at the heart of this study, I organized life story interviews with 15 women and men who came to live in Finland after seeking asylum. Their interviews were recorded, transcribed and then analysed using the Listening Guide (LG). An analytical step was developed called letting stories speak to hear Kurdish refugee´s life story approach experiences. These were interviewed face-to-face life story interview approach. In all the interviews were done at the participants' home. The interviews were conducted in Kurdish and translated to English. The LG method enables an understanding and represented the active role the Kurdish refugee plays in the construction of their own life stories.

654   The Role of the Italian Civic Organizations in the Integration Process of Migrants and Refugees

Mariann Domos

Italy is one of the key actors in the ongoing international "migration crisis" in the Mediterranean region. Since the early 2000s, immigration has increased considerably and it revealed difficulties in handle the complexity of this phenomenon. The Italian migration policy didn't offer exact answers, and managed it in different ways, but when we talk about migration and its management, we cannot disregard the issue of integration. In Italy there is a broad civil society and some of them try to handle the mass migration in the local level. These bottom-up social co-operations put in connection the Italian people with immigrants through various projects. Their importance is to recognize the integration is a key issue: those who choose to stay in the country need to be helped to become a useful element in the society and the reduction of the cultural gap need to be a base for a more successful migration policy. These organizations can transfer the knowledge to local policies, programs and actors and they can help prepare action plans to policy level or they can integrate their programs into the mainstream services. Such as they can help to rethink the provision of services to migrants and ethnic minorities and undertake the necessary organizational changes to adapt these services. And it is important to note that the number of regular immigrants in Italy has come up to 5 million, representing 8.4% of the total population.[3]

Some of the civil organizations is very interesting and particular initiative, for example the 'centro sociale' or the faith-based organizations. But why are they so important along with the integration? And the success of the local action is always a question, does it work in the policy level too? In the presentation I prove to show an overview of the challenges of Italian integration policy nowadays. A very important goal of the author is to show and demonstrate the role of civic organizations in the Italian migration issue. In the presentation I would like to introduce some special initiatives such as the 'centro sociale' and the 'ecclesiastic-based' civic organizations and emphasize the unique world of these initiatives. The lecture analyses and tries to group them while presents their different types of services and its importance along with the integration.

The paper, based especially on empirical experiences, is the result of two years research in Italy with different scholarships.

663   Potential Diaspora Direct Investment in Wales

Sarah Louisa Birchley

This paper presents the results of a feasibility study to ascertain the appetite for a Welsh Diaspora Direct Investment (DDI) fund. Diaspora are a potential source of talent and skills and enablers of economic growth (Kuznetsov, 2010). Many countries have been working to better understand their diaspora and how they can harness their social and financial capital for the benefit of the home country. There are various engagement strategies used to reach out to the diaspora, these strategies are explicit and systematic policy initiatives aimed at developing and managing relationships between homelands and diasporic populations (Boyle, Kutchin and Ancien, 2009). It is through such strategies that initiatives such as DDI can be encouraged and managed. DDI differs from international remittances in that remittances involve the sending of money to family members, DDI focuses on direct investments. DDI is also thought to be more stable than other types of foreign direct investment particularly during unfavorable economic conditions, because of the emotional connections of diaspora members to their country of origin.

Wales, with a population of 3.1 million, has an estimated 3 million Welsh diaspora. The Welsh government launched its International Strategy in 2020, setting out their approach to international engagement. It highlights the steps they will take to ensure Wales has an increasing profile and influence in the

---

[3] https://www.tuttitalia.it/statistiche/cittadini-stranieri-2019/

world, part of which is to engage the diaspora. *GlobalWelsh* (GW) is a diaspora organization with a mission to build on the networks and norms of reciprocity and trustworthiness that characterize groups of people in a diaspora. They believe that building such networks will develop a type of social capital that has the potential to be a stimulus of financial capital for the economic development of Wales. *GlobalWelsh* has already begun the smart utilization of digital technologies for connecting their diaspora through their *Connect* platform and have engaged in an Investor Portal to support Welsh businesses. Yet, Wales is yet to have a coordinated approach to DDI. This research targeted members of the diaspora through GW and key stakeholders to determine the type of financial investment the diaspora would engage in. This would help determine if a DDI fund could be beneficial for Wales. A survey was conducted among the diaspora and interviews were held with key stakeholders. Findings show that although there is an appetite for a DDI fund for Wales, there are many precursors to a successful fund being established. The results of this study will not only provide guidance for Wales as it moves forward but may also serve to inform policy and practice in other diaspora organizations.

References

Boyle, M., R. Kitchin, and D. Ancien. (2009). *The NIRSA Diaspora Strategy Wheel and Ten Principles of Good Practice*, National University of Ireland.

Kuznetsov, Y. (2006). *Diaspora Networks and the International Migration of Skills: How Countries Can Draw on Their Talent Abroad. Washington*, DC: World Bank.

743   Asylum policy and labour exploitation among asylum seekers and refugees in Italy. First research results

Natalia Maria Szulc

Background

In recent years we have witnessed a paradigm shift in the management of forced migration and integration of asylum seekers and refugees. The international community (headed by The Agenda 2030 and The Global Compact on Refugees) have taken a common position - to increase private sector involvement in the socio-economic integration of forced migrants.

Aim

Mapping private sector engagement in the socio-economic integration of refugees and asylum seekers in the host country. Identifying the role of the private sector, as well as the inhibiting and activating factors and the range of activities. Moreover, the research will attempt to answer the question of how the private sector can contribute to solving labour exploitation among forced migrants.

Methodology

Qualitative and quantitative analysis of data collected during a six-month field research in Italy. I conducted structured and semi-structured interviews with private sector actors involved in the forced migrants environment. The same applies to local and national authorities, and civil society actors. Research includes in-depth case studies on the private sector's engagement.

Results

Taking a multidimensional approach, I will present the first findings and developments of the research. The research fills a gap in the discussion on the nature of private sector engagement in refugee socio-economic integration in Europe. The profile of engagement in Italy and the adopted methodology will allow further exploration of the phenomenon in other host European countries.

2B   Education and Migration
Chair Amina Ghezal, University of Exeter, UK

803   Bilingualism, Language Proficiency and Educational Achievements: Are all subjects equal?
       Hamutal Kreiner and Svetlana Chachashvili-Bolotin
809   Language: the key to integration? Exploring the complex role of language in integration processes
       Helen McCarthy
887   "My Tuvaluaness starts with my language": language use and preservation of the Tuvaluan diaspora in New Zealand
       Amina Ghezal
699   From Root to Route: The Case of Syrian University Students in Istanbul As Active Agents of Transnational Spaces and Identities
       Seyma Karamese

803   Bilingualism, Language Proficiency and Educational Achievements: Are all subjects equal?

Hamutal Kreiner and Svetlana Chachashvili-Bolotin

In a world of rising immigration, understanding the impact of language proficiency on educational achievements is important even for second-generation immigrant (SGI) students. This research examines bilingualism and language aptitude in educational achievements by comparing non-immigrant background students and SGI students.

The novelty of the current research is twofold. First, the distinction between different learning subjects as a function of the teaching language (verbal topics and studying foreign language). Second, the study's conceptual framework combines both sociological and sociolinguistics approaches. According to the sociological approach, the family background of immigrant students, such as parental educational level and economic means, makes a crucial contribution to educational achievements (Lissitsa & Chachashvili-Bolotin, 2019; Portes & Rumbaut, 2001). Regarding the sociolinguistic approach, most SGI students are Heritage Bilingual (HB) students, those whose home spoken language is not the dominant language of the larger (national) society. As a result, they may have more limited vocabulary, slower comprehension, and lesser fluency. On the other hand, these HB students may have the advantages in meta-linguistic skills due to simultaneous acquisition, in terms of executive functions etc. (Maluch & Kempert, 2017; Schwartz & Gorbatt, 2016). Therefore, we can postulate that after controlling for SES family background, SGI students will show lower achievement than non-immigrant background students in subjects that depend on context language due to differences in comprehension during classes. In contrast, SGI students will show higher achievements when studying foreign language compared to the non-immigrant background students due to their developed metalinguistic skills.

To examine our hypotheses, we used Israeli Ministry of Education databases for all grade-12 students in the Jewish sector who earned high school matriculation certification in 2014-2017. We analyzed the differences between two groups of Israeli-born students: SGI students whose both parents emigrated from the Former Soviet Union (FSU) (N=19,133) and students with a non-immigrant family background (N=154,467). The total sample was 173,600 students. It is important to emphasize that the FSU immigrants in Israel is large enough demographically to support the continuous use of the Russian language. (Remennick, 2017). Russian has become a third most spoken language of the country (Yelenevskaya & Fialkova, 2017). Thus, most Israeli-born children of the FSU immigrants are HB speakers. Using hierarchical linear regression models, we compared achievements in subjects taught in the local language (such as Hebrew, Civic, Math) and foreign language (English) between these two groups.

Analysis of achievements as reflected in the national matriculation exams database revealed both advantages and disadvantages in matriculation grades related to parental linguistic background. In verbal topics as well as in Mathematics, non-immigrant background students gained the highest grades and SGI students scored lowest. Controlling for Hebrew grades decreased or diminished these differences. In contrast, in English as a foreign language, SGI students did not exhibit disadvantage compared to non-immigrant background students. Moreover, after controlling for Hebrew grades, SGI students gained the highest grades in English. The practical implications of these findings may inform policy makers as to educational policy and intervention programs aimed at improving educational achievements among immigrant populations.

References

Lissitsa, S., & Chachashvili-Bolotin, S. (2019). Enrolment in mathematics and physics at The advanced level in secondary school among two generations of highly skilled immigrants. *International Migration, 57*(5), 216-234.

Maluch, J. T., & Kempert, S. (2017). Bilingual profiles and third language learning: The effects of the manner of learning, sequence of bilingual acquisition, and language use practices. *International Journal of Bilingual Education and Bilingualism*.

Portes, A., & Rumbaut, R. G. (2001). *Legacies: the Story of the Immigrant Second Generation*. New York: Russell Sage Foundation.

Remennick, L. (2017). Generation 1.5 of Russian-Speaking Immigrants in Israel and in Germany: An Overview of Recent Research and a German Pilot Study. In L. Isurin & C. Riehl (Eds.), *Integration, Identity and Language Maintenance in Young*

Immigrants: Russian Germans or German Russians? (pp. 69-98). Amsterdam: John Benjamins Publishing.

Schwartz, M., & Gorbatt, N. (2016). 'Why do we know Hebrew and they do not know Arabic?'Children's meta-linguistic talk in bilingual preschool. *International Journal of Bilingual Education and Bilingualism, 19*(6), 668-688.

Yelenevskaya, M., & Fialkova, L. (2017). Linguistic Landscape and what it tells us about the integration of the Russian language into Israeli economy. *Вестник Российского университета дружбы народов. Серия: Лингвистика, 21*(3).

809   Language: the key to integration? Exploring the complex role of language in integration processes

Helen McCarthy

Mastering the destination language is often described by politicians as fundamental to migrants' integration. This is, in part, due to language's symbolic role in the building of imagined national communities and identities. In the UK, this idea has becoming increasingly widely circulated in discussions about a post-Brexit immigration system. Thus in public imaginaries, speaking English is a key element of showing that migrants are able to contribute and are committed to the destination country.

Academic accounts also often identify language as a key aspect of integration. While recent conceptualisations have focused on the processual and interactional nature of integration, seeking to more accurately capture the multi-dimensional and dynamic nature of these processes, most still provide fairly superficial accounts of the role of language. These often fail to grapple with the complex role that language plays in society, acting both as medium of communication as well as a marker of identities. It is this dual role of language that makes understanding its role in integration processes so complex.

Drawing on mixed-methods empirical work with Spanish citizens living in the UK, this paper seeks to unpack this complexity with a more nuanced analysis of the role that language plays in a range of integration processes. As an understudied population, this group provides an in interesting case study: migration from Spain is fairly recent – having increased substantively in the last decade. This group is highly educated but still arrive with barriers in English language competence. Using findings from an online survey and 27 in depth qualitative interviews, the paper draws on a rich data-set to build a multi-faceted account of integration processes.

Through exploring the relationships between English language skills and people's social connections and sense of belonging, the paper highlights the complex and highly subjective role that language plays across a range of integration processes. The findings reveal how differences in people's ability to invest time and money in language learning, both before and after arrival in the UK, affects long term outcomes. Linking back to broader integration theories and models, the paper demonstrates that integration processes proceed through a multiplicity of languages and argues that this must be made more explicit in academic accounts.

887   "My Tuvaluaness starts with my language": language use and preservation of the Tuvaluan diaspora in New Zealand

Amina Ghezal

Post-migration, immigrants' native languages play a vital role in preserving their native culture, identity, and ties with the homeland. Language preservation is a source of empowerment for many immigrant communities, connection to cultural heritage and unity as a diaspora in the host-place. This research has been conducted to explore Tuvaluan immigrants' culture, place attachment and belonging to the motherland. This research aims to highlight the role of language use and preservation in the immigrants' lives and understand their transnational activities and their socio-political discourses of immigration and of being foreign nationals in New Zealand. Throughout the analysis of forty interviews with Tuvaluan immigrants in New Zealand, following a *Talanoa* approach (a traditional Pacific conversation and storytelling method), Tuvaluans have expressed that "Te 'Gana Tuvalu" or Tuvaluan language is a constructive element of their territorial and national identity, and a gateway towards understanding the Tuvaluan culture, ancestral knowledge and history. Tuvaluan immigrants equate the Tuvaluan language with a sense of distinctiveness, pride, and Tuvaluan culture continuity in the host-place post-resettlement. In this respect, language is given prime importance in Tuvaluans' houses, community, cultural events and religion, despite the hardships of preserving it, especially among the younger generations. Therefore, the constant use and preservation of Te Gana Tuvalu is an essential condition to maintain and preserve the Tuvaluan identity and culture, thus preserving attachment to and transnational ties with Tuvalu the homeland.

699   From Root to Route: The Case of Syrian University Students in Istanbul As Active Agents of Transnational Spaces and Identities

Seyma Karamese

Approximately 4% of Turkey's population are recently arrived, Syrian migrants, escaping from the harsh conditions of war in their country (Erdoğan, 2018). As a result of conditions in the region and its generous open-door policy, Turkey is now host the world's largest community of Syrians displaced by the ongoing conflict. According to the statistics of Directorate General of Migration Management, Turkey's Syrian migrant population is more than 3 million in mid-April 2019 (Interior Directorate General of Migration Management (IDGMM), 2019). This number, which is more than the population of many European countries, has produced many consequences and transformations within the cities of Turkey by touching each ordinary person's life from different aspects. Istanbul with its highest urban population makes discussion possible to understand these transformations by focusing on dialectical relation between space and identity in urban context. This dialectical relation directly related to youth students' daily life because they are using different places, creating new sense of places with new cultural forms, transforming and negotiating their identities, trying to be integrated education system and touching different social groups. In other words, they not only produce new sense of place but also negotiate their identities through this place making process. In this sense, I will mainly examine the daily life routine of youth Syrian university students to clarify the co-construction process of identity and sense of place.

As qualitative research methods, 30 in-depth interviews and 2 focus groups were conducted with students whose age over 18 between in Istanbul. Moreover, field research was supported by participant observations and taking notes. I will mainly contribute to debate on youth and migration studies by showing the tendency among young migrant population. It is found that this group coming with forced migration not only part of transnational places but also in the future they will be agent of transnational identities. This is because, these students by obtaining Turkish citizenship and getting education in Turkey will be directly part of Turkish society. However, at the same time they have transnational networks in other countries such as friend groups, relatives and professional links, they would like to live both in Turkey and another country - mostly in Syria or any European country- after education and they are planning to be part of international work life. This shows a tendency towards product of interconnecting flows of routes rather than roots (Massey, 1994). The concept of routes better describes their mobility and transnational ties.

Thus, the interrelation between routes and roots is vital because a completely rooted sense of identity is challenged with the mobility of these students so using "routes" is more appropriate to understand the transnational place perceptions and identity construction of Syrian students in Istanbul.

2C   Youth Migration
Chair: **Ana Vila Freyer, Universidad Latina de México, Mexico**
676   The Impact of Deferred Action for Childhood Arrival (DACA) on Educational and Career Goals: A mixed-method study of DACA eligible students at a California public university
Nicole Dubus
511   Recognition and Exercise of the Social Right to Education. Challenges and Opportunities in a Multicultural Inclusion perspective
Elena Girasella
680   The Obama Administration's Central American Minors (CAM) Program (215-217): A Safe and Legal Path to the U.S.?
Chiara Galli
497   Teachers' Perceptions of Integration of Immigrant School-Students: Ideal versus Reality - The Israeli Case
Adi Binhas

676   The Impact of Deferred Action for Childhood Arrival (DACA) on Educational and Career Goals: A mixed-method study of DACA eligible students at a California public university

Nicole Dubus

Research Problem: The immigration policy known as Deferred Action for Childhood Arrivals (DACA) was developed to address the needs of children brought to the United States when they were young and have no clear path toward citizenship. This study examines the experiences of DACA eligible and recipient college students from one public university in California.

Theory: Critical Relations Theory is used to understand the experiences of the participants.

Methods: This was a mixed method study using a survey of DACA students (n=107) that focused on their experiences, and in-person interviews from key informants (n=4) who provide resources for DACA students, and from interviews of DACA students (n=7).

Findings: The qualitative data complemented the quantitative data in showing the additional stressors DACA students experience that impact their graduation and career outcomes, such as family obligations, work obligations, financial strain, mental health, academic strain, and fear.

Conclusions: To be helpful to this population, educators, policy makers, social support agencies, and immigration advocates need to be involved. It is important to understand the layered barriers that make it difficult for DACA students to succeed.

Keywords: DACA (Deferred-Action-for-Childhood-Arrivals), University, Immigration, Migration, United States

511   Recognition and Exercise of the Social Right to Education. Challenges and Opportunities in a Multicultural Inclusion perspective

Elena Girasella

The slight increase in the number of refugees who had access to university education in 2019 is far from the UNHCR's target of the inclusion of 15% of the refugee population in tertiary education by 2030 (UNHCR, 2019) and it is reasonable to assume that the SARS-CoV-2 coronavirus pandemic will explain its negative effects even in this topic. This work is intended to contribute to the affirmation of the right to education as a social right. The contribution is based on the assumption that the enhancement of the knowledge and skills of migrants, refugees and asylum seekers represents one of the main levers of inclusion and development. Investing in education and facilitating access to the highest levels of education not only guarantees full personal development but it also generates indisputable added value to the entire community. The assessment of a positive impact that goes beyond the private sphere is justified by the quantity and quality of the migration flows in this century. Notwithstanding these simple remarks, the choice to undertake an educational path is still residual. It is, in fact, one of the most difficult paths to deal with, starting from the problem of demonstrating the level of previous studies by the documents. Regardless of age, precondition, motivation and expectations, the reception system implemented by the host countries causes the loss of the background of knowledge and skills which, on the contrary, should be recognised and further supported. The chosen point of view looks at the migration phenomenon as a matter of high political value, it can be ascribed to the capacity of institutions to guarantee sustainability and inclusion, through processes that, first of all, enhance human resources brought by the migration phenomenon and, moreover, that include in the social system people of different cultures and languages. The level of inclusion of immigrants is certainly related especially to the politics and legislative acts that the legal system adopts to overcome cultural, ideological and religious differences. In this framework, it must be considered that the concept of integration does not correspond to that of homologation and that the government intervention will be all the more effective the more it will be able to ensure coexistence and compatibility between different cultures, through its different institutional structures, within the constitutional principle of pluralism and that of equality, and, at the same time, guaranteeing to the immigrants an adequate level of rights, especially the social ones. Looking at the Italian university system we will try to give an account of its most recent evolution in the indicated direction. To do this, we will consider the legal framework and we will examine how it leads to the necessity to expand the sphere of social rights to be recognised to the individuals, besides any status linked to citizenship. Lastly, by illustrating the main experiences emerging from the Italian context, we will examine the way the contribution of universities in favour of the inclusion of migrants, refugees and asylum seekers is expected to become increasingly important.

References

Benhabib Seyla, Another Cosmopolitanism, Oxford University Press, Oxford 2006;

Cassese Sabino, Stato in Trasformazione, Estratto in Rivista Trimestrale di Diritto Pubblico Anno LXVI Fasc. 2 – 2016. Milano, Giuffrè Editore (2016);

Davies Sarah R., Research staff and public engagement: a UK study. Springer, 2013;

IOM, Views on the Roadmap for the EU's New Pact on Migration and Asylum, August 2020, https://eea.iom.int/publications/iom-views-roadmap-eu-new-pact-migration-and-asylum;

UNHCR, Doubling our impact third country higher education pathways for refugees, 2019 https://www.unhcr.org/5e5e4c614.pdf.

680   The Obama Administration's Central American Minors (CAM) Program (215-217): A Safe and Legal Path to the U.S.?

Chiara Galli

Created by the Obama administration after a record surge in unaccompanied child migration, the Central American Minors (CAM) program was meant to allow children whose lives were at risk in Honduras, El Salvador, and Guatemala to join their parents in the United States. Programs like CAM that allow individuals to obtain refugee status from their home countries, and thus avoid perilous journeys to reach countries of asylum, have been touted as "solutions" to refugee crises. However, this chapter demonstrates that CAM was an inadequate solution. Ignoring the role of U.S. immigration policy in producing the very conditions it claimed to solve, the program was designed to benefit an excessively narrow group of individuals. Poor implementation lead to processing delays that meant resettlement goals were never met and children who applied were placed at even greater risk as they waited at length in dangerous home countries while their applications were assessed.

497   Teachers' Perceptions of Integration of Immigrant School-Students: Ideal versus Reality - The Israeli Case

Adi Binhas

Over the years, Israeli society has moved from a melting pot to a multiculturalist understanding of integrating immigrant students into the Israeli educational system. Our article attempts to disentangle these dynamics in the context of school's classrooms which are targeted to immigrant students. Specifically, we focus on teachers' views about teaching and the integration of immigrant students in the new society. To do so, we examine the existent educational policy and training in this regard. We ask what guidelines are stated by the official educational policy – Do these guidelines entail a normative discourse that stresses a melting pot or multiculturalist approach towards integration of the immigrant students? Are these guidelines reflected in teachers' views? To address these questions, we used a qualitative method that included twenty interviews with teachers and the teams that work with immigrant students in four affluent high-schools in the Tel-Aviv area. The immigrant students arrived during the last five years and come from France, Ukraine and English-speaking countries. Findings revealed that both official policy and teachers' views involve various profiles of a national-hegemonic (melting pot) and multiculturalist approaches. Moreover, they indicate a lack of professional guidance for teachers in their work immigrants.   Conclusions suggest that in an era of globalization, on which the multicultural discourses are salient, especially when immigrants are from Western countries, both the host country and the immigrants themselves are ambivalent with regard to meaning of societal integration. Thus, we suggest that a clearer immigration policy is on due.

2D   AMERM Panel: Pandémie (French)

Chair: Mohamed Khachani, AMERM, Morocco

655   L'Afrique et la pandémie du Coronavirus, quels effets sur la migration ?
Mehdi Lahlou

668   Le droit de la famille en migration : quels conflits, quelles solutions ?
MALIKA BENRADI

690   Délivrance des documents d'identité et intégration socio-économique des migrants, réfugiés et leurs enfants au Maroc
Hajar EL MOUKHI

655　L'Afrique et la pandémie du Coronavirus, quels effets sur la migration ?

Mehdi Lahlou

Les effets immédiats de la pandémie du Coronavirus, qui a affecté la planète depuis le début de l'année 2020 et les mesures prises à travers le monde pour la contenir ont soudainement bloqué l'économie mondiale, en poussant au confinement d'une partie de la population mondiale et en fermant la plupart des pays sur eux-mêmes, ont rendu ceux parmi eux qui disposent de peu de moyens encore plus fragiles.

Dès le printemps 2020, il est très vite apparu que ce sont les populations les plus pauvres et les plus précarisées socialement dans les pays riches et, plus encore, dans les pays en développement, qui ont subi en termes de chômage, de baisse d'activité et de revenus les conséquences de la crise sanitaire. Or, si dans les pays développés les Etats ont pu mettre en place, unilatéralement ou en groupe – comme cela a été le cas de l'Union européenne - de nombreuses mesures économiques, financières et sociales de nature à atténuer le poids de la crise sur leurs populations, dans les pays moins nantis, où les Etats sont faibles ou défaillants, le coronavirus a rapidement aggravé les conditions de vie de nombreuses catégories sociales. Cela en raison de la forte dépendance des économies de ces pays par rapport au commerce mondial ou au tourisme international et en raison de l'importance de l'activité économique informelle et du manque - ou de l'insuffisance - de la protection sociale en leur sein. Parallèlement, les problèmes de chômage, de faim ou de malnutrition, déjà prégnant dans ces mêmes pays, sont devenus encore plus accentués.

Et, de fait, la crise sanitaire mondiale a révélé au grand jour les problèmes structurels, internes comme externes, que connaissent les pays en développement, notamment en Afrique. Soit des problèmes qui renforcent les incitations à la migration, quelles que soient les risques que les migrants prennent pour cela.

Dans ce sens, pendant toute la période au cours de laquelle les frontières aériennes, terrestres et maritimes, en particulier entre l'Europe et les pays africains, étaient presque totalement bloquées, les flux migratoires des rives sud de la Méditerranée vers les rives nord ont fortement diminué. Toutefois, avec ce qui s'est passé à ce propos entre la Tunisie et l'Italie ou entre l'Afrique de l'ouest et du nord et les Îles Canaries, il semble bien que le potentiel de migration depuis le continent n'ait pas disparu. Au contraire, les effets (actuels et futurs) des crises économiques et sociales, qui continueront sans doute de s'aggraver, suggèrent que les incitations à migrer à la recherche de subsistance ou de meilleures conditions de vie deviendront très probablement plus fortes.

Ainsi, même si les retombées de la COVID-19 sur la santé ont été ressentis avec moins d'intensité, en termes relatifs, sur les Africains, ceux-ci ont vu leurs conditions de vie se détériorer fortement suite à la pandémie. Et, au-delà de ses effets néfastes immédiats, les projections sur l'impact des retombées socioéconomiques de la pandémie sur la sécurité alimentaire, le chômage ainsi que les revenus et la croissance économique en Afrique donnent une image plutôt sombre. Notamment dans l'optique qu'elles pourraient conduire un plus grand nombre de personnes, désespérées, hors de leur pays d'origine, quel qu'en soit le coût.

Dans cette communication nous traiterons de la situation née en Afrique suite à la pandémie et nous en présenterons les principales indications, notamment en termes de baisse de revenus, d'augmentation de chômage ou d'exacerbation des tensions sécuritaires, avant de revenir sur les évolutions enregistrées au cours de l'année 2020 en rapport avec la migration et ce qui pourrait en advenir à court et moyen termes.

668   Le droit de la famille en migration : quels conflits, quelles solutions ?

Malika Benradi

Partout au monde, la question migratoire a soulevé de très nombreuses problématiques, abordées sous différents angles : politique, économique, juridique, social, culturel…, interpellant directement les politiques d'intégration dans les pays d'accueil, qui évoluent au gré des conjonctures politiques et économiques.

En ce qui concerne la vie publique des migrants, le principe de la territorialité des lois, fondement de la souveraineté des États, a dominé la gestion des relations avec les migrants, quels que soient leur pays d'origine, son régime politique, ses lois nationales, ou ses valeurs culturelles… : les droits social, pénal, administratif, commercial, foncier… des pays d'accueil s'imposent aux migrants sur la base de leur lieu de résidence dans le pays d'accueil.

Cette logique d'imposer aux migrants l'arsenal juridique du pays d'accueil n'a pas pu être étendue ni imposée au droit de la famille. Par respect au principe de la personnalité des lois en matière de statut personnel, les migrants se voient appliquer, sur le territoire des pays d'accueil, leur propre droit de la famille, sur la base de leur nationalité d'origine. Il est considéré, par ailleurs, comme l'expression de l'identité culturelle des migrants et renforce leurs liens avec le pays d'origine.

Cependant, l'application de ce principe, fondé sur la nationalité d'origine du migrant, va obliger les pays d'accueil à appliquer sur leurs territoires un droit, dont les fondements et le référentiel, est en grande contradiction avec l'ordre juridique des pays d'accueil, dans sa dimension politique inhérente au respect de l'ordre public.

Si pendant longtemps l'ordre juridique des pays d'accueil, au niveau législatif, doctrinal et jurisprudentiel, a eu recours à l'ordre public atténué pour permettre la réception du droit de la famille des pays musulmans, dont sont originaires des millions de migrants en Europe, force est de constater qu'aujourd'hui, l'ordre public devient de plus en plus sévère et écarte de plus en plus l'application du droit de la famille aux migrants musulmans. Sous prétexte, d'assurer plus facilement l'intégration des migrants musulmans, les plus éloignés de la culture judéo-chrétienne, dominante en Europe, le critère de rattachement à la nationalité d'origine est écarté au profit du critère de la loi du domicile permanent, en l'occurrence la loi de leur résidence permanente dans les pays d'accueil.

La présente communication entend d'une part, lever le voile sur les conflits de lois voire de culture que soulève la réception du droit de la famille des migrants musulmans en Europe, dont le référentiel du droit de la famille est éminemment religieux : il permet la répudiation, la polygamie, ne reconnaît pas la filiation en dehors des liens du mariage, consacre des inégalités de genre en matière d'héritage…Et d'autre part, interpeller les politiques d'intégration en Europe, notamment dans leurs dimensions politique et socio-économique, et questionner le pouvoir des négociations menées par les pays musulmans en la matière, compte tenu de l'apport financier important des migrants au profit des pays d'origine.

690   Délivrance des documents d'identité et intégration socio-économique des migrants, réfugiés et leurs enfants au Maroc

Hajar El Moukhi

Resume

Ces dernières années, plusieurs publications académiques ou institutionnelles ont abordé l'intégration économique et l'insertion sociale des migrants et des réfugiés au Maroc[4], ce qui n'est pas le cas des apatrides. À première vue, cette population ne suscite pas intérêt imminent puisqu'un seul cas a été enregistré apatride en 2017, selon le bureau marocain des réfugiés et apatrides. Or, l'étude menée par des chercheures de l'Association Marocaine d'Études et de Recherches sur les Migrations (AMERM)[5] a pointé le doigt sur le risque

---

[4] - Fatima Ait Ben Lmadani (dir.), 2016, La politique d'immigration. Un jalon de la politique africaine du Maroc ? Cas de la régularisation des migrants subsahariens, Publications de l'AMERM.
Ministre Délégué auprès du Ministre des Affaires Étrangères et de la Coopération Internationale, Chargé des Marocains Résidant à l'Étranger et des Affaires de la Migration, 2018, Politique Nationale d'Immigration et d'Asile : RAPPORT 2018 https://marocainsdumonde.gov.ma/wp-content/uploads/2019/01/Politique-Nationale-dimmigration-et-dAsile-_-Rapport-2018.pdf
Ministère Chargé des Marocains Résidant à l'Étranger et des Affaires de la Migration, ?, Guide pratique pour faciliter votre intégration au Maroc, https://marocainsdumonde.gov.ma/guide-pratique-pour-faciliter-votre-integration-au-maroc/ Plateforme Nationale Protection Migrants, 2017, ETAT DES LIEUX DE L'ACCES AUX SERVICES POUR LES PERSONNES MIGRANTES AU MAROC : Bilan, perspectives et recommandations de la société civile ; http://www.pnpm.ma/wp-content/uploads/2017/12/Rapport-PNPM-11_2017_ACCES-AUX-SERVICES-POUR-MIGRANTS-AU-MAROC.pdf
[5] Malika Benradi (dir.), 2019, La prévention de l'apatridie chez les migrants et leurs enfants en Afrique du Nord : le rôle des pays d'accueil et des pays d'origine dans l'enregistrement des naissances et la délivrance des documents d'identité : Le cas de l'Égypte et du Maroc : Rapport Maroc, Publications de l'AMERM : http://amerm.org/wp-content/uploads/pdf/publications/AMERM_Rapport-Apatridie-Migrants-fin_2019-FR.pdf

d'apatridie qui pourrait avoir lieu si les politiques publiques relèguent au second degré la question de la protection juridique des migrants et réfugiés qui se trouvent sur son territoire. Cette protection, au-delà de la régularisation de leur situation juridique, passe également par l'intervention auprès des consulats des pays d'origine afin de faciliter l'obtention des documents d'identité de cette population.

La compréhension de la relation entre la délivrance des documents d'identité et l'intégration socioéconomique n'est pas aussi simple. L'interdépendance entre les deux variables fait que la prise de la bonne décision qui pourrait concilier entre les intérêts des différents intervenants interpelle plusieurs disciplines et exige une réelle volonté politique des décideurs du pays d'accueil et des pays d'origine. La délivrance des documents d'identité, devient, par conséquent, la clé de voûte pour une réelle insertion socio-économique des migrants et réfugiés mais également pour garantir les droits de leurs enfants à s'inscrire à l'état civil, avoir une éducation, bénéficier des soins de santé et vivre dans une certaine paix sociale. Mais en même temps, le chemin à parcourir pour obtenir ces documents d'identité n'est pas parsemé de fleurs.

Pour plusieurs migrants, demandeurs d'asile et réfugiés, cette question ne constitue pas une priorité. Ce qui prime c'est avoir un revenu qui leur permette d'effectuer les dépenses les plus élémentaires, sachant que la vulnérabilité de cette catégorie de la population rend plusieurs en quête de survie. Cette lutte quotidienne entrave la recherche d'obtention de ces documents prouvant leur identité, d'autant plus que pour les demandeurs d'asile et les réfugiés cette question passe à l'oubliette quand elle est conditionnée par un contact quelconque auprès des consulats de leurs pays d'origine.

À travers ce projet d'article, nous allons essayer d'apporter un autre regard sur ce thème. Notre objectif est d'arriver à une meilleure compréhension de cette interdépendance entre la délivrance des documents d'identité et l'intégration socioéconomique des migrants et réfugiés, qui, souvent, n'est traitée que de passage dans les articles et études traitant de l'apatridie.

Pour mettre en lumière cette facette occultée, nous allons nous baser sur une revue de littérature théorique et empirique qui traite aussi bien de l'apatridie que de l'intégration socioéconomique des migrants au Maroc. Ce deuxième aspect bien qu'il a suscité un intérêt croissant de la part des chercheurs, des décideurs politique et de la société civile au Maroc, n'a pas abordé le risque d'apatridie. D'où l'intérêt de rapprocher les deux thématiques.

Mots clefs : apatridie, documents d'identité, Maroc, intégration socioéconomique.

---

698   La fuite des compétences = Défis et opportunités pour le développement

Zekri Ahmed

Nous sommes aujourd'hui témoins d'un de ces processus historiques engendrant la transformation de la production, antérieurement isolée de l'activité scientifique, en un processus scientifiquement organisé, plus exactement en un complexe Science-Industrie, où les connaissances sont devenues puissance productive immédiate ou « puissance matérialisée du savoir » ou plus précisément « Knowledge intensive »

Savoir et Pouvoir étaient déjà inséparables. Ont-ils jamais cessé de l'être ? Il y a longtemps déjà Francis Bacon pu l'affirmer : « Knowledge is power »
Le passage d'une compétitivité basée principalement sur la productivité, les coûts et la production de masse à une compétitivité où la qualité, l'innovation et la personnalisation du produit sont les éléments clés de la réussite. Et, à l'heure où les entreprises se digitalisent et l'intelligence artificielle révolutionne la façon de faire, la capacité des entreprises locales à recruter des profils qualifiés devient, de jour en jour, plus délicate. La réhabilitation conséquente du scientifique comme agent de production dans la mesure où les capacités d'innover et de créer sans cesse des produits nouveaux déterminent le succès ou l'échec de toute entreprise.

Dans ces nouvelles conditions de compétitivité, les ressources humaines qualifiéesdeviennent un élément central dans la stratégie de ce fait, les définitions de l'exode des cerveaux sont souvent contradictoires et de tonalités différentes pour des politiques, des économistes, des chercheurs de leurs pays de départ ou de résidence. Ce drainage des cerveaux (brain drain) recouvre la perte du personnel hautement qualifié lié aux départs d'un pays vers un autre.
La pénurie des talents est un fait sur le marché de l'emploi, et elle est amplifiée par le phénomène d'exode des cerveaux. Ces départs, sous le regard impuissant des pays d'origine et parfois avec leur accord taciten'est pas propre au Maroc, certes, mais qui a atteint des proportions parfois inquiétantes, selon les derniers chiffres fournis par le ministre de l'Éducation nationale de la formation professionnelle de l'enseignement supérieur et de la recherche scientifique.

Le Maroc enregistre le 2ème taux de fuite des cerveaux le plus élevé dans la région du Moyen-Orient et de l'Afrique du Nord (MENA). Ainsi, plus de 20.000 experts marocains hautement qualifiés dans divers domaines ont choisi de travailler à l'étranger sans compter les 50.000 Marocains qui font leurs études à l'étranger.

La fuite des cerveaux est le drame par excellence.« C'est comme enlever la moelle osseuse du corps économique et social. ». L'État marocain forme avec les deniers publics des compétences qui, à la fin de leur cursus universitaire, s'iront ailleurs. ».   On constate une inversion des flux en faveur des pays développés, car aujourd'hui le flux d'argent qui part du Sud vers le Nord est de loin supérieur à l'aide qui vient des pays du Nord.« De toutes les ressources que possède un pays, les plus importantes ce sont les ressources humaines. Leur perte impacte cruellement le développement d'un pays de manière générale, encore plus un pays comme le Maroc qui en a besoin pour émerger. En fait, nous pédalons dans le vide. Nous formons des gens pour, au final, parer au déficit laissé par les départs, d'où la volonté actuelle d'attirer des talents internationaux, notamment de subsahariens. Ainsi, on devient à la fois victime et acteur de ce transfert de ressources humaines à l'échelle planétaire. Non seulement nous sommes victimes de ces flux totalement contre-productifs, mais nous participons en plus à l'aggravation des pays qui se trouvent à notre sud ».

Parmi les causes figurent, sans ordre de priorité, les conditions de travail, les crises économiques et les conditions salariales, les caractéristiques des recherches, la disparité entre l'offre et la demande de travailleurs qualifiés face à l'expansion de l'enseignement supérieur par rapport à l'économie du pays et à l'environnement politique, etc.

Cette hémorragie des ressources humaines interpelle politiques et scientifiques dans un environnement international de mobilité des cerveaux et d'émergence de la société de la connaissance.

Diverses solutions sont proposées qui comportent entre autres la poursuite de la politique du retour (return option), l'encouragement de la mobilisation de la diaspora (diaspora option), l'amélioration des conditions de travail, des salaires, de l'équipement des laboratoires, d'intégration régionale, mais aussi l'instauration d'un climat de confiance et de sécurité.

Cette inversion de l'exode des cerveaux (reverse brain drain) ou ce gain de cerveaux (brain gain) prend lentement corps avec des politiques incitatives de protection des libertés, de facilités d'exercice du métier et de reconnaissance sociale des chercheurs qui retournent au pays.

L'examen de ce phénomène renvoie à une problématique à dimensions différentes :

1. Quelle est la dimension de cette forme de migration et comment a-t-elle évolué ?

2. Quelles sont les logiques qui soutendent cet exode de ces compétences ?

3. Quelles sont les incidences du phénomène dans le pays d'origine (Maroc) et dans les espaces d'accueil ?

4. Ces incidences sont-elles purement économiques ou également sociales, politiques voire même culturelles ?

5. Quelles sont les perspectives d'avenir et quelles solutions peut-on envisager pour faire de ces compétences expatriées un atout pour le développement de leurs pays d'origine ?

1002   La protection juridique internationale des migrants (PJIM)

Ali El Mhamdi

La PJIM procède des droits humains en tant que normes universelles impératives qui reconnaissent et protègent la dignité de tous les êtres humains sans distinction aucune.

Les différentes situations humaines vécues pour l'accomplissement de tout projet migratoire engendrent des vulnérabilités de toutes sortes qui rendent nécessaire une protection internationale des migrants . L'ONU s'y est attelée en faisant adopter un socle de règles qui se déclinent en cinq catégories ci-après:

- Les instruments juridiques relatifs aux droits humains.

- La convention sur la protection des droits des travailleurs migrants et des membres de leur famille

- Le Droit pénal international contenu essentiellement dans les deux protocoles de Palerme, l'un vise à prévenir, réprimer et punir la traite des personnes et l'autre vise à lutter contre le trafic illicite de migrants.

- Le droit international du travail objet des conventions et normes élaborées par l'OIT.

- Le droit des réfugiés objet de la convention de Genève du 1951.

Les normes précitées ont été confortées par des législations nationales plus ou moins protectrices et des conventions régionales dont notamment celles adoptées par le Conseil de l'Europe, l'OEA et l'OUA. Les unes et les autres ont fait l'objet de traités internationaux qui ont emporté en son temps l'adhésion quasi- unanime des États.

Leur adoption a été favorisé par l'évolution la doctrine juridique qui reconnait à partir de 1945 l'individu come sujet de droit international en lui accordant des droits subjectifs fondamentaux connus sous le concept des droits humains. IL en résulte une triple obligation à la charge de l'Etat comme corollaire : celle de respecter, de protéger et garantir. D'un autre coté la justice pénale internationale peut désormais demander des comptes à des individus criminels qui violent le droits humains.

Le contrôle de l'application des droits humains est assuré par des instituions et des mécanismes dédiés dont notamment le Haut Commissariat aux droits de l'homme, la Commission de la condition de la femme l'OIT, l'OIM et les différents Comités de suivi.

Sur le terrain, l'application de la PJIM rencontre des obstacles multiples au premier rang desquels la persistance de la discrimination des personnes en fonction de leur nationalité et la souveraineté absolue des Etats en matière de gestion des flux migratoires.

Depuis sa création, l'ONU n'a cessé d'œuvre pour faire admettre l'exigence de la protection des droits des migrants dans les politiques publiques aux plans national et international ; si les progrès enregistrés en la manière sont indéniables , les échecs et les déficits n'en sont pas mois évidents et la communauté internationale se doit d'y remédier.

Sur la base d'enseignements puisées dans des travaux académiques et pratiques en l'objet

nous proposerons dans notre communication un état de lieu avec ses ombres et lumières assorti d'explications nécessaires et des pistes de réflexion en vue d'une meilleure protection des droits des migrants pour l'avenir. tel est l'objet et la finalité de la présente communication .

2E   Migration Governance
Chair: Gökay Özerim, Yaşar University, Turkey
653   Migration and Governance: The Case of Filipino and Indonesian
       Irregular Migrants Workers in Sabah, Malaysia
       Omer Faruk Cingir and Thirunaukarasu Subramaniam
674   Sons of the Yellow Emperor: Official Chinese knowledge production on
       migration and mobility
       Carsten Schafer
876   Migration Focused NGOS: Changing Funding Mechanisms, Political
       Advocacy, and Efficiency
       Jessica Marie Felder

653   Migration and Governance: The Case of Filipino and Indonesian Irregular Migrants Workers in Sabah, Malaysia

Omer Faruk Cingir and Thirunaukarasu Subramaniam

Every year, millions are displaced in the world and they are becoming refugees or asylum seekers or immigrants. Especially in Asia, migration is more common and usual phenomena because of unemployment, geographical features and lack of semi-professional workers. Malaysia is also an important destination for immigrants. According to data from World Bank, Malaysia is one of the most crowded countries in terms of immigrant population in the Southeast Asian Countries (World Bank Group, 2016). Moreover, according to statistics in 2012, the number of foreign workers in Malaysia has almost reached 2.8 million (Tajari & Affendi, 2015). Malaysia which attracts thousands of workers especially from Indonesia and the Philippines, is also attempting to turn its irregular migrant population into legal temporary legal workers (Koser, 2007). Some measures recognize the positive contribution of migrants and migration to economic welfare, to national prosperity and to development. However, other measures react to migration and to migrants as threatening phenomena. These measures can have negative consequences, including violations of the human rights of migrants and their families (Inter-Parliamentary Union, 2015). However, Malaysia has not ratified the 1951 Geneva Convention on Refugees and the 1967 Protocol (Kassim & Zin, 2011). In light of this information, the regulation and management of immigrants in Malaysia are becoming more important. The lack of efficient migrant worker regulations in Malaysia leads to migrants to head for irregular channels. According to ILO and IOM report (2017), the irregular migration compared with regular migration resulted in less time, less cost, and fewer problems in terms of migrants. Especially Sabah with porous borders has become the main destination for Indonesian and Filipino irregular immigrants.

This study aims to provide suggestions that will help other researchers who will conduct field research on immigrants and to provide ground for new discussions. In particular, the data that obtained in the field study in Sabah, Malaysia one-to-one surveys, semi-structured interviews and participatory observations with Indonesian and Filipino irregular immigrants will be analyzed. The most common difficulties and problems faced by migrants, ethical issues, cultural and social dilemmas will be discussed. The last part of this study will focus on how migrants produce solutions to these problems. Thereby humanitarian and moral dimension of immigration policy will be emphasized. With this special case of Filipino and Indonesian immigrants, general immigrant issues and policies implemented against them will be studied.

674   Sons of the Yellow Emperor: Official Chinese knowledge production on migration and mobility

Carsten Schafer

From its very beginning in the 1930s, the development of migration studies was closely interlinked with Western nation-state building processes. As a result, migration studies have reproduced notions originally defined by European and North American immigration politics - such as "refuges" or "asylum seekers"; its resources are mostly invested in measuring the degree of integration of immigrants. Yet, not only China's nation building process differs much from those of most European states, but also the country's experience with international migration. While Europe hosts the largest number of international migrants, China is the world's leading emigration country. Not surprisingly, the way in which "migrants" are categorized and imagined and notions such as "migration" and "border" are conceptualized, studied and politicized in China is quite different from European mainstream approaches. Chinese knowledge production is characterized by a strong China-centrism and methodological nationalism that produces essentializing discourses on race, culture, and belonging. These paradigms also affect the establishment of migration politics and border regimes, as well as boundary making processes based on ethnicization and culturalization. Against this background, I aim to systematically reflect the cultural, ideological and historical contexts that shape the production of knowledge on migration in China as well as the thereby arising group-related border imaginations. This study is based on a qualitative content analysis of official Chinese documents, Chinese think-tank publications and other Chinese research. We cannot understand international mobility without understanding such non-Western notions of migration. By mapping different geographic "epistimologies" and their influences on migration and boundary making, I want to understand the conditions of possibilities for future cross-cultural cooperation in both politics and research between Europe and China.

876   Migration Focused NGOS: Changing Funding Mechanisms, Political Advocacy, and Efficiency

Jessica Marie Felder

This dissertation investigates the impact of government funding on NGOs that deal with immigration-related issues. Government-NGO relationships can vary greatly. Prior work suggests that relationship dynamics may be elitist when cooptation is the norm, pluralist where capacity building is emphasized, or feature resource dependence when NGOs are reliant on government funding. However, the rise of bid-based funding calls into question these traditional notions of government-NGO relationships. I propose a new government-NGO relationship heuristic which I refer to as 'delegatory.' Delegatory relationships are where governments take a more hands-off approach to NGOs, and simply focus on performance metrics. In this study, I will use both surveys and interviews to understand where particular relationship dynamics are characteristic across European countries and how these relationships impact NGOs' behavior and efficiency. My purposes are to (1) better understand immigration-related NGOs and (2) propose a theory that better fits emerging patterns of government-NGO funding and cooperation.

2F   Welbeing and Migration

Chair: *Apostolos G Papadopoulos, Harokopio University, Greece*
500   Nordic Welfare Chauvinism: A Comparative Analysis of Welfare
       Chauvinism in Norway, Sweden, Finland and Iceland.
       David Andreas Bell
528   Second immigrant generation in the Norwegian welfare state
       Bard Smedsvik
647   Review of Mental Health Presentations in Asylum Seekers Attending
       the Emergency Department
       Jacqueline Eleonora Ek
902   Deep dive in the well-being of Romanian migrants in Greece
       Apostolos G Papadopoulos and Loukia-Maria Fratsea

500   Nordic Welfare Chauvinism: A Comparative Analysis of Welfare Chauvinism in Norway, Sweden, Finland and Iceland.

David Andreas Bell

Using data from the European Social Survey collected in 2016/2017, we analyze welfare chauvinist attitudes in what is often maintained to be the most generous welfare states; Norway, Sweden, Finland and Iceland. Welfare chauvinism is often understood as maintaining that the benefits provided by the welfare state should primarily be given to the native population, while immigrants are to be excluded from these benefits. We find that the attitude of wanting immigrants to never get equal rights to social benefits is near non-existent in the four Nordic countries. However, Finland, Norway and to some degree Sweden are in the top tier in Europe when it comes to respondents maintaining that immigrants need to obtain citizenship before they are to be given equal rights to social benefits and services. We further analyze these welfare chauvinist attitudes by exploring how attitudes towards welfare benefits, satisfaction towards these benefits and different forms of anti-immigrant attitudes may relate to welfare chauvinist attitudes in the four countries.

528   Second immigrant generation in the Norwegian welfare state

Bard Smedsvik

This paper exploits administrative data from Norway to study immigrant second generation performance in the domestic labour market, compared to first generation and non-immigrant population. The Norwegian welfare state and its generous unemployment insurance scheme provide an ideal background for our quantitative analysis. We apply a dualistic definition of labour, in which we define reception of unemployment subsidy as a proxy of an individual's position as an insider or outsider in the labour market (Rueda, 2006).

Previous literature (Borjas, 1993; Algan et al. 2010; Feliciano and Lanuza 2017) has highlighted that second generations often perform better than their parents with respect to education outcomes and labour market participation, which is a feature that is confirmed in our data. However, we compare for the first time the performance of the second generation to *both* the first generation *and* the non-immigrant population. In this way, rather than providing a simplistic comparison of the second generation of immigrants with respect to their parents, we contribute with a thorough assessment of the labour market status of the immigrant second generation in the Norwegian labour market. Has the immigrant second generation closed the gap with the non-immigrant population? What are the determinants of the remaining gaps?

Background literature: there is an ongoing debate on the impact of immigration on labour markets. A special concern is how immigrants often end up in low-skilled low-wage work, often called outsider-work (Elstad and Heggebø, 2020). This raises a concern that children of immigrants to a larger extent are born into lower socioeconomic class, making welfare, mobility and social inequality important aspects for the life course of this group. Portes and Zhou (1993) apply the concept of 'modes of incorporation' as a useful theoretical tool to understand second generation integration to the labour market. According to this theory, the societal context immigrants arrive to plays a decisive role in their offspring's life. Our focus is on the institutional and political dimension, especially how mobility ladders work for immigrants and their children in the host country.

Preliminary results: the preliminary results of the analysis of the incidence of unemployment insurance across the distinct groups, show that the first-generation immigrants receive around 2-3 times higher amounts than the non-immigrant population in unemployment benefits, indicating a rather weaker integration in the labour market. The second immigrant generation, although it performs better than the first generation, still receives up to 2 times (for the lowest deciles of the income distribution) the amounts received by the non-immigrant population. Overall, these preliminary results indicate that the second generation has still a long path to go to achieve full integration in the Norwegian labour market, contrary to what previous studies have pointed out.

References

Algan, Y., Dustmann, C., Glitz, A., & Manning, A. (2010). The Economic Situation of First and Second-Generation Immigrants in France, Germany and The United Kingdom. Economic Journal, 120(542), F4-F30.

Borjas, G. J. (1993). The Intergenerational Mobility of Immigrants. Journal of Labor Economics, 11(1), 113-135.

Elstad, J. I., & Heggebø, K. (2020). 'Crowded out'? Immigration Surge and Residents' Employment Outcomes in Norway. Nordic Journal of Working Life Studies.

Feliciano, C., & Lanuza, Y. R. (2017). An Immigrant Paradox? Contextual Attainment and Intergenerational Educational Mobility. American Sociological Review, 82(1), 211–241.

Portes, A., & Zhou, M. (1993). The New Second Generation: Segmented Assimilation and Its Variants. The Annals of the American Academy of Political and Social Science, 530, 74-96.

Rueda, D. (2006). Insider-Outsider Politics in Industrialized Democracies: The Challenge to Social Democratic Parties. American Political Science Review, 99(1), 61-74.

647   Review of Mental Health Presentations in Asylum Seekers Attending the Emergency Department

Jacqueline Eleonora Ek

Background

Boat movement across the Mediterranean continues to be a humanitarian challenge. Irregular immigration and applying for asylum is both a lengthy and mentally demanding process. Those doing so are often faced with multiple challenges, which can adversely affect their mental health[1],[2]. Between January and August 2020, Malta disembarked 2 162 people rescued at sea, 463 of them between July & August[3]. To better understand the spatial dimensions of this humanitarian crisis, this study aims to Review discrepancies in the management of Asylum Seekers attending the Emergency Department (ED) with Acute Mental Health presentations as compared to local residents with the same presentations.

Method

In this retrospective study, an analysis of 17 795 consecutive ED attendances in a Mediterranean frontline country was done to look for discrepancies in the medical management of Asylum Seekers vs Local Residents presenting to ED with Acute Mental Health Presentations.

Results

Of the ED attendances, 92.3% were local residents and 7.7% were non-locals. Of the non-locals, 13.8% were asylum seekers and 86.2% were other-non-locals. Acute mental health presentations were seen in 1% of local residents, this increased to 20.6% in asylum seekers.

When evaluating the presenting complaint, over half the attendances of asylum seekers presented with deliberate self harm 56.4%, this number was considerably lower in local residents 28.9%. [1]Contrastingly, in local residents the most common presenting complaint was suicidal thought/ low mood 37.3%, the incidence was similar in asylum seekers at 33.3%. Similarities were also seen with regards to aggressive/erratic behavior, in asylum seekers 15.4% and in local residents 14.5%.

Main differences included 12.8% of asylum seekers presenting with refused oral intake while only 0.6% of local residents presented with the same complaints. 7.7% of asylum seekers presented with a reduced level of consciousness, no local residents presented with this same issue.

Management in evaluating these issues involved the use of computed tomography (CT) to rule out organic cause for altered mental state. A CT scan was used in 12% of local residents and in 35.9% of asylum seekers.

A number of medications were used varying from standard analgesia and fluids to psychiatric treatment and general anesthetics. The most common treatment administered to asylum seekers was supportive fluids 15.4%, the most common in local residents was benzodiazepines 15.1%.

Conclusion

Results showed multiple disparities in health management. A meeting was held between entities responsible for migrant health in Malta including the Emergency Department, Primary Health Care, Migrant Detention Services and Malta Red Cross. Currently national quality-improvement initiatives are underway to form new pathways to improve patient centred care. These include an interpreter unit, centralised handover sheets and a dedicated migrant health service.

References

Magzoub Toar, Kirsty K O'Brien, Tom Fahey; Comparison of self-reported health & healthcare utilisation between asylum seekers and refugees: an observational study\(https://pubmed.ncbi.nlm.nih.gov/19566954/

Cetta Mainwaeming, Constructing a Crisis: the Role of Immigration Detention in Malta. (http://www.humanrightsmalta.org/uploads/1/2/3/3/12339284/centre_on_migration_ policy_and_society_university_of_oxford_oxford_uk_constructing_a_crisis_the_role _of_immigration_detention_in_malta_2012_detention_irregular_immigration_migrat ion_policy_asylum.pdf)

UNHCR, The UN Refugee Agency, Malta Factsheet (https://www.unhcr.org/mt/wp-content/uploads/sites/54/2020/09/Malta-Sea-Arrivals-and-Asylum-Statistics_UNHCR_August2020.pdf)

902   Deep dive in the well-being of Romanian migrants in Greece

Apostolos G Papadopoulos and Loukia-Maria Fratsea

Over the last thirty years Greece was transformed from an emigration to an immigration country. During that time, international migration flows contributed to new socioeconomic realities in Greece. In this context, the collapse of the socialist regime the geographical and cultural proximity of the Greece and Romania enabled the emergence of various forms of mobility between the two countries. In addition, since 2007, Romanians' access to the Greek labour market has become easier due to the accession of their country to the EU. However, the statistical and empirical evidence suggests the existence of a hierarchy of stratified rights regarding entry, residence and employment which has impacted on the social position and well-being of Romanian migrants in Greece. Despite the sings of economic recovery ten years following the downturn, the ongoing Covid – 19 pandemic has implications on the livelihoods and the mobility of migrants and natives alike.

Drawing from an empirical research in the context of the IMAJINE Project ("Integrative Mechanisms for Addressing Spatial Justice and Territorial Inequalities in Europe IMAJINE" received funding from the EU Horizon 2020 Research and Innovation Programme, under Grant Agreement No. 726950), our paper aims at situating the aspirations, agency and well-being of Romanian migrants during and after the economic recession in two regions of Greece, and to inquire into and interpret their material well-being and their sense of belonging. The migrants' own narratives about their well-being are analysed in relation to their social trajectories, spatial movement(s), and settlement patterns in Greece. Moreover, their perceptions of their living conditions and well-being both in Romania prior to their migration and today are interrelated to the construction of their current subjective well-being and livelihoods. The paper concludes with a critical discussion regarding the implications of the lockdown on migrants' standard of living, employment conditions and mobility.

2G   Communication and Migration

Chair: Vildan Mahmutoglu, Galatasaray University, Turkey

549   International Student Migration and Polymedia: The Use of Communication Media by Bangladeshi Students in Germany
Md MatiulHoque Masud

557   Visual representations of the refugee experience from those experiencing it. A case study of refugees from Syria into Greece
Anastasia Chalkia, Joanna George Tsiganou, Martha Lembesi

584   Speaking to not communicate as a state practice: the communication as border
Mafalda Carapeto

599   Content-analytical study of migrants in the leading Ukrainian media
Liudmyla Leonidivna Yuzva

549   International Student Migration and Polymedia: The Use of Communication Media by Bangladeshi Students in Germany

Md Matiul Hoque Masud

Tertiary-level students from Bangladesh usually migrate to Germany for the purpose of higher studies. These international student migrants use communication media to maintain connections with family members and friends in Bangladesh and social networks with friends, classmates, and Bangladeshi community members in Germany. Drawing on the experiences of Bangladeshi student migrants in Germany and using polymedia theory, this paper investigates how the migrant students use the polymedia environment to maintain the transnational social networks and connections. This paper is based on qualitative data derived from 18 in-depth interviews with Bangladeshi migrant students in Germany. Findings suggest that using the polymedia environment, Bachelor migrant students receive emotional support from their family members back home, while Masters and PhD students are responsible for providing emotional and practical support to their left-behind families, relatives, and friends. Migrant students' media usage with families and friends living in Bangladesh is influenced by their marital status and gender as well as their familial and social structure in Bangladesh. Their use of communication media with the members of the Bangladeshi community and foreign classmates living in Germany is comparatively less frequent and more education-oriented.

557   Visual representations of the refugee experience from those experiencing it. A case study of refugees from Syria into Greece

Anastasia Chalkia, Joanna George Tsiganou, Martha Lembesi

The usual tools we, the sociologists, use in our study of the social experience are based on transcribing textualised information to meaningful knowledge. However, within the mounting vein of visual sociology during the recent decades, new means have been added, which when used solely or additionally, might help us to comprehend more fully narratives of life experiences. Our proposed paper focuses on the travelling and host experiences into Greece of refugees from Syria and it is based on a qualitative research conducted in 2019-2020 with Syrian refugees incomers to Greece. It is in the scope of the proposed paper to address the framing of the refugee experience not only in terms of the discourse resulting out from the face-to-face interviews with our research population but mainly in terms of the visual representations of the refugee experience as exhibited in their own snap-shots. Our conclusions are therefore based on two distinct types of mediation. The mediation of an interpreter and the mediation of a visual instrument. Conscious of the methodological issues involved we have tried to avoid misinterpretations and misconceptions by carefully and diligently addressing respondends' own stories on the visual material they have generously offered to us. There are these stories we wish to share with the scientific community indicating that inferences on cultural diversification might not hold the strong face validity attributed to them.

584 Speaking to not communicate as a state practice: the communication as border

Mafalda Carapeto

In this communication I aim to discuss immigrants' perceptions on the Portuguese State by looking into the experiences of foreign residents with the Portuguese Borders and Foreigners Office (Serviço de Estrangeiros e Fronteiras, hereafter SEF). SEF is responsible for applying the Act n. ° 23/2007 of 4th July that has defined the new legal framework for the entry, permanence, exit and removal of foreigners from national territory. I choose to address the perspective of migrants by shedding light on the assessment of their *encounter with the state* (Sharma and Gupta, 2006; Gupta and Sharma, 2006), that is with state agents enrolled in the bureaucratic process of entering, staying and removal from national territory. Specifically, the perception that migrants have about the form of communication provided by the state agents in SEF, that guides the bureaucratic processes. By communication I mean not only the language but also the type of information and the way the information is handled by the state agents, working in SEF.

Policy implementation by state agents in bureaucratic agencies, such as SEF, can be conceived as the work of "street-level bureaucrats" (Lipsky, 1980), that is, people whose professional functions require that they "interact directly with citizens in the course of their jobs, and have substantial discretion in the execution of their work" (Lipsky 1980, 193). Implementation, either for practical or political reasons - the black box as it is known - becomes a social field where discretion has been acknowledged as ubiquitous (Ham and Hill, 1986) and unavoidable, and not necessarily an obstacle to the realization of policy objectives, but as a case of expertise that allows for the bureaucrat to solve a problem (Evans and Harris, 2004).

Literature have been referring that bureaucrats are hardly solely the "guardians of the procedure', but regulations are reinterpreted and redefined at the implementation level, exercising their power over its territory and especially at its borders. Thinking of borders as polysemic disturbs the idea of the inside and the outside, the national and the foreigner, or the idea that borders define only the space around the territories. Borders are physical and imagined; are material and experiential (King, 2016; Brown, 2017); are dispersed everywhere, wherever the movement of information, people and things happens and has to be controlled (Balibar, 2004). Borders are practices that are reproduced, every time we decide who can or cannot enter / cross / stay. Presenting themselves differently to different people, these state practices (Seabra Lopes, 2018), geographically dispersed, besides the dimension of policing, are also deeply bureaucratic. Consequently, being in unsuspected places, as is the case of the various SEF divisions, spread across the country, where the communication factor is crucial to the unfolding of the immigrants' processes in order to obtain or remain with their legal status.

This research takes an ethnographic approach and combines methods and data from different sources. Data were collected through semi-structured interviews and informal conversations, policy documents available on the internet and grey literature namely the internal reports produced by state institutions.

Bibliography

Balibar, Étienne. 2004. We, the people of Europe? Reflections on Transnational Citizenship. Princenton University Press.

Brown, Wendy. 2017. Walled States, Waning Sovereignty. Zone Books.

Evans, Tony and Harris, John. 2004. 'Street-level Bureaucracy, social work and the (exaggerated) Death of Discretion'. British Journal of Social Work, 34, 871-895.

Gupta, Akhil e Sharma, Aradhana. (2006). 'Globalization and Postcolonial States.' Current Anthropology, 47(2): 277-307.

Ham, Cristopher, and Michael Hill. 1986. Introduzione all'analisi delle politiche pubbliche [Introduction to the Analysis of Public Policies]. Bologna: Il Mulino.

King, Natasha. 2016. No Borders: The politics of Immigration Control and Resistance. Zed Books.

Lipsky, Michael. 1980. Street Level Bureaucracy: Dilemmas of the Individual in Public Services. New York: Russell Sage Foundation

Seabra Lopes, Daniel. 2018. O Estado por Dentro: Uma Etnografia do Poder e da Administração Pública em Portugal. Fundação Francisco Manuel dos Santos.

Sharma, Aradhana e Gupta, Akhil. 2006. "Introduction" in The anthropology of the state: a reader. Blackwell Publishing.

599 Content-analytical study of migrants in the leading Ukrainian media

Liudmyla Leonidivna Yuzva

Modern societies are characterized by rapid informatization and, often, excessive consumption of media products, which vividly illustrate the statistics of Desjardins (Desjardins 2016). It is also indisputable that the media are often the "thought leaders" that shape the opinion of the average person.

In recent years, Ukraine has seen a decline in tolerance for immigrants and people of other nationalities. One of the reasons for this situation may be the coverage of migration by the mainstream media.

Within the framework of the international grant study 'Migrants. Analysis of media discourse on migrants in Poland, the United Kingdom, Ukraine, Albania and the Czech Republic' (MAD) we conducted an empirical study of coverage of the topic of migration in different types of media.

One of the most powerful methods of studying documents, including media, in the social sciences is content analysis (Krippendorff 2004). Therefore, it was he who acted as a basic method in the study of information coverage of migrants, refugees, migrants and workers in the leading Ukrainian media. Additionally, automated semantic analysis was used in the study.

Research methodology. The time frame of the study covers 4 years: from January 1, 2015 to December 31, 2018. The sample consists of 15 leading

Ukrainian media of various types (Internet media, print media and television) and various forms of ownership (public and private). These are:

• Internet media: Ukrainian Pravda, Censor.net, Radio Svoboda, Strana, 24.ua;

• TV channels: UA: Pershiy, Ukraine, 1 + 1, Inter, ICTV;

• Press: Government Courier, Vesti, Segodnya, Den, Gazeta in Ukrainian.

The sample is automated, based on the use of the Mediateka tool. In total, more than 39,000 publications mentioning keywords were recorded in these media during the period, a third of which were processed on the basis of step-by-step selection - about 12,000. Coding is latent, manual. The technique of coding the key of posts is applied. The key words were: migrants, refugees, migrants, IDPs (internally displaced persons), workers (as a nationally labeled concept).

Additionally, automated (artificial) semantic analysis (ASA) was used to better understand the semantic cores of media discourse. The ACA allowed us to analyze the socio-demographic dimension of the media discourse on migrants. And also to study and interpret socionyms, political names, cultural names, ethnonyms and confessional names that were used for different types of migrants.

One of the results of the study was the finding that during 2015-2018, the Ukrainian media paid the most attention to the migration crisis, which affected the European Union, and later escalated in the United States. This issue was raised in September 2015, when the war in Syria caused a large influx of illegal migrants (in the media they are often also called refugees) to European countries. Since then, the topic of migrants has not disappeared from the pages of newspapers, Internet sites and television programs throughout the study period. In terms of the number of reports, it was even ahead of the domestic hot topic - IDPs from Donbass and Crimea.

END OF FIRST DAY

3A   Migration and Integration

Chair: Fanny Christou, Lund University, Sweden and Migrinter, University of Poitiers, France

671   (Im)mobility practices of refugees and (non-removed) asylum seekers struggling for access to resources: exploring integration processes in three Northern Italian cities
Iraklis Dimitriadis

715   Refugee Integration and State "Legitimation Crisis": A Study of the Host and the Rohingya Communities in Cox's Bazar, Bangladesh
Md Reza Habib

740   Social and solidarity economy through the analysis of the Little Palestine in Berlin: integration, citizenship and identity in diaspora
Fanny Christou

746   Social cohesion in multiethnic and multicultural societies Republic of North Macedonia
Agron Rustemi

671   (Im)mobility practices of refugees and (non-removed) asylum seekers struggling for access to resources: exploring integration processes in three Northern Italian cities

Iraklis Dimitriadis

Labour market insertion and welfare services are two of the main dimensions shaping refugee integration (Ager and Strang 2008; Olwig 2011). On the one hand, refugees often experience difficulties in the labour market due to the lack of individual resources, and because they have to face structural constraints in the host country and hostility in local contexts. On the other hand, access to welfare rights varies across countries, and it may also depend upon the local tiers of asylum governance that is stance of local authorities towards refugees and asylum seekers (Hinger et al. 2016).

Italy saw an increase in flows of people seeking international protection since 2015. To respond to the needs of new arrived people the Italian government introduced extraordinary measures which have not been adequately implemented (Campomori 2018). Municipalities have not demonstrated interest in sharing the burden of the reception of RAS, and the evaluation of international protection applications took very long time. Another problematic aspect has been considered the establishment of private reception facilities (mostly in Northern Italy) in areas that did not favour refugee integration. In the meantime, the stance of local communities where refugees and asylum seekers were settled became increasingly hostile in many cases, whereas the rise the populist government coalition of 2018-2019 ruled by the M5S and the League promoted restrictive migration policies, which hindered further the already problematic refugee integration process (Ambrosini 2019).

This article examines the means by which refugees and asylum seekers face structural constraints and restrictive policies in Northern Italy where the majority of migrant population is concentrated. The study is part of the H2020 MAGYC project and draws on 44 semi-structured interviews with key informants (professionals and volunteers of reception facilities, trade unionists and lawyers with expertise on immigration) and refugees and asylum seekers. Fieldwork research was conducted from October 2019 to February 2021. The article explores forms of (im)mobility of refugees and asylum seekers (RAS) to cope with lack of support in labour market insertion and welfare services. It adopts a comparative approach considering practices of people living in Milan (city of Refuge), Busto Arsizio (hostile city towards migrants) and Como (border city).

Preliminary results show that refugees and asylum seekers implement a series of mobility practices to access jobs and welfare services in Milan, while mobility (or immobility) to Como emerges as a practice to access welfare services in a city where civil society's involvement in the asylum governance considerably increased in the last years. People's capacity to overcome obstacles through (im)mobility practices depends upon their financial capital, cultural resources (knowledge of Italian language and how to navigate the administration system) and social ties which interplay with characteristics of the socio-economic local context. Although legal status is generally considered an important resource that migrants mobilise to achieve their goals (Moret 2017), it seems that this does not always happen in the Italian case due to the introduction of restrictive policies, hostility in local contexts and peculiarities of the reception system regarding dispersal of migrants across the country. The paper also discusses the impact of COVID-19 pandemics to refugees and asylum seekers' (im)mobility practices and reflects on the practical implications of the means that migrants employ to improve their lives.

Bibliography

Ager, A., and A. Strang. 2008. "Understanding integration: A conceptual framework." Journal of Refugee Studies 21(2):166–191.

Ambrosini, M. 2019. The Imaginary Invasion: How the Discourse on the "Refugee Crisis" Has Impacted Italian Politics and Society. Ed. A. Rea, M. Martiniello, A. Mazzola, and B. Meuleman. The Refugee Reception Crisis in Europe. Polarized Opinions and Mobilizations. Éditions de l'Université de Bruxelles.

Campomori, F. 2018. "Asylum seeker reception policies in Italy: Weaknesses and contradictions." Politiche Sociali 5(3):429–436.

Hinger, S., P. Schäfer, and A. Pott. 2016. "The Local production of Asylum." Journal of Refugee Studies 29(4):440–463.

Moret, J. 2017. "Mobility capital: Somali migrants' trajectories of (im)mobilities and the negotiation of social inequalities across borders." Geoforum(November):0–1.

Olwig, K. F. 2011. "'Integration': Migrants and refugees between Scandinavian welfare societies and family relations." Journal of Ethnic and Migration Studies 37(2):179–196.

715 Refugee Integration and State "Legitimation Crisis": A Study of the Host and the Rohingya Communities in Cox's Bazar, Bangladesh

Md Reza Habib

The Rohingyas – an ethnic group of Myanmar- are considered as one of the most persecuted community worldwide. Nearly 1.3 million Rohingyas crossed the Bangladesh border from 1978 to 2017 on account of oppressive and discriminatory actions led by the military government of Myanmar. Currently, the Rohingyas are living in over 30 temporary camps in Ukhia and Teknaf sub-districts of Cox's Bazar district in Bangladesh, where in the past few years the Rohingya population has grown three times the local population.

Habermas' (1975) theory on "legitimation crisis" is very significant to interpret and explain the current socio-cultural, economic, political and environmental conditions of Cox's Bazar after the arrival of the Rohingya. The study found that the recent involuntary migration of Rohingya into Bangladesh has created an unequal socio-economic opportunity for the host community- such as employment in the local labour market, inefficiency and injustices in delivery of services-- in food procurement and consumption, education, health, transport, housing, and other basic needs. Furthermore, the environment and natural resources (forest, lands, and water) have been mismanaged and destroyed in the process of resettling Rohingyas. The locals perceive that the host government and UN agencies are giving more priority to the Rohingyas than them.

Deploying Habermas I argue that these conflicts are creating problems of "social integration" between the Rohingya and the locals despite some socio-cultural similarities between the host community and Rohingyas, such as language and religion (that is similarities of "lifeworld"). The crisis has a deeper political implication, as the identity of the (deserving) citizen and its rights to local and national resources is getting pitted against the identity of the refugee non-citizens, who are being perceived by the locals as the (non-deserving) users of the resources, at the cost of the citizen. Consequently, a large section of the host community has lost their confidence and trust towards the capacity of the democratically elected government, and UN agencies to manage and govern the situation, and it points at the deeper "legitimation crisis" at the systemic level.

The main purpose of the study is to explore the effect of Rohingya migration on the social and system integration process that leads to a crisis of legitimacy in Bangladesh. This study has adopted a qualitative method of analysis and total of 20 interviews were taken. The respondents are covered from Rohingyas, local community leaders, host community, journalists, union council representatives, religious leaders, government and NGO officials. Moreover, for analysis secondary data has been drawn from reports, articles, web resources, and newspapers.

Finally, I suggest that the host government, UN and non-government stakeholders have to make sure access to equal opportunities and delivery of services for both communities and contribute to building a cohesive and peaceful society for all.

740   Social and solidarity economy through the analysis of the Little Palestine in Berlin: integration, citizenship and identity in diaspora

Fanny Christou

Based on a fieldwork that has been conducted among the Palestinian community in Berlin in 2019, this presentation aims to explore the initiatives and strategies of this diaspora in the field of social and solidarity economy, also called third sector. In this respect, this paper aims to critically engage with the concepts of integration and citizenship that need to take into account the plural spheres of migrants' participation, thus allowing a better understanding of belonging and identity. In addition, by questioning and analysing how the third sector is invested by the Palestinians in Berlin, this study seeks to provide with new insights regarding the plurality of the negotiation of integration and citizenship in the German host country.

This paper is based on a bottom-up approach in order to shed light on the role played by migrants, such as the Palestinians who have been historically settled in Germany. The original character of this presentation thus shows the importance of migrant communities which are nevertheless still too often analysed through the prism of the so-called migratory crisis. Indeed, the analysis of migrant practices in the field of social and solidarity economy can provide with a new framework, strengthening our understanding of the role members of middle eastern diasporas, such as the Palestinian one in its diversity, can play in the dynamic development of our European societies. In addition, this paper aims to bring a new approach regarding the social and solidarity economy: source of employment, springboard for integration and citizenship, creator of plural identities, this third sector needs to be considered as an increasingly important source of social participation and economic development.

By questioning theoretical and conceptual models, this work is based on three main ambitions: 1/ the articulation between the politics of integration in Germany with the possibility to deconstruct this concept based on the analysis of the processes that have been developed by a specific group of migrants (Palestinians) in Berlin, 2/ the necessity to shed light on social and economy solidarity and its dynamics through the development of a specific Palestinian third sector, source of integration and citizen belonging, 3/ the socio-political meaning of the Palestinian practices and strategies in the third sector and the ways they can foster a new diasporic identity.

Thus, after a general overview on the Palestinian presence in Germany, this presentation will analyse the evolution of the German politics of migration, integration, and citizenship, articulated with the social and solidarity sector that is invested by the migrants' communities and that contribute to the development of the so-called « Little Palestine ».

Mots-clés : Palestinians, Berlin, social and solidarity economy, integration, citizenship, identity

References

Barwick C., 2017, « L'accueil des réfugiés à Berlin : une question clé aux multiples enjeux », Allemagne d'aujourd'hui, vol.3(221), p. 95-106

Bayat A., 2013, Life as Politics. How Ordinary People Change the Middle East, Standford, Standford University Press (deuxième edition)

Blanc J., 2014, « Une théorie pour l'économie sociale et solidaire », Revue internationale de l'économie sociale et solidaire, n°331(93), p. 118-125

Dubslaff V., 2016, « Crise des réfugiés et crispations identitaires : l'Allemagne en proie au national-populisme », Allemagne d'aujourd'hui, vol. 2(216), p. 20-28

Erdal M. B. & Oeppen C., 2003, « Migrant balancing acts: Understanding the interactions between integration and transnationalism », Journal of Ethnic and Migrant Studies, 39(6), p. 867-884

Ghadban R., 2005, « The impact of Immigration Policies on Palestinians in Germany », in Shiblak A., The Palestinian diaspora in Europe. Challenges of Dual Identity and Adaptation, Institute of Jerusalem Studies and Palestinian Refugee & Diaspora Center, p. 32-43

Gouverneur M., 2012, L'économie sociale et le tiers secteur en Allemagne et en France, Bruxelles : Think tank pour la solidarité

Ostergaard-Nielsen E., 2003, « The Politics of Migrants' Transnational Political Practices », The International Migration Review, 37(3), p.760-786

Ronzy M., 2006, Regard sur les pratiques d'intégration en économie sociale et solidaire, Reliance, 2006, vol. 1(19), p. 70-77

Weiss K., 2018, « Les principes de la politique allemande d'intégration – un modèle pour l'intégration », in Weiss K., Roth R., Voges M., Allemagne : quel modèle d'intégration ? Contributions sur les grands principes de la politique d'intégration, le rôle du système de formation, l'action des communes et l'engagement citoyen, Paris, Fondation Friedrich-Ebert, p. 2-3

746   Social cohesion in multiethnic and multicultural societies Republic of North Macedonia

Agron Rustemi

Multiculturalism is closely associated with "identity politics," "the politics of difference," and "the politics of recognition," all of which share a commitment to revaluing disrespected identities and changing dominant patterns of representation and communication that marginalize certain groups. Multiculturalism is also a matter of economic interests and political power; it demands remedies to economic and political disadvantages that people suffer as a result of their minority status.

Study of the development of democracy, the role of the State, the emergence of new nationalisms and new xenophobic and racist types of behavior, and of the role of "ethnico-national" or "linguistico-cultural" minorities is the core problem. The contribution of the social sciences in such a sensitive area should help in devising solutions for the promotion of democracy and the prevention of conflicts brought about by the confrontations inherent in the strengthening of the multicultural and multi-ethnic character of the Republic of North Macedonia.

The article will surely attract attention as in scientific circles and the general public because in itself incorporates an issue that has been and still is a core problem in functioning and developing democracy and the idea of universal human rights in general and in particular in the Republic of North Macedonia.

3B   Education and Migration

836   GEMILLI project - Gender, Migration and Illiteracy

Margarida Barroso

Gender, Migration and Illiteracy. Policy and Practice for Social Integration (GEMILLI) is a project funded by the EC Marie Sklodowska-Curie Actions, that analyses the intersections of gender, migration and illiteracy and its implications for social integration. GEMILLI proposes a comprehensive approach and research strategy, able to advance knowledge and to inform the development of effective policies to promote the integration of migrant women with low literacy.

What do we know about illiterate migrant women?

- Literacy is a social practice shaped by relations of power and sociocultural determinants (Street, 1984, 2012)

- Gender is a structuring dimension of illiteracy

- Women represent 2/3 of the world's adult population unable to read or write (UNESCO, 2000, 2004)

- Gendered ideologies are associated with distinct expectations and investments in education for boys and girls (Unesco, 2000)

- Women constitute 48% of the worldwide migration and 52,4% of Europe's international migration (IOM, 2018)

- The number of migrants from countries with high levels of illiteracy and low levels of schooling has increased in Europe (IOM, 2018)

- Female migration is no longer exclusively associated with a male-dependent role

- Migrant's education has been analysed mainly from the perspective of children (Spencer and Cooper, 2006)

- Disaggregated data on illiteracy – literacy level, migration status, gender – is still lacking.

Aims and Objectives

- To compare two country-cases representative of new and old immigration countries, Spain and France, regarding the definition, development and implementation of concrete measures to address the social integration of migrant women with low literacy;

- To understand how integration programmes are implemented locally and how fieldwork practice relates to the institutional context and to European and national policy guidelines;

- To understand the impacts of social integration policies and practices in individual biographies.

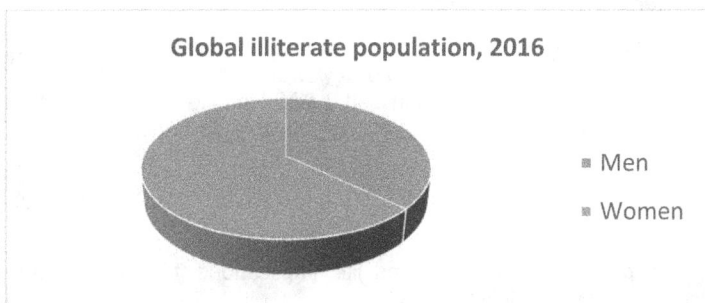

Global illiterate population, 2016

- Men
- Women

Source: Unesco, 2016

Approach and Methods

- Analysis of the institutional context

- Analysis of policy and normative documents addressing gender, migration and illiteracy

- Analysis of key migrant integration indicators

- Organisational case studies in local institutions offering literacy and language courses, with specific programmes for women

- Documental analysis

- Systematic observation of practice
- Semi-structured interviews with fieldwork professionals
- Analysis of 20 biographies of migrant women without or with low levels of formal education

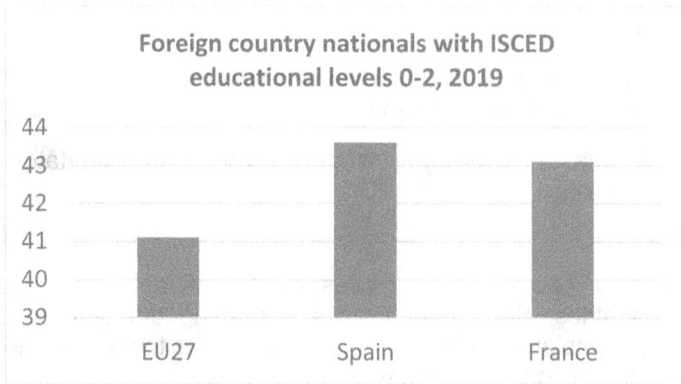

Foreign country nationals with ISCED educational levels 0-2, 2019

44
43
42
41
40
39

EU27   Spain   France

Source: Eurostat, 2020

References

International Organization for Migration (2018), Migration Data Portal: https://migrationdataportal.org/themes/gender.

Spencer, S. and B. Cooper (2006), *Social Integration of Migrants in Europe: a Review of the European Literature*, Oxford, COMPAS.

Street, B.V. (1984), *Literacy in theory and practice*, Cambridge, Cambridge University Press; Street, B.V. (2012), "Contexts for literacy work: New literacy studies, multimodality and the 'local and the global'", in Tett, L., M. Hamilton and J. Crowther (eds), *More powerful literacies*, Leicester, National Institute for Adult Continuing Education

UNESCO (2000), "Literacy for All: A United Nations Literacy Decade", Discussion Paper, Paris, UNESCO

UNESCO (2004), "The plurality of literacy and its implications for policies and programmes", Position Paper, Paris, UNESCO

749   Inclusive Education from The Perspective of Immigrant Parents: The Lithuanian Case

Vaiva Chockevičiūtė and Ausra Simoniukstyte

Access to education is recognized as a fundamental human right. It is identified as a key means of preventing social exclusion and poverty and an important way of supporting the inclusion of the most vulnerable groups (European Commission, 2002). The concept of inclusive education that had been developed during last decades and had replaced the concept of "integration", reflected a shift from a needs-based to a rights-based educational agenda (Pirrie, Head, & Brna, 2006). Thus, inclusive education by definition strives to provide equal educational opportunities for every child. Lately, there has been an increasing recognition of the importance of inclusive education for neutralising and overcoming social and ethno-cultural stratification. Accordingly, in Lithuania, since 2011 an inclusive education has been claimed to be "the most important political goal" of the national education system (The Law on Education of the Republic of Lithuania, 2011). Inclusive education has become even more relevant with the increasing number of immigrants from non-EU countries to Lithuania (EMN, 2020).

The educational situation of the most vulnerable groups, such as immigrant and refugee children, can provide a clue into the praxis of inclusion and disclose the significant gaps and challenges on the way of its implementation. The present study aims to bring refugee and immigrant mothers' perspective on implementation of inclusive education in Lithuania. The study presents the results of qualitative in-depth interviews with immigrant/refugee parents and NGO representatives, volunteers and assistants who help immigrant families to cope with various problems they face after arriving into the host country. The interviews were carried out with one immigrant and six refugee parents from Syria, Tajikistan Turkey, Ukraine, and four NGO representatives. The data was collected in Vilnius, in January-March, 2020. The interviews analysed in the paper were initially conducted as a part of Erasmus+ project "Teachers Competencies for Social Inclusion of Migrants and Refugees in Early Childhood Education".

The interview findings have revealed the following parents' expectations towards education of their children and accompanying problem areas of inclusive education: the preparedness of teachers to work with culturally diverse groups of students; close collaboration between teachers and parents; avoidance of ethnocentric approach in teaching; cultural diversity as opposed to monocultural environment of school; culturally diverse teaching content; sense of belonging to a school community. The interview data raises questions about the role of interculturalism in education system instead of ethnocentric multiculturalism which might be dysfunctional in a pluralistic society (Sue, Sue, 2008). It also invites to discuss the key tension in contemporary identity politics between cultural complexity and simplification (noted by Thomas Hylland Eriksen, 2019) and its impact on education.

888 Mobility and Education in Nigeria: Accounts from The COVID-19 Era

Ishaq Abdulkarim Aliyu, Maryam Liman, Sadiq Abubakar Muktar

Nigeria, the most populous country in Africa recorded its first corona virus (COVID-19) case in Lagos State. The spread to other states was mainly due to returnees from other infected states within Nigeria and from countries of the world. Nigerian students from around the world also returned home when schools closed down and opted for on-line classes. Following the increase in the number of infected people, all schools in the nation were closed. An on-line survey of some Nigerian students studying both in Nigeria and abroad revealed the latter and those in private universities within the country have online classes while those in Nigerian public schools do not have that as an alternative. All the students from Nigerian universities are home due to the compulsory closure of all schools within the nation while those studying abroad came back home due to fear of experiencing lockdown in a foreign country, fear of shortage of funds, food and basic supplies, loneliness and also fear of falling sick without any family around. 2% of the students have tested positive for the Corona virus and they form part of returnee students from Cyprus back to Kano through the Nnamdi Azikiwe International Airport, Abuja. The Nigerian Center for Disease Control (NCDC) and Kano State Ministry of Health has full details of all the students and has kept in touch with them throughout the 14days isolation period recommended for all returnees. The authorities constantly advised the students through text messages to adhere to COVID 19 protocols by always wearing face masks when in public, keeping a distance of at least 2metres from the next person and washing of hands with soap.

References

Eriksen T.H. (2019) Cultural Complexity in Vertovec S. (ed.) (2019) *Routledge International Hanbook of Diversity Studies*. London and New York: Routledge, p. 376.

European Commission (2002). *Joint Report on Social Inclusion*, p. 48.

European Migration Network Lithuania (2020). *Migration in Numbers*. Available at: https://123.emn.lt/en/#chart-14-desc (accessed 15-01-2021).

Pirrie, A., Head, G., & Brna, P. (2006). *Mainstreaming pupils with special educational needs. Edinburgh: Scottish Executive Education Department*.

Sue D.W., Sue D. (2008). *Counselling the Culturally Diverse: Theory and Practice. New Jersey: John Wiley & Sons*, p. 85.

The Law on Education of the Republic of Lithuania (2011). Available at: https://eacea.ec.europa.eu/nationalpolicies/eurydice/content/legislation-38_en (accessed 15-01-2021).

519 International education, digital worlds and entrepreneurial awareness: a case study based on the experience of Chinese students in France

Claudia Astarita

Abstract: Globalization has triggered a remarkable growth in the number of international students enrolling in institutions outside their countries of citizenship. Students' experiences of transnational mobilitiestend to have a deep and significant impact on their identities, on their views of themselves, their families and friendship networks, their country of origin, their host country, and the world. This paper explores the impact of transitional mobility from another perspective, the one of students' understanding and actual exploitation of entrepreneurial opportunities in the host country. Grounded on a longitudinal study conducted among Chinese students based in France, this article highlights if, how, and under which circumstances students' mobility is understood and exploited as a new source of economic opportunities, as well as the role played by real and digital Chinese communities already residing in the host country to push newcomers into new entrepreneurial paths and experiences. Also, the paper starts reflecting on the consequences of these entrepreneurial experiences in a host country on the same students that are expected to go back to the People's Republic of China after completing their studies in France. About the contributor: Claudia Astarita is lecturer at Sciences Po Lyon and researcher at the Lyon's Institute of East Asian Studies (IAO). She is also an associate Fellow at the Asia Institute, the University of Melbourne, and International Relations Analyst for South Asia at CeMiSS, Centre for Military and Strategic Studies, in Rome. She obtained her Ph.D. in Asian Studies from Hong Kong University in early 2010. Her main research interests include China's political and economic development, Chinese and Indian Foreign policies, East Asian regionalism and regional economic integration, Asian Civil Society, and the role of media and memory (both official and unofficial) in reshaping historical narratives in Asia

915   Understanding migrants' identities: the Role of Universities and communities

Olivia M. Joseph-Aluko

The last decade has witnessed increasing and intensifying waves of population movements, which have led to drastic shifts in demographic composition in many nations around the world, with a corresponding growth in social unrest and economic instability that challenges nations' ability to progress in achieving the Sustainable Development Goals (SDGs). There is a pressing need for academics and higher education institutions in general to engage with policymakers and local communities to develop initiatives aimed at addressing demographic changes in ways that promote sustainable development by aiding migrants' acculturation and economic integration and helping host societies learn ways to tolerate and ultimately embrace growing socio-cultural and linguistic diversity. This study explores universities' initiatives to contribute to efforts by international agencies, the private sector, and governments at various levels to engage in outreach to local communities in the goal of integrating migrants and promoting greater social cohesion between host communities and newcomers in a manner that contributes to positive development outcomes.

Methodology

This study examines primary and secondary documents and websites published by higher education institutions in the developed and developing worlds to identify degree programs, faculty centres and university institutions, initiatives, and partnerships related to migration and demographic change.

Findings

Higher education institutions in the United States, Australia, and Europe have devoted increasing amounts of resources toward incorporating migration studies into core curricula, including diverse disciplines such as sociology, political science, public service and social work, law, English, history, anthropology, international affairs, education, and urban planning. Graduates are being prepared for careers in governmental agencies at various levels, policy think tanks and firms, community-based non-profits and non-governmental organizations, international agencies, and advocacy and public interest organizations. Major initiatives have encompassed studies of how host populations understand and respond to immigration, legal clinics advocating for migrant rights, outreach programmes aimed at educating and promoting understanding between immigrants and receiving communities, and work with policymakers to devise measures that safeguard the rights and dignity of migrants and refugees. Other outreach programmes promote physical, mental and behavioural health and health education or provide entrepreneurship assistance and vocational training to migrants and refugees. A few institutions such as University of the People in Pasadena, California, USA, and Entraide Universitaire in Paris, France, and the University of Canberra have engaged in efforts to provide higher education opportunities to refugees.

Conclusion

Despite increasing efforts by universities, societies in Western, developed nations remain hostile to migrants and refugees due to the continued escalation of negative media and political narratives. It is critical that other social institutions become more involved in social and economic integration efforts to develop more open societies. Exploring efforts to integrate migrants into local communities helps to enhance our understanding of the migration processes and wider consequences for societies, including issues of governance, human rights, socio-cultural diversity, development and citizenship that shape migrants' life chances.

References

African Centre for Migration & Society. (2019). our research themes. Retrieved from http://www.migration.org.za/

Cornell Center for Social Sciences (2019). Immigration resources. Retrieved from http://socialsciences.cornell.edu/immigration/immigration-resources/

European Master in Migration and Intercultural Relations. (2019). The EMMIR programme. Retrieved from https://www.emmir.org/programme

Ferede, M.K. (2016). *Engaging the diaspora: Potential for sub-Saharan African universities*. Policy Brief, OECD Programme on Innovation, Higher Education and Research for Development. Retrieved from https://www.oecd.org/sti/Engaging%20the%20Diaspora_Ferede.pdf

Kothari, A., MacLean, L., Edwards, N. & Hobbs, A. (2011). Indicators at the interface: managing policymaker-researcher collaboration. *Knowledge Management Research and Practice*, 9(3), 203-214.

Uhawenimana, T.C. (2012, 26 August). Higher education needs to engage in outreach-based research. *University World News*. Retrieved from https://www.universityworldnews.com/post.php?story=20120822164106621

United Nations. (2017, 5 April). Speakers discuss migration-driven demographic challenges, role of international assistance, as population and development commission continues session. Retrieved from https://www.un.org/press/en/2017/pop1058.doc.htm

United Nations Department of Economic and Social Affairs. (2012). Issues Brief 15 -

Migration and sustainable development. Retrieved from https://sustainabledevelopment.un.org/index.php?page=view&type=400&nr=544&m enu=124

University of the Witwatersrand. (2019). The Forced Migration Studies Programme, University of the Witwatersrand (FMSP). Retrieved from https://www.eldis.org/organisation/A35104

Vega, D. (2013, 21 May). *We need to increase diversity in policymaking.* Center for American Progress. Retrieved from https://www.americanprogress.org/issues/race/news/2013/05/21/64024/we-need-to-increase-diversity-in-policymaking/

Yale MacMillan Center Program on Refugees, Forced Displacement, and Humanitarian Responses. (2019). Retrieved from https://refugee.macmillan.yale.edu/

3C Turkiye'nin Goc Deneyimi
Chair *Yakup Çoştu, Hitit University, Çorum, Turkey*

564 The Influence of Migration on the Cultural History of Islam A Review in The Context of the Quranic Commentary Studies of Early Period

Ömer Dinç

It should be noted that one of the main factors of the spreading of the Islamic religion to a wide geography from the earliest periods is the migration. When we consider the migrations of the Prophet from Mecca to Medina and the first Muslims to Abyssinia, it can be expressed as a historical reality that immigration influences the spreading of Islam more effectively and quickly. In addition, following the Prophet's period, the migration of muslims to various cities and regions, it is seen that they generally perform the activities of explaining and interpreting the Qur'an in terms of calling people to the religion of Islam and in particular the formation of religious culture. As these activities allow Islam to be accepted in many geographies outside the Arabian peninsula, at the same time, they leaded on the cultural formation of Muslims to become increasingly widespread. Especially we see tahat in the process of interpretation of the

89

Qur'an, many companions of the Prophet Muhammad went various places and created a tafsir school on their own axis. For example Ibn Mas'ud migrating to Iraq from Mecca directed the region's Islamization process and he established a school by explaining and interpreting the Qur'an that he learned from the Prophet. This can be seen as a good example of the contribution of the migration factor to the development of Islam's intellectual dimension. In addition, the Muslims in these regions learning the Qur'an's explanation and interpretation transmitted this experience to the other regions and this became a tradition in the context of the activities of Qur'anic interpretation.

In this study, to which regions some companions of the Prophet migrated in order to teach and explain the Qur'an after the period of the Prophet Muhammad will be analyzed. This will be followed by the discussion of how the works they carried out in these regions influenced the development and progress of Islam. In addition, how the people taught by these companions migrating to the outside of the Arabian Peninsula transmitted this experience to the other people by way of migration to the other regions and the effects of this will also be handled.

622   The COVID-19 Pandemic and Syrian Women Refugees in A Gender Perspective

Senem Gürkan ve Erkan Perşembe

The COVID-19 pandemic, which has had impact on the whole world, undoubtedly affected each and every individual. The literature on pandemic has shown that people in vulnerable / disadvantaged groups with special conditions such as poverty, old age, disability, gender-based discrimination, refugee and asylum, are affected more negatively and / or exposed to discrimination compared to other segments of the society.

Specifically, in Turkey, Syrians under temporary protection, on one hand, have been trying to cope with the problems such as integration, poverty, unemployment, hunger, etc.; on the other hand, have faced with some problems stemming from the pandemic period. Gender inequality, which is one of the sources of these problems, has caused these women to be negatively affected both before and during the pandemic period. As the relevant literature states, the pandemic process has paved the way for the end and / or slowdown of actions on gender discrimination in recent years. Therefore, the acquisitions are eliminated and the inequal status have deepened and caused new problems.

The aim of this study is to reveal the consequences of the COVID-19 pandemic on Syrian women refugees in Samsun in a gender perspective. Within this respect, these research questions were tried to be replied:

1. How has the COVID-19 pandemic had effects on Syrian women refugees from a gender perspective?

2. Has the gender role stress of Syrian women refugees in Samsun showed differences according to their age?

3. Has the gender role stress of Syrian women refugees in Samsun showed differences according to their marital status?

Methodologically, the research was conducted through the periods and methods of qualitative and quantitative, that is, mixed research paradigms. The participants of the study were 32 Syrian women refugees living in İlkadım, Canik and Atakum districts of Samsun province. The qualitative dimension of the study was carried out through grounded theory while the quantitative dimension was carried out through correlational survey model. The data were collected by the researchers themselves by using in-depth interview technique through online interviews to minimize the risk of the transmission of the virus. A semi-structured interview form and questionnaire form were used and ethical consent was taken before the research. The semi-structured observation form included Feminine Gender Role Stress Scale (FGRSS), together with demographic and open-ended questions, to measure the gender role stresses of the participants.

Three-step qualitative research model was conducted to the qualitative data. To the quantitative data set, on the other hand, One-Way Analysis of Variance (ANOVA) was applied to reveal whether the gender role stress of Syrian women refugees in Samsun showed differences according to their age; and Independent Samples t-Test was applied to reveal that of their marital status.

The findings of the study have put forth that the gender effects of the COVID-19 pandemic on Syrian female refugees living in Samsun can be divided into 7 themes. These effects are, respectively, increase in economic difficulties, increase in household responsibilities, increase in domestic violence, psychosocial effects, increase in health problems, decrease in women's participation to social life and increase in polygamy. The analysis conducted to reveal whether the gender role stress of Syrian women refugees in Samsun showed differences according to their age have demonstrated that there is no statistically significant difference between these two variables. Moreover, the analysis conducted to reveal whether the gender role stress of Syrian women refugees in Samsun showed differences according to their marital status have demonstrated that the married participants experience higher levels of gender role stress than those of the single ones. As a result, the COVID-19 pandemic has reinforced the gender-based discrimination faced by Syrian women refugees, one of the disadvantaged groups; and gender inequalities have deepened within this period. It is thought that the social impact of the pandemic was felt more in women and that these women lost some of the acquisitions they gained until the pandemic in the context of gender equality.

835   Sicilya'ya İlk Müslüman Göçü ve Tesirler

Mehmet Azimli

Avrupa'da aydınlanmaya en fazla tesirin Endülüs üzerinden olduğu genel bir kabuldür. Oysaki Avrupa'daki Reform ve Rönesans hareketlerinin İtalya üzerinden yayıldığını düşünürsek; başka bir sebep aramak lazımdır. Bu da Sicilya'daki ileri bir medeniyetin bu hareketlenmelere yaptığı katkı ile olmalıdır.

Sicilya'daki Müslüman kültürü tarafından üretilen bilgi ve teknolojinin İtalya yoluyla Batıya taşınması, gerek mimaride gerek bilimsel alanlarda gerekse de Batının kilisenin dini hegemonyasından kurtulmasında çok önem arz etmektedir. Bu manada bugünkü Batının bütün dünyaya iftiharla sunduğu; Allah ile insan arasına girmeyen ve özgürce yaşanılan bireysel din algısı Müslüman

Sicilya'dan gelen bir tesirdir. Bu esasında süreç boyunca Batıda laikliğin ilk adımlarının atılmasına da sebep olmuştur.

Sicilya'da siyasi olarak Müslüman dünyanın kullandığı usuller alınmakla birlikte zirai alanda Batının bilmediği yeni zirai metotlar Batıya aktarılırken mimaride yepyeni usuller kilise mimarisine tesir etmiştir. Sicilya üzerinden elde edilen yığınlarca kitap Batı dillerine çevrilerek Avrupa'nın sınıf atlamasına katkı sağlanmıştır. İdrisi'nin Kral II. Roger'a sunduğu "Kitabu'r-Rucar" bunun en güzel örneğidir. Bu eserinde dünyanın yuvarlaklığını savunan İdrisi ayrıca küre biçimindeki bir dünya haritası da sunmuştur.

Kategorik olarak söylersek; Sicilya üzerinden Batıya giren pusula; dünyayı keşfetmesine, kağıt; bilimsel patlama yapmasına, barut; askeri üstünlük elde etmesine sebep olurken matematikte Batının bu gün kullandığı rakamlar da bu kategoriye dahil edilebilir.

Bildirimizde İslam öncesi Sicilya'nın durumu aktarıldıktan sonra Sicilya'nın Müslümanlar tarafından fethi ayrıca Müslümanların hakimiyetinden sonra Normanlar döneminde Sicilya'nın durumu ve Sicilya İslam Medeniyetinin Batıya tesirlerinden maddeler halinde bahsedilecektir. Bu etkiler siyasi etki, mimari ve sanatsal etki, ilmi etki, zirai etki, endüstriyel etki, dil ve edebiyat yönünden etki şeklinde aktarılabilir.

1025   Göç Aydınlanma Sağlar mı? -Karşılaşma ve Yüzleşme Pratiği Olarak Göç ve Kimliğin Dönüşümü

Mehmet Evkuran

Anlam ve değer arayışı, gelişmişlik düzeyi ne olursa olsun düşünce ve duygu (akıl ve arzu da denebilir) varlığı olan insanın vazgeçilmez bir sorunudur. Kimlik tanımlamaları değer ve anlam arayışlarına bağlı süreçlerdir. Kimlikler boşlukta oluşmaz; zaman ve mekân bağlamlarında tanımlanır ve gelişir. Bu nedenle zamanın ve mekânın değişmesi/dönüşmesi ile birlikte, kimlik krizlerinin ortaya çıkması sürecin doğal bir sonucudur. Zaman-mekân ve kimlik ilişkilerindeki sorunları ya da imkânları tetikleyen temel olgulardan birisi göçtür.

Toplumlar sorunlarını çözmeye çalışırken, tarihlerinde yer alan figürlere yönelik özdeşleştirmelere başvururlar. Özdeşlik, yeni olanın sürpriz yanlarını gidermekte ve yaşanan krizi yabancı olmaktan çıkarmaktadır. Yanı sıra sorunları çözmek için gerekli olan zihinsel saflık, odaklanma, motivasyon ve eyleme geçme gibi unsurları sağlamaktadır. Yaşanan sorun ve sıkıntının yeni bir eşey olmadığı eskiden bu yana karşılaşılan bilindik bir durum olduğunu algısı, toplumsal iletişimi ve dayanışmayı sağladığı gibi toplumsal-tarihsel kimliği de yeni şartlar bağlamında yeniler ve güçlendirir. Ancak kimliğin izlediği bu yöntemin sıkıntıları da bulunmaktadır. Karşılaşılan sorunları özdeşleşme üzerinden sürekli olarak geriye dönük analojilerle karşılaşma eğilimi, yeni ve farklı olanların gözden kaçırılmasına yol açacaktır. Her olayın kendi biricikliği ve tarihsel tikelliği içinde ele alınması gerekir. İnanca ya da ideolojiye süreklilik kazandırma adına geriye dönük analojilerle dolu bir dünya inşa etmek, hayatın canlı akışının dışında kalmak, zorlanmak ve hayatı zorlamak, fanatikleşmek gibi sorunlar doğuracaktır.

Müslüman coğrafyanın kendi içinde yaşanan ya da Avrupa ve ABD'ye yönelik göçlerin kendilerine özgü koşulları ve sonuçları vardır. Bu göçler, doğurduğu siyasal, ekonomik ve toplumsal problemlerin dışında daha kökende kimlik ve değerlerle ilgili sorunları tetiklemiştir. Özellikle zamana ve mekâna aşırı bağlı kimlikler bu süreçte daha derin savrulmalar yaşamaktadır.

Bu çalışmada zaman-mekân değişmesinin kimlikler üzerindeki etkileri, sorunları çözerken sadece inanca sarılmanın olumlu-olumsuz sonuçları, özdeşliklerin yararları ve sakıncaları üzerinde durulacak, olgu merkezli yaklaşımın gerekliliği tartışılacaktır.

700   Salgin Döneminde Uzaktan Eğitim ve Yabanci Uyruklu Öğrenciler: Çorum İl Merkezi Örneği

Yakup Çoştu

2020 yılı başından itibaren COVID 19 salgını tüm dünyada hızlı bir şekilde yayılım göstermiş ve başta sağlık alanı olmak üzere ekonomik, sosyal ve kültürel hayatın tüm alanlarında önemli değişim ve dönüşümlerin yaşanmasına neden olmuştur. Günümüzde yaşanan salgının etkilediği alanlarından bir başkası da eğitim alanı olmuştur. Hastalığın yayılım hızını yavaşlatma ya da durdurma adına örgün eğitim alanında bir takım uygulamalar yürürlüğe konulmuştur. Bu uygulamaların başında ise, uzaktan eğitim modeli yer almaktadır. Bu model, öğrencilerin zaman ve mekan bağlamında birbirlerinden ve öğrenme kaynaklarından uzak olmayı içermektedir. Yapılan araştırmalara göre, çeşitli kitle iletişim imkanları üzerinden yürütülen bu eğitim modelinde, eğitimsel kaynaklara ulaşabilme ya da onlardan yararlanma eşitliğinde ciddi sorunların ortaya çıktığı belirlenmiştir. Özellikle, dezavantajlı gruplar bu süreçten en çok etkilenenler olmuştur.

Kendi anavatanlarının dışında azınlık olarak bulunan göçmenlerin, ev sahibi topluma uyum sağlama süreçleri sosyal bilimciler tarafından ele alınan önemli araştırma konuları arasında yer almaktadır. Özellikle, genç kuşak göçmenlerin ev sahibi topluma yönelik sosyal ve kültürel uyumunda, okullaşma ve dil öğrenimi önemli rol oynamaktadır. Çünkü eğitim, göçmenler için yeni sosyal ortamlara ve hayat şartlarına uyum sağlamanın ve geçmişin travmatik anılarından uzaklaşmanın önemli bir aracıdır. Ülke genelindeki yabancı uyruklu göçmen nüfusu dikkate alındığında, Türk eğitim sistemi için göçmen öğrenciler konusu, artık göz ardı edilemez bir gerçek haline dönüşmüştür.

Türkiye'de COVID 19 salgını sürecinde örüğün eğitimde, uzaktan eğitim modeline geçilmiştir. Buda, beraberinde birtakım eşitsizliklerin oluşmasına neden olmuştur. Bu eşitsizliklerden hiç kuşkusuz dezavantajlı gruplar içerisinde yer alan göçmen öğrencilerde etkilenmiştir.

Çorum il merkezinde, İçişleri Bakanlığı Göç İdaresi Genel Müdürlüğü'nün yayınladığı istatistiklere göre, 17.02.2021 tarihi itibariye, geçici koruma kapsamında 3.212 Suriyeli bulunmaktadır. İkamet izni ile Çorum'da yaşayan göçmen sayısı 2.098 kişidir. Uluslararası koruma kapsamında yer alan ve uluslararası koruma arayan göçmen sayısı ise 12.000 civarındadır. Çorum il genelinde Milli Eğitim Müdürlüğüne bağlı okullarda (ana sınıfı, ilkokul, ortaokul ve lise) okuyan yabancı uyruklu öğrenci sayısı ise, toplam 3.374'tür.

Bu bildirinin temel konusunu, Çorum il merkezinde ikamet eden göçmen toplulukların İl Milli eğitim Müdürlüğüne bağlı ilkokul, ortaokul ve liselere kayıtlı öğrencilerinin salgın (COVID 19) sürecinde uzaktan eğitimden faydalanma durumlarının tespit edilmesi oluşturmaktadır. Bu kapsamında, uzaktan eğitime katılım, derse devam, ders başarı durumu, okul-öğrenmen-veli irtibatı gibi hususlar eğimde fırsat eşitliği kapsamında betimsel olarak araştırılacaktır. Bahsi geçen konu, araştırmanın çalışma grubunu oluşturan, Çorum İl Merkezinde yabancı uyruklu öğrencilerin olduğu ilkokul, ortaokul ve liselerde görev yapan ve sınıflarında yabancı öğrenci bulunan öğretmenler ve okul idarecileri ile yapılacak yarı yapılandırılmış mülakat tekniği üzerinden araştırılacaktır.

3D   Communication and Migration

Chair Vildan Mahmutoglu, Galatasaray University, Turkey

708   The role of social media in the construction of "illegal" migration routes:
Experiences of Syrian migrants
Nadide Schwarzenberger and Yelda Özen

872   Representation of Syrian Refugees in Bianet.Org and Hürriyet
Newspaper: A Comparative Study of Alternative Media and Mainstream
Media
Derya Kurtuluş

639   Anti-immigrant narratives in times of real crisis. An automated content
analysis of Italian political communication on social media
Anita Gottlob and Luca Serafini

708   The role of social media in the construction of "illegal" migration routes: Experiences of Syrian migrants

Nadide Schwarzenberger and Yelda Özen

The war commenced in Syria in 2011 has created a massive immigration wave in which Syrian individuals have been migrating from Syria to Europe for "better conditions"; however, this migration makes migrant policies for securing borders become strictdue to the concern of socio-cultural changes. The growing crisis leaded the Syrian to seek "illegal" ways of immigration. On 14th -15th of September 2015, thousands of people organized by way of Facebook gathered together in Edirne and demanded to be allowed to pass on Europe by walking throughout Balkans.This movement has paved the way for a foresight that social media is highly influential in the process of irregular immigration.It is clear that social media as the basic necessity of network society within the information age offers Syrian individuals, who intend to immigrate, the ways of the globalizing world or in Castells's words, new routes constructed "in the timeless landscape of computer networks and electronic media".From this point of view, this study aims to understand how the Syrian individuals, as the main subject of the immigration, experience this processand form the illegal migration routes in their own words and to reveal the crucial role of social media in the process. To achievethis aim, in-depth interviews with 26 Syrian immigrants who went through the illegal immigration routes arriving at or captured in Austria and who reside in Austria's Linz city and its surrounding towns were conducted and systematic observation notes were taken. According to findings,it can be said that social media and sharing networksas new communication technologies have the role in creating an illegal immigration way in which the actor, the potential immigrant dominates.The Syrian individual has planned almost every step through cyber nets with a holographic impression on his/her mind before going on the road and therefore has made the illegal immigration way safe. From findings, every steps of Syrian migration resembles "migration network stairs" in this study. Network theory Which emphasizes community network based on kinship ties, ethnic identity and friendship in the process of migration,seem to have power to explain the first steps of Syrian migration from Syria to neighbour countries; however following steps need different new types of net, in other words cyber nets, which create virtual migrant community, functional in giving support each other and coping with various risks encountered in the route of migration to Europe.In addition, the Syrian migrant' experiences during the route to Europe indicate that immigration has class-based and gender-based aspects. This immigration is observed as a middle-class and male-dominated story. On the one hand, the route of migration interlaced with cyber nets make women invisible and make men dominated in the whole process; on the other hand migrants who have professional occupation, educated and with high digital literacy could reach the target country.

872   Representation of Syrian Refugees in Bianet.Org and Hürriyet Newspaper: A Comparative Study of Alternative Media and Mainstream Media

Derya Kurtuluş

Since March 2020, as in the rest of the world, news on both mainstream media and alternative news platforms in Turkey was heavily related to Covid 19 pandemic, and vaccination studies, quarantines and measures that came into our lives with the pandemic.

One of the most important issues on the agenda shortly before March 2020, which was the date of the first case declared officially, was the news related to Syrian refugees who were protesting on the Greece border of Turkey.

This study aims to comparatively examine how Bianet, as an alternative media source, and Hurriyet, as the mainstream media press, did make news on the events ongoing after the statement given by Edirne Governor's Office, which tells that they will allow Syrian refugees to cross border between Turkey and Greece on 27 February 2020, and the rights violations that the Syrian refugees, of which majority was refugees from Istanbul, faced with this unilateral transition freedom explanation.

At the time when Syrian refugees have become a kind of bargaining element with the European Union, and, accordingly, where the refugee crisis came, irregular crossings over the Aegean Sea by boat were let unchallenged by the state, and in the investigations made on the basis of discourse it was observed that they were encouraged. In the news framing of Hürriyet, as an example of a progovernment press organ, while reporting this situation, they emphasized "humanitarianism of Turkey" and "aggrievement" that the country experienced due to the refugee population, on the other hand, bianet.org website have made news on the difficulties experienced by refugees with the rights-based approach that constitutes websites publishing policy. The present study attempts to discuss the ideological background of two news sources and their approach to the refugee issue through mainstream media and alternative media reporting perspective.

The news published on the online edition of Hürriyet newspaper and on the bianet.org website between 25 February 2020 and 25 March 2020 were searched for the keywords 'Syrian', 'refugee', 'refugee', 'immigrant' and the results were analyzed using a critical discourse analysis method. The underlying reason for choosing this date range is that it covers the period when the rumor of allowing passage across borders began to spread and the period when waiting collectively at the border was prohibited due to covid 19. When 'the fact that Syrian refugees have not been featured in the mainstream media as much in the last year after Covid19 pandemic became the main topic in Turkey as well' was taken into consideration, the reporting of protests and government discourses on protests taking place in Edirne and the North Aegean in February 2020 represents an area worth studying at the point reached where 10 years were passed after the open-door policy of Turkey started in April 2011, which allowed Syrian Refugees to enter the country.

639 Anti-immigrant narratives in times of real crisis. An automated content analysis of Italian political communication on social media

Anita Gottlob and Luca Serafini

In Europe, the topic of immigration is highly divisive on social media, and immigrants are often framed in terms of risk to the society by right-wing populist (RWP) communication and media. In this work, we explore how the topic of migration varies in political communication and online media when the host-society is occupied with managing 'real' risks through automated-content analysis. More specifically, we used the health crisis of the COVID-19 pandemic in Italy as a case study for what we termed a 'tangible crisis'. Here, we identified two periods related to growing cases of COVID-19 in Italy which we termed 'waves of tangible crisis', assuming that in these two periods the risk stemming from COVID-19 was strongly perceived by the Italian population. We contrasted our observations to the periods between the two waves.

We first used a dictionary related to migration to compare the salience and engagement on posts by Italian media and politicians on Facebook during the first and second wave of COVID-19 infections in Italy. Our sample included a total of 276809 posts of four Facebook pages of media outlets, and 71875 posts on eight Facebook pages of political parties. We then operationalized risk narratives on migration by constructing a risk- and threat dictionary.We further examined how engagement on both, social media timelines by political leaders and mainstream media sites online developed over time.

This work focuses on the communication of populist parties mainly on the far-right (such as the Lega and Fratelli d'Italia) and the 5 Star movement, which is classified as a 'transversal' (Mosca & Tronconi, 2019).

We compare the posts of these parties to those of mainstream and left-leaning parties. Recent evidence suggests that anti-immigration references surfaced as 'the most distinguishing factor of Right Wing Populist communication on Facebook' (Heiss & Matthes, 2020). Further, we also explore posts by far-right and right wing media compared to mainstream media, as previous empirical evidence suggests that migration is often framed as a risk and threat to the host society in right-wing media outlets (Wodak and Khosravinik, 2013).

Our findings suggest that the political discourse and risk narratives on immigration decreased during times of 'tangible crisis' for right-wing populist parties and news media.

Our results further show that within the two periods of high infection rates of COVID-19 in Italy, the salience of migration related posts as well as engagement for those pages generally decreased for RWP and anti-establishment parties in comparison to the other parties, and periods of lower infection rates. Concerning risk-related posts, we found a similar trend. All together, our findings suggest that the political discourse on migration as well as the exposure to the topic for Facebook Italian users decreased. Crucially, this happened also at a time when key policies regarding immigration and regularization of migrants were discussed by the Italian government, receiving unexpectedly low reactions. Drawing on prior theories on risk perception and crisis discourses, this leads us to theorize that anti-immigrant communication loses its strength during times of tangible crises.

References

Abbondanza G., Balio F., The electoral payoff of immigration flows for anti-immigration parties: the case of Italy's Lega Nord, European Political Science, 17 (3), 378–403.

Barberá, P., Jost, J. T., Nagler, J., Tucker, J. A., & Bonneau, R. (2015). Tweeting from left to right: Is online political communication more than an echo chamber? Psychological science, 26(10), 1531-1542.

Beck, U. (1992). Risk society: Towards a new modernity (Vol. 17). sage.

Beck, U., Giddens, A., & Lash, S. (1994). Reflexive modernization: Politics, tradition and aesthetics in the modern social order. Stanford University Press.

Beck, U. (1996). The Reinvention of Politics. Rethinking Modernity in the Global Social Order. Polity Press.

Boomgaarden, H.,McLaren, L., & Vliegenthart, R. (2017). News coverage and public concern about immigration in Britain. International Journal of Public Opinion Research, 30(2), 173-193.

Burgess, A., Wardman, J., & Mythen, G. (2018). Considering risk: placing the work of Ulrich Beck in context.

Bracciale, R., & Martella, A. (2017). Define the populist political communication style: the case of Italian political leaders on Twitter. Information, Communication & Society, 20(9), 1310-1329.

Boberg, S., Quandt, T., Schatto-Eckrodt, T., & Frischlich, L. (2020). Pandemic populism: Facebook pages of alternative news media and the corona crisis--A computational content analysis. arXiv preprint arXiv:2004.02566.

Bonaccorsi, G., Pierri, F., Cinelli, M., Flori, A., Galeazzi, A., Porcelli, F., ... & Pammolli, F. (2020). Economic and social consequences of human mobility restrictions under COVID-19. Proceedings of the National Academy of Sciences, 117(27), 15530-15535.

Blumler, J. G., & Kavanagh, D. (1999). The third age of political communication: Influences and features. Political Communication, 16(3), 209–230. doi:10.1080/105846099198596

Cecchi S. (2011), The criminalization of immigration in Italy: extent of the phenomenon and possible interpretations, Italian Sociological Review, 1 (1), 34–42.

CrowdTangle Team (2020). CrowdTangle. Facebook, Menlo Park, California, United States

Chouliaraki, L., & Zaborowski, R. (2017). Voice and community in the 2015 refugee crisis: A content analysis of news coverage in eight European countries. International Communication Gazette, 79(6-7), 613-635.

Wildavsky, A., & Dake, K. (1990). Theories of risk perception: Who fears what and why? Daedalus, 41-60.

Douglas, M. (2013). *Risk and blame.* Routledge.

Ernst, N., Engesser, S., Büchel, F., Blassnig, S., & Esser, F. (2017). Extreme parties and populism: An analysis of Facebook and Twitter across six countries. Information, Communication & Society, 20(9), doi: 10.1080/1369118X.2017.1329333

Eberl, J. M., Huber, R. A., & Greussing, E. (2020). From Populism to the 'Plandemic': Why populists believe in COVID-19 conspiracies.

Gerbaudo, P. (2014). Populism 2.0: Social media activism, the generic internet user and interactive direct democracy. In Social Media, Politics and the State: Protests, Revolutions, Riots, Crime and Policing in the Age of Facebook, Twitter and YouTube (pp. 67-87). Taylor and Francis. DOI: 10.4324/9781315764832

Giddens, A. (1990). *The Consequences of Modernity*, Polity Press.

Giddens, A. (1991). *Modernity and self-identity: Self and society in the late modern age.* Stanford university press.

Hall, S. 1993. Culture, community, nation. Cultural Studies 7:349- 63.

Heidenreich, T., Eberl, J. M., Lind, F., & Boomgaarden, H. (2019) 'Political migration discourses on social media: a comparative perspective on visibility and sentiment across political Facebook accounts in Europe', Journal of Ethnic and Migration Studies, 1-20.

Heiss, R., & Matthes, J. (2020). Stuck in a nativist spiral: Content, selection, and effects of right-wing populists' communication on Facebook. Political Communication, 37(3), 303-328.

Hollway, W., & Jefferson, T. (1997). The risk society in an age of anxiety: situating fear of crime. British journal of sociology, 255-266.

Maltone-Bonnenfant, C. (2011). L'immigrazione nei media italiani. Disinformazione, stereotipi e innovazioni. Line@ editoriale, (3), 62-78.

Mazzoleni, G., & Bracciale, R. (2018). Socially mediated populism: the communicative strategies of political leaders on Facebook. Palgrave Communications, 4(1), 1-10.

Musarò P., Parmiggiani P. (2017), Beyond black and white: the role of media in portraying and policing migration and asylum in Italy, International Review of Sociology, 27 (2), 241-260.

McLaren, L. M. (2010) 'Cause for Concern? The Impact of Immigration on Political Trust', Policy Network.

McLaren, L., Boomgaarden, H., & Vliegenthart, R. (2017). News coverage and public concern about immigration in Britain. International Journal of Public Opinion Research, 30(2), 173-193.

Miłkowska-Samul, K. (2018). Il discorso anti-immigrazione: migranti, immigrati, profughi, rifugiati nei social media italiani. J. Łukaszewicz.

Pierri, F., Artoni, A., & Ceri, S. (2020). Investigating Italian disinformation spreading on Twitter in the context of 2019 European elections. PloS one, 15(1), e0227821.

Reuters Institute For the Study of Journalism. (n.d.). Digital News Report 2017. https://www.digitalnewsreport.org/survey/2017/

Reuters Institute For the Study of Journalism. (n.d.). Digital News Report 2019. https://www.digitalnewsreport.org/survey/2019/

Reuters Institute For the Study of Journalism. (n.d.). Digital News Report 2020. https://www.digitalnewsreport.org/survey/

Sniderman P. M., HagendoornL. PriorM.(2004). Predisposing factors and situational triggers: Exclusionary reactions to immigrant minorities. American Political Science Review, 98,35-49 DOI: http://dx.doi-org.uaccess.univie.ac.at/10.1017/S000305540400098X

Slovic, P. (1999) 'Trust, emotion, sex, politics, and science: Surveying the risk-assessment battlefield', Risk analysis, 19(4), 689-701.

Slovic, P., Finucane, M. L., Peters, E., & MacGregor, D. G. (2004). Risk as analysis and risk as feelings: Some thoughts about affect, reason, risk, and rationality. Risk Analysis: An International Journal, 24(2), 311-322.

Tusikov, N., & Fahlman, R. C. (2009). Threat and risk assessments. Strategic thinking in criminal intelligence, 147-164.

Urso A. (2018), The politicization of immigration in Italy. Who frames the issue, when and how, Italian Political Science Review, 48 (3), 365-381.

Vilella, S., Lai, M., Paolotti, D., & Ruffo, G. (2020). Immigration as a Divisive Topic: Clusters and Content Diffusion in the Italian Twitter Debate. Future Internet, 12(10), 173.

McCombs, M. E., Shaw, D. L., & Weaver, D. H. (2014). New directions in agenda-setting theory and research. Mass communication and society, 17(6), 781-802.

Wodak, R., KhosraviNik, M., & Mral, B. (Eds.). (2013). Right-wing populism in Europe:

Politics and discourse. A&C Black.

World Health Organisation, Corona Virus Disease (COVID-19) Pandemic, https://www.who.int/emergencies/diseases/novel-coronavirus-2019.

3E   Migration Governance

634   Urban Forced Migrants in the City of Tel-Aviv: From Arrival to Resettlement City?

Lilach Lev Ari

The purpose of this presentation is to discuss possible policy avenues regarding the transition of the city of Tel-Aviv from being an arrival to a resettlement city. This review paper refers to theories and various qualitative and quantitative secondary data sources.

Two-thirds of all refugees worldwide live in urban areas. They travel to a small number of cities: 'Arrival cities,' which function as hubs for initial integration and transit, and are often the end destination of the refugees' journeys, by becoming a resettlement city (Bose 2018; IOM, 2015). After the initial stage of immigration, an arrival city has the potential to become a 'resettlement city,' which enables forced migrants to reconstruct their lives regarding social infrastructure, housing amenities and utilities (Dachaga and Uchendu- Chigbu (2020).

During the past decade, a considerable number of asylum seekers (60,000) have migrated from African countries to Israel via Egypt. Their migration push motives were mainly the ongoing and bloody wars on the African continent as well as corruption, severe poverty, hunger, economic and politically unstable structures in their countries of origin. Israel became a preferred destination for many African forced migrants (Fargues 2017). Most asylum seekers came to Israel from Eritrea (Muller 2018). The number of asylum seekers in Israel today is approximately 31,052 (Population and Immigration Authority 2020).

Two thirds of asylum seekers in Israel found their way to the metropolitan Tel-Aviv area; More than a third (37%, 13,655 people) of them in the southern neighborhoods of the city of Tel Aviv (Vinograd et al. 2018). In these poor neighborhoods they live in crowded conditions of poverty and inferior sanitation.

Even before the migrants' arrival, these neighborhoods suffered from crowdedness, prostitution, gambling, illegal drugs and crime, low housing values and multi ethnic, racial social and cultural environment (Cohen and Margalit 2015). The local residents in and around these neighborhoods feel that their rights have been trampled on by thousands of migrants, crammed into these areas. As a result, these residents' life quality has been dealt a mortal blow, in an area in which they, too, are struggling with life difficulties in Israel. Hence, the tension between these two groups is increasing (Israel Affordable Housing Center 2018).

Since Israel does not see itself as a destination country for non-Jewish migration, any migrant to Israel who has no Jewish lineage is subject to status regulation under the Entry to Israel Law or the Anti-Infiltration Law. This attitude considers the migrants a significant strategic threat to the national interests of the State of Israel (Ben-Nun 2017). In this context, asylum seekers, as *non-Jewish* forced migrants, who reside in the country for several years, have slight chances to be fully integrated or receive refugee status. However, in the context of the city of Tel Aviv, it might possibly become a resettlement city, similarly to arrival cities elsewhere. Therefore, new policy trajectories should be implemented in order to reconstruct multicultural interactions aimed to diminish hostility, encourage integration, positive and constructive resettlement activities.

Bibliography

Ben-Nun, G. (2017) Seeking asylum in Israel: Refugees and the history of migration law. London and New York: I.B. Tauris.

Bose, P. S. (2018) Welcome and Hope, Fear, and Loathing: The Politics of Refugee Resettlement in Vermont. Peace and Conflict: Journal of Peace Psychology, 24(3), 320–329.

Cohen, N. & Margalit, T. (2015) 'There are really two cities here': Fragmented urban citizenship in Tel Aviv. International Journal of Urban and Regional Research, 39, 666-686.

Dachaga, W. & Uchendu-Chigbu, E. (2020). Understanding tenure security dynamics in resettlement towns: Evidence from the Bui Resettlement Project in Ghana. Journal of Planning and Land Management, 1(2), 38-49.

Fargues, P. (2017). Four decades of cross-Mediterranean undocumented migration to Europe: A review of the Evidence. International Organization for Migration (IOM) and the UN Migration Agency.

International Organization for Migration (IOM) (2015). World migration report 2015—Migrants and cities: New partnerships to manage mobility. Retrieved from http://publications.iom.int/books/world-migration-report-2015-migrants-and-cities-new-partnerships-manage-mobility#sthash.OFstnNsn.dpuf

Israel Affordable Housing Center (2018). Strategical plan: Decentralization and integration of asylum seekers and rehabilitation of southern Tel Aviv.

Retrieved from

https://95a8002f-7213-49ea-b9cc-3740efc65539.filesusr.com/ugd/976b1a_c4327c1257a8408ca86430117a9

44072.pdf [Hebrew].

Muller, T. R. (2018). Realizing rights within the Israeli asylum regime: A case study among Eritrean refugees in Tel Aviv. African Geographical Review, 37(2), 134-145.

Population and Immigration Authority (2020). Israel's *Foreigners' Data*. June 2010. Retrieved from https://www.gov.il/BlobFolder/generalpage/foreign_workers_stats/he/%D7%A0%D7%AA%D7%95%D7%A0%D7%99%20%D7%96%D7%A8%D7%99%D7%9D%20%D7%91%D7%99%D7%A9%D7%A8%D7%90%D7%9C%20%D7%A8%D7%91%D7%A2%D7%95%D7%9F%201%202020.pdf [Hebrew].

Vinograd, A., Ron, O. with Shany, Y. (2018). Asylum seekers: A legal framework for geographic distribution in Israel. Jerusalem: The Israel Democracy Institute [in Hebrew].

580   Street Level Bureaucrats in Local Migration Governance: Going Beyond the Responsibilities

Elif Topal Demiroglu

As municipalities become more interested in immigration issues and become more active in different dimensions of migration policy, local government bureaucrats have more and more effective roles in local governance of migration. As conceptualized defined by Lipsky, street-level bureaucrats are front-line workers who use discretion power in daily encounters within the legal framework defined for them or their institutions.[6] These public servants implement immigration policy in a way that "translat[e] the intent of the policy into reality"[7]. In this study, the experts of the municipalities' migration units are considered as street-level bureaucrats within the framework of Lipsky's definition. It is claimed that the roles of these bureaucrats go beyond using discretionary power to shape the approach of the municipality to immigration as a whole in the field of migration governance, where the legal framework is indeed very ambiguous. Although this argument is parallel with the concept of municipal activism put forward by Spenser and Delvino[8], this study shows that it is not only the municipality as an institution, but also the street level bureaucrats act to mediate the immigrants and the local people and take initiatives. Particularly, municipalities where the institutional capacity is not at a level to respond to non-citizens, it is seen that street-level bureaucrats have two important roles in the process of responding to the increasing population that challenge the municipalities. The first of one is the management of daily life, and the second is that they are the means and supporting actors of local governance

---

[6] Lipsky, M (1980). Street-Level Bureaucracy: Dilemmas of the Individual in Public Services, New York, NY: Russell Sage Foundation.

[7] Ismail W, Ariffin R and Cheok CK (2017). Human Trafficking in Malaysia: Bureaucratic Challenges in Policy Implementation, *Administration and Society* 49, 3

[8] Spencer, S and Delvino, N (2019). Municipal Activism on Irregular Migrants: The Framing of Inclusive Approaches at the Local Level, *Journal of Immigrant & Refugee Studies*, 17:1, 27-43, DOI:10.1080/15562948.2018.1519867

arrangements. In this context, while the study also focuses on the local turn [9] approach in local migration governance literature, it is argued that besides other factors affecting local immigration policies, institutional factors such as the structure and functioning of the local bureaucracy, as well as the individual attitudes and relations of bureaucrats are also effective in shaping local responses. In this context, it discusses the key role of street-level bureaucrats in local governance in the light of the findings of the field research, which consist of face-to-face interviews with migration unit experts in six district municipalities of Istanbul and the follow-up of different activities of these units for immigrants. Thus, it has been observed that the personal relations, professional experiences and the story of "otherness" of the street-level bureaucrats are effective in the local migration governance process.

623   Differential Inclusion at the Localities: A Study of Turkey's Municipalities

Reha Atakan Cetin

Being situated on the European Union's borders and as a candidate member, Turkey hosts more than 3,5 million refugees, making it the world's largest refugee-hosting country. While the government's open-door policy has been persistent, the inclusion of these communities has not followed a top-down approach with strategically planned national-level policies. Coupled with the impact of the domestic political and economic instabilities, the lack of centralized policies resulted in precarious conditions where refugees are left with marginalization and discrimination. On the other hand, local governments have pursued policies for refugee integration. While existing research discussed the broader implications of local policies, a critical perspective is necessary to examine how local structures pursue these policies differently based on multiple identities and 'deservingness.' Addressing the heterogeneity of refugee identities; this article examines the various ways in which the local governments in Turkey's most urbanized areas (Istanbul, Ankara, and Izmir) realize their policies for integration. It aims to go beyond the literature and reflects on the discursive socio-spatial policy dimensions where these communities' differential inclusion/exclusion are negotiated at the intersections of race, ethnicity, gender, sexual orientation, education levels, and socioeconomic status. The article utilizes primary (in-depth key informant interviews with the representatives of municipalities and partnering civil society organizations) and secondary sources (institutional papers and policy/project reports). Following critical discourse and policy analysis procedures, it suggests that local governments reinforce refugee marginalization and exclusion by including/excluding certain groups/identities from their local integration policies and strategies which limits the refugees' urban survival and resilience mechanisms.

---

[9] Scholten, P. and Penninx, R. (2016). The Multilevel Governance of Migration and Integration, In: Garcés-Mascarenas, B. and Penninx, R. (eds.) *Integration Processes and Policies In Europe*. Cham/Heidelberg/New York: Springer International Publishing, 91-108.

629 Governing migration through housing: "Overt interventionism" and bordering practices in accommodation and support services

Regina C Serpa

Sanctions and conditionality represent interventions commonly deployed in both housing and immigration policy – as strategies designed to ensure compliance and influence behaviour change. The ultimate sanction in immigration law mirrors that in housing policy – the effect of deportation and eviction is to enforce expulsion. On a less severe scale, welfare conditionality is nevertheless a means to coerce, persuade and ensure compliance with immigration and housing regulation. This paper examines how British and Dutch housing services are implicated in policing migration and national security through the use of 'overt interventionism' (Watts et al, 2017) to illustrate the 'bordering practices' that operate in everyday services (Paasi, 2009). Such interventions can be through: the exercise of force (such as the eviction of failed asylum seekers and deportation of homeless EU migrants); coercion (including restricting eligibility to state support and imposing behavioural contracts); and influence (for example, by 'support' service workers advocating voluntary repatriation).

Using a comparative, critical analysis to examine migration governance policy, this paper demonstrates *how* immigration and border controls are heavily implicated in systems claiming to offer welfare support. The paper demonstrates how the thesis of crimmigration (Stumpf, 2006) can be used to explain *why* housing and welfare is implicated in immigration control through a study of two seemingly disparate national contexts - the United Kingdom and the Netherlands. The striking similarities between these (ostensibly) neoliberal and social democratic approaches to migration governance develops crimmigration theory and helps to facilitate new (conceptual and empirical) tools - to enable the provision of locally based, inclusionary practices.

References

Paasi, A. (2009) Bounded spaces in a 'borderless world': Border studies, power and the anatomy of territory. *Journal of Power*, 2 (2), 213–234.

Stumpf, J. (2006). The crimmigration crisis: Immigrants, crime, and sovereign power. *American University Law Review*, 56, 367-419.

Watts, B., Fitzpatrick, S., & Johnsen, S. (2018). Controlling homeless people? Power, interventionism and legitimacy. *Journal of Social Policy*, 47(2), 235-252.

3F Health and Migration

778   Italian asylum reception system and health challenges: The Apulian case

Antonella Biscione, Gul Ince-Beqo, Michela Camilla Pellicani

The aim of this research is to contribute to the literature on migration and health, particularly asylum seekers' health access at the first reception centers in Apulia, the southeastern region of Italy; one of the main Mediterranean routes for asylum seekers heading for Europe. For this purpose, we use data collected within the project AMIF "Prevention 4.0", funded by the European Commission and the Italian Ministry of the Interior and aimed at creating an integrated system of prevention, diagnosis, treatment and rehabilitation of asylum seekers and holders of international protection on the regional territory. The survey drafted to retrieve information not available in other database features mostly closed-ended questions.

Our main findings show that the centers, throughout the reception process, guarantee the protection of health and medical care to all guests. Moreover, results highlight that in the reception process, the medical service therefore appears decisive and the absence of a constant control of health status can cause the worsening of not visible symptoms, creating further psycho-physical problems.

648   Evaluation of the Relationship Between Language Barriers and Psychiatric Admissions in Migrated Residents Attending the Emergency Department in Malta

Christopher Giordimaina, Jacqueline Eleonora Ek, Michael Spiteri, Pierre Agius

Research Problem: The immigration policy known as Deferred Action for Childhood Arrivals (DACA) was developed to address the needs of children brought to the United States when they were young and have no clear path toward citizenship. This study examines the experiences of DACA eligible and recipient college students from one public university in California.

Theory: Critical Relations Theory is used to understand the experiences of the participants.

Methods: This was a mixed method study using a survey of DACA students (n=107) that focused on their experiences, and in-person interviews from key informants (n=4) who provide resources for DACA students, and from interviews of DACA students (n=7).

Findings: The qualitative data complemented the quantitative data in showing the additional stressors DACA students experience that impact their graduation and career outcomes, such as family obligations, work obligations, financial strain, mental health, academic strain, and fear.

Conclusions: To be helpful to this population, educators, policy makers, social support agencies, and immigration advocates need to be involved. It is important to understand the layered barriers that make it difficult for DACA students to succeed.

862   Quickly Adapting to COVID-19 in a Chicago Refugee Clinic and Hospital Endoscopy Program

Benjamin Hirsch Levy III, Leibe Arroyave

Objective

During COVID-19, our Antillas refugee clinic in Chicago (which serves approximately 60% of the refugees in the state of Illinois) successfully transformed our medical practice in key ways to safely take care of patients.

Methods

During March and April 2020, we converted our clinics to telemedicine. This allowed us to expedite refugee patient care in a safe manner – to avoid gatherings of patients in waiting rooms, to simplify transportation issues, and to continue serving patients even during the mandatory lockdown. We quickly worked with the IT department at our hospital to launch a secure, encrypted video telemedicine program that patients could easily access by clicking on an email or text through "Doxy." For those refugees without access to a smartphone or computer, we provided secure encrypted phone telemedicine options through "Doximitry." We maximized use of both our certified interpreters in clinic (previous refugees themselves) and the use of a subcontracted language line (Pacific Interpreters).

We provided COVID-19 testing to all refugee patients in order to expedite care. Patients were counseled and educated after their tests resulted. We designed specialized instructions concerning transportation and COVID-19 PCR testing prior to any outpatient procedures.

We improved safety mechanisms in all perioperative areas included increased physical distancing between patient bays and increased use of physical barriers separating patients. In order to increase compliance of wearing of masks in the hospital (and for our refugee patients in the community), we educated patients through instruction forms, posters, letters, and frequent verbal reminders.

We also launched a COVID-19 PCR screening programming prior to any endoscopy procedures such as esophagogastroduodenoscopies and colonoscopies. During March 2020, we worked with a Plexiglas company in Chicago to design intubation/endoscopy boxes that allowed airway monitoring while preventing aerosolized virus from spreading during procedures.

The Gastroenterologists and Anesthesiologists at our hospital acquired Powered Air Purifying Respirators to use when taking care of COVID-19 positive refugee patients during emergency procedures.

Results

We increased compliance for the wearing of masks in the perioperative areas from 60% in mid-March to 100% in June 2020 through these educational programs. Our mask wearing educational programs improved consistent and constant wearing of masks to prevent transmission of COVID-19.

Patients were required to get a COVID-19 PCR test 2-3 days in advance of their endoscopy in order to minimize the potential for hospital transmission. Through this program, we identified many asymptomatic COVID-19 patients who had no idea they were sick and potentially spreading the virus at home, at work, and in the community. Each time a patient was diagnosed, the Gastroenterologist and/or Internal Medicine physician called refugees to provide care and education. This COVID-19 refugee screening program drastically reduced the potential for virus spread.

Conclusion

Through creative adaption in clinic and at our hospital endoscopy program, we expedited medical care in a safe manner. Our Antillas refugee clinic and hospital also helped prevent COVID-19 virus transmission within our Chicago refugee communities and at the hospital.

553   Exploring the Impacts of Migration on Iranian Students Wellbeing

Forouzan Rostami and Mohmmad Mobin Rostami

Migration is the movement of people across a specified boundary for the purpose of establishing a new or semi-permanent residence. With up to 2% of the world's population living outside of their country of birth, the potential impact of population mobility on health and on use of health services of migrant host nations is increasing in its importance. Historically this movement was nomadic, often causing significant conflict with the indigenous population and their displacement or cultural assimilation. Qualitative method was used to this research. Present study draws on interviews, with 7 interviews with UPM student's emigrants. Results illustrate immigrant status may impact family stress and uncertainty, health outcomes, and educational attainment and may result in increased social isolation for students in immigrant families.

3G   Return Migration

Chair Selda Dudu, University of Seville, Spain

839   "From here to the border I'm Mexican, and from the border over there I'm American": A look inside return migration and its complexities
        Edgar Emmanuell Garcia-Ponce, Irasema Mora-Pablo, M. Martha
        Lengeling
673   Turkish Returned Immigrants' Income by Gender Perspective
        Selda Dudu and Teresa Rojo

839   "From here to the border I'm Mexican, and from the border over there I'm American": A look inside return migration and its complexities

Edgar Emmanuell Garcia-Ponce, Irasema Mora-Pablo, M. Martha Lengeling

This presentation reports on the findings of a study which aimed at examining the life stories of two young return migrants who belong to the same family, but who have experienced several migratory moves between Mexico and the US. Through a narrative approach and semi-structure interviews following a retrospective perspective, the results show how the two return migrants' continuous transformations are complex and continual, redefining all aspects of self along the lines of sense of belonging, ethnicity and professional identity. We learn how these return migrants reposition themselves by using their English language skills while pursuing a professional identity. The results in turn reveal the importance of knowing more about the transnational experience of these young return migrants, how they interpret their past and current experiences and how they construct their future professional identity.

The complex socio-political relationship between Mexico and the United States has created for years the migration of Mexicans looking for "the American dream". This represents a challenge to the kids of those families who pursue better economic opportunities, as they need to manage complex identity and educational issues in both sides of the border (Darvin & Norton 2014; Despagne & Jacobo-Suárez 2019)

The mobility between the two countries is not always possible for young migrants, as they usually depend on their parents' decision and migratory status. For those who experience this back and forth movements between the two countries, they may start experiencing a sense of inferiority, based on the disadvantageous position in relation with the American citizens, and this includes feeling part of the community or feeling rejected (Hernández-León et al. 2017).

The Cross-Border Social Network Theory goes beyond transnationalism, and it might help to understand the capacity of the individual to mobilize different resources that go beyond ethnic and kinship networks. This theory is intended to be a more dynamic approach to understanding return migration identifying different types of returnees, as they might portray different levels of preparation and readiness (Hazan 2014). An interesting approach in this view is how the individual can prepare for his/her return to the country of origin. In terms of readiness, the individual feels that he/she has accomplished the original goals for emigration or that he/she can have strong opportunities in the country of origin. His/her skills, knowledge and experiences acquired in the host country, give him/her a feeling that this increases his/her human, social and linguistic capital, something that he/she can mobilize to facilitate his/her successful reintegration in the country of origin (Cassarino 2008).

The two participants portrayed here come from the same family, but they have experienced different life paths across the two countries. Their interpretations of such experiences were significantly different. We will trace their biographies to illustrate the different patterns in their identity formation and how their experiences have shaped who they are and who they want to become.

673   Turkish Returned Immigrants' Income by Gender Perspective

Selda Dudu and Teresa Rojo

Thousands of Turkish migrants return to their homeland each year and join the labour force. Each one returns with new skills, which increase their chance to find a better job than their jobs before the migration. However, income determinants are different for women and men, which also impact their earnings. Adopting a gender perspective, this paper investigates if migration experience has different effects on women and men's determinants of labour income. The paper utilizes the Household Labour Force Surveys data of Turkey between 2009 and 2018. The main findings of regression analysis suggest that being a woman had a -0.16% impact on the labour income compared to being a man in the total labour force population. Surprisingly, this negative impact outgrew to -18% for the Turkey-born women population with migration experience. Working without job security has a greater negative impact with -0.59% on Turkey-born returned immigrant women. However, job-skill and education have a higher positive impact on Turkey-born returned immigrant women's labour income in all job-skill and education levels than Turkey-born returned immigrant men's labour income. This study concludes that gender, age, education level, job experience, employment type, and job informality are determinants of the Turkish population's labour income. The effect level of these determinants is to the detriment of women. Job informality has a great negative impact on Turkey-born returned immigrant women's labour income.

552   Gendered experiences of educational migrant returnees in Covid-19 times

Chiedza Mutsaka Skyum

An African University with students from over 40 countries had no choice but to encourage students to return to their home countries when Covid-19 hit. They feared having the students 'stuck' in lockdown far away from their families. Flights were scheduled and students flew home. It was declared that there would be no interruption to the students' learning as classes would continue online. However, in the students' home countries, societal barriers existed that hindered some students from being able to continue with their classes. In many societies, girls and women are responsible for doing the majority of childcare tasks and domestic work in a household. Teachers began to receive emails from female students who could not dedicate the needed time for their classes. One had multiple siblings that were not in school and needed homeschooling and care, another's father was forced out of his job so her mother became a vendor and she in turn did the cooking and cleaning, and another was caring for her ill grandmother who needed palliative care. The family expectations and the de-prioritisation of their education by their families has affected their educational journeys. Without Covid-19, they would have continued as resident students whose time was fully committed fully to their studies. This article will share the experiences of a few of these students, examine some gendered migration theory and consider the Institutional response - it will also detail some techniques for differentiation used by teachers to ensure that when these students did find the time, they were able to catch up and still achieve the learning outcomes.

12:15-12:45 BREAK

Day Two 7 July 2021 Wednesday

Day Two 7 July 2021 - 12:45-14:15
4A   Migration and Integration
Chair: Sadaf Mahmood, Government College University Faisalabad, Punjab, Pakistan
847   Integration Challenges of Pakistani Diaspora into West European Societies; a Gender Sensitive Analysis with a Focus on Germany
       Sadaf Mahmood, Beatrice Knerr, Izhar Ahmad Khan
861   Experiences of social insertion of professional Mexican migrants in the United States
       Lilia Dominguez Villalobos, Monica Laura Vazquez Maggio,
662   Mobilities, Networks and Changes of Chinese Migration: Case study on Barcelona Metropolitan Area
       Yuelu He
864   Experiences of social and psychological adaptation and identity formation of immigrant Turkish students in North Cyprus: Preliminary results
       Aysenur Talat Zrilli and Şerif Türkkal

847   Integration Challenges of Pakistani Diaspora into West European Societies; a Gender Sensitive Analysis with a Focus on Germany

Sadaf Mahmood, Beatrice Knerr, Izhar Ahmad Khan

In the 21st century, integration of immigrants has become a challenge for different countries in European Union. Most of the immigrants preferred to stay in Europe because of its high income and better quality of life. The proper integration of immigrants can help the host societies to increase their benefits from immigrants. Social scientists tried to find the factors that hindered the immigrants' socio-economic integration in host societies.

As per Pakistan foreign mission in Germany, in early 2017, numbers of Pakistanis in Germany were 90500 (Amjad, 2017). Around 30,000 of these settlers reached Germany after 2015 (Haider, 2018). All these statistics show that numbers of Pakistanis are increasing, as more people move to Germany for education, employment and asylum. Majority of these Pakistanis are males, but recently number of females is also growing. Concerns related to social integration of Pakistani migrants across Europe are subject of numerous studies. New social integration laws introduced, require certain characteristics before accepted into Germany (BBC News, 2016). In the present paper, our focus is to determine the integration of Pakistani immigrants with a focus on Germany, one of the major host countries. A gender sensitive analysis has been applied to compare the situation of Pakistani male and female respondents and to analyze their social integration issues. Are the male and female respondents facing same intensity of integration problems or the problems differ by gender was the main research question? We considered David Lockwood's (1964) theory of social system as the basis for the present study to describe the concept of Pakistani immigrants' integration in Germany. Several studies found that education, duration of stay in the host society, and interaction with other nationalities helped in integration (Thapa, 2005; Syed *et al.*, 2006; Cohen, 2007; Dalgard and Thapa, 2007; Haque, 2012; Laurentsyeva & Venturini, 2017; Wessendorf & Phillimore, 2018).

The empirical data was gathered from Pakistanis living in Germany by using the survey method. Pakistani individuals above 18 years and living in Germany for more than three months on a legal status were included in the sample. 264 respondents were interviewed in different cities of Germany. Equal numbers of men and women (132) each were interviewed.

The variables primarily focused were availability of Halal food, freedom in following religious rituals, practices and knowledge of German and English language and social interaction with Germans, Pakistanis and other nationals. These variables were tested with various background variables such as education, skills, age, marital status and being employed. The results found through ordinary least square (OLS) regression model, that knowledge of English language, level of comfort when interacting with Germans and frequency of meeting with other nationalities are strongly related to integration of members of both gender in Germany. The friendly attitude and acceptance of host society is significantly related to integration. Interestingly, English language proficiency seemed to be significantly affecting the integration in German society for better than German language itself. These accounts are valuable in shaping policy measures and are highly relevant beyond the focus of these countries.

References

Amjad, R. (2017). The Pakistani diaspora: Corridors of opportunity and uncertainty. Lahore: Lahore School of Economics.

BBC News. (2016, 4 14). Germany moves towards new integration law for migrants. Retrieved from BBC News: https://www.bbc.com/news/world-europe-36048397

Haider, S. (2018, 06 05). Why are Pakistanis so successful at finding jobs in Germany. Retrieved from Deutsche Welle: https://www.dw.com/en/why-are-pakistanis-so-successful-at-finding-jobs-in-germany/a-44083455

Laurentsyeva, N., & Venturini, A. (2017). The Social Integration of Immigrants and the

Role of Policy-A Literature Review. Intereconomics, 285-292. doi:DOI: 10.1007/s10272-017-0691-6

Wessendorf, S., & Phillimore, J. (2018). New Migrants' Social Integration, Embedding and Emplacement in Superdiverse Contexts. Sociology, 123-138. doi:https://doi.org/10.1177%2F0038038518771843

Dalgard, O. S., & Thapa, S. B. (2007). Immigration, social integration and mental health in Norway, with focus on gender differences. Clinical Practice and Epidemiology in Mental Health, 3(1), 24-34.

Haque, K. (2012). Iranian, Afghan, and Pakistani Migrants in Germany: Muslim Populations beyond Turks and Arabs. Chloe: Beihefte zum Daphnis, 46(1), 193-206.

Lockwood, D. (1964). Social integration and system integration, in: Zollschan, K. and Hirsch, Walter (eds.), Explorations in Social Change. Routledge and Kegan: London, 244-251

Syed, H., Dalgard, O., Dalen, I., Claussen, B., Hussain, A., Selmer, R., & Ahlberg, N. (2006). Psychosocial factors and distress: a comparison between ethnic Norwegians and ethnic Pakistanis in Oslo, Norway. BMC public health, 6(1), 1-9.

Thapa, S. B., & Hauff, E. (2005). Gender differences in factors associated with psychological distress among immigrants from low-and middle-income countries. Social psychiatry and psychiatric epidemiology, 40(1), 78-84.

861 Experiences of social insertion of professional Mexican migrants in the United States

Lilia Dominguez Villalobos, Monica Laura Vazquez Maggio

En años recientes han surgido diversos estudios que analizan las condiciones de inserción laboral y el nivel de ingreso de migrantes profesionistas mexicanos que viven en Estados Unidos. Sin embargo, poco se conoce respecto a cómo ellos viven la experiencia social de encontrarse en una nueva sociedad, la norteamericana. Con base en un estudio que utilizó métodos mixtos, en este artículo se exploran diversos temas de la identidad de estos migrantes: ¿Se sienten mexicano-norteamericanos, mexicanos o norteamericanos? ¿Conservan su lengua materna en el hogar? ¿Qué contactos mantienen con familia y amigos en México? ¿Viven experiencias de discriminación? Al final, exploramos si consideran que su decisión para emigrar a los Estados Unidos fue adecuada, si existe el deseo de un posible retorno a México, y si sí, cuáles son los obstáculos para ello.

662 Mobilities, Networks and Changes of Chinese Migration: Case study on Barcelona Metropolitan Area

Yuelu He

Chinese population in Spain has been constantly increasing since the end of 20th century even in the economic crisis of 2008. Till 2020 Chinese ethnic group has become the sixth largest migrant population in Spain and the third largest in Barcelona Metropolitan Area. Despite a growing scholarly interest on Chinese migration in Spain, there is still a lack of study on demographic changes of influx of Chinese migration to the host society over the recent decades. Likewise, what is not yet clear is their residential mobilities and localization patterns, although this approach plays a central role to understand the heterogeneity of socioeconomic and cultural characteristics of Chinese ethnic group in Spain, as well as their different migration trajectories.

This work analyzes characteristic of residential patterns of Chinese population in Barcelona Metropolitan Area and their intra-municipal mobilities in the area. Building on both quantitative and qualitative data, this research uses data from Residence Variance Statistics (EVR) collected by the National Institute of Statistics (INE) and qualitative material of 25 structured in-depth interviews with Chinese residents in Barcelona. Our preliminary findings indicate that Chinese ethnic group is highly concentrated in a handful of municipalities and scarcely moves once they settle down. Yet limited as their mobilities are, these intra-municipal mobilities have been found to be surprisingly intensive and deeply rooted in social networks within the ethnic group.

864 Experiences of social and psychological adaptation and identity formation of immigrant Turkish students in North Cyprus: Preliminary results

Aysenur Talat Zrilli and Şerif Türkkal

The present study holds a constructivist perspective about identity implying that individuals have an active role in the process of constructing their own realities, i.e., in understanding and presenting who they are and where they belong in the society (Berzonsky, 1992). According to Berzonsky (1992), people employ problem-solving strategies in the face of changing contextual conditions, which determine the construction of their identity styles. These identity styles are 'informational style', 'normative style' and 'diffuse avoidant style'. According to this theory, these styles, reflect individuals' information processing and problem-solving strategies in general (Berzonsky, 1992).

In the context of migration identity becomes an even more complex matter as migrants' acculturation experiences, defined as changes that occur in the cultural patterns of groups, when these come into continuous first-hand contact with other groups (Redfield, Linton & Herskovits, 1936), creates new challenges. In this context, immigrant groups need to make certain decisions regarding their own cultural patterns and those of the majority culture. According to a model developed by Berry (1997), immigrant groups can choose to follow different strategies from among available options of integration, separation, assimilation or marginalization. The strategy chosen will depend on the degree to which immigrants seek to adopt elements from the majority culture and retain their own cultural patterns. The process of making these decisions as well as the acculturation strategy chosen by the immigrants will likely affect the concerned individuals' identity constructions.

The disciplines of psychology and sociology have developed their own traditions of dealing with issues related to individuals' and groups' identity processes, but to our knowledge, there are not many studies incorporating theories from these different fields. Therefore, the present study aims to bridge this gap by approaching the issue of identity formation by migrant groups and its relationship to their psychological well-being from an interdisciplinary perspective incorporating Berzonsky's 'identity styles' (Berzonsky, 1992), Berry's 'acculturation strategies' (Berry, 1997) and constructionist sociological theories about ethnic identity (Cornell and Hartmann 2007). Additionally, to our knowledge, acculturation and identity processes of second-generation immigrants from Turkey in North Cyprus has not been extensively studied. The present study aims to contribute to filling this gap in research by focusing on second generation immigrants from Turkey who are pursuing university education in North Cyprus. For that purpose, the study will be drawing on data from semi-structured individual and focus group interviews. It will endeavour to make discernible this populations' acculturation strategies and identity styles, the relationship between these two and their impact on psychological well-being. It also aims to explore whether or not and in what ways certain acculturation strategies and identity styles are regarded as sources of stress in these students' everyday lives.

References

Berry, J. W. (1997). Immigration, acculturation and adaptation. Applied Psychology: An International Review, 46, 5–68.

Berzonsky, M. D. (1992). Identity Style and Coping Strategies. *Journal of Personality, 60 (4),* 771-788.

Cornell, S. & Hartmann, D. (2007). *Ethnicity and Race: Making Identities in a Changing World. Second Edition.* Thousand Oaks.

Redfield, R., Linton, R., & Herskovits, M. (1936). Memorandum on the study of acculturation. *American Anthropologist, 38,* 149–152.

4B   Education and Migration

Chair Süreyya Sönmez Efe, University of Lincoln, United Kingdom

819   "Brain Drain" Migration As Another Consequence of Corruption in the Republic of Kosovo
       Adrianit Ibrahimi and Besa Arifi

756   Highly skilled migration in Russia: history, current trends and prospects
       Alexander Subbotin and Vladimir Iontsev

758   Objective and subjective variables behind the working conditions of tertiary educated Mexican migrants in the United States
       Lilia Dominguez Villalobos and Monica Laura Vazquez Maggio

731   Academic Brain Drain: The Case of North Macedonia
       Blerta Ahmedi-Arifi

819 "Brain Drain" Migration As Another Consequence of Corruption in the Republic of Kosovo

Adrianit Ibrahimi and Besa Arifi

Within a decade (2008-2018) more than 344.000 Kosova citizens decided to leave Kosova and search for a better life in the EU countries (European Policy Institute of Kosovo, 2019, p. 8). This is approximately 20% or 1/5 of the entire resident population of the Republic of Kosova. Only during the irregular migration crisis of 2012-2015, approximately 125.000 citizens of Kosova have been registered as asylum seekers in the European Union countries (Halili Xhevdet, Ibrahimi Adrianit, 2017, pp. 90-91). Among those asylum seekers from Kosova, more than 75% belong to the 0-34 age group. This age group represents the majority of the population and the working power in the Republic of Kosova. Moreover, the citizens from Kosova who emigrated had higher levels of education on average than the resident population, resulting in a significant brain drain from the Republic of Kosova during the past decade (World Bank Group, 2018, p. 21).

On the other hand, the Republic of Kosova is still struggling in the fight against corruption especially grand corruption. Consequently, the performance of the Republic of Kosova in the Corruption Perception Index (CPI) for 2020 is disappointing again. Transparency International has ranked the Republic of Kosova only as no. 104/180 with a 38/100 score in the 2020 Corruption Perception Index (Transparency International, 2020). The struggle of the Republic of Kosova with corruption is confirmed also from the "Kosovo 2020 Report" of the European Commission where is concluded that *"Kosovo is at an early stage in the fight against corruption and has made limited progress in this area"* (European Commission, 2020, p. 5).

Migration as a phenomenon is ubiquitous because it is just another concomitant of globalization. However, if more than 20% or 1/5 of the population leaves the country within a decade, this shall be a concerning topic for discussion in Kosova, especially if this trend is still going on. It is undisputable that corruption is among the main reasons for such a migration crisis from Kosova. This because in the ears of the youth in Kosova, corruption means nothing better than unemployment, poverty, nepotism, inequity, injustice, and insecurity. Every person has only one life and tries to make the best of it, especially if he/she has put hard work into his/her education or else. From this point of view, the brain drain from Kosova has been massive in the 21st century. Germany remains the most preferred final destination of migrants from Kosova (GAP Institute, 2020, pp. 27-29). Meanwhile, the health system, the IT sector, the construction sector, the social workers, and the craftsman's in Kosova are among the most damaged sectors from brain drain (Balkan Policy Research Group, 2020, p. 21).

Bibliography

Balkan Policy Research Group. (2020). *Kosova: Trendet e migracionit kërkojnë një qasje të re strategjike*. Prishtina: Norwegian Embassy in the Republic of Kosova. Retrieved February 25, 2021, from https://balkansgroup.org/wp-content/uploads/2020/10/Kosova_Trendet-e-Migrimit-kerkojne-nje-qasje-te-re-strategjike-13.10.2020.pdf

European Commission. (2020). *Kosovo 2020 Report.* European Commission. Brussels: European Commission. Retrieved February 24, 2021, from https://ec.europa.eu/neighbourhood-enlargement/sites/near/files/kosovo_report_2020.pdf

European Policy Institute of Kosovo. (2019). *The Great Escape.* Prishtina: EPIK. Retrieved February 24, 2021, from https://cdn.website-editor.net/8a3b242c12494d76b2b60ea75852e5f4/files/uploaded/THE%2520GREA T%2520ESCAPE.pdf

GAP Institute. (2020). *Emigrimi i fuqisë punëtore të Kosovës në Gjermani.* Prishtina: The Expert Council of German Foundations on Integration and Migration. Retrieved February 25, 2021, from https://www.institutigap.org/documents/82484_emigrimi_gjermani_.pdf

Halili Xhevdet, Ibrahimi Adrianit. (2017, December 8). Causes for the Irregular Migration crisis: Case of Kosovo. *Strategos, 1(2), 2017, 79-98, 1*(2), 79-98. Retrieved February 24, 2021, from https://papers.ssrn.com/sol3/papers.cfm?abstract_id=3086822

Transparency International. (2020). *Transparency International - the global coalition against corruption,* CPI 2020. (Transparency International) Retrieved February 24, 2021, from Corruption Perception Index 2020: https://www.transparency.org/en/cpi/2020/index/ksv#

World Bank Group. (2018). *Western Balkans Labor Market Trends 2018.* World Bank. Washington: World Bank. Retrieved February 24, 2021, from http://documents1.worldbank.org/curated/en/565231521435487923/pdf/124354-Western-Balkans-Labor-market-trends-2018-final.pdf

756   Highly skilled migration in Russia: history, current trends and prospects

Alexander Subbotin and Vladimir Iontsev

In this study, we examine some historical aspects of intellectual migration in Russia, modern features and future prospects of this process. When the Russian Empire was dynamically developing at the beginning of the Romanov dynasty, especially under Peter I and Catherine II, it actively attracted highly skilled specialists. The reason for that is understanding of the state authorities of the need to modernize the military, trade and construction sectors. The current Russian situation is diametrically opposite, i.e. the country faces an intensive outflow of highly qualified specialists abroad.

The study is based on both the publicly available statistical data of the Russian Federal State Statistics Service (Rosstat) and data from published materials in various publications. We employ a range of methods from comparative demography as well as systematic and comparative-historical methods widely used in theoretical research in sociology.

One of the main features of intellectual migration in Russia is the current demographic situation, which can be designated by the concept of demographic crisis. The authors provide their own definition of this term, highlighting that one of its characteristic features are qualitative negative changes, and which should not be confused with such notion as depopulation.

From 2002 to 2009, the number of emigrants with higher education decreased two times, and it has increased by almost eight times from 2009 to 2019. The current stage of Russia's socio-economic development shows that the instability of the conditions in which highly skilled specialists exist can convince them to emigrate to more stable countries having more normal arrangement. It is also noted in our study that Russian migration official data is based on de-registration or renunciation of citizenship, which leads to that Russian official statistics underestimate the real scale of emigration from Russia.

The conclusion of the study considers proposals to improve the management of highly skilled migration. Authors complete that the most promising development option for both Russia and other countries is to encourage return intellectual migration.

758 Objective and subjective variables behind the working conditions of tertiary educated Mexican migrants in the United States

Lilia Dominguez Villalobos and Monica Laura Vazquez Maggio

This paper contributes to the field of study of skilled migration by employing a different database from the one commonly used to study labor-market placement; our database was collected through an online questionnaire answered by Mexican migrants with tertiary education (TE) living in the United States. Through analysis of a set of both objective and subjective variables (not available in any other official database), we developed a statistical profile of their working and income conditions (high, medium and low) and we corroborate much of what is in the literature, that is, that the concept of human capital is insufficient to analyze job outcomes of tertiary educated (TE) migrants. We find that variables that increase the probability of being located at the high-income stratum for both men and women are having a command of English and having a job offer prior to arrival in the United States. For both men and women, feeling discriminated because of having an accent decreases the likelihood of being in the high-income bracket. Other variables matter for men and not for women (and vice versa); for example, suitability of the knowledge acquired in Mexico mattered only for men and academic degrees (master's and doctoral) and migratory status mattered for women but not for men. While being a professional or an entrepreneur/manager and specializing in a STEM (Science, Technology, Engineering and Mathematics) area increase the probability of high income for men, for women the profession, and the specializations that increase the likelihood of being in this stratum are economic-managerial, education, humanities and the arts.

731 Academic Brain Drain: The Case of North Macedonia

Blerta Ahmedi-Arifi

Skilled labour is an important asset for any country in the development process and the emigration of skilled individuals presents a threat of a 'brain drain' which can affect growth, development and the quality of education. Brain drain in this research represents the loss of academic staff and researchers from a source country to a recipient country. Using survey data this study investigates the factors affecting academic staff's decision on migration. It critically examines brain drain in higher education institutions in North Macedonia and its implications. Most of the academic staff intends to migrate to more developed countries mainly because of low standards of living and wages, political influence in universities and lack of promotion possibilities based on merit. The recent pandemic opened new possibilities of academic staff and researchers to work or emigrate 'virtually' without the need to be physically present there. These possibilities should be explored and could be attractive as well for the skilled emigrants to transfer their knowledge to their colleagues and institutions in the home country, i.e. 'virtual return'. Based on the finding this paper proposes policy recommendations for institutions to explore strategies on how to best use the skills of academic and research staff for improving socio-economic benefits, and most importantly commitment to implementing these strategies.

4C   Youth Migration

Chair: Afzalur Rahman, University of Chittagong, Bangladesh

505   Unaccompanied Minors Inclusion in Greece: An Empirical Research
        Dimitrios Georgiadis
512   Sense of Belonging of Migrant Children in Poland
        Anzhela Popyk
645   Female Refugee Students and Sense of Belonging in Schools
        Sonja Aicha van der Putten

714   "The young and the restless": Second generation Chinese migrants in
        Thessaloniki
        Georgia Sarikoudi

505   Unaccompanied Minors Inclusion in Greece: An Empirical Research

Dimitrios Georgiadis

From the period from 2015 to 2016, Greece experienced an unprecedented influx of migrants and refugees fleeing war and deprivation in their home countries in the Middle East and south Asia, or in search of a better and safer life in the EU. The closure of the border between the former Yugoslav Republic of Macedonia and Greece in early March 2016 left thousands of refugees and migrants stranded in Greece –often without adequate accommodation, healthcare, and access to education, with about 60 percent of them being women and children and 40 percent men.

Children are among of the most vulnerable members of our society and it is our shared responsibility to protect, nurture and care for them. Children separated from their caregivers are particularly susceptible to exploitation, abuse and neglect.

Most of the unaccompanied minors arriving in Greece, are boys, while their age ranges between 14 to 18 years old. Greece is a cultural crossroads between

East and West and a major entry point for refugees to the EU. It is estimated that according National Center for Social Solidarity, more than 2.800 unaccompanied children (UAC) sought asylum in Greece, most came from Syria, Afghanistan, Iran, Iraq, and Somalia. Although the number is quite high, Greece did not manage to ensure an adequate response. Upon their arrival in a host country, UAC have expectations towards the new country (living conditions, health and education system, asylum process) and goals that they would like to achieve. Most of the times, their expectations are not met in the reality. For a period of time, they have to live in camps, until their registration is completed, and then they will be referred to other care facilities. However, in Greece, the shelters do not have enough space for all the UAC, and for this reason, children may have to live in camps (in specific sections named 'Safe Zones').

The aim of this research is to examine the perceptions of unaccompanied minors regarding education and the labor market. The sample of the research was 120 unaccompanied minors. The survey was conducted between January and March 2020. The analysis of the results launched that the majority of the participants in the research have encountered hostile behavior at school by their classmates, while a small percentage by their teachers. They are often confronted with racial, ethnic, religious and cultural discrimination, while receiving suspicion, rejection and racism from Greek society. The consequence of the above is school dropout, marginalization and consequently social exclusion.

512   Sense of Belonging of Migrant Children in Poland

Anzhela Popyk

Immigrant children have recently become a prevalent matter in Polish media, as an unprecedented number of 53 thousand foreign-born children have attended Polish schools in the 2019/2020 academic year (The Ministry of National Education) . While this might be a novel phenomenon in the country, media, politicians and scholars worldwide have drawn attention to the issues of migrant children for the last few decades.

Transnational practices, within two or more transnational social or geographical fields, greatly affect the formation of the sense of identity and belonging (Wodak and Krzyżanowski, 2007, Cuervo and Wyn, 2017), and lead to the appearance of "dual" Perez-Felkner (2013) identities of the first and second-generation migrants. The sense of belonging depends on the young migrants' movement, identity and place. Cross-border migration affect the shift of belonging over the space and its redevelopment in a new social field. If belonging is not recreated in a new society, the feeling of displacement takes over it (Hout et al. 2014). The migrants' sense of belonging is not constructed merely by the individuals, but is shaped by their feeling as being "at home", in the meaning of "place-belonginess", and the socio-spatial inclusions/exclusions, which refer to the "politics of belonging" (Yuval-Davis 2006). The first analytical dimension, "place-belonginess", indicates that 'home' stands for migrant's feeling comfortable, secure and attached to the certain place over time. A young migrant may belong to multiple physical and social places, such as household, peer groups, school, community, city and nation, in the host country, home country and cross-border communities. This multi-level attachment acknowledges that migrants' belonging is a multi-scalar (Hout et al. 2014) and multi-sited concept.

This paper presents how migrant children negotiate own sense of belonging in Poland, that has been a homogeneous country with a short history of immigration. The results of the study indicate that primary school children's sense of belonging is greatly influenced by their families and kins, as well as the parents' religion and culture. Teenagers, however, tend to negotiate the sense of belonging over the spaces and are likely to experience the identity shift under the influence of school, peers and media in the host country.

The research was based on the child-centred approach. Qualitative research methods were used in the project. Research techniques, chosen for the study, were primarily semi-structured interviews. The research consisted of two modules conducted simultaneously: with migrant children, their parents, and teachers (total number of the interviews 49).

References

Cuervo H., & Wyn J. (2017). A longitudinal analysis of belonging: Temporal, performative and rela-tional practices by young people in rural Australia. *Young*, 25 (3), 219–234.

Huot, S., Dodson, B., & Laliberte Rudman, D. (2014). Negotiating belonging following migration: exploring the relationship between place and identity in Francophone minority communities. *The Canadian Geographer*, 58(3), 329–340.

Perez-Felkner, L. (2013). Socialization in childhood and adolescence. In:DeLamater, J. & Ward, A. (Eds) *Handbook of social psychology*. Dordrecht: Springer, 119-149.

Wodak, R., & Krzyzanowski, M. (2007). Multiple Identities, Migration and Belonging: 'Voices of Migrants'. In: Caldas-Coulthard, C-R., & Iedema, R. (Eds.), *Identity Trouble: Critical Discourse and Contested Identities*. London: Palgrave Macmillan, 95-119.

Yuval-Davis, N., Wemyss, G., & Cassidy, K., (2018). Everyday Bordering, Belonging and the Reorientation of British Immigration Legislation. *Sociology*, 52 (2), 228-244.

645   Female Refugee Students and Sense of Belonging in Schools

Sonja Aicha van der Putten

There are over 50 million children from refugee backgrounds under the age of 18 years old worldwide today. Due to the unique cognitive, social, and emotional needs of developing children, the United Nations Convention on the Rights of the Child recommends that countries make special provisions for refugee student populations. Education plays an essential role in creating a sense of belonging and preserving hope amongst adolescents from refugee backgrounds.

To better understand the significance of sense of belonging on students from refugee backgrounds, this study used narrative inquiry to collect data from seven-female adolescent students from refugee backgrounds in one Canadian secondary school. The study triangulated data from interviews, observations, field note journals, and artwork to better understand students' experiences. A strength-based lens framed students as being resilient, resourceful, and optimistic of their futures, despite the on-going challenges that they continued to experience upon resettlement.

Findings indicated that a sense of belonging was influenced positively and negatively by feelings of inclusion/exclusion both in the community and amongst peer groups, teacher-student relationships, and the availability of support services. The female experience was also uniquely influenced by additional familial obligations and responsibilities.

The study concluded that schools that are able to foster a positive sense of belonging amongst students from refugee backgrounds increase their pro-social outcomes and decrease their negative well-being outcomes. The positive academic, behavioural, and psychological outcomes of students who feel a strong sense of belonging in school results in improved self-efficacy, motivation and reduced social-emotional distress.

714   "The young and the restless": Second generation Chinese migrants in Thessaloniki

Georgia Sarikoudi

In Greece, Chinese immigrants appeared mainly at the end of the 1990's. The changes in the legislation allowed Chinese traders who until then probably working in other European countries, to develop commercial activity in Greece. The majority of those who came to Greece settled in both major urban centers, Athens and Thessaloniki.

The literature regarding the Chinese immigration in Greece is quite limited. The few studies that exist (Kokkali 2009; Tontsev 2007; Theodoraki 2013) are preoccupied with the immigrants entrepreneurship and the emergence of multicultural spaces in the urban landscape. However, very few studies have focused on this community, and even less is known about Chinese immigrant families. There is no information and how the second generation experiences its diversity and demonstrate defiance against the parental dominance and its expectations.

In this presentation I would like to examine how young Chinese in Thessaloniki struggle to negotiate their identity and their position within their family and towards the local community following their own personal needs and desires. I will explain that through the daily spontaneous actions and moments they reject the hegemonic identity imposed on them by their parents and they try to renegotiate their rules and freedoms within their family and in the new host country.

919   Human Dignity and the Gendered Motivations for Migration among Iranian International Students in Canada

Erfaneh Razavipour Naghani

While various cultural, social, political and economic factors are recognized as push and pull factors contributing to human migration (Kazemi, Baghbanian, Maymand, and Rahmani 2018; Preston 2014; Tsapenko 2015; Van Hear, Bakewell, and Long 2012), this study explores how human dignity (HD) and gender play a role in students' decision for migration. Drawing on in-depth interviews with 10 women and 10 men Iranian international students in Montreal and 4 Iranian students (2 women and 2 men) who left Canada, we were inspired by elements from Kianpour (2016) and Oleinik (2016) to apply a framework of HD to analyse the data. Four themes emerged as being key to Iranian international students' motivations to migrate: 1) influence of family, friends and social networks, 2) freedom and equality, 3) looking for security, and 4) seeking fulfilment and appropriate status. We offer a discussion of how our findings compare and contrast with the existing literature on international students and HD and conclude with observations about how having an awareness of gender dynamics and students' demand for human dignity could strengthen the support offered to students in Iran and to international students in Canada.

1048   Female Refugee Students and Sense of Belonging in Schools

Sonya Van Der Putten

Over 40% of individuals from refugee backgrounds are children, and there are over 50 million displaced children under the age of 18 globally today (Refugee and Migrant Children, 2020). Due to the unique cognitive, social, and emotional needs of developing children, the United Nations Convention on the Rights of the Child recommends that countries make special provisions for refugee student populations (UN Convention, 2019). A critically important way to do so, is through education. Education plays an essential role in creating a sense of belonging and preserving hope amongst children from refugee backgrounds (Kia-Keating & Ellis, 2007).

School environments that are able to foster a positive sense of belonging in refugee students increase their academic, behavioural, and psychological outcomes and decrease their negative well-being outcomes. In this study, the sense of belonging amongst female secondary students from refugee backgrounds in one Canadian secondary school was studied. Study participants were government sponsored refugees who had arrived in Canada with one or more family members, either directly from active conflict zones or via a refugee camp in a secondary host country. Participants were of Middle Eastern, South Asian and East African origin. Narrative inquiry was used to collect data, which was triangulated from interviews, observations, and field note journals, to better understand students' experiences. A strength-based lens was applied which framed students as being resilient, resourceful, and optimistic about their futures, despite the ongoing challenges they continued to experience upon resettlement.

Findings indicated that a sense of belonging was influenced negatively by feelings of exclusion in school, where participants felt socially isolated by their Canadian-born peers, and felt that their teachers, outside of their English Language Learner classes, treated them and their unique learning needs with indifference. Support services available in the school and wider community were found to be supportive of the needs of study participants and their families, but the heightened demand placed on these services meant that participants were unable to access them when needed most. Gender-based responsibilities and expectations, both in the home and at school, also influenced the experiences of belonging amongst study participants.

The study concluded that schools that are able to foster a positive sense of belonging amongst students from refugee backgrounds increase their pro-social outcomes and decrease their negative well-being outcomes. The positive academic, behavioural, and psychological outcomes of students who feel a strong sense of belonging in school resulted in improved self-efficacy, motivation and reduced social-emotional distress. In order for this to happen, however, the unique learning needs and challenges faced by these students must be addressed through an equity-based approach, where resources and supports are put in place that are tailored to the identified needs of students from refugee backgrounds, including specific issues faced by female students.

Young people from refugee backgrounds strengthen the social fabric of Canadian society. As Canada continues to welcome thousands of families from refugee backgrounds annually, supporting refugee children in schools, while recognizing the disproportionate impact of the challenges faced by female students from refugee backgrounds, is paramount to fostering a strong sense of belonging, and successful settlement for refugee families in Canadian society.

References

Kia-Keating, M., & Ellis, B. H. (2007). Belonging and Connection to School in Resettlement: Young Refugees, School Belonging, and Psychosocial Adjustment. *Clinical Child Psychology and Psychiatry, 12*(1), 29-43.

Refugee and Migrant Children Crisis. (2020). UNICEF Canada. Retrieved January 18, 2020, from https://www.unicef.ca/en/donate/child-refugee-crisis

UN Convention on the Rights of the Child. (2019). United Nations Human Rights: Office of the High Commissioner. Retrieved January 18, 2020, from http://www.ohchr.org/en/professionalinterest/pages/crc.aspx.

4E   Migration Governance

498   Central American forced migration in transit through Mexico. Immigration ban and safe third country

Jorge Morales Cardiel

Central American forced migrations are made up of a collective that has been historically excluded and marginalized from capitalist development processes that also fulfilled specific functions within the new international division of labor in constant subordination. These Central American Migrants face the systematic violence when they crossing the borders derived for the restrictions on the free movement imposed by United State and Mexico governments, on the sidelines of the international human rights treaties signed by these countries, and on the other hand, for the growing interference of organized crime in collusion with the migration authorities of Mexico.

The fact of turning Mexico into a supposed "third safe country" represents a new political chapter of a long novel of Mexican subordination on the issue of forded migration to its North American peer, in the same way, the political asylum system in Mexico is collapsing as the requests for asylum continue to increase. This immigrant's ban affected who fled from Central American, whom crossed in transit through Mexico and tried to take cover under the Migrant Protocol Protection (MPP), due a recent emblematic case of the migrant caravans taking off in 2018, an exodus of forced migrants leaving Central America crossing Mexico with the intention of surrendering to the US border patrol to request international protection.

Since the implementation of this program, these migrants return back to the border cities of Mexico where they suffer the same persecution of organized crime and all systemic violence of the Mexican State. United States immigration ban does not consider the long record of human rights violations towards forced migration from Latin America, a lot less if these migrants flee from poverty and violence because from Washington administration is encouraging countries like Guatemala to sign safe third country despite the fact that the majority of the asylum seekers come from these nation.

The long-term impact highlights the incompatibility between human rights and forced migration, an incompatibility that has characterizes Trump's administration, refers to the lack of greater ethical considerations in the contexts of humanitarian crises in which these human displacements found beyond the restrictive and border-containment policy decisions prevail. This happens when the responsibility inherent to the condition of any State for the protection of immigrants as people in vulnerable situation disappears. The humanitarian crisis of forced migrations on the border between Mexico and United States will continue to deepen alarmingly, also even more in a context of pandemic.

Therefore this ban represents one of the most complex and controversial issues to continue to re-conceptualize the concept of forced migration for existing legislations, for now in the year 2020 it´s in a dead end for asylum seekers and in terms of migratory transit considering the role of countries like in Mexico another gray area towards the political treatments of this situation being a "Safe third country" when the asylum seekers suffered there all possible human rights violations.

558   The resilience of the diaspora has shaped the institutional framework (Moldova case study)

Olga Coptu

The Moldovans' migration process changes have led to the reorientation of political forces towards members of diaspora. The growth of diaspora and its role in the national elections had required the adaptation of the state institutions and elaboration of migration policies. At various stages, diaspora's involvement in developing migration and social policies has fluctuated. It has been conditioned by diaspora's level of trust towards the central government and the authorities' openness towards diaspora.

The consolidation of diaspora associations and the participation at the annual diaspora Congresses led to several initiatives that contributed to creating an institutional framework for migration and diaspora. Such an institution became the Office for Diaspora Relations (Bureau for Relations with Diaspora - BRD)[10], created in 2012 within the State Chancellery. The head of BRD reports directly to the Prime Minister. The BRD's status entitles the bureau to coordinate state policy on Migration and Diaspora Development (DMD)[11]. BRD consolidated its positions in 2017, when it took over the elaboration and implementation of the "Reintegration Plan for Migrants[12] " from the Ministry of Health, Labour and Social Protection.

Migration governance has become one of the Government's priorities by 2014, when the ruling party won an overwhelming victory in diaspora. Diaspora gradually became the electoral catalyst of pro-European parties, but only a few politicians knew how to capitalize on it. Subsequent reshuffles in the Government have led to a declining interest in the diaspora. The situation has

---

[10] GD no. 780 of October 19, 2012, the creation of the BRD (with the status of General Directorate).
[11] GD 725 of September 8, 2017, approved the Mechanism for the coordination and implementation of the state policy in the field of diaspora, migration and development (DMD) by the central and local public authorities.
[12] In 2017, BRD developed and coordinate the implementation of the Plan actions on the reintegration of returned citizens from abroad for the years 2017-2020.

worsened since the November 2016 elections, culminating in a Diaspora's court case versus the Republic of Moldova's Government. In the last elections, there was an unprecedented turnout of the diaspora. The diaspora's growing interest in the country's political processes, politicians' hostile statements towards diaspora and governmental decisions have all influenced the diaspora's massive vote.

Lately, diaspora became aware of its catalyst role in the political life in Moldova. Therefore, diaspora can increase its influence in the future, but it must become an active player in political parties in Chisinau. Leastways, diaspora should get involved in developing policies for migrants and in stimulating relations with state institutions.

The proposed article will examine the diaspora's resilience and how it has shaped the institutional framework. The methodological approach is grounded on the analysis of documents drafted by public institutions and publicly available information about Moldovan migrants.

571   Humanitarian assistance in the MENA region - The case of Hungary and Turkey in a comparative perspective

Tamas Dudlak

As recent public and scholarly inquiries started to express interest in the political developments in Turkey and Hungary from a comparative perspective, it is timely and relevant to analyze, compare and review the rise of humanitarian politics pursued by the respective governments of these countries. This paper suggests that both countries try to build a better image of themselves in the international arena through state-related humanitarian activism and seek influence in specific – culturally and ideologically related – external environments even beyond their regional impact. It is interesting to see how their spatial positionality would affect how they negotiate their identities concerning humanitarianism and how anti-migrant states are trying to foster audiences as humanitarian actors at home, on the EU level, and in the Middle East. In Hungary, the government has a clear anti-migrant stance, and its humanitarian activity is mainly motivated by the mitigation of the root causes of migration by helping the local communities affected by various crises. In Turkey's case, lately, there is a tendency towards the same (dispositive) approach as the government tries to force the return of Syrian refugees by providing them support in their original Syrian environment.

For comparison, this paper analyses different projects of various state agencies of Hungary and Turkey, all related to their activities in the MENA region. The fields of action of these state institutions or government-related organizations range from disaster relief aid, education assistance, post-conflict reconstruction, direct investment to culturally related (language, religion) assistance for conflict-ridden societies. In the analysis, it is essential to see the driving factors behind the selection process of the projects, how the respective governments communicate these initiatives, and in general, what are the leading causes of the emergence of humanitarianism both in Turkey and Hungary?

4F   Health and Migration

Chair: Jeffrey H. Cohen, Ohio State University, USA

A Homing Journey: Notions of Home during the COVID-19 pandemic
Alejandra Castellanos Breton, Jose Guillermo Ricalde Perez, Lisa Marie
Perez Sosa

551 No Escape: Refugee Experiences in the COVID-19 Lock-down in
Malaysia
Hui Yin Chuah, Melati Nungsari, Sam Flanders

554 Assessment International Migrants Challenges during COVID-19
Pandemic
Forouzan Rostami and Mohmmad Mobin Rostami

578 General and Health-Related Networks and Social Capital during the
COVID-19 pandemic: An Ego Network Analysis of Lusophone
Immigrants and Portuguese Natives
Paulo Sousa Nascimento

510   A Homing Journey: Notions of Home during the COVID-19 pandemic

Alejandra Castellanos Breton, Jose Guillermo Ricalde Perez, Lisa Marie Perez Sosa

From March 2020 until today, the media and the governments have bombarded society with the phrase 'Stay at home', the most common recommendation to combat the COVID-19 pandemic. The constant uncritical use of the term 'home' brought up several questions and became an invitation to re-think: What is home? How does it feel? And how is it built up? Home is primarily related to everyday life experiences, which involves different temporalities, spaces, and settings.

The process of attaching a sense of home to one's life is what Paolo Boccagni (2017) refers to as 'homing'. This process includes the evolving ways of understanding home according to specific cultural and social standards; the ways of cultivating it as an emotional and relational experience; and the ways of orienting one's multiple social practices. In short, homing as a process aims to reproduce, reconstruct, and possibly rebuild meaningful home-like settings, feelings, and practices.

However, in western society, the heteronormative model of 'home' has come to be the lens that informs and molds the experience of home remaining as a preferred model that neglects space for differences (Ahmed,et al., 2003). Therefore, the present article shows how notions of home among the current LGBTQI+ Erasmus Mundus master students have been shaped during the COVID-19 pandemic. This research is relevant for understanding migrants' everyday life as a unique domain that provides multiple meanings of home that might disrupt its fixed and heteronormative notion.

This study uses a qualitative approach based on photovoice methods, in-depth interviews, and a focus group. The results show how the COVID-19 pandemic created a new space for the LGBTQI+ Erasmus students to understand and review how they lived their sexual orientation during their home experience with themselves and their families. This also brought reflections on the importance of the body, placing it as an active agent that creates new sites of attachments. The COVID-19 pandemic also deconstructed the usual romanticized and positive connotation of home by adding a constant feeling of fear and discomfort, limiting their homing options as wanted. The government's mobility and migration restrictions illustrated how external circumstances shape the process of homing and might create forced experiences. Therefore, the students created new meanings of inhabiting internal and external spaces. Finally, due to the COVID-19 measures, memories became a way to recreate and bring up home-like elements from the past lacking in the present. In this way, they tried to seek a sense of home by adding and subtracting symbolic meanings to objects, places, relationships, and memories. In conclusion, their testimonies show that they are continuously becoming at home through practices of rooting and uprooting.

Bibliography

Ahmed, S., Castañeda, C., and Fortier, A.-M. (2003). Uprootings/Regroundings. Questions of Home and Migration. New York: Berg. https://doi.org/10.4324/9781003087298

Boccagni, P. (2017). Migration and the search for home. Mapping domestic spaces in Migrants everyday lives. New York : Springer Nature. https://doi.org/10.1057/978-1-137-58802

551   No Escape: Refugee Experiences in the COVID-19 Lock-down in Malaysia

Hui Yin Chuah, Melati Nungsari, Sam Flanders

The academic literature surrounding issues related to the pandemic is rapidly expanding every day. We know, for example, that low-income students are disproportionately affected by school shutdowns in America (Chetty et al. 2020), that individual choices tied to fears of infection seemed to be the reason for the collapse in economic activity in the U.S. rather than the legal shutdown orders (Goolsbee and Syverson 2021), and that the structure of social networks play a very important role in the geographic spread of the disease (Kuchler, Russel, and Stroebel 2020). The studies surrounding the impacts of the pandemic in emerging economies, however, is sparse and focusing only on the general population with little to no regard for vulnerable populations, such as refugees and displaced persons. Although some attention has been given to understanding and measuring the health risks of refugees in camps and urban slums (Ahmed 2020; Raju and Ayeb-Karlsson 2020; Truelove et al. 2020; Vince 2020), there have not been many attempts to address the experiences of refugees within a country, and to understand the economic and social impacts of the pandemic.

This paper adds to the literature surrounding the impact of COVID-19 by presenting a qualitative study of forced migrants' experiences in Peninsular Malaysia. The paper also aims to answer: (i) how has refugee trust towards authority figures (e.g. the government and public health officials) changed throughout the pandemic, (ii) how has this impacted their compliance and attitudes towards public health measures? The paper is divided into two parts. In the first part, we conduct in-depth, semi-structured interviews with 20 community leaders from eight independent refugee (ethnic) groups based on five different dimensions: economic, social, security, health, and communication of information during the pandemic. Based on grounded theory (Charmaz and Belgrave 2018; Strauss and Corbin 1997), we then build a theoretical framework to explain the experience of a refugee in Malaysia during the pandemic. In particular, we find that the experiences of the refugees mediate their trust in authority figures during the time of the pandemic.

Using this model, we then conduct a comparative qualitative study between two refugee groups - 11 Rohingyas and eight Syrians - to specifically probe the impact of identity on the experience of an 'average' refugee who is neither a leader nor representative of their community. The two main findings were the following: that identity was a truly defining factor in determining a refugee's experience - the Rohingyas, for example, faced significantly more economic difficulty and hardship than the Syrians - and that an experience of a refugee community leader is vastly different than an "average" refugee. Most of our respondents in the second part had not received any assistance from local NGOs or Malaysians - this is vastly different than the experience of the community leaders, who themselves were a part of the distribution supply chain of food and cash aid from local NGOs. Thus, the main policy recommendation is that organizations and governments should pay more attention to choosing a diverse range of "injection points" into refugee social networks in order to maximise the spread of aid.

References

Ahmed, Mabrur. 2020. 'Preventing Disaster: COVID-19 and the Rohingya in Bangladesh'. *LSE Blog* (blog). 3 April 2020. https://blogs.lse.ac.uk/southasia/2020/04/03/preventing-disaster-covid-19-and-the-rohingya-in-bangladesh/.

Charmaz, Kathy, and Linda Liska Belgrave. 2018. 'Thinking About Data With Grounded Theory'. *Qualitative Inquiry* 25 (8): 743–53. https://doi.org/10.1177/1077800418809455.

Chetty, Raj, John N. Friedman, Nathaniel Hendren, and Michael Stepner. 2020. 'The Economic Impacts of COVID-19: Evidence from a New Public Database Built Using Private Sector Data'. *NBER Research Working Paper Series* 27431.

Goolsbee, Austan, and Chad Syverson. 2021. 'Fear, Lockdown, and Diversion: Comparing Drivers of Pandemic Economic Decline 2020'. *Journal of Public Economics* 193 (January): 104311. https://doi.org/10.1016/j.jpubeco.2020.104311.

Kuchler, Theresa, Dominic Russel, and Johannes Stroebel. 2020. 'The Geographic Spread of COVID-19 Correlates with the Structure of Social Networks as Measured by Facebook'. *NBER Research Working Paper Series* 26990.

Raju, Emmanuel, and Sonja Ayeb-Karlsson. 2020. 'COVID-19: How Do You Self-Isolate in a Refugee Camp?' *International Journal of Public Health* 65 (5): 515–17. https://doi.org/10.1007/s00038-020-01381-8.

Strauss, Anselm, and Juliet M. Corbin, eds. 1997. *Grounded Theory in Practice*. London: Sage Publication.

Truelove, Shaun, Oirt Abrahim, Chiara Altare, Andrew Azman, and Paul Spiegel. 2020. 'COVID-19: Projecting the Impact in Rohingya Refugee Camps and Beyond'. *SSRN Electronic Journal*, January. https://doi.org/10.2139/ssrn.3561565.

Vince, Gaia. 2020. 'The World's Largest Refugee Camp Prepares for Covid-19'. *BMJ* 368 (March): m1205. https://doi.org/10.1136/bmj.m1205.

554   Assessment International Migrants Challenges during COVID-19 Pandemic

Forouzan Rostami and Mohmmad Mobin Rostami

Migration defines as any person who has changed her/his country of usual residence, distinguishing between short- term migrants and long-term. The estimated number of International migrants has increased over the past five decades.Covid-19 crisis is increasing pressure on migrants as well as stable employment to sustain themselves and their families. The paper shows how, concerns about the impact of Corona virus on the ability of minorities and migrants. This article also indicates the current global health crisis would intensity social and economic inequalities, political, international students, families Children vulnerability across mobility in the Corona virus outbreak.

578   General and Health-Related Networks and Social Capital during the COVID-19 pandemic: An Ego Network Analysis of Lusophone Immigrants and Portuguese Natives

Paulo Sousa Nascimento

Social networks and social capital are acknowledged as determinants of health, playing a protective role in immigrant's mental health. Such determinants face changes over the time spent by immigrants in the destination country, studying their influence is crucial. Yet, most studies only address general/important matters networks, instead of also considering specific/health-discussion networks, which may elicit peripheral ties acting as bridges to access health resources. Because disruptive events (e.g., COVID-19) can also modify the structure/functions of networks, reducing their social capital and limiting access to certain resources, the analysis of both networks is crucial to explore their transformation, power, and constraints. The present study aims to 1) compare the characteristics of general and specific networks, to depict their changes and social capital oscillations; 2) extend that comparison by analyzing networks specificities of Lusophone immigrants and Portuguese natives; and 3) funnel the analysis to evaluate network fluctuations according to immigrant's length of time in Portugal during the COVID-19 pandemic.

A convenience sample of egocentric networks (general and health) was collected through name generators (collecting alters name), name interpreters (for alters attributes) and position generator (for social capital) between July and December 2020. The sample comprised 71 egos (n = 53 natives, n = 18 immigrants). E-net software was used to assess networks composition, heterogeneity, homophily (gender, age, education attainment, alters immigrant status) and structural holes. Networks were also characterized in terms of social capital (alters occupations) and alters proximity level.

General networks had higher degree than health networks, despite the latter being more constrained. Gender homophily occurred on both networks, with age heterophily being higher among health networks. Social capital increased on health networks. General networks of Lusophone immigrants and Portuguese natives also had higher degree, but natives presented more efficient networks. Constraints increased among native's health networks, which were age heterophilic. Immigrants ties were more diverse, with status homophily being higher among natives' networks, where more ties were shared with other natives. Natives had more social capital on both networks. Finally, immigrants living in Portugal for less than 2 years had lower social capital and denser networks, yet smaller and less efficient health networks, compared to those living in the country for more than 5 years with less dense but more efficient networks, particularly health networks.

Lusophone immigrants and Portuguese natives have smaller health networks, mostly comprising family members and friends. Also networks for both groups have more women alters, as they may be more prone to effective health discussions. Age heterophily among health networks may be due to networks composition (more family members) increasing constraints but diversifying health experiences. The migration process disrupts social capital contributing to less efficient networks among immigrants. As residency time decreases, social capital and efficiency decline: ties with natives are limited and access to effective resources may be impaired. Studies on migrant's general and specific networks are relevant as informative on social health determinants and interaction patterns, helping stakeholders on health decision making processes particularly among disruptive contexts.

4G   Migration Theory: New Debates

Chair: Ruchi Singh, Prin. L. N. Welingkar Institute of Management
   Development & Research, India

687   Water and forced migration: perspectives of human rights
   Megumi Nishimura
718   Understanding the presence of the culture of migration in Kerala
   R.B. Bhagat and Sulaiman KM
732   Measurement of Ethnic Diversity and Its Effect with the Recent In-
   Migration Rate
   Tiara Maureen
757   Extraterrestrial Migration and the Transportation Model for a Space
   Colonization and Manufacturing System: Analyzing the Risks of Artificial
   Orbital Debris Accumulation
   Stefani Stojchevska

687 Water and forced migration: perspectives of human rights

Megumi Nishimura

This paper analyze how water shortage aggravated migration to the cities. Depite the water shortage due to the global climate change among MENA and sub-Saharan as well as the Middle East countries, it hardly causes the outbreak of major war. This does not mean, however, the costs are distributed evenly and equally among various social groups.

In fact, the water shortage caused forced migration due to the local water conflicts to the cities' slum areas, althgouh the access to usable water is increasiingly perceived as human rights issues.

The paper examines how the costs are distributed for aquiring water and inter-state conflicts by examining the water-related forced migration, such as irrigation problems or food shortages. More broadly, the issue will be related to a larger theoretical problem how mitigation of inter-state conflicts are incurred costs among non-organized domestic actors, such as farmers, water users.

718 Understanding the presence of the culture of migration in Ke

R.B. Bhagat and Sulaiman KM

Migration from Kerala to the Gulf region has converted to a major subject of debate in academic circles since the 1970s oil boom. Through active engagement with migrant recruiters, the Keralites (People of Kerala) has built a sophisticated network that enables, facilitates, and promotes labour migration. It is evident that many of the theories of migration, from the broad structural theories to theories that attempt to account for migrant agency, are relevant to the Kerala case. Migration, as a culture, or the normalization and internalization of movement, is connected to the motivations to migrate. The structure of migration and its history and the continuity that characterizes movements past and present for most sending communities creates a "culture of migration" that supports movers and non-movers. It facilitates network building between origin and destination populations (Cohen, 2004). I argue that the outcomes of a culture of migration are felt not just by the migrants themselves but also by their relatives and by Kerala as a whole.

In this paper, a step was taken to establish the culture of migration theory through the qualitative data collected from the study area (Calicut-Kerala). The attempt to develop the theory through qualitative data was considered due to many facets of the culture of migration have been described qualitatively. Based on Cohen (2004), by "culture of migration", this study means to make three arguments. First, migration is widespread and had a historical presence in Kerala. Second, the decision to migrate is one that people make as part of their everyday experiences (familial and social). Third, Keralites consider the decision to migrate as a path towards economic well-being. This paper will try to address these arguments. The historical narratives and the media contents collected as part of this study shows that migration is widespread in Kerala and had a historical presence by pointing out-migration became an easier process;

by the end of the 19th century, almost all households in Kerala have been notably affected by Gulf migration. According to Mathew et al. (2003), migration has deeply and visibly influenced every perspective of life, including economic, social, political, cultural and even religious viewpoints of the Malayalee in Kerala.

According to the New Economics of Labour Migration concept, they were revealing that the decision to migrate is in part arranged by all adult members of a migrant's family. Further, the qualitative narratives show how the family and community influence the migration decision of its member. The involvement of the household in migration decision was visible from the beginning of the gulf migration. Soon after that, Kerala's people became more aware of the opportunity they have if they can take the risk of crossing the sea and making it into the gulf. Families forced unemployed youths to migrate. Finally, the result in-depth interview conducted among potential future migrants shows that most of them believe that if they have to make progress in their standard of living and social status, migrating to the gulf is a better way to do it. The findings validate the arguments this study made about the culture of migration. Kerala does have a culture of migration. Though it is at times latent, the culture of migration is activated by specific, culturally defined circumstances.

References

Cohen, J. (2004). The Culture of Migration in Southern Mexico. Austin: University of Texas Press.

Massey, D. S., Arango, J., Hugo, G., Kouaouci, A., Pellegrino, A., & Taylor, E. J. (1998). Worlds in motion: Understanding international migration at the end of the millennium. Oxford: Clarendon Press.

Zachariah K.C, Mathew E.T, and Rajan S.I. (2003). Impact of Migration on Kerala's Economy and Society. International Migration.

732   Measurement of Ethnic Diversity and Its Effect with the Recent In-Migration Rate

Tiara Maureen

Ethnic diversity has its appeal to study. Measures of ethnic diversity that have been used in many studies are the Ethnic Fractionalization Index (EFI) and the Ethnic Polarization Index (EPOI). EFI shows the level of ethnic heterogeneity. While EPOI is used to identify the existence of several ethnic groups that are relatively huge and almost the same. The value of the EPOI can indicate the conflict potential from the existence of ethnic groups. Indonesia is known for its ethnic diversity. In 2010, Statistics Indonesia classified 1,343 ethnic groups into 31 major ethnic groups based on the results of the 2010 Population Census (SP2010) as a source of data for local development planning needs. Ethnic diversity can be sourced from the high flow of migration that causes changes in ethnic composition. Provinces in Indonesia that changing ethnic composition are Riau and Riau Islands. According to the results of SP2010, Riau Islands is the province with the highest rate of recent in-migration in Indonesia at 15.88% and the Riau Province at 6%. Recent in-migration reflects the displacement state of five years ago. Research on the in-migration behavior of ethnic groups is still relatively small. Research of ethnic groups in-migration behavior according to the characteristics of migrants is useful to see how ethnic groups are distributed and can be compared between regions. Thus, this study aims to obtain the ethnic composition, in-migration patterns of ethnic groups, and to measure ethnic diversity, and to see the effect of in-migration on ethnic diversity in Riau and Riau Islands in 2010. The data used is the secondary microdata SP2010 which covers 10% of the population of the Riau and Riau Islands Province in 2010. The analytical method used is a descriptive analysis of the ethnic composition and its in-migration patterns according to age, sex, and area of residence. The measure of ethnic diversity used is EFI and EPOI with quadrant analysis. Simple regression analysis is used to see the effect of recent in-migration on EFI and EPOI. The results showed that the composition of migrants according to ethnic groups between Riau and Riau Islands Province was not much different. The largest percentage of migrants are Javanese, Batak, Minangkabau, and Malay. Recent in-migration in ethnic groups tends to be carried out by male migrants, aged 23-54 years, and live in urban areas. Both provinces have high EFI and middle EPOI values. Five regencies have a quite high EFI and high EPOI values. The regencies with high EPOI may need attention because the conflict potential may be higher. Simple regression analysis shows that recent in-migration has a positive effect on EFI and a negative effect on EPOI. However, EFI and EPOI only show levels of ethnic diversity and potential opportunities for conflict. EFI and EPOI are not the main determinants of conflict but can be important indices that can help make better policies.

References

Ananta, A. (2016). Changing ethnic composition and potential violent conflict in Riau Archipelago, Indonesia: an early warning signal. *Population Review, 45(1)*.

Arifin, E., Ananta, A., Utami, D., Handayani, N., & Pramono, A. (2015). Quantifying Indonesia's Ethnic Diversity:Statistics at National, Provincial, and District Levels. *Asian Population Studies, 11(3)*, 233-256.

Badan Pusat Statistik. (2011). *Kewarganegaraan, Suku Bangsa, Agama, dan Bahasa Sehari-Hari Penduduk Indonesia: Hasil Sensus Penduduk 2010*. Jakarta: Badan Pusat Statistik.

Esteban, J., Mayoral, L., & Ray, D. (2012). Ethnicity and Conflict: An Empirical Study. *American Economic Review, 102(4)*, 1310-1342.

Montalvo, J., & Reynal-Querol, M. (2005). Ethnic Polarization, Potential Conflict and Civil Wars. *American Economic Review 95(3)*, 796-816.

Raymer, J., Smith, P., & Giulietti, C. (2011). Combining Census and Registration Data to Analyse Ethnic Migration Patterns in England from 1991 to 2007. *Population, Space and Place, 17(1)*, 73 - 88.

757 Extraterrestrial Migration and the Transportation Model for a Space Colonization and Manufacturing System: Analyzing the Risks of Artificial Orbital Debris Accumulation

Stefani Stojchevska

While emphasizing the importance of migration in relation to the survival of mankind, its manifestation may not be generally conceivable in the following decades, considering that we are currently living in the geological epoch of the Anthropocene – which by itself brings along the obligation to continuously fight against various hazardous environmental issues, such as global warming. By contrast, the concept of extraterrestrial migration, although initially envisaged within science fiction literature, may be slowly moving toward the scope of scientific factuality and technological feasibility. Disregarding the continuous discoveries of exoplanets, who only descend extraterrestrial migration into oblivion, its origination has tendencies to strongly resemble orbiting objects identical to the International Space Station (ISS). Such manifestations can be further advanced by physical aspects contained within a specifically developed "Transportation Model for a Space Colonization and Manufacturing System", which represents only a Q-GERT simulation at the moment.

The Space Colonization and Manufacturing System (SCMS) ordinarily consists of six major subsystems whose names correspond to the physical location that they occupy within the Earth-Moon system: (1) Low Earth Orbit, (2) Geostationary Earth Orbit, (3) Low Lunar Orbit, (4) Unstable Lagrangian Point Two, (5) Stable Lagrangian Point Four, and (6) Stable Lagrangian Point Five. Since the SCMS requires for an Earth Space Station (ESS) to reside in Low Earth Orbit (LEO), while a Satellite Solar Power Station (SSPS), considered as the major product of the SCMS, will be constructed in Geostationary Orbit (GEO), it would initially utilize two Earth orbits. However, ever since the launch of Sputnik 1 in 1957, artificial orbital debris has begun to accumulate in Earth orbit, where its increasing growth is becoming life-threatening to astronauts and orbiting space objects. Hence, an important question simultaneously arises: Does artificial orbital debris pose a serious threat to extraterrestrial migration?

This research paper correspondingly analyzes the official space environment statistics data published by the National Aeronautics and Space Administration (NASA) and the European Space Agency (ESA) regarding the expected evolution of the number of orbital objects larger than 10 cm in LEO and the relative associated number of catastrophic collisions from 1957 up to the 23th century, as well as number fragmentation events and missions to LEO and GEO from 1960 to 2020. Additionally, mankind is limited in solving the artificial orbital debris issue regarding the Kessler Syndrome which can be primarily analyzed given the collision frequency of artificial satellites, from 1970 to 2020. In order for the possible structure of a SCMS to hold great potential for creating permanently habitable objects in the near future, underlying philosophical, anthropological, ethical and legal constructs must be scrutinized as well. Particularly considering the law and governance on extraterrestrial migration, the 1967 Outer Space Treaty contains no specific provisions of extraterrestrial migration envisioned within the presented model, which is why space jurisprudents and policy-makers must focus on pushing the limits of migration and simultaneously prove that mankind can and will thrive within an unfathomable environment such as outer space by breaking through the new epoch of the Anthropocosmos.

14:15-14:30 BREAK

Day Two 7 July 2021 Wednesday

Day Two 7 July 2021 - 14:30-16:00
5A   Migration and Integration
Chair: Ana Vila Freyer, Universidad Latina de México, Mexico
567   Successful migrant integration: Case Study Șomcuta Mare, Romania
       Razvan Dacian Carciumaru
569   Would you please tell me, which way I ought to go? Central Americans
       crossing by or settling in Guanajuato
       Ana Vila-Freyer
570   Refugee Integration in the United States and Germany: A Comparative
       Study
       Alvina Ahmed
574   Uses and Gratifications of Digital Diasporic Media Amongst Same-
       Language Minorities: A Qualitative Case Study on the Venezuelan
       Immigrant Communities in Chile and in Colombia After the Refugee
       Crisis (2015 - onwards)
       Matthias Erlandsen

567   Successful migrant integration: Case Study Șomcuta Mare, Romania

Razvan Dacian Carciumaru

The guidelines contained in the programmatic documents at European level and the dynamic nature of migratory flows in the region require a permanent adjustment of national policies related to social realities in Romania, as well as institutional development to meet the challenges imposed by proper management of the phenomenon. The management of the migration phenomenon is based on the participation of all institutions with competencies in this field, through a participatory management and through inter-institutional, national and international cooperation. The aim of the present study is to diagnose the phenomenon at certain times and in certain conceptual and organizational frameworks, but it can represent a reference point for future analyzes on the guidelines of the national program for the integration of migrants.

In Romania there are six regional centers of accommodation and reception of asylum seekers strategically placed on the national territory. "Regional Center for Accommodation and Processing of Asylum Applications", from Bucharest, is the first center built in Romania to serve this purpose. There is a similar center in the north side of the country, in Șomcuta Mare, Maramureș county, which is part of the present study. Other centers are in Giurgiu, Galați, Rădăuți and Timișoara, all placed near the borders of Romania.

The paper addresses, from two perspectives, the phenomenon of integration of both refugees and migrants in local communities, a topical issue facing the European Union. One of them is the perspective on government policies, and the other refers to the practical implementation of these policies.

Several important approaches include the analysis of secondary sources (literature on integration, published at national and European level) and a quantitative research, analysis of data from public institutions.

There is worth mentioning that an integration program, part of an EU project, was implemented within the "Regional Center for Accommodation and Procedures for Asylum Seekers", from Șomcuta Mare, during 2017-2020. The project addresses both refugees, who come from conflict areas, especially from Syria recently, as well as foreigners who come from countries outside the European Union and who are in Romania for various purposes.

This integration program is not mandatory, but according to the recent legislative changes in the field, the asylum seeker is required to enroll in this program, if he wants the support of the Romanian state, including financial assistance.

The research question to be tested in this theoretical analysis is whether the response of the Romanian authorities to the crisis of 2015 was according to the main lines of the EU The paper will generally examine the procedure for registering an asylum application and the forms of protection offered by the state or, in some cases, return assistance, in order to determine whether the steps taken regarding integration policy were in the proper direction.

In what concerns the methods used in order to validate the hypothesis, the present paper examines the context that determined the emergence of EU integration policy and the contributions to the national legislation from the EU countries. Moreover, the empirical part of this analysis will take into consideration the perception of nationals regarding the EU migrant integration policy and their attachment to the European values.

The main objectives of the integration program should be aimed at ensuring the socio-economic conditions aspiring to cultivate values in order to promote human interests and ensure risk minimization.

569   Would you please tell me, which way I ought to go? Central Americans crossing by or settling in Guanajuato

Ana Vila-Freyer

Young Central Americans migrants seek to go as far north as possible away from their communities of origin. The north has become Guatemala, somewhere in Mexico, an asylum-refugee camp on the Mexican northern border, the United

States. Some might even seek Canada. The growing visibility of this northward movement has exposed a shifting position in the political response in Mexico, ranging from letting them pass as if unseen, to securing the border due to pressure from the U.S. government over the past 20 years (Giorguli, García, & Masferrer, 2016; Gonzales & Steven, 2017; Torre, Destino y asentamiento en México de los migrantes y refugiados centroamericanos, 2020). Diving for safety, migrants have been changing the routes and strategies to become visible in order to ensure protection and, more specifically, finding a safe place to continue their lives (Torre & Mariscal, 2020; Glockner, 2019; Silva, 2015; Torre & Yee, México ¿una frontera vertical? Políticas de control del tránsito migratorio irregular y sus resultados, 2007-2016, 2018). This movement change stands on demographic and economic transformations in different regions of Mexico, as in Guanajuato, that could require this low-skilled, but necessary, labor in traditional sectors. Henceforth these chapter emphasize in the importance of reflecting on the construction of consensus that would allow the establishment of sanctuary cities in the state.

570   Refugee Integration in the United States and Germany: A Comparative Study

Alvina Ahmed

The 2015-16 refugee crisis has seen millions of refugees flee their native lands in the Middle East and North Africa and arrive in Western countries, namely in the United States and in European nations. As a result, the Western nations faced a number of hurdles, from processing asylum applications to integrating refugees into the labour market and society at large. Although certain policies in a handful of nations proved effective in aiding to resettle the asylum seekers, the overwhelming responses from Western citizens and refugees suggest that the global response to the crisis had been inadequate. Previous literature has concluded that refugees in the United States typically face a number of challenges despite having varying levels of financial and social support; when comparing refugees with other migrants, the former usually take longer to become economically self-sufficient and integrate into American culture.[13] Furthermore, studies have mentioned that many refugees in the United States report having language barriers and emotional trauma years after initially arriving in the nation.[14] Similar studies have been conducted regarding refugee integration in Germany. According to Brücker et al, refugees arriving in Germany during the 2015-16 have integrated into the German labour market more effectively than refugees who sought asylum in Germany before 2015; the percent of refugees who self-reported possessing proficient German language skills increased from 12 percent in 2015 to 41 percent in 2017.[15] Furthermore, almost 25% of refugees who had completed integration programs provided by

---

[13] Tran, Van and Francisco Lara-Garcia. A New Beginning: Early Refugee Integration in the United States, 2020, pp 117-143.
[14] Tran, Van and Francisco Lara-Garcia. A New Beginning: Early Refugee Integration in the United States, 2020, pp 117-143.
[15] Brücker, H, et al. Integrating Refugees and Asylum Seekers into the German Economy and Society: Empirical Evidence and Policy Objectives, Dec. 2019, pp. 5–36.

the Bundesamt für Migration und Flüchtlinge (BAMF) after initially arriving in 2015 found employment by the second half of 2017.[16] This research uses refugee integration programs in the United States and Germany as case studies; using structured focused comparison, this study compares language acquisition, job placement, and social integration of refugees who gained asylum in the United States and Germany in and after 2015. The results of the structured focused comparison indicate that refugees arriving in Germany were more likely to have been economically self-sufficient and socially integrated into Western society than those arriving in the United States. The study examines some factors that may have caused the differences between the effectiveness of integration programs in the two nations. These findings would be helpful in anticipating challenges in refugee and migrant integration programs in the future.

574   Uses and Gratifications of Digital Diasporic Media Amongst Same-Language Minorities: A Qualitative Case Study on the Venezuelan Immigrant Communities in Chile and in Colombia After the Refugee Crisis (2015 - onwards)

Matthias Erlandsen

According to the literature, mass media are an essential institution in the migration process (Park, 1920, 1922, 1925). Several studies, particularly those in sociology and social psychology, demonstrate that along with other institutions, mass media are one of the first to emerge every time a new group of migrants settles (Hickerson & Gustafson, 2016).

However, these studies mostly focus on societies that do not share the same language. Therefore, their conclusions are apparent when they state that "ethnic media" helps navigate the hosting society and learn the local language for the newly-arrived immigrants.

Drawing on Park's ideas on "Ethnic and Foreign Media," and considering the new patterns in South-South human migration, especially in Latin America and the former colonies, this study aims to, on the one hand, to distinguish the concept "Ethnic Media" from "Diasporic Media" regarding digital media created by and for migrant communities—particularly those sharing the same language;

On the other hand, this research aims to analyze and document new Uses and Gratifications (Katz, Blumler, & Gurevitch, 1973) that Venezuelan migrants in Chile and Colombia report over their experiences after consuming two different local news outlets of this kind: "El Vinotinto" in Chile, and "El Venezolano Colombia" in Colombia.

This research is based on an exploratory qualitative research (Creswell & Plano Clark, 2018), which involves online one-on-one interviews with migrants in both Chile and Colombia to detect new categories of uses and gratifications.

Preliminary conclusions demonstrate that there are new uses and gratifications. In the first category, audiences report using this type of media to promote entrepreneurship and professional services, access to censored news in

---

[16] Brücker et al. "Zweite Welle der IAB-BAMF-SOEP-Befragung"

Venezuela, and as a channel of humanitarian aid. They report legal compliance in the migration process in the gratifications category, stronger bonds with Venezuela's daily life, and an ethnonationalism without community-building.

References

Creswell, J. W., & Plano Clark, V. L. (2018). *Designing and Conducting Mixed Methods Research* (3rd ed.). Thousand Oaks, CA: SAGE.

Hickerson, A., & Gustafson, K. L. (2016). Revisiting the immigrant press. *Journalism, 17*(8), 943-960. doi:10.1177/1464884914542742

Katz, E., Blumler, J. G., & Gurevitch, B. (1973). Uses and gratifications research. *Public Opinion Quarterly, 37*, 509-523.

Park, R. E. (1920). *Foreign language press and social progress.* Paper presented at the National Conference of Social Work, Chicago, IL.

Park, R. E. (1922). *The immigrant press and its control.* New York; London: Harper & Brothers.

Park, R. E. (1925). The immigrant community and the immigrant press. *American Review, 3*, 18-24.

5B   History of Migration

Chair: Caner Tekin, University of Bochum, Germany

547   Human movement from Turkey to Western Europe: A historical and theoretical assessment in the international migration context
Mehmet Rauf Kesici

603   Building Borders in the Wake of Empire: Missionaries, Religious Identity, and the Greco-Turkish Population Exchange, 1922-1923
Eulogio Kyle Romero

661   Changing Trends in Research on Turkish Migrants in Germany
Genevieve Golden Soucek

850   Perception of 1864
Melike Batgıray Abboud

800   Internal Migration and Higher Education in Turkey: University Expansion between 197-1975
Caner Tekin

547   Human movement from Turkey to Western Europe: A historical and theoretical assessment in the international migration context

Mehmet Rauf Kesici

This study aims to investigate the changing phases and forms of human movement from Turkey to Germany and the UK from a comparative historical perspective and in a multi-theoretical framework. Its main purpose is to analyse the individual and structural factors which initiate and perpetuate migration between these countries.

The research is based on two field studies, a literature review and, a multiple theoretical perspective. The first field study conducted in London, UK, between

September 2014 and September 2015. The second one carried out in the Ruhr Region (Ruhrgebiet), Germany, between January 2017 and December 2019.

This study clarifies that these migration waves have been initiated by several factors including socioeconomic differences, demographic disparities, political distinctions and conflicts. The migration is also perpetuated by proceeding dissimilarities, the culture of migration, social networks and ethnic economies in Germany and the UK. However, it deals with these migration waves in general, not in details, and uses only the appropriate migration theories.

The study, employing theoretical approaches and field studies, presents a deeper insight into the motives for migration and the reasons which push people to leave Turkey and attract them to move to Germany and the UK while the existing studies on migration from Turkey to Western Europe do not use both the field studies and theoretical perspectives.

References

Abadan-Unat, N. (1995). Turkish migration to Europe. *The Cambridge survey of world migration*, 279-284.

Akgündüz, A. (1993). Labour Migration from Turkey to Western Europe (1960–1974) An Analytical Review. *Capital & Class, 17*(3), 153-194.

Arango, J. (2018). Explaining migration: a critical view. *International Social Science Journal, 68*(227-228), 105-117.

Hagen-Zanker, J. (2008). Why do people migrate? A review of the theoretical literature. *A Review of the Theoretical Literature (January 2008). Maastrcht Graduate School of Governance Working Paper No.*

Icduygu, A. (2006). A panorama of the international migration regime in Turkey. *Revue européenne des migrations internationales, 22*(3), 11-21.

Kesici, M. R. (2020). The Visibility of an Invisible Community's Labour Exploitation in an Ethnic Economy: A Comparative Study on Kurdish Movers in the United Kingdom. *Migration Letters, 17*(3), 461-470.

King, R., Thomson, M., Mai, N., and Keles, Y. (2008). 'Turks' in the UK: Problems of Definition and the Partial Relevance of Policy. *Journal of Immigrant & Refugee Studies, 6*(3): 423-434.

Lee, E. S. (1966). A theory of migration. *Demography, 3*(1), 47-57.

Martin, P. L. (1991). *The unfinished story: Turkish labour migration to Western Europe: with special reference to the Federal Republic of Germany* (Vol. 84). International Labour Organization.

Massey, D. S., Arango, J., Hugo, G., Kouaouci, A., Pellegrino, A., & Taylor, J. E. (1993). Theories of international migration: A review and appraisal. *Population and development review, 19*(3), 431-466.

Meyers, E. (2000). Theories of international immigration policy—A comparative analysis. *International migration review, 34*(4), 1245-1282.

Oğuz, G. (2012). *EU enlargement and Turkish labour migration*. UNU Press.

Ravenstein, E. G. (1885). The laws of migration. *Journal of the statistical society of London, 48*(2), 167-235.

Ravenstein, E. G. (1889). The laws of migration. *Journal of the royal statistical society*, 52(2), 241-305.

Sirkeci, I., Bilecen, T., Coştu, Y., Dedeoğlu, S., Kesici, M. R., Şeker, B. D., Tilbe, F., & Unutulmaz, K. O. (2016). *Little Turkey in Great Britain*. London: Transnational Press London.

Sirkeci, I., & Cohen, J. H. (2016). Cultures of migration and conflict in contemporary human mobility in Turkey. *European Review*, 24(3), 381-396.

Sirkeci, I. (2009). Transnational mobility and conflict. *Migration Letters*, 6(1), 3-14.

Wallerstein, I. (1974). *The Modern World-System*, New York: Academic Press.

Wickramasinghe, A. A. I. N., & Wimalaratana, W. (2016). International migration and migration theories. *Social Affairs*, 1(5), 13-32.

603 Building Borders in the Wake of Empire: Missionaries, Religious Identity, and the Greco-Turkish Population Exchange, 1922-1923

Eulogio Kyle Romero

Refugees are a constant symptom of war. Between 1922 and 1923 over two million Greeks and Turks were forced out of their homes in an unprecedented crisis of refugee migration. Unlike most instances of refugee crisis, however, these Greeks and Turks were forced out by international arrangement rather than by war. Indeed their marginalized status as refugees occurred in order to end a conflict: the Greco-Turkish War. Signed in 1922, the Lausanne Treaty authorized Turkey and Greece to denaturalize and expel any ethnic Greeks living within Turkish borders and any ethnic Turks residing in Greece. The newly made League of Nations approved of the treaty, arguing that separation would prevent more violence in the region. Only one problem remained, however: identifying the prospective refugees. To accomplish this, the treaty dictated that any Greek Orthodox Christians in Turkey would be identified as Greek, and any Muslims in Greece would be Turks. In practical terms, this meant that the new nation of Turkey denaturalized many Greek Orthodox ethnic Turks who claimed long lineages in the Ottoman Empire and Greece forced out any Muslim despite their skin color, ethnicity, or ancestry or, indeed, their wishes. The Lausanne treaty empowered Turkey and Greece to expel their marginalized religious communities in order to form homogeneous states with strictly defined religious borders.

My paper analyzes the role of the international community and Western missionaries in contributing to this discourse on religious separation. It follows how an eclectic mix of U.S. aid workers and State Department officials conceived of the Eastern Mediterranean in the wake of the unprecedented brutality of World War I as a fundamentally religious space. As the Ottoman Empire collapsed, these Americans increasingly identified strong nation-states as the only possible solution to the famines and violence of the post-WWI world, which they understood to be caused by inter-religious violence, eventually leading to tacit support for ethnic violence and expulsion on the assumption that it would lead to lasting peace. These changing notions of sovereignty led these actors to build new relationships with the Greek and Turkish governments through the connective network of the League of Nations. This new political nexus between U.S. aid groups, the consolidating ethno-states of Greece and Turkey, and the newly emergent League of Nations led to not only explicit support for the concept of a "population exchange" but extensive infrastructural aid. Since Anglo-American missionaries in the Middle East characterized Islam, rather than national or ethnic character, as the cause of conflict in the region, humanitarian institutions targeted aid at Christian refugees, sanctioning only certain types of movement. Interestingly, this type of religious segregation gelled with new Turkish plans to expel Christian minorities. In the liminal historical space caused by the Ottoman Empire's collapse religion operated as a key factor in constructing new nations.

References

Barnett, Michael. *Empire of Humanity: A History of Humanitarianism*. Ithaca: Cornell University Press, 2013.

Clark, Bruce. *Twice a Stranger: The Mass Expulsions that Forged Modern Greece and Turkey*. Cambridge: Harvard University Press, 2009.

Fassin, Didier. *Humanitarian Reason: A Moral History of the Present*. Berkeley: University of California Press, 2012.

Kieser, Hans-Lukas. *Nearest East: American Millenialism and Mission to the Middle East*. Philadelphia: Temple University Press, 2010.

Ozsu, Umut. *Formalizing Displacement: International Law and Population Transfers*. Oxford: Oxford University Press, 2015.

Philliou, Christine. *Biography of an Empire: Governing Ottomans in an Age of Revolution*. Berkeley: University of California Press, 2011.

661   Changing Trends in Research on Turkish Migrants in Germany

Genevieve Golden Soucek

Changing Trends in Research on Turkish Migrants in Germany
Soucek, Genevieve

Introduction

Turks started immigrating to Germany in the 1960s and 1970s as guest workers, or "Gastarbeiters." Around 3 to 5 million Turks have moved to Europe in the past few decades, with a majority settled in Germany (Sirkeci & Cohen, 2016). Between 2010 and 2016 about 1.35 million migrants came to Germany, of which about 850,000 were Muslim (Pew Research Center, 2017). A little less than half of these migrants were refugees and about 86 percent of the refugees were Muslim. Today, as more Muslim refugees settle in Germany, there has been a rise in xenophobia among Germans and Turkish migrants often must confront ethnic discrimination (Sirkeci, Cohen & Yazgan, 2012). The goal of this research is to review what topics related to the physical and mental health of first- and second-generation Turkish migrants to Germany are chosen for research and how those topics relate to changes in treatment of Turkish immigrants in Germany since the early 2000s.

Many factors and environmental pressures impact the health of an individual and their community. Broadly these factors can be political, social, economic, ethnic and cultural. When looking at Turkish migrants in Germany, some of the major topics influencing their health and wellbeing include social welfare and emergency care use, physical and cognitive health, smoking, labor market and education integration, familial and intergenerational transmission, a sense of belonging and identity, citizenship and host culture adoption and ethnic retention, return migration intentions, and alienation by the host culture in Germany. I used these topics as domains for research and found that the prevalence of these topics, which appear throughout research on Turkish immigrants in Germany, have shifted from 2001 to 2019.

Originally, I did not intend to address the shift in research topics. I found this significant change after organizing a series of resources on the status of Turkish immigrants in Germany. After surveying work on Turkish migrants who have settled in Germany, what became clear was the increasing pressures, particularly discriminatory pressures, affecting the community and the impacts of those pressures on the health of the community. I later focused on the shift in research topics and contexts in which the research was framed, either looking at Turks compared to other Turks or Turks compared to Germans, and how pressures affecting health arise or are associated with research. I compiled sources by searching for articles on demographics of Turkish migrants in Germany and their health. After finding 29 sources covering different aspects of physical and mental health of first- and second-generation Turkish migrants in Germany, I identified research domains and summarized each. I noted how the information in each article was relevant when looking at its application in the world and how the outcomes in the articles were addressed by the authors. Then I organized the articles by year starting in 2001 and ending in 2019. I looked at major events and changed in Germany in each of those years and discovered how events influenced the research being done and the way issues were addressed.

Since the early 2000s there has been a shift in focus from looking at the culture and health of Turkish migrants in Germany to a need for Turks to assimilate. I also noticed that acculturative pressures and xenophobia influenced issues. Furthermore, issues that were generally seen as health concerns in Germany have slowly become "Turkish problems," that need to be fixed so Turkish migrants and their children will appear "Germanized." These themes in shifting research have adverse effects on Turkish migrants, change research and change German perceptions of Turks in Germany. This creates new problems and issues for Turkish migrants and children of migrants as they navigate life in Germany.

Status of Turkish Migration to Germany

An increase in the number of Turks migrating to Germany in the 1960s and 1970s was motivated by labor exchange agreements between Germany and Turkey (Sirkeci & Cohen, 2016). These migrants came as guest workers on contracts. Many Germans believed that the Turks who came as the guest workers would return to Turkey at some point. However, in the 1980s and

1990s, the main purpose of migration to Germany changed as Kurdish refugees escaped political oppression. Kurds dispersed around Europe, with the majority going to Germany. These migrants settled in Germany, began their families and there is now a large Turkish community of Turks and German-Turks. The discrimination and xenophobic biases against Turks and Germans of Turkish descent from German natives is in part due to a fear of Turkish migrants entering their country and starting families. Because the largest migrant group in Germany is from Turkey, issues surrounding Turkish migrants in Germany are prominent in the media and politics. This creates controversy over Turkish migration and communities in Germany and makes these individuals and communities a target for xenophobic actions. I argue that the status of Turks in Germany has not changed, but rather the population has grown and in response to this growth, German attitudes towards them have shifted.

Status of Research on Turkish Migration to Germany

Between 2001 and 2019 the topics of study in research on Turkish migrants shifted. There was a decrease in articles focused on physical and mental health among Turks in Germany. At the same time, there was an increase in articles that compare Turkish and German native health outcomes.

In 2014, there is a noticeable increase in the number of articles that look at the health of Turks in Germany compared to that of German natives. One important topic covered in these articles is smoking. Several articles compare rates of smoking among Turkish men and women to native-born German men and women (Katharine Reiss et. al., 2015). There was a higher number of Turkish smokers than German smokers (Katharine Reiss et. al., 2014) and it was recommended that Turkish smoking rates should be lowered to more closely match those of Germans. This makes smoking a Turkish health issue rather than a general health issue. Turks can be seen as a problem because they are practicing an unhealthy habit. A habit that was initially a "German" trait to be addressed, has become a Turkish problem.

In addition to the shift in the context of the research

completed, there was a decrease in the variety of topics covered from the period between 2001 and 2013 and then between 2014 and 2019. Some topics are present in both periods, emergency care and welfare, cognition, belonging and distress and family and intergenerational transmission, and some only in the first, like physical health, and some that appeared in the second, such as return migration intentions. Between 2001 and 2013 there were topics regarding physical health, family and intergenerational transmission, the labor market, education, citizenship and host culture versus ethnic retention, emergency care and welfare, belonging and identity and how it leads to distress and alienation by the German host culture. Research with the main topic focused on physical health, education, the labor market, alienation by the host culture and citizenship and host culture versus ethnic retention were not present in the articles between 2014 and 2019. However, smoking and return migration intentions were present in that period. The decrease in research variety and representation while the Turkish population in Germany grows leads me to ask why?

Summaries of Articles and Periods

Between 2001 and 2019 there are a variety of topics of investigations regarding Turkish migrants in Germany. However, there is a noticeable shift in the research topics and the context in which they are described, and conclusions drawn. Between the years of 2001 and 2013, many of the articles regarding Turkish migrants in Germany compare physical and mental health within the Turkish migrant population and with Turks in Turkey (Figure 1). On the other hand, between 2014 and 2019 there is an increase of research done on Turkish migrants in Germany that compares the health of Turks in Germany to that of native Germans rather than to that of other Turks (Figure 2). The percentage of research in a Turkish context dropped from 81 percent to 50 percent and the percentage of research in a German context rose from 19 percent to 50 percent. In about half of the articles between 2014 to 2019 the health of Turkish migrants and the children of Turkish migrants were compared to the health of Germans. However Turkish migrants face environmental, political and social pressures that Germans do not. These factors impact health in significant ways and must be included when comparing health outcomes. Germans, unlike Turkish immigrants, do not face discrimination, pressures of acculturation and xenophobia.

Not only did the context in which the research was done change, but the research domains changed as well. Between 2001 and 2013 there was a fairly diverse distribution in research topics and domains (Figure 3). The domain of physical health made up 23.8 percent of research. Research on family and intergenerational transmission, labor market, education, and alienation by host culture included 9.5 percent each; citizenship and host culture versus ethnic retention represented 19 percent; emergency care and welfare 4.8 percent; belonging, identity and distress 9.5 percent; and cognition represented 4.8 percent. In this period there were no articles on smoking or return migration, which becomes an important domain between 2014-2019 (Figure 4). Between 2014 and 2019, smoking made up 25 percent of the research represented. Belonging, identity and distress made up 12.5 percent; family and intergenerational transmission 12.5 percent; return migration intentions included 25 percent; emergency care and welfare was 12.5 percent, and cognition was also 12.5 percent of all research reviewed. In this period certain topics that were present between 2001-2013 are missing, including: physical health, labor market, education, citizenship and host culture versus ethnic retention, and alienation by host culture. While there are articles covering these topics, in my generalized survey they were not present, highly visible or accessible. The shift in contexts and research is not natural and instead reflects how patterns of interest have changed as well as how funding and attitudes are changing.

Importance of these Trends

These findings show how research is affected by and responds to shifting opinions and changing patterns of state support. Specifically, reviewing these pieces shows how German responses to Turkish migrants and German-Turks impact issues that are critical if Turks are to settle safely. There was a significant change from focusing on Turkish culture and health before 2014. After 2014 the focus on Turks in comparison to German natives in regards to health increased. In addition, a focus on how to "fix" what was assumed to be a Turkish problem reflected a shift in investigation. The average age of Muslims in Germany is younger than that of native Germans and Muslims also have more children on average than Germans (Pew Research Center, 2017). With this in mind, even if migration to Germany stopped, the Muslim population in Germany would continue to grow.

While there are several reasons for the changes in study and positioning of the Turkish community in Germany, I argue that this shift is due at least in part to increasing xenophobia as Germans realize that many Turks do not intend to return to Turkey. A 2011 study on the views of German youth on Turks in Germany found that many German youth did not have negative views on Turks in Germany (Benz, 2012). By 2017, the situation was different. The PRC found that while many Germans have positive views on and attitudes toward refugees, many German adults think more refugees in the country increases the chances of terrorism (Pew Research Center, 2017). Many Germans think that Muslims want to be part of a distinct community and will not adopt German customs or integrate into Germany. This contributes to the increase in funding and research encouraging acculturation of Turks.

A citizenship test for Muslim immigrants put into place in Baden Wuerttenbug in 2006, created political controversy and was debated in the media. The test drew a great deal of criticism (Ramm, 2010). Among outcomes of the test, it "Islamized" Turkish immigrants and brought attention to Turks living in Germany as some politicians and "Islam experts" in academia tried to reform the anti-immigration policies in Germany. On the other hand, politicians can also use the xenophobia present in Germans who fear that refugees and Muslim immigrants increase the likelihood of terrorism to fuel anti-immigration agendas, therefore inspiring more xenophobia and distrust of Muslim and Turkish immigrants. Different themes or research should be targeted to fix problems and depoliticize the portrayal of migrants and refugees. This in turn will affect health and wellbeing and sense of belonging among Turkish migrants in a more positive way.

Figure 1. Research Trends on Turkish Migrants in Germany 2001-2013

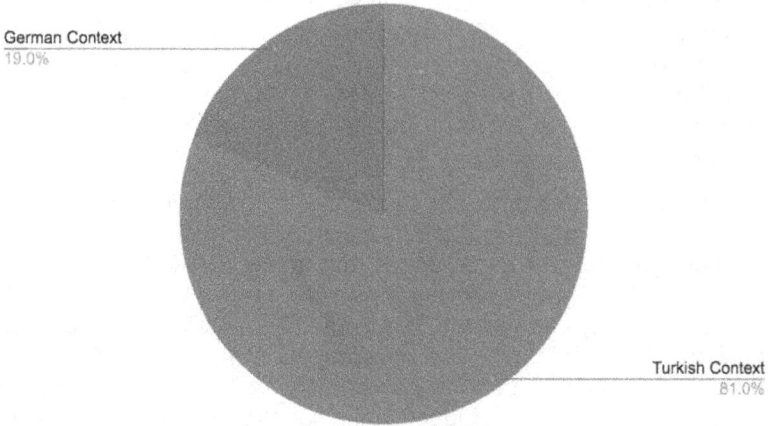

Research Trends on Turkish Migrants in Germany 2001-2013

German Context
19.0%

Turkish Context
81.0%

Figure 2. Research Trends on Turkish Migrants in Germany 2014-2019

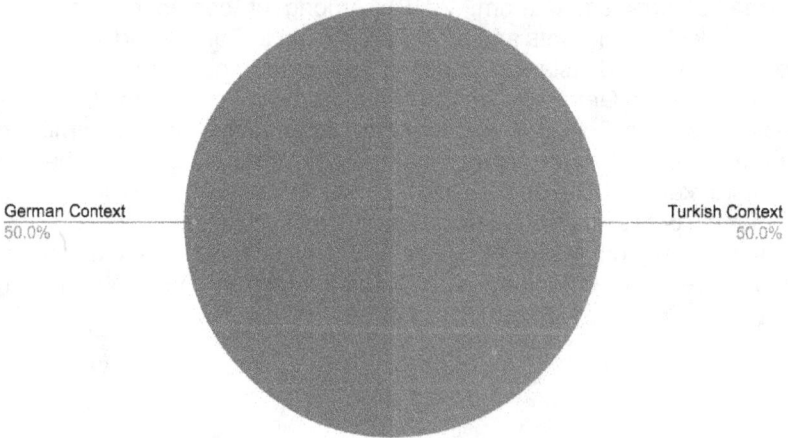

Research Trends on Turkish Migrants in Germany 2014-2019

German Context
50.0%

Turkish Context
50.0%

Figure 3. Distribution of Research by Topic 2001-2013

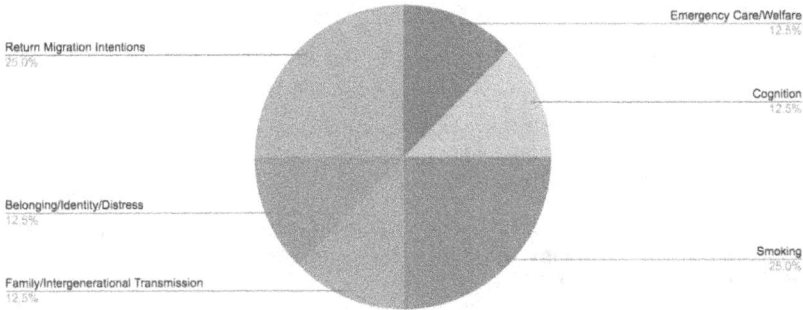

Distribution of Research by Topic 2014-2019

Figure 4. Distribution of Research by Topic 2014-2019

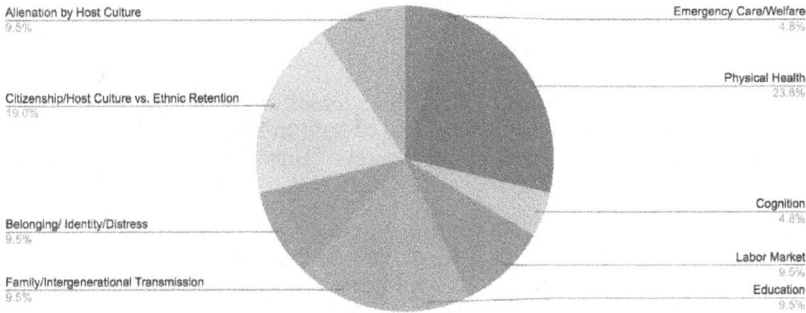

Distribution of Research by Topic 2001-2013

References

Aichberger, M. C., Bromand, Z., Heredia Montesinos, A., Temur-Erman, S., Mundt, A., Heinz, A., Rapp, M. A., & Schouler-Ocak, M. (2012). Socio-economic status and emotional distress of female Turkish immigrants and native German women living in Berlin. *European psychiatry : the journal of the Association of European Psychiatrists, 27 Suppl 2*, S10–S16. https://doi.org/10.1016/S0924-9338(12)75702-4

Becker, B. (2009). Immigrants' emotional identification with the host society: The example of Turkish parents' naming practices in Germany. *Ethnicities, 9*(2), 200–225. https://doi.org/10.1177/1468796809103460

Becker, B. (2013). The impact of familial activities on the verbal and non-verbal skills of children of Turkish immigrants in Germany. *International Research in Early Childhood Education, 4*(1), 91-104. doi:10.4225/03/5817e68869b29

Benz, C. (2012). "'Türkenproblematik' 2011: Views of German Youth Towards the Turkish Minority." *Clocks and Clouds, 2*(1). Retrieved from http://www.inquiriesjournal.com/a?id=1612

Biedinger, N., Becker, B., & Klein, O. (2015) Turkish-language ability of children of immigrants in Germany: which contexts of exposure influence preschool children's acquisition of their heritage language?: *Ethnic and Racial Studies*, (38)9, 1520-1538. doi: 10.1080/01419870.2015.1005641

Crul, M., & Schneider, J. (2009). Children of turkish immigrants in Germany and the Netherlands: The impact of differences in vocational and academic tracking systems. *Teachers College Record*, *111*(6), 1508-1527. https://www.tcrecord.org/content.asp?contentid=15333

Diehl, C., & Liebau, E. (2015). Turning back to Turkey – Or Turning the Back on Germany? *Zeitschrift Für Soziologie, 44*(1), 22-41. doi:10.1515/zfsoz-2015-0104

Ehrkamp, P. & Helga Leitner (2003) Beyond National Citizenship: Turkish Immigrants and the (RE)Construction of Citizenship in Germany: *Urban Geography*, (24)2, 127-146, doi: 10.2747/0272-3638.24.2.127

Ehrkamp, P. (2005) Placing identities: Transnational practices and local attachments of Turkish immigrants in Germany: *Journal of Ethnic and Migration Studies*, (31)2, 345-364, doi: 10.1080/1369183042000339963

Erkal, M. Z., Wilde, J., Bilgin, Y., Akinci, A., Demir, E., Bödeker, R. H., Mann, M., Bretzel, R. G., Stracke, H., & Holick, M. F. (2006). High prevalence of vitamin D deficiency, secondary hyperparathyroidism and generalized bone pain in Turkish immigrants in Germany: identification of risk factors. *Osteoporosis international : a journal established as result of cooperation between the European Foundation for Osteoporosis and the National Osteoporosis Foundation of the USA, 17*(8), 1133–1140. https://doi.org/10.1007/s00198-006-0069-2

Ersanilli, Evelyn & Koopmans, Ruud, 2009. Ethnic retention and host culture adoption among Turkish immigrants in Germany, France and the Netherlands: A controlled comparison. Discussion Papers, Research Unit: Migration, Integration, Transnationalization SP IV 2009-701, WZB Berlin Social Science Center.

Ersanilli, E. & Koopmans, R. (2010) Rewarding Integration? Citizenship Regulations and the Socio-Cultural Integration of Immigrants in the Netherlands, France and Germany. *Journal of Ethnic and Migration Studies*, (36)5, 773-791, doi: 10.1080/13691831003764318

Euwals, Rob and Dagevos, Jaco and Gijsberts, Mérove and Roodenburg, Hans, Immigration, Integration and the Labour Market: Turkish Immigrants in Germany and the Netherlands (March 2007). IZA Discussion Paper No. 2677, Available at SSRN: https://ssrn.com/abstract=978762 or http://dx.doi.org/10.2139/ssrn.978762

Euwals, R., Dagevos, J., Gijsberts, M., & Roodenburg, H. (2010). The Labour Market Position of Turkish Immigrants in Germany and the Netherlands: Reason for Migration, Naturalisation and Language Proficiency. *International Migration Review, 44*(3), 513-538. doi:10.2139/ssrn.978780

Humphrey, M. (2011). The Securitization and Domestication of Diaspora Muslims and Islam: The case of Turkish immigrants in Germany and Australia. *International Journal on Multicultural Societies, 11*(2), 136-154. www.unesco.org/shs/ijms/vol11/issue2/art2

Kietzmann, D., Knuth, D., & Schmidt, S. (2017). (Non-)utilization of pre-hospital emergency care by migrants and non-migrants in Germany. *International journal of public health, 62*(1), 95–102. https://doi.org/10.1007/s00038-016-0904-y

Kotwal A. A. (2010). Physical and psychological health of first and second generation Turkish immigrants in Germany. *American journal of human biology : the official journal of the Human Biology Council, 22*(4), 538–545. https://doi.org/10.1002/ajhb.21044

Pew Research Center. (2017, November 29). The Growth of Germany's Muslim Population. Retrieved November 14, 2020, from https://www.pewforum.org/essay/the-growth-of-germanys-muslim-population/

Krist, L., Keller, T., Sebald, L., Yesil-Jürgens, R., Ellert, U., Reich, A., Becher, H., Heuschmann, P. U., Willich, S. N., Keil, T., & Liman, T. G. (2019). The Montreal Cognitive Assessment (MoCA) in a population-based sample of Turkish migrants living in Germany. *Aging & mental health*, *23*(1), 30–37. https://doi.org/10.1080/13607863.2017.1396577

Kristen, C., Reimer, D., & Kogan, I. (2008). Higher Education Entry of Turkish Immigrant Youth in Germany. *International Journal of Comparative Sociology*, *49*(2–3), 127–151. https://doi.org/10.1177/0020715208088909

Morawa, E., & Erim, Y. (2014). Acculturation and depressive symptoms among Turkish immigrants in Germany. *International journal of environmental research and public health*, *11*(9), 9503–9521. https://doi.org/10.3390/ijerph110909503

Phalet, K., & Schönpflug, U. (2001). Intergenerational Transmission of Collectivism and Achievement Values in Two Acculturation Contexts: The Case of Turkish Families in Germany and Turkish and Moroccan Families in the Netherlands. *Journal of Cross-Cultural Psychology*, *32*(2), 186–201. https://doi.org/10.1177/0022022101032002006

Porsch-Ozcürümez, M., Doppl, W., Hardt, P. D., Schnell-Kretschmer, H., Tuncay, M., Akinci, A., Bilgin, Y., & Klör, H. U. (2003). Impact of migration on Helicobacter pylori seroprevalence in the offspring of Turkish immigrants in Germany. *The Turkish journal of pediatrics*, *45*(3), 203–208.

Ramm, C. (2010) THE MUSLIM MAKERS: How Germany 'Islamizes Turkish Immigrants. *International Journal of Postcolonial Studies*, (12)2, 183-197, doi: 10.1080/1369801X.2010.489692

Reiss K, Breckenkamp J, Borde T, et al. (2014) Smoking during pregnancy among Turkish immigrants in Germany-are there associations with acculturation? Nicotine & Tobacco Research. *Official Journal of the Society for Research on Nicotine and Tobacco*. 17(6), 643-652. DOI: 10.1093/ntr/ntu237.

Reiss, K., Schunck, R., & Razum, O. (2015). Effect of Length of Stay on Smoking among Turkish and Eastern European Immigrants in Germany--Interpretation in the Light of the Smoking Epidemic Model and the Acculturation Theory. *International journal of environmental research and public health*, *12*(12), 15925–15936. https://doi.org/10.3390/ijerph121215030

Riphahn, R. T., Sander, M., & Wunder, C. (2010). The welfare use of immigrants and natives in Germany: The case of Turkish immigrants. *International Journal of Manpower, 34*(1), 70-82. doi:10.1108/01437721311319665

Sirkeci, I., Cohen, J. H., & Yazgan, P. (2012). Turkish culture of migration: Flows between Turkey and Germany, socio-economic development and conflict. *Migration Letters, 9*(1), 33-46. doi:10.33182/ml.v9i1.201

Sirkeci, I., & Cohen, J. H. (2016). Cultures of Migration and Conflict in Contemporary Human Mobility in Turkey. *European Review, 24*(3), 381-396. doi:10.1017/s1062798716000119

Steinmann, J. (2019). One-way or return? Explaining group-specific return intentions of recently arrived

Polish and Turkish immigrants in Germany. *Migration Studies*, (7)1, 117-151. https://doi.org/10.1093/migration/mnx073

Tarner, I. H., Erkal, M. Z., Obermayer-Pietsch, B. M., Hofbauer, L. C., Bergmann, S., Goettsch, C., Madlener, K., Müller-Ladner, U., & Lange, U. (2012). Osteometabolic and osteogenetic pattern of Turkish immigrants in Germany. *Experimental and clinical endocrinology & diabetes : official journal, German Society of Endocrinology [and] German Diabetes Association, 120*(9), 517–523. https://doi.org/10.1055/s-0032-1321808

Wengler, A. The health status of first- and second-generation Turkish immigrants in Germany. *Int J Public Health* 56, 493–501 (2011). https://doi.org/10.1007/s00038-011-0254-8

Zielke-Nadkarni, A. (2003). The Meaning of the Family: Lived Experiences of Turkish Women Immigrants in Germany. *Nursing Science Quarterly, 16*(2), 169–173. https://doi.org/10.1177/0894318403251797

850   Perception of 1864

Melike Batgıray Abboud

Circassian Migration transformed into the mass movement in the second half of the nineteenth century after the Tsarist Russia's oppressions in the area. Although it was investigated deeply, public opinion about the Circassian migration fell on stony ground. The article aims to understand how the process of migration was perceived by immigrants and how it was passed on to generations, how it was reproduced by third and the fourth generations and tries to understand their perceptions and feelings about migration.

The purpose of this study was to show the perception of migration in the public's memory in the light of my experiences during the field researches I conducted in different cities of Turkey where the migrants were settled by the Ottoman Empire, not to reveal historicity. The method of the study was oral history. The study tries to explain how the immigrants' grandchildren perceives and explains the "1864".

My research findings indicate that, although the Ottoman Empire's archive was relatively fertile to understand the settlements of the Circassians, there were great numbers of cases which did not reflect the Ottoman archival documents such as "lost villages". During the study, the term "lost village" was used for the abandoned or vanished villages which were given to the Circassians to settle by the Ottoman Empire. Although the first settlement history of the villages could be seen in the archival documents, it is impossible to understand the reason of being "lost" of these villages without field research and oral history. Thanks to the oral history, immigrants' unregistered stories during the road to Ottoman land filled some important gaps in migration studies thanks to the memories which were passed down by word of mouth.

The another purpose of the research was to understand the ordinary immigrant who could not find a place himself in the archival documents, and the ordinary immigrant who we need to know in point of fact. It should not be forgotten that, migration was formed by individual concerns. At that point, historian needs to know people's own concerns to understand the process in addition to written documents.

As a result, this study has two purposes: the first is to understand the current migration perception of the descendants of the immigrants that started in 1856, and the second, more methodologically, is to reveal how useful oral history will be to historians in migration studies.

800   Internal Migration and Higher Education in Turkey: University Expansion between 197-1975

Caner Tekin

The relationship between migration and higher education has not been a much-discussed subject in the literature concerning Turkey's migration history. If anything, Turkey's higher education guidelines from the 1950s developed, among other things, as a response to population change, urbanisation, and demands of the ever-increasing high school graduates for university education.

This study addresses a part of this period and discusses the relevance of the higher education policy for urbanisation, increasing student demands for university placements, socioeconomic development in cities and nation-state development between 1970 and 1975, during which 9 new public universities were founded in the province. To this end, it investigates the relevant amendments in the higher education law, their debates in the parliament (parliamentary minutes), and the State Planning Organisation's five-year development reports regarding this era. The study thus aims to give historical insights into the debates between governments, political parties, and the bureaucracy over Turkey's higher education policy and migration management.

5C   Latin America y migracion (Spanish)
Chair: Pascual Garcia-Macias, Universidad Tecnica Particular de Loja, Ecuador
587   Aporofobia y nacionalismo: el rechazo al inmigrante (pobre)
Laura Natalia Rodriguez Ariano
594   Retos para la Adaptacion Economiica y Social de la Poblacion Inmigrante Venezolana en el sur de Ecuador
Jessica Andrea Ordonez
609   International migration from Central America and Mexico to the United States in 221 in the face of structural crises, the Covid 19 and the Biden government
Rodolfo Garcia Zamora and Selene Gaspar Olvera
611   Migracion de jubilados en las playas del noroeste mexicano
Pascual Garcia

587 Aporofobia y nacionalismo: el rechazo al inmigrante (pobre)

Laura Natalia Rodriguez Ariano

Las migraciones tienen un papel fundamental en la historia. Implican un proceso de integración demográfica de culturas distintas, es decir, no existe un sentido universal de las migraciones y las condiciones históricas e integridad se han ido transformando paulatinamente.

Gran parte de las migraciones del siglo XXI son forzosas y no van en busca de un sueño, suerte y fortuna, van en busca de un trabajo, huyen de sus países de origen debido a los problemas políticos, sociales y económicos. Algunas externalidades negativas de las migraciones a nivel mundial son discriminación, violencia e intolerancia que desatan las diferentes fobias hacia el que es considerado diferente, el otro, el que no pertenece al lugar, ya sea por tener características físicas, ideológicas y costumbres distintas.

Actualmente vivimos en un mundo, donde el ser humano ha denotado más distinciones entre el <<*nosotros y el ellos*>> haciendo una fuerte alusión hacia la otredad, lo que le es distinto, lo que no es parte de su entorno. El rechazo frente a esta otredad resulta un factor inamovible para las personas, donde muchos dejan a flor de piel sus *espíritus animales* y el poder adquisitivo juega un papel fundamental al diferenciar y menospreciar a otro ser humano por su capacidad adquisitiva. Se trata de un problema de pobreza, característica común entre la población, **aporofobia.**

Una de las principales problemáticas a nivel mundial y que se presenta con gran frecuencia en contra de la población inmigrante, la aporofobia es clave importante para entender los conflictos políticos y sociales en la actualidad. Sin justificar ningún tipo de rechazo, esta provoca odio a la población de bajos recursos. Lo anterior, aunado a la intolerancia por raza, etnia, preferencia sexual, religión o extranjería propicia una animadversión aún más grande.

Los diferentes tipos de intolerancia disfrazadas de *fobias* propician una nueva forma de realizar política, donde los gobernantes de varios países, utilizan mecanismos de exclusión como parte de sus campañas y discursos políticos para conseguir un resultado favorable dentro del voto popular. En donde, no tienen mucho por ofrecer y buscan a quien *echarle la culpa* de los problemas coyunturales en los que se encuentra su país, prometiendo acabar con los *causantes* de su inestabilidad social, económica y política.

Este mal presenta una tesis que afirma ser un mecanismo de defensa biológico. A pesar de que existen varios discursos de lo políticamente correcto y de igualdad entre los seres humanos, sólo quedan en discurso, las acciones muestran lo opuesto. Lo que es un hecho, es que la aporofobia es una realidad desde tiempo atrás.

594 Retos para la Adaptacion Economiica y Social de la Poblacion Inmigrante Venezolana en el sur de Ecuador

Jessica Andrea Ordonez

El objetivo de este estudio es analizar las actitudes xenofóbicas y discriminatorias con respecto a este colectivo, los cuales les imponen límites en los niveles de poder y disfrute de sus derechos. Este estudio de tipo cualitativo y cuantitativo que parte de una encuesta de percepción dirigida a la población total del cantón Loja, sur de Ecuador, en el mes de diciembre de 2020, donde se utilizó un muestreo aleatorio simple. Se determinó la percepción, positiva y negativa, sobre las personas respecto de la presencia de inmigrantes de origen venezolano en la mencionada ciudad.Se determina que la población lojana considera que el número de inmigrantes venezolanos que hay en la ciudad es elevado, estos son tratados con desconfianza, se considera que influyen en la reducción de los salarios e incremento del desempleo de los lojanos. Los locales desconocen que los migrantes al igual que los nativos son personas portadoras de derechos y, que deberían aprender la cultura local.

609 International migration from Central America and Mexico to the United States in 221 in the face of structural crises, the Covid 19 and the Biden government

Rodolfo Garcia Zamora and Selene Gaspar Olvera

At the beginning of 2021, new migrant caravans from Central America are announced, the record of 40 billion dollars of remittances in Mexico and a new, less restrictive immigration policies of the Government of President Biden. The new caravans were stopped in Honduras and Guatemala with strong pressure from the United States, Mexico offers to collaborate with the new government of that country in migration policy in the region and Biden offers to suspend the construction of the wall, promote the legalization of 11 million undocumented immigrants, support the legalization of 600 000 "dreamers", reverse the separation of 500 children from their families, re-establish the asylum and refugee policy and announce an investment of 4 billion dollars for the development of Central America. All this undergrowth of Covid 19 in the region and an economic collapse. In the absence of economic development strategies in the migrant's countries of origin, their reactivation and migration will depend on the reactivation of the United States economy, its investments and migration policies in the region.

611 Migracion de jubilados en las playas del noroeste mexicano

Pascual Garcia

En los últimos treinta años, en el contexto de la globalización económica las migraciones han adquirido mayor importancia a nivel mundial, no sólo los flujos dirección del Sur al Norte, sino también entre regiones del Sur al Sur y en los últimos años, ha tomado un auge del Norte a Sur con determinados flujos migratorios como los de los pensionados (provenientes del norte económico) que buscan un mayor nivel de calidad de vida al final de su vida. Los cambios radicales en los medios de transporte y en las tecnologías de la información, así como el envejecimiento de la población de los países ricos, los impactos negativos de las políticas económicas de ajuste estructural en el norte y el deterioro de la calidad de vida de los jubilados, conlleva el plantearse migrar a sitios donde su bienestar no se vea mermado.

En cuanto a estos migrantes pensionados son considerados por algunos como turistas residenciales, ya que no encajan en los marcos teóricos y en el arquetipo de migrante trabajador proveniente de países subdesarrollados y que emigra a países con mejores condiciones económicas. Tampoco es un turista normal, puesto que sus estancias se prolongan durante meses o incluso años. Esta ambigüedad y discrepancia de conceptos hacen que actualmente no se encuentre bien definida la tipología de migración que ellos realizan, algunos teóricos la definen como "migración privilegiada" (Croucher, 2012); mientras otros estudiosos la catalogan como "turismo residencial" (Huete y Mantecón, 2011); otras perspectivas lo enfocan a la manera de "estilos de vida migratorios" o *life style migration*" (O´Reilly y Benson, 2009); incluso hay quienes basan sus estudios en las comodidades o amenidades que los lugares de acogida les brindan utilizando el término de "*amenities migration*" (Bustamante, 2012; Pera, 2008); existen otros investigadores que cimientan sus estudios en los procesos de envejecimiento "*aging migration*" o "*aging in place*" utilizando el término para describir a la persona que vive en un lugar por elección propia y con fines de envejecer el tiempo necesario que la vida le permita (Johansson et al., 2012). Finalmente otros estudian el vínculo entre el lugar donde radican los adultos mayores y los cambios que producen en dichas comunidades (Prisuta, Barrett y Evans, 2006).

Sun embargo, la mayor parte de la literatura sobre este tema no ahonda en dilucidar las razones por las cuales los adultos mayores deciden dejar su país de origen. Se obvian las razones bajo un discurso de la oferta y de las virtudes que poseen los sitios de destino (playas, bajos costos de vivienda, buen clima todo el año, tranquilidad, etcétera) pero los contextos de salida y estructuras económico, político y sociales se omiten. De tal manera que, como lo comenta Hayes (2013), es necesario desarrollar una perspectiva que vaya más allá del enfoque sustentado en la elección racional y que a su vez integre estructura y agencia en el análisis, donde exista un análisis minucioso de los procesos sociales. Para de esta manera; poder conceptualizar mejor el fenómeno de esta migración y ampliar el concepto y dimensiones de estos agentes transnacionales jubilados.

5D   Gender, Sexuality and Migration
Chair: Wendelmoet Hamelink, University of Oslo, Norway
681   Masculinities at The Crossroad: War, Migration and Urban Poverty in The Case of Syrian Men in Ankara
Saeid Mozafari
786   The refugee journey: Gendered narratives of displacement, loss and hope by Syrian Kurdish women
Wendelmoet Hamelink

681   Masculinities at The Crossroad: War, Migration and Urban Poverty in The Case of Syrian Men in Ankara

Saeid Mozafari

Many countries around the world have to face with the social, political and economic effects of forced migration as a humanitarian problem. In this regard, due to the outbreak of Syrian Civil War and its geopolitical position in the Middle East, Turkey has been hosting diverse migrant groups including Syrian refugees whose numbers is almost four million. Such a considerable population of Syrian refugees has become an important issue to be studied. Consequently, there is a substantial increase in the researches focusing on different aspects of Syrians' lives in Turkey especially with regard to women and children. However, despite the antagonistic relations between war, forced migration, poverty and masculinity, the question of the masculinities of Syrian refugees in Turkey has remained untouched. Accordingly, this study by focusing on the Syrian men living in Ankara's lower-class neighborhoods aims to draw an image of the impacts of the crucial conditions such as the war, the forced migration and the poverty on their masculinities. In this context, this study intends to answer the question that what are the forms of masculinities in crises and how are they perceived? How new masculinities are mediated through the conditions of forced migration and urban poverty in the case of Syrian refugee men in some neighborhoods in Ankara? Therefore, in order to probe the essence of the interactions between such conditions and masculinities, this study uses qualitative research methods. Data collection techniques consist of in-depth semi-structured interviews with 17 Syrian men and doing observations in their homes where interviews took place. Moreover, in order to have an extensive understanding of everyday life of urban poor Syrian families, observations have done in the neighborhoods where mostly lower-class Syrians live. In this way, research findings indicate that the catastrophic effects of the civil war in Syria, the forced migration and the harsh conditions of poverty in Turkey paved the way for a multilayered crisis in Syrian men's masculinities. Furthermore, other dimensions of crisis in masculinities were determined by factors such as religious conservatism and the age of participants which helped them to ignore and conceal the existing crisis. The patriarchal regime intertwined with religion or age also provides Syrian refugee men with the opportunity of reproducing crisis-ridden masculinities. For instance, some Syrian refugee men describing himself as a conservative persons feel deficient as father due to the change in their employment position but at the same time they hold that they are the ones who say the last word in the family. However, younger Syrian men also by accepting their inability in fulfilling their gender role expectations, emphasizing on importance of consultation in domestic responsibilities especially with their wife.

786   The refugee journey: Gendered narratives of displacement, loss and hope by Syrian Kurdish women

Wendelmoet Hamelink

This paper investigates the narratives of Syrian Kurdish women who settled in Turkey and Scandinavia during the Syrian war. Based on life story interviews with 20 women, the paper will focus on the specific challenges that women were facing during the process of deciding to leave, traveling, and staying in places along the route. Women talked about what made them leave Syria at a particular moment; about what loss they suffered because of leaving their homes, relatives and country behind; and about what they gained or are hoping for. The research takes a narrative and biographical approach (Halfacree & Boyle 1993) in order to gain insights into the ways in which the women's journeys were influenced by their longer personal and intersectional histories, and cultural histories of women's mobility and intergenerational family relations (Anthias 2012). Rather than only focusing on the direct context of the war, women's journeys are life events that, as this study argues, can only be understood within these larger histories (Thomas & Dommermuth 2020).

The paper will also pay attention to the refugee journey as a process; most journeys did not have a straightforward, planned character from A to B, but unfolded over time while traveling from one place to the next, first within Syria, and then abroad. Often, women had expected to return to their homes sooner or later but realized on the way that returning had become impossible. Staying in different places along the route informed their decisions what to do next. Women often talked about this process in a gendered way: being a woman gave someone different options for how and where to go than being a man. Moreover, the journey could lead to a renegotiation of gender roles, in which women began to see themselves differently and took on different roles (Vaiou 2012 pays attention to this issue). Although Migration Studies has increasingly paid attention to the gendered nature of migration (Marchetti 2018, Mahler & Pessar 2006), this continues to be an understudied area, especially in the context of conflict and violence. The study aims to fill this gap, both through its long-term biographical approach as well as its gendered perspective.

References

Anthias, Floya. (2012). "Transnational mobilities, migration studies and intersectionality. Towards a translocational frame." *Nordic Journal of Migration Research* 2 (2): 102-110.

Halfacree, Keith H. and Paul J. Boyle. (1993). "The challenge facing migration research: the case for a biographical approach." *Progress in Human Geography* 17 (3): 333-348.

Mahler, Sarah J. and Patricia R. Pessar. (2006). "Gender matters: ethnographers bringing gender from the periphery toward the core of migration studies." *International Migration Review* 40 (1): 27-63.

Marchetti, Sabrina. (2018). "Gender, migration and globalisation: an overview of the debates." *Handbook of migration and globalization*, ed. Anna Triandafyllidou, Cheltenham/Northampton: Edward Elgar Publishing: 444-457.

Thomas, Michael and Lars Dommermuth. (2020). "Internal Migration and the Role of Intergenerational Family Ties and Life Events." *Journal of marriage and family*. DOI: 10.1111/jomf.12678.

Vaiou, Dina. (2012). "Gendered mobilities and border crossings: from Elbasan to Athens. *Gender, Place and Culture* 19 (2): 249-262.

789   Gender differences in post-crisis emigrations from Spain

Sandra Lopez-Pereiro

The map of migrations in Spain has changed dramatically during the last decades. The country started the new century becoming a major destination of migration for the first time in its history. However, this trend was challenged by the 2008 crisis and its further consequences, which caused a decrease in the number of arrivals and the activation of new emigrant flows. More than a decade after 2008 and before the COVID crisis, macroeconomic indicators showed signs of recovery, but the labour market was still terribly damaged and characterised by high levels of insecurity and bad labour conditions. Consequently, emigration flows showed a decrease, although they were far from stopping completely.

When dealing with a migration phenomenon that seems strongly connected to working conditions and precarity, gender can play an important role which deserves attention. Some aspects highly marked by gender such as inequality on the labour market, differences in expectations and caring responsibilities are important elements which influence migratory trajectories and discourses. On the other hand, the European Union offers a wide range of scenarios regarding employment, conciliation, co-responsibility and labour relations. Different countries also mean having different political and labour frames to escape from precarity, so they can be chosen by migrants in accordance with different points of view and priorities. The significance of these factors is higher in the intra-European migration's scenario, where other constrictive factors connected to movement restrictions lose their importance.

The aim of this research is to identify the gender differences in trajectories, motivations, and discourses of the after-crisis Spanish migrants. In order to fulfil it, a qualitative research has been developed, since the objects of study since are more suitable for this kind of approach. Moreover, the lack of accuracy of official migration data makes it difficult to identify gender differences by using quantitative methods, since data do not cover all the migrants and they do not offer interesting variables to analyse. Semi-structured interviews to post-crisis emigrants from Spain were developed, focusing on their trajectories, discourses and projects. They were carefully analysed by using discourse analysis techniques. A gender perspective was applied to the analysis, as well as a caring-centred approach.

The result is an exploratory map of the detected gender differences. The topic seems to be an interesting line of research which could be enormously enriched by new and richer migration data sources.

*This research is embedded within a thesis dissertation in progress and the NUEMIG project, funded by the Spanish Ministry of Economic Affairs.

815 Countering Discrimination and Hate Speech: Gender, Culture and Migration in New Media Environment

Selçuk Çetin and Tuğba Asrak Hasdemir

After the beginning of civil war in Syria in 2011, very significant number of Syrian people had to leave their country and emigrate by force. Many migrants were displaced to the different regions of Turkey. Today, in the World, Turkey is the country in which the largest number of Syrian migrants live. At the beginning, Syrian people were located are in refugee camps. In time, they have moved to the different regions and cities of Turkey in relation to the sudden and huge increases in the number of migrants people. Nowadays, Syrians are one of the migrant groups who become the new actors of social and business life in Turkey. They are now encountering local people more often in different part of Turkey. Unfortunately, the encounters between Syrians migrants and local people does not result in understanding and accepting each other in general. Some negative attitudes are demonstrated towards Syrian migrant people and we can detect signs of this negativity towards Syrians in media environment including the digital media. Racist-discriminatory and hate speech content can be easily circulated in digital media environment by finding supporters. Étienne Balibar purported that new modality of racism as "racism without race" is quite different from racism based on biological heredity (Balibar & Wallerstein, 2000). According to him, neo-racism now tends to be focused on "cultural differences". In the case of negative tone and attitudes towards migrant people, neo form of racism preserve the pillars of segregation. The concept of neo-racism and discussions around this concept will be useful in addressing the issue in relation to racist-discriminatory attitudes towards to the migrant people in new media environment. Beside it, hate speech themes which are defined and described by the studies conducted in Hrant Dink Foundation to assess the "hate speech in the media" will be helpful in the analysis of hate speech content in new media environment (Güvengez, at all, 2020) This paper aims to elaborate racist-discriminatory discourses against Syrian migrant in a famous and most visited new media platform, *Ekşi Sözlük* (in Turkish). Like *Urban Dictionary* which is known worldwide, *Ekşi Sözlük* is a crowdsourced online dictionary. Within the scope of the study, the contents under the heading "Syrian Migrants" will be analyzed with Van Dijk's critical discourse analysis method (Dijk, 1988). His analysis especially will focus on the racist-discriminatory discourses in relation to the genders and culture. Furthermore, this paper will be concluded with certain suggestions on what is to be done to create awareness and eliminate racist-discriminatory discourses in the new media environment.

References

Balibar, E., & Wallerstein, I. (2000). Irk, Ulus, Sınıf. İstanbul: Metis.

Güvengez, S., Özkan, Ş., Saç, E., Sert, G., Söyler, M., & Tekin, F. (2020). Medyada Nefret Söylemi ve Ayrımcı Söylem 2019 Raporu. İstanbul: HDV Yayınları.

Van Dijk, Teun A. (1988). News as Discourse. New Jersey: Lawrence Erlbaum Associates Publication.

5E Migration, Politics and Law

Chair: *Ülkü Sezgi Sözen, University of Hamburg, Germany*

691 Non DAC donors and migration flows in the Third World
Megumi Nishimura
703 How do country of birth and citizenship affect perceptions of crime?
Gianluca Bortoletto
726 "They Know We Can't Go to the Police: Narratives on Violence and Robbery from Sub-Saharan African Transit Migrants in Istanbul
Abdirashid Diriye Kalmoy

691 Non DAC donors and migration flows in the Third World

Megumi Nishimura

One of the most constroversial phenomenon in the recent world politics is the increasingly aggresive economic assistance and foreign aids of Non-DAC donors (non members of the OECD's Development Assistance Committee), such as China, India, Brazil, Saudi Arabia, and Russia. Their foreign aids cover the divergent areas, such as medical, agricultural, and epidmiological assistance as well as vast investments in strategic resources.

This paper addresses the issue whether and how their aids differ from those of the OECD-DAC on the impacts of migration or population flows in the Third World in Asia and Africa. The case study includes South Africa, Ethiopia, the DRC, and Angola

703 How do country of birth and citizenship affect perceptions of crime?

Gianluca Bortoletto

The link between immigration and the crime rates, especially in the host countries, has been extensively studied in the previous literature. In this study, I explore how country of birth and citizenship at individual-level, defined as EU, non-EU or native (e.g., a person living in Italy who is born in another EU country will be categorised as a EU-born, non-EU if born in a non-EU country and native if born in Italy and the same holds for citizenship) affect crime perceptions at household-level. I explore this research question in a repeated cross-sectional framework using data form the European Survey on Income and Living Conditions (EU-SILC) for a pool of European countries over the period 2004-10. I also consider the interaction effect of citizenship and country of birth with other variables that the literature predicts to be relevant in affecting crime rates. I do not find evidence of a significant impact of country of birth or citizenship on crime. Also, while other factors, such as socio-economic status, population density in the area of living and others, are significant and present a robust effect on crime perceptions, the effect of country of birth and citizenship and of their interaction terms is very context-dependent and not robust to different specifications. Further research should be conducted perhaps combining household data with the characteristics of the neighbourhood where the household lives.

726 "They Know We Can't Go to the Police: Narratives on Violence and Robbery from Sub-Saharan African Transit Migrants in Istanbul

Abdirashid Diriye Kalmoy

Migrants face on daily basis different forms of violence and violations in the migration routes and destinations from police, border patrols, human smugglers, gangs, thieves, guides, local inhabitants and from other fellow migrants. Istanbul has become over the years one of the most consequential destination and gateway to "fortress" Europe. Given the city's proximity to the Greek and Bulgarian borders, it has become a crucial nexus in a complex and global-wide network of migrants' trails, routes and destinations. The subject matter of this study is sub-Saharan African Transit migrants who are stuck and live in Istanbul's Aksaray and Tarlabaşı districts and how they face violence, racism and robbery which have become widespread in these migrant-preferred spaces. While Aksaray and Tarlabaşı have become safe haven for diverse groups of migrants, they have also become "hell" during the night as gangs and thieves unleash violence and robbery. Moreover, transit migrants face death, violence and assistance in the Aegean Sea and in the borderlands between Turkey, Greece and Bulgaria during the migration process. Furthermore, these two districts are portrayed in the Turkish media and social discourses as drug-infested and red-light districts where state laws are non-applicable once darkness falls. My study is based on twenty ethnographic interviews conducted with sub-Saharan African transit migrants. While the districts of Aksaray and Tarlabaşı and their residents are demonized in the social and political discourses and sensationalised by the media, my study aspires to give primacy to the narratives and accounts of their residents, and how they lead their day to day lives amid economic and social precarity, "illegality", violence, racism, solidarity, assistance and robbery. The objective of my study is to give voice and agency to the narratives, voices and perspectives of migrants as they transit through Istanbul to Europe. This study aims to contribute to the burgeoning studies of sub-Saharan African transit migrants in Turkey and also challenge scholarly works that implicitly or explicitly disregard migrants' narratives, life-stories, accounts, perspectives and views in the migration experiences and processes.

5F Religion and Migration

Chair: Eric M Trinka, James Madison University, USA

525 Buddhism, International Humanitarian Law, and the Protection of Internally Displaced People
Christina Anne Kilby

546 Representations of the Holy Land: The Impressions of Two Transnational Populations of Living and Working in the Kingdom of Saudi Arabia

Simeon S Magliveras and Sumanto Al Qurtuby

525 Buddhism, International Humanitarian Law, and the Protection of Internally Displaced People

Christina Anne Kilby

Displacement is a common consequence of armed conflict that entails acute suffering and loss of protection. The prevention of displacement and the protection of displaced people are integral concerns of International Humanitarian Law (IHL), which prohibits displacement unless a civilian population's security requires it, and which also requires appropriate provisions for the safety, shelter, health, hygiene, nutrition, and family unity of the displaced.[17] While refugees fall under the protection of the United Nations, internally displaced people or IDPs remain within the bounds of their state of citizenship or habitual residence. When that state is at war, the government on which displaced people should normally rely for protection and assistance may be unable or unwilling to provide for their welfare. Furthermore, respect for the sovereignty of states can hinder international humanitarian intervention on behalf of IDPs. For this reason, IDPs are particularly vulnerable to prolonged suffering and lack of protection during times of armed conflict, even though they are included in the provisions of IHL.

The objective of this research presentation is to investigate several intellectual resources that Buddhist tradition offers for analyzing the causes of displacement, the responsibilities of sovereign governments, and the protection of displaced people. I employ a critical-constructive approach to analyzing Buddhist texts in order to probe the implications of karma, the gift of fearlessness,[18] and the five precepts of Buddhist practice[19] for building a Buddhist ethic of IDP protection that aligns with the mandates of IHL. This research is part of a larger project initiated by the International Committee of the Red Cross that explores intersections between Buddhism and IHL in order to enhance the understanding and implementation of IHL in Buddhist-majority societies.[20]

---

[17] Customary IHL Rules 129 and 130 prohibit forced displacement of domestic or occupied populations. Rules 131, 132, and 133 outline the requirements of protection and care for the displaced. Rule 24 requires displacement of civilians from the vicinity of military objectives. From the *IHL Database: Customary IHL*, accessed at https://ihl-databases.icrc.org/customary-ihl/eng/docs/v1_rul on February 22, 2021.
[18] Here I build on the research I published in "The Global Refugee Crisis and the Gift of Fearlessness." *Journal of Buddhist Ethics.* Vol. 26: pp. 307-327.
[19] I draw in particular on the *Upāsakaśīlasūtra (The Sutra on Upāsaka Precepts)* and on the *Abhisanda Sutta* (On Rewards), from the *Anguttara Nikaya* 8.39.
[20] The project website is hosted at https://blogs.icrc.org/religion-humanitarianprinciples/category/

546   Representations of the Holy Land: The Impressions of Two Transnational Populations of Living and Working in the Kingdom of Saudi Arabia

Simeon S Magliveras and Sumanto Al Qurtuby

Focusing on both professional and "unskilled" Filipino and Indonesian expatriates in Saudi Arabia, this paper examines how these two transnational communities envisage their lives in the Kingdom. Saudi Arabia's Filipinos and Indonesians are interesting because (1) the two groups comprise the Kingdom's largest Southeast Asian transnationals and (2) the Filipinos are mostly Catholic while Indonesians are generally Muslim. This paper explores the different imaginations, perceptions, and impressions about Saudi Arabia. Moreover, Indonesia and the Philippines have shared similar geographies, colonial pasts, and in the contemporary world, use immigration as a development strategy. Saudi Arabia, as are other Gulf countries, are magnets for Filipinos and Indonesians. Saudi Arabia affords foreign workers relatively high salaries, economic prosperity, political stability, and, for Muslims, easy access to Makkah and Madinah. This paper studies (1) underlying motives of Filipino and Indonesian migrants in the Kingdom, (2) their perceptions about Saudi society, and (3) their strategies of making a living in Saudi Arabia. This paper suggests that Filipinos come to Saudi Arabia for one set of moral/secular (economic) imperatives, while Indonesians are driven by a different mix of secular and religious/moral imperatives. In conclusion, although the two communities seem to have different motivations, they share the same impression towards Saudi Arabia as a good site for making a living.

770   The Role of Interreligious Dialogue and Outreach in Strengthening Social Inclusion in Europe: the case of Network for Dialogue

Aleksandra Djuric Milovanovic and Amjad Mohamed-Saleem

Since the beginning of the "migrant crisis" in 2015, many European countries have been struggling with not only the influx but how to ensure cohesive integration into the host communities. Whilst part of the challenge has been dealing with host communities that are polarised between 'for' and 'against' migration, the real challenge is the 'Anxious Middle' who are those who are not strongly against migration but have a number of concerns about the effect of migration on their society (Katwala and Somerville 2016). Facts, figures and moral messaging appear to be ineffective in tackling these real concerns. What has been found to be really useful are programs that support a real connection between communities and create programs that build trust with each other (Moretti and Bozon 2017). Enabling more positive interactions between refugees and migrants and the local host community by coming together and learning from each other as well as about each other can provide the basis for a deeper relationship. In this case local community based organisations, such as faith based associations and inter religious bodies, are well placed to bridge

buddhist-circles/. Accessed on February 22, 2021.

the communities, offer opportunities for volunteering and to offer these opportunities for connection and greater humanisation of the migrants (Fiddian-Qasmiyeh 2011;). When such connections are based on interreligious and intercultural dialogue, these can foster empathy, understanding and mutual respect (Abu-Nimer and Smith 2016). However the role of religion and dialogue in promoting social inclusion and migration has not been extensively researched, especially not from a comparative perspective. There is often too few empirical studies that place a value on this unique perspective especially from a transnational context where across the migration trail, networks of religious organisations can work and coordinate with each other to support refugees and migrants (Mavelli, Wilson 2017).

This paper focuses on the role of religious leaders, inter religious bodies and faith-based organisations (FBOs) and their grassroots work with refugees and migrants in building social cohesion across Europe, through exploring the experience of the Network for Dialogue, a European platform of organizations, including faith-based ones, set up by the International Dialogue Centre, KAICIID in 2019. This paper will analyse the grassroots experiences of religious actors in refugee and migrant support in the past years from several European countries included in the Network, namely: Sweden, Croatia, Austria, Greece and Italy. The argument that will be put forward is that whilst interreligious and intercultural dialogue are vital, FBOs benefit from a peer network that supports learning and the enhancement of practice of interreligious dialogue. The paper draws the conclusion that policy makers need to recognise the importance of such connections and the potential role played by FBOs in promoting social cohesion. Thus, entities like the Network for Dialogue that seek to build the field of dialogue within the specific area of refugee support, are useful in creating a mechanism for exchange between grassroots dialogue actors and policy makers.

Works Cited

Abu-Nimer, Mohammed, and Renata K Smith. 2016. "Interreligious and intercultural education for dialogue, peace and social cohesion." International Review of Education (Springer) 62 (4): 393-405.

Ballinger, Steve, Rutter, Jill, and Katwala, Sunder. 2017 "How to win the argument for refugee protection", British Future

British Red Cross. 2019 "Evaluation of the Open Arms Project", British Red Cross

Dempster, Helen, and Hargrave, Karen. 2017. "Understanding Public Attitudes towards Refugees and Migrants". ODI Working Papers

Fiddian-Qasmiyeh, Elena. 2011. "Introduction: Faith-based humanitarianism in context of forced displacement", Journal of Refugee Studies 24(3), 429-439.

Hawkins, Stephen. 2019 "Speaking to Core Beliefs: Communicating about Immigration in 2019-2020". More in Common

Katwala, Sunder, and Will Somerville. 2016. "Engaging the Anxious Middle on Immigration Reform: Evidence from the UK Debate." Migration Policy. May. Accessed January 2021. www.migrationpolicy.org/research/engaging-anxious-middle-immigration-reform-evidence-uk-debate.

Orton (2012). Building migrants' belonging through positive interaction. Strasbourg: Council of Europe. Available at: https://www.coe.int/t/democracy/migration/Source/migration/EnglishMigrantBelongi ngWeb.pdf

Mavelli, Luca, and Wilson, Erin (eds.). 2017. The Refugee Crises and Religion: Secularism, Security and Hospitality in Question. London, New York: Rowman & Littefield.

Moretti, Sebastian, and Tiziana Bozon. 2017. "Some Reflections on the IFRC's approach to Migration and Displacement." International Review of the Red Cross (ICRC) 99 (1): 153-178.

517   Textual Placemaking as an Act of Religious Coping in ancient Judaism and the Biblical Corpus

Eric M Trinka

This paper provides an answer to the broad question of how religious texts function in contexts of mobility and migration.

The Babylonian exile of Judean populations in the 6th century BCE resulted in the movement of peoples from Judea to Mesopotamia and Egypt, among other places. As part of their incursions in the land of Judah, Babylonian forces destroyed the Jerusalem Temple. In the wake of changing worship paradigms that were informed by the Temple's destruction and resultant shifting centers of religious power, textually bound forms of religiosity grew in both prominence and pluriformity. Among those changes which took place is an aspect of religious experience that likely predated the official constitution of Judaism, but which came to fullness in light of the Exilic and post-Exilic periods. This element of Judahite religiosity is one by which practitioners came to understand their sacred texts as inhabitable spaces. In this matrix, narratives of Israel's origins and experiences of coming to know their God functioned not only as historical retellings or as theological metanarrative, but as omni-temporal sites of religious engagement and re-enactment that placed recipients of the texts square in the middle of the migratory journeys told within the texts. This paper draws on the methodologies of cultural psychology and religious coping (Pargament; Kanal & Grzymała-Moszczyńska, 2019), acculturation studies (Berry 2019; Alba & Foner (2015), placemaking (Knott, 1998, 2016; Knott & Vásquez, 2014), role theory (Sundén) and broader studies of textual engagement in contexts of migration and diaspora in order to explore transitions in thinking and praxis/performance regarding the role of religious texts in the lives of ancient Jewish migrant/diasporic communities in Babylon and Egypt. The textual corpus around which this study will be focused is Psalmodic literature and extra-biblical religious literature from these various communities.

5G   Migration Research: New Debates
Chair: Süreyya Sönmez Efe, University of Lincoln, United Kingdom
787   New patterns of migration in Mediterranean: North-South
Boutaina Ismaili Idrissi

787   New patterns of migration in Mediterranean: North-South

Boutaina Ismaili Idrissi

The foreign migration to Morocco mainly Spanish and French has deep historical roots. Being an old phenomenon that has been fueled by economic, social and even cultural reasons since the second half of the 20th century, this phenomenon has gained momentum in recent years especially in the aftermath of the 2008-2009 global economic crisis.

The latest available data shows the increasing part of French and Spanish migrants among total migrants residing in Morocco. Many factors could explain this trend some of which are the political stability and the economic dynamism in which the country has embarked thanks to the accelerate pace of reforms engaged recently as part of an ambitious goal to improve its integration within the globalization.

Alongside these important factors, Morocco's geographical proximity, its culture of tolerance and its cost of living affordable for European standards could also stand as attractive factors that explain why some French and Spanish citizens choose Morocco as a country of residence.

This paper will emphasize the key features of this new pattern of migration in the Mediterranean region, which shows that migration flows are not inevitably in one way, i.e. South-North. It could enable a North-South dynamic that may be of great value added to host countries such as Morocco at various level: reinforcement of local demand in the case of retired migrants; setting up of new businesses that create jobs at the local level; a source of expertise to local firms actually challenged by the shortage of skills and competencies…

In other words, the paper will shed light on this new form of migration based on the case of Morocco, its dynamics, and features and to what extent it is due to structural or cyclical factors. It will tackle, therefore, the main policy responses that need to be deployed by so as to grasp the opportunities associated with this type of migration. Other specific aspects will be examined mainly in connection with cultural and socioeconomic integration of French and Spanish Migrants and how this could be used as a strong argument to pledge for a new paradigm of migration within the Mediterranean region.

With the view of the multidimensional aspects to be covered, the paper will be based upon a systemic approach and will rely on both qualitative and quantitative tools to assert the key findings. This paper is intended to enrich Morocco's options to promote and take advantage from this type of migration.

630   The Role of High-Skilled Migrants in Home Country's Innovation Development: A Theoretical Account

Irma Baneviciene and Vilmante Kumpikaite-Valiuniene

Background and purpose.

Research shows that high-skilled migrants had positively influenced innovation process in host counties (Ozgen *et al.*, 2013; Nathan, 2014; Laursen *et al.*, 2020). Scientific literature is abundant with the research on high-skilled migrants' impact on host country's economy and innovation process. However, there is still lack of scientific data and research in regards to high-skilled migrants' influence on home country's innovation development. Therefore, *the purpose* of this article is to present analysis of what elements of high-skilled migrants' contribution to home country's innovation development are being analyzed in current scientific literature.

Methods

Narrative literature review was performed to analyze the elements of high-skilled migrants' contribution to home country's innovation development. I have searched Google Scholar database for articles published in 2010 and newer in regards to high-skilled migrants and home country's innovation development.

Results

Based on Zaidi (2018) I grouped high-skilled migrants' effect on home country's innovation development into three groups: 1) product, 2) process, and 3) business model innovations. According to analyzed scientific migration literature, these groups include following elements of innovations:

- **Product innovation:** knowledge flows between host and home countries; patent citations; business network building and diaspora; entrepreneurship and companies with ties to home country; returning high-skilled migrants with additional knowledge and experience help to foster innovation in home country; remittances invested into product innovation.

- **Process innovation:** international trade - high-skilled migrants facilitate export/import from home country, build business networks between both countries, establish production, R&D or retail branches in home country; returning high-skilled migrants bring with them experience and knowledge for process improvements as well; remittances invested into process innovation.

- **Business model innovations:** high-skilled migrant's entrepreneurship experience in host countries; business knowledge spillover extending to home countries through business networks or branches; communication through diaspora; return migration.

Conclusions

Theoretical analysis of current scientific literature in regards to high-skilled migrants' contribution to home country's innovation development highlighted many different elements, which could be grouped into the main three groups. However, analysis revealed there is a need to research in more detail how high-skilled migration affects innovation in home country.

References

Laursen, K. *et al.* (2020) 'Mounting corporate innovation performance: The effects of high-skilled migrant hires and integration capacity', *Research Policy*, 49(9), p. 104034. doi: 10.1016/j.respol.2020.104034.

Nathan, M. (2014) 'The wider economic impacts of high-skilled migrants: a survey of the literature for receiving countries', *IZA Journal of Migration*, 3(1), p. 4. doi: 10.1186/2193-9039-3-4.

Ozgen, C., Nijkamp, P. and Poot, J. (2013) 'The impact of cultural diversity on firm innovation: evidence from Dutch micro-data', *IZA Journal of Migration*, 2(1), p. 18. doi: 10.1186/2193-9039-2-18.

Zaidi, A. (2018) *Three Types of Innovation - Product, Process and Business Model, Management Insights*. Available at: https://mdi.com.pk/management/2018/05/three-types-innovation/ (Accessed: 12 January 2021).

904   How perceiving refugees as threat may backfire on German's health: An integrated threat theory approach

Saskia Judith Schubert

It is largely known, under which conditions members of host countries such as Germany perceive refugees as threatening, and express negative attitudes. However, little attention has been given to implications that subjective perceptions of threat among the host community may have for their own psychological health. Using Integrated Threat Theory, the current study examined the relationships between perceived threats, person-centered antecedents for intercultural settings and ill-being among Germans, who reflected on the incoming refugees. A random sample (N= 1000) was recruited, which matched the German census regarding central demographics. Participants completed a cross-sectional online survey with validated self-report measures. Assessments covered four perceived threat types (intergroup anxiety, symbolic and realistic threat, negative stereotypes), their person related antecedents (national identity as German, quantity and quality of intercultural contact) and psychological health (distress). Applying structural equation modeling, we found that high national identification as German was related to greater perceptions of symbolic/realistic threat, stronger negative stereotypes and, to a lower extent, to intergroup anxiety. Vice versa, a high quality of intercultural contact was associated with a decrease of all four threat types. The quantity of intercultural contact with refugees was not related to perceived threat. In terms of health outcomes, lower psychological distress was predicted by lower intergroup anxiety and less perceived realistic/symbolic threat, yet better quality of intercultural contact and greater national identity as German. Taken together, perceiving refugees as a threatening outgroup may signify a self-harming health risk, while high quality intercultural relations may directly and indirectly enhance psychological health.

627 Appropriating the Global Neoliberal Humanitarianism: Humanitarianism Narratives of Local Humanitarian Actors working with Syrian Refugees in Turkey

Hande Sözer

This presentation contributes this emerging literature critical of moralizing humanitarianism and pointing out to its political economic dimension (Reid 2010, Fassin 2011, Ticktin 2011). Specifically, it historicizes and contextualizes contemporary humanitarianism by arguing that contemporary global humanitarianism is neoliberal in political, economic and moral premises and that the emerging global neoliberal humanitarianism has complicated manifestations in the local contexts. The presentation examines the global neoliberal transformation of humanitarianism by focusing on its local manifestation by focusing on the narratives of local humanitarian actors working with Syrian refugees in Turkey. The presentation has the following argument: at the humanitarian space regarding Syrian refugees in Turkey, local state and non-governmental humanitarian actors do not assemble global neoliberal humanitarianism to the local context; on the contrary, they re-construct the neoliberal discourse in line with their own local political, economic, and social priorities.

The presentation utilizes data from fieldwork which includes 80 semi-structured interviews with people working at the local branches of the self-proclaimed humanitarian organizations in 2014-2017. These organizations include the local branches of the state institutions and international, regional, national and local non-state organizations working with Syrian refugees. The field sites include Gaziantep, Hatay, Osmaniye, Mardin, Edirne, Çanakkale, İzmir, Antalya and Şanlıurfa.

The presentation has two central parts: First, it theoretically examines the neoliberal transformation of humanitarianism. The literature recognizes that humanitarianism has always been a product and outcome of the existing political economic context (see Barnett and Weiss 2008, 2011; Reid-Henry 2014; Duffield 2019). Contemporary humanitarianism is a result of and reproduces the neoliberal political economic and moral principles (Sözer 2020). The neoliberal transformation of humanitarianism can be seen at the organization of the humanitarian actors (states as "just a partner" and non-state humanitarian actors as professionals of "a sector"); at the renewed operations of humanitarianism (via "marketization"); at the formation of its "target groups" (via "economization" and "responsibilisation"); and at the self-designated aims of humanitarian engagement (via recalibration to building resilience). Such neoliberal transformation infiltrated into Turkish humanitarian engagement with Syrian refugees as well.

Second, the presentation calls for examining global humanitarian transformations by not just just historicizing but also contextualizing. Therefore, it examines the forms of humanitarian engagement regarding Syrian refugees in Turkey. It sees this engagement not as a distortion of the Western forms of humanitarianism yet a path open to bear the complexities. To ground this point, the presentation examines local humanitarianisms as seen by the local humanitarian actors and focuses on three widespread dichotomies in these actors' narratives: *the official vs civilian humanitarianism* dichotomy as of who should control humanitarian space; *political vs technical humanitarianism* dichotomy as of how to do humanitarian engagement; and *the Western-centric and local* humanitarianism dichotomy as of what purpose humanitarianism serves. An examination of these dichotomies reveals that local humanitarians working with Syrian refugees in Turkey utilize these already existing dichotomies in the Turkish political context, appropriate them by using neoliberal jargon or premises yet in line with their own already existing political dispositions.

References

DUFFİELD, M. (2019). "Post-Humanitarianism: Governing Precarity through Adaptive Design," *Journal of Humanitarian Affairs*, 1(1), 15-27.

FASSİN, D. (2011). "Noli me tangere: The moral untouchability of humanitarianism". *Forces of compassion: Humanitarianism between ethics and politics*, 35-52.

REİD-HENRY, S. M. (2014). "Humanitarianism as liberal diagnostic: humanitarian reason and the political rationalities of the liberal will-to-care". *Transactions of the Institute of British Geographers*, 39(3), 418-431.

SÖZER, H. (2020). Humanitarianism with a neo-liberal face: vulnerability intervention as vulnerability redistribution. *Journal of Ethnic and Migration Studies*, 46(11), 2163-2180.

TİCKTİN, M. I. (2011). *Casualties of care: Immigration and the politics of humanitarianism in France*. Univ of California Press.

16:00 END OF SECOND DAY_____YOK

Day Three 8 July 2021 Thursday

Day Three 8 July 2021 - 10:45-12:15
6A   Work, Employment and Migration
Chair Suzanne Menhem, Lebanese University, Lebanon
561   Work and New Moral Economy among Albanian Domestic Workers in Greece
Ajay Bailey, Armela Xhaho, Erka Caro
635   A Watched Pot: Food and the Everyday Resistance of Filipino Domestic Workers in Italian Households
Sophia Iosue
818   Global care chains with new actors: Au-Pairs
Tuana Bildircin

598   Migrant and domestic workers in Lebanon facing economic crisis and
       COVID-19 in Lebanon.
       Suzanne Menhem

561   Work and New Moral Economy among Albanian Domestic Workers in Greece

Ajay Bailey, Armela Xhaho, Erka Caro

The Greek labor market is highly segregated in terms of gender and nationality. Albanian women migrant workers in Greece are mainly concentrated in female-dominated occupations, such as service sector and domestic work. Domestic work is widely perceived as a socially under-evaluated occupation, bearing the social stigma. The very fact that migrants are segregated in these types of occupations adds another layer of stigmatization. Moreover, domestic work takes place inside the private sphere and, as such, it is easy to dismiss the formal labor regulations. Besides this, nor the relationship between the employer and employee in this kind of job is perceived in terms of employment relationship, neither workers are perceived as workers with their human and labor rights, thus making them more vulnerable. This paper deepens conceptual understanding of employee-employer relations in domestic labor sector and related *exchange* practices by building on new moral economy theory to analyze such kind of informal relations and practices. The moral economic perspective is broadly understood as a system of economic transactions that invoke social relationships and moral norms of society. This framework explains that, on one hand, all kinds of economic activities are influenced and structured by moral sentiments and norms and, on the other, these particular norms may be negotiated, diminished or reinforced by economic pressures. The research question we address in this paper is how Albanian women in domestic sector experience and negotiate the "unwritten" working relations in domestic sector and how they position themselves within such relations. The article is based on 19 biographic interviews with the Albanian migrant women in Greece who worked as domestic workers. All interviews were held in Athens in Greece over a two-year period March 2014-November 2016. The study showed that, while the relationship between workers and employers could be mutually beneficial and positive, these relationships were often highly dynamic, complex, unequal, and exploitative. These stories illustrate how the household work can reproduce relations of inequality and reinforce power hierarchies. The narratives shed light into the exploitative and coercive relations, which are embedded in the notions of new moral economies. Interestingly, they show how economic value of productive work was understood in exchange of reproductive labor, underpinned by expectations of "servitude". The study reveals how social and economic relations are, therefore, constructed and shaped through the exchange of interpersonal dynamics and emotions, which are invoked and depend on and influence of moral/ethical sentiments, norms, and behaviors.

635   A Watched Pot: Food and the Everyday Resistance of Filipino Domestic Workers in Italian Households

Sophia Iosue

Food is an essential consideration in domestic workers' daily lives. For many, it is critical to their relationships with their employers. Yet, few studies in the domestic worker literature have examined food's social meaning. Building on my experience as part of the staff in a Milanese household, in this study I highlight that foodways are a critical and overlooked analytical tool for studies of domestic work. I use 'foodways' – a deliberately broad term that refers to 'symbolic communication . . . social boundaries, and the production of identity' related to food (Vivanco, 2018) – to examine the intricate power balance between domestic workers and their employers. Thus, I offer a new perspective on domestics, highlighting that they are disciplined through foodways, but they simultaneously enact resistance through these same channels.

Scott and de Certeau provide useful frameworks for studies of resistance – particularly, the notions of 'everyday resistance' (Scott, 1990) and cooking as an embodied act of resistance (de Certeau, 1984). Seminal studies in the domestic worker literature (Hondagneu-Sotelo, 2007; Rollins, 1985) support the observation that food is important to domestics, but few focus explicitly on foodways. Those that do examine food primarily as a substance employers use to subjugate their employees. Contrastingly, I build on the literature that examines domestics' agency (Harzig, 2006) to explore domestics' everyday negotiations with their employers.

I conducted 16 interviews between March and April 2020. I selected Milan because of my rapport with the domestic worker community after working there and because Milan has the highest concentration of Filipino domestic workers in Italy. I used Facebook and community representatives as entry points to the community. Just before leaving for my fieldwork, Milan became an epicenter for Covid-19 in Europe, and I transitioned all fieldwork to video calls. Through a combination of virtual and classic snowballing, I interviewed 14 female domestic workers, one male, and one adult daughter of a domestic worker. I fully transcribed and coded the interviews using thematic analysis.

Concurrent with the dominant literature, foodways discipline the domestics I spoke with. But, crucially, domestics simultaneously express resistance through these same channels in three distinct but overlapping ways. First, they strategically employ their food knowledge in displays of resistance that disrupt the narrative of maternalism, and thus, the 'victim' narrative. Second, through foodways, domestics capitalize on their liminality to make material gains in order to resist narratives of economic inequality. Finally, domestics use opposing social relations around foodways to claim space.

Food occupies an important space within the household/workplace, and it deserves more attention in the literature. Employers use food to discipline domestics, but at the same time, domestics use foodways to express resistance. Domestics tangibly resist their employers' domination, but they also more abstractly resist narrative domination by expressing their agency through foodways. Thus, foodways are critical to assessing the contradictory power dynamics that exist between domestics and their employers.

References Cited

De Certeau, M. 1984. *The Practice of Everyday Life*, translated by Steven Rendell. Berkeley: University of California Press.

Harzig, C. 2006. 'Domestics of the World (Unite?): Labor Migration Systems and Personal Trajectories of Household Workers in Historical and Global Perspective'. *Journal of American Ethnic History* 25(2/3): 48—73.

Hondagneu-Sotelo, P. 2004. 'Immigrant Women and Paid Domestic Work: Research, Theory, and Activism'. In *The Blackwell Companion to Sociology*, ed. Judith R. Blau, Malden: Blackwell Publishing, pp. 423—436.

Rollins, J. 1985. *Between Women: Domestics and Their Employers*, Philadelphia: Temple University Press.

Scott, J.C. 1990. *Domination and the Arts of Resistance: Hidden Transcripts*. New Haven: Yale University Press.

Vivanco, L. 2018.'Foodways'. *A Dictionary of Cultural Anthropology*, Oxford: Oxford University Press.

818   Global care chains with new actors: Au-Pairs

Tuana Bildircin

In this paper, I look whether the case of Au-Pair programs present a case for "global care chains" in terms of inequalities of the international system. I will focus on the European Union as a case study and argue that Europe creates its own periphery in terms of care work. In that sense, continuation of the capitalist system is sustained with outsourcing care work, deepening international inequalities (Fraser, 2016). Au-Pairs are growing in number and a special form of youth migration, hiding its structural inequalities of class, gender and race behind the frame of "education" and "gap year." After all, it is as Cox (2007) says, "they are migrant domestic workers who are constructed by official discourses as neither workers nor migrants but as participants in a 'cultural exchange' programme" (p. 282). The result of this is that creation of deregulated areas of work with neoliberalism even in an already highly deregulated area since it is considered "private sphere." Although the image tells something else, the picture of networks and Au-Pair migration resembles the traditional global care chains. On the other hand, they do not require any prior experience, and they are paid less than traditional migrant care workers. These Au-Pairs constitute the "transnational human capital" and an alternative way for child care for families in Europe, depending on their class position (Gerhards, Hans, & Carlson, 2017). That can be the first step to the formation of a transnational care chain, and the system requires it for its continuation. There is a constant need by the capital for a "squeezable labour force" (Floya & Lazaridis, 2000). This flexibility is given by these migrant women who have no security and contributes to the reproduction (Hess, 2009). In fact, Chuang (2012, p. 269) also claims, "the "cultural exchange" rhetoric used in the au pair program regulations and practice reifies harmful class, gender, and racial biases and tropes that feed society's stubborn resistance to valuing domestic work as work worthy of labor protection." This relationship is dangerous for both sides since it is born out of the need for a cheap solution to the childcare and creates a dependency relationship with those without a balance between work and family life.(Stenum, 2011).

References

Chuang, J. A. (2012, August 15). The U.S. Au Pair Program: Labor Exploitation and the Myth of Cultural Exchange. *Harvard Journal of Law & Gender*, s. 2012-46.

Cox, R. (2007). The Au Pair Body. *European Journal of Women's Studies, 14*(3), 281–296.

Floya, A., & Lazaridis, G. (2000). *Gender and Migration in Southern Europe. Women on the Move.* Oxford: Berg.

Gerhards, J., Hans, S., & Carlson, S. (2017). *Social Class and Transnational Human Capital.* New York: Routledge.

Hess, S. (2009). *Globalisierte Hausarbeit.* Wiesbaden: VS Verlag für Sozialwissenschaften.

Hess, S., & Puckhaber, A. (2004). *Feminist Review*, 65-78.

Stenum, H. (2011). *Abused Domestic Workers in Europe: The case of au pairs.* Brussels: European Parliament.

598   Migrant and domestic workers in Lebanon facing economic crisis and COVID-19 in Lebanon.

Suzanne Menhem

The migrant and domestic workers in Lebanon are experiencing financial hardship due the economic recession following the uprising of October 2019, the dollar crisis and COVID-19. Lebanon identified the first human case in February 2020, and declared the lockdown on March 15th to deal with the spread of the epidemic. Confinement measures don't allow migrant and freelance domestic workers to work remotely due to the nature of their jobs. Additionally, they are being blocked with no source of income since the country is on lockdown and households are quarantined; that has caused many to suffer job and income losses, a reduction or a suspension of their wages as Lebanese employees who have lost their jobs and find themselves in a critical situation and unable to pay migrant workers at a market exchange rate of 4000 LBP; to say the least migrant are in dire situation. Their number is close to 270,000 according to the Ministry of Labor in 2018; this is excluding the irregular labor force that is hard to estimate. The foreign population represents up to 5.5% (excluding Syrian and Palestinian refugees). According to the daily report published by the Ministry of Health, in May 2020, 8% of foreigners are infected.

This study aims to address the issue of COVID-19 and its socio-economic and health impact on the daily lives of migrant and domestic workers in Lebanon as well as their return to their home countries.

Methodologically, the qualitative approach will be applied for this study realizing in-depth interviews with migrant and domestic workers, Lebanese employees, and experts. The results will shed the light for a possible social policy related to this situation in Lebanon as a way to secure their rights.

6B   Space and Migration

Chair: Simeon Magliveras, King Fahd University of Petroleum and Minerals, Saudi Arabia

612   Interethnic Contact and Social Capital in European Immigrant Neighborhoods
Rui Carvalho

616   Being offline and online in a situation of forced immobility: the example of the Brenner border in northern Italy
Claudia Lintner

665   Refugees Social Relations and Local Community Perception: A Transnational Urbanism Analysis
Akino Midhany Tahir, Aswin Baharuddin, Darwis Darwis, Ikrana Ramadhani

682   Social network ties and the connections to city destinations among urban refugees in Uganda
Francis Anyanzu and Nicole DeWet-Billings

612   Interethnic Contact and Social Capital in European Immigrant Neighborhoods

Rui Carvalho

European cities have been receiving growing numbers of international migrants and facing rising challenges related to increased ethnic diversity in the last decades. These recent developments have led to a growth in the number of empirical studies examining the effects of migration-driven ethnic diversity for the livelihoods and social cohesion of European neighborhoods and cities. Contrarily to the negative effect of ethnic diversity on community cohesion found in well-known studies focusing on the United States (Putnam, 2007; see Portes and Vickstrom (2011), for a critique), existing studies in Europe have produced more mixed results (for reviews, see Dinesen et al., 2020; and Van der Meer and Tolsma, 2014). One transversal finding though is the mediating effect that having social, and particularly interethnic, contacts at the neighborhood level has on the association between ethnic diversity and community social cohesion. This finding begs the question of what factors influence the establishment (or not) of interethnic contacts at the neighborhood level, particularly in ethnically diverse neighborhoods, i.e. in those areas where people are directly exposed to members of other ethnic groups. In an attempt to contribute to this scholarship, in this work, I query: What sociodemographic and attitudinal elements are associated with the formation of interethnic contacts of different types and degrees of intimacy (i.e. strength of tie) in European ethnically diverse neighborhoods? I answer this question by using data from a unique survey applied to the residents of twelve multiethnic neighborhoods located in four

European cities (Bilbao, Spain; Lisbon, Portugal; Thessaloniki, Greece; Vienna, Austria). Using several logistic regression models predicting interethnic contacts of various types and degrees of intimacy, I find that: (a) migration background, i.e. being an immigrant or not, is the single most important predictor of neighborhood interethnic ties; (b) claiming a religious affiliation, regardless of what that affiliation is and for both immigrants and the autochthonous population, is associated with overall lower levels of interethnic contact with neighbors; (c) engaging in the neighborhood's associational life is related to higher levels of weak interethnic ties but also with more conflictual interactions (negative contacts); and (d) stronger ties seem to be associated more with sociodemographic elements (e.g. migration background, occupational status, educational levels), while one's attitudes, values, practices, and neighborhood social capital (e.g. religious beliefs, civic participation, anti-immigration attitudes, neighborhood perceptions and attachments) are more strongly associated with weaker ties and negative interactions. These and other results, which I discuss in light of the existing scholarship on interethnic contacts and on the effects of ethnic diversity on social cohesion and social capital, show the value of considering different types and levels of intimacy of contact, as well as attitudinal variables, in studies of the determinants and conditions of interethnic contact (at the neighborhood level). Altogether, this shows the importance of viewing interethnic contact and social capital as multifaceted concepts, whose various dimensions are influenced differently by different demographic, cognitive and behavioral individual-level factors.

References

Dinesen, Peter T., Merlin Schaeffer, and Kim M. Sønderskov (2020). "Ethnic Diversity and Social Trust: A Narrative and Meta-Analytical Review." *Annual Review of Political Science*, 23 (1): 441-465.

Portes, Alejandro and Erik Vickstrom (2011). "Diversity, Social Capital, and Cohesion." *Annual Review of Sociology*, 37 (1): 461-479.

Putnam, Robert D. (2007). "'E Pluribus Unum': Diversity and Community in the Twenty-First Century; The 2006 Johan Skytte Prize Lecture." *Scandinavian Political Studies*, 30 (2): 137-174.

Van der Meer, Tom G. and Jochem Tolsma (2014). "Ethnic Diversity and its Effects on Social Cohesion." *Annual Review of Sociology*, 40 (1): 459-478.

616   Being offline and online in a situation of forced immobility: the example of the Brenner border in northern Italy

Claudia Lintner

This article focuses on the concrete policies of exclusion and border practices in the northern Italian border zone and their impact on refugees' immobility experiences as both online and offline actors. In doing so, the article has adopted a multidimensional understanding of mobility, as a physical as well as a virtual experience. It is shown that new forms of involuntary or forced immobility are instigated as a result of migration and border regimes. However, the development of new technologies have challenged the mainly physical understanding of mobility and immobility. Indeed, more than ever before, social media platforms, phone applications, etc. have released mobility from its purely physical meaning by adding the virtual dimension of mobility.

Additionally, and crucial to the chapter's line of argument, there is an emerging strand of studies that focuses less on the individual benefit of ICT in refugees' trajectories and more on questions related to access and affordability capabilities. By adopting a qualitative research approach, the results show, that in the Italian-Austrian border zone, the physical mobility of refugees and thus the spaces where they are permitted to be, have been systematically reduced and limited. However, the policies and practices of exclusion no longer discriminate and marginalize on a physical level but have also been effective in reducing the virtual dimension that characterizes mobility. In order to exercise this form of mobility, having access to connectivity, as well as electricity and thus relying on digital infrastructures that are accessible for all (for example, free internet provided via Wi-Fi hotspots throughout the city) is crucial. Instead, as the mapping and analyses of the data show, public connectivity provided by public Wi-Fi hotspots has changed from a human right into an instrument of power that has imposed new inequalities and new exclusion forms.

665 Refugees Social Relations and Local Community Perception: A Transnational Urbanism Analysis

Akino Midhany Tahir, Aswin Baharuddin, Darwis Darwis, Ikrana Ramadhani

The increasing gap between resettlement needs and UNHCR's annual submissions from year to year has made more refugees live in protracted situations in transit countries. Until 2020, 1.813 refugees registered with UNHCR live in Makassar City and spend more than three years waiting for their application—placement to a third country or return to their home country. Living in urban areas forces refugees to engage with the public and have ample opportunities to interact with local communities in public spaces—streets, markets, public transportation, and parks.

This research is qualitative research using a case study approach to provide an in-depth understanding of refugees' cases in Makassar and perceptions of local communities. With the RDI UREF research team's approval, this study uses data from a Placemaking research in Makassar in 2019, obtained through in-depth interviews with youth refugees and a baseline survey of local youths regarding their perceptions of people from different groups. The study used a purposive sampling strategy, involving all refugees and local youths who participated in the placemaking research. Official documents from international organizations and the city government are also the sources of data in this study.

The data obtained were analyzed using the spiral technique. The first loop is reading and memoing, then entering the process of describing and classifying, categorizing the data into themes that contextualize with the framework from literature, which will focus on how refugees maintain their social relations of transnational ties.

Using the theory of transnational urbanism from Michael Peter Smith, this research concludes that refugees in Makassar who have registered with UNHCR and receive basic needs assistance from the International Organization for Migration (IOM), are not fully connected to socioeconomic opportunities. The refugee-related policy framework in Indonesia does not permit refugees to work formally. However, at the same time, refugees are connected to cultural and consumption practices that they find in the city. Registration and legal recognition are essential matters for refugees because they can open up opportunities to access public services available in cities. This condition happened in Makassar after a joint legal framework was agreed upon by the City Government and IOM. However, empirical evidence related to this is lacking.

Refugees in Makassar are involved in the ideas of "freedom" living in third countries through sophisticated information and communication networks. This condition makes refugees have no desire or 'need' to maintain their social relations with the local community. Public places in the neighborhood, such as parks, are not yet a place for the two groups to socialize and express their identity. The perception that local youth have towards refugees is the result of contestation on the meaning of place by various actors; the refugees themselves, local communities, governments, and international organizations that are intertwined with each other and then influence how the place "represents" particular groups.

References

Creswell, John W., and Cheryl N. Poth. 2018. *Qualitative Inquiry and Research Design: Choosing Among Five Approaches*. Fourth ed. London: SAGE Publications.

Smith, M. P., 2000. *Transnational Urbanism: Locating Globalisation*. New York City: Wiley.

Tahir, A., Dwiyani, R., Sagala, S. & Viartasiwi, N., 2019. *Secondary Cities and Forced Migration*. Jakarta, ISOCARP.

UNHCR, 2019. *Global Trends Forced Migration 2018,* Geneva: UNHCR.

Wolcott, H.F. 1994. Transforming qualitative data: Description, Analysis, and Interpretation. Thousand Oaks, CA: Sage.

Tahir, Akino M., Nino Viartasiwi, and Risye D. Yani. 2019. *Constructing a Shared Identity: Engaging Youth in Creative Placemaking for Social Integration of Urban Refugees in Indonesia*. Bandung: Resilience Development Initiative.

682   Social network ties and the connections to city destinations among urban refugees in Uganda

Francis Anyanzu and Nicole DeWet-Billings

Cities have become important places of destinations for forced migrants in Sub Saharan African countries. In these cities, where state assistance and protections are not readily available or channelled to forced migrants in camps, social networks have played significant roles. In particular, ties formed through family, kinship, friendship, ethnic and organisational networks have been instrumental in access to livelihood opportunities in cities (Omata, 2012; Crush and Tawodzera, 2017). Migration decisions have also been shaped by connections through kinship ties (Shaffer, Ferrato and Jinnah, 2018). Refugees have often used their social networks to relocate from camps to cities (Palmgren, 2013).

In spite of the interest in social networks as source of social capital and pull factors for refugee flows, little is known about how these social networks influence the flow or refugees to city destinations. The objective of this study is to identify the social network ties that influence the flows of refugees to cities and examine how these ties channel refugees to urban areas.

In depth interviews from biographical narratives of migration trajectories were used to capture the patterns of flows and the personal and organizational networks involved in the refugee flow to urban areas. The study area is Kampala, the capital and commercial city of Uganda

The preliminary findings in this suggests that weak ties – rather than strong ties – in transit and at the city destination are important ties connecting refugees to city destinations. These weak ties constitute un specified co-nationals, unknown transporters (truckers, motorcycle taxis at borders) and friends of friends or relatives. While weak ties for refugees from bordering countries operate mainly at transit points by providing transport to specific destinations, weak ties for refugees from non-bordering countries influence refugees' movements through provision of unsolicited information about the destinations.

The study concludes that while insecurities may be the primary drivers of population movement, social network ties connect refugees to specific destinations.

References

Crush, J., & Tawodzera, G. (2017). *Comparing Refugees and South Africans in the Urban Informal Sector*. Cape Town: Southern African Migration Programme

Omata, N. (2012). *Refugee livelihoods and the private sector: Ugandan case study.* RSC,

Working paper 86. Oxford: University of Oxford

Palmgren, P. A. (2013). Irregular networks: Bangkok refugees in the city and region. *Journal of Refugee Studies, 27*(1), 21-41.

Shaffer, M., Ferrato, G., & Jinnah, Z. (2018). Routes, locations, and social imaginary: a comparative study of the on-going production of geographies in Somali forced migration. *African Geographical Review, 37*(2), 159-171. DOI: 10.1080/19376812.2017.1354308

6C   Youth Migration
Chair: Pinar Yazgan, Sakarya University, Turkey
499   Learning Levels of Children from Short-Term Migrant Families:
      Evidence from Rural India
      Leena Bhattacharya

499   Learning Levels of Children from Short-Term Migrant Families: Evidence from Rural India

Leena Bhattacharya

At the global level, over 762 million individuals migrate internally, where a very high proportion can be classified as seasonal, temporary or short-term migrants. India and China, the two most populous countries have a very high share of internal migrants. Literature in China has provided robust evidence that children from migrant families have lower learning levels than their counterparts from non-migrant families (Zhang et al., 2014; Zhao et al., 2014). Despite the presence of 10.7 million children in rural short-term migrant families in India, such studies have not been done in the Indian context. To the best of our knowledge, this is the first study which uses a nationally representative data to enquire, what happens to the learning levels of children from short-term migrant families in rural India? We explore this question for children aged 8-11 years using India Human Development Survey 2011-12 data. Results indicate that that each age, children from short-term migrant families acquire lower language and mathematics levels than children from non-migrant families. Acknowledging the possibility of endogeneity, we instrument the presence of short-term migrant in the family using lagged district proportion of short-term migrants in 2007-08 and the lagged proportion of workers in manufacturing industry in other districts of the state in 2009-10 using National Sample Survey Organisation's Employment and Unemployment Surveys. Additionally, we assess the potential impact of omitted variable bias in our estimates using a novel method developed by Oster (2019). Our results remain robust to both the methods. Next, we examine one of the possible mechanisms to retain learning levels of children in the Indian policy context. Under the Right to Education Act of 2009, Indian education policy suggests that local government authorities can operate seasonal hostels to protect the right to education of children from short-term migrant families. We use a unique primary data collected from a very high out-migration-prone Indian state of Odisha in 2019 and examine whether left-behind children in seasonal hostels are able to retain their learning levels. We find that percentile rank of language and mathematics of left-behind children were not different from that of children from non-migrant families whereas percentile rank of migrant children were lower. Our results are not affected by omitted variable bias (Oster, 2019). Restricting our analysis to children from migrant families, we find that left-behind children in seasonal hostels have the highest percentile rank. Overall, the results suggest that encouraging migrants to leave their children behind in hostels can be effective in protecting child's right to education.

References

Oster, E. (2019). Unobservable Selection and Coefficient Stability: Theory and Evidence. *Journal of Business and Economic Statistics, 37*(2), 187–204. https://doi.org/10.1080/07350015.2016.1227711

Zhang, H., Behrman, J. R., Fan, C. S., Wei, X., & Zhang, J. (2014). Does parental absence reduce cognitive achievements? Evidence from rural China. *Journal of Development Economics, 111*, 181–195. https://doi.org/10.1016/j.jdeveco.2014.09.004

Zhao, Q., Yu, X., Wang, X., & Glauben, T. (2014). The impact of parental migration on children's school performance in rural China. *China Economic Review, 31*, 43–54. https://doi.org/10.1016/j.chieco.2014.07.013

516   Parent-Child Interactions: Perceptions of Migrant Children with Low and Significant Levels of Internalized Symptoms

Kristel Tardif-Grenier

Purpose

Canada welcomes a growing number of immigrants to ensure its economic vitality, and among these migrants are a considerable number of families with children (OECD, 2018). In this regard, it is well documented that the significant changes that often characterize the migratory journey can lead to changes in family dynamics, such as increased cohesion or conflict (Patterson, 2002). Especially if the cultural gap between the country of origin and the host country is important (Erel, 2013). Among all the actors in the child's sphere having a significant influence on their life, parent-child interactions play a primary role and represent an important developmental context, particularly for mental health (Morris et al., 2017). While family risk factors in a migration context are well documented, little is known about what characterizes the families of immigrant children who are more resilient.

Contrary to the deficit centered and victimizing logic, it is therefore interesting to focus on what characterizes family dynamics in children who present positive adaptation following immigration. Indeed, the family can play a stress-buffering role during the migration experience and contribute, through interaction with children's adaptive strategies, to their adaptation (Hodes et al., 2008). However, much of this knowledge about peri-migration family dynamics is based on adult or adolescent accounts, and very little is known about how this transition affects the family lives of children (White et al., 2011). Understanding their perspectives is essential to comprehend children's migratory experience (Moskal & Tyrrell, 2016). This study aims to determine what characterizes the parent-child interactions of recently migrated children who develop fully and well.

Methodology

This study focuses on the family representations of 33 children (6-13 years) who recently immigrated to Canada. Participants were divided into two groups according to whether they had a low (n= 23) or clinically significant (n= 10) level of internalized symptoms (measured with Dominic Interactive; Kuijpers et al.,

2014). These groups were compared to document the family dynamics in the context of migration as perceived by children who experience this critical transition by manifesting more or fewer symptoms, thus identifying potential risk or resilience factors.

Findings

In both groups, children reported a positive view of their family and increased time spent with the father following migration. However, children with fewer symptoms perceived a greater diversity in shared interactions with their parents following migration. Children who had a clinical level of symptoms focused on family cohesion and the importance of being loved. These results suggest that more diverse interactions with parents following migration could be associated with resilience among children and reflect the importance of the different spheres of parental involvement.

Originality/value

Very few studies have documented this phenomenon using the perspective of children themselves. This exploratory research will help guide future studies to identify resilience factors for internalizing symptoms in migrant children by drawing attention to essential elements from their perspective.

References

Erel, U. (2013). Troubling or ordinary? Children's views on migration and intergenerational ethnic identities. In McCarthy, J.R., Hooper, C.A. and Gillies. V. (Eds.), *Family troubles?: Exploring changes and challenges in the family lives of children and young people* (pp.199-208). Bristol University Press.

Hodes, M., Jagdev, D., Chandra, N., & Cunniff, A. (2008), Risk and resilience for psychological distress amongst unaccompanied asylum seeking adolescents, *Journal of Child Psychology and Psychiatry, 49*, 723–732. doi: 10.1111/j.1469-7610.2008.01912.x.

Kuijpers, R. C.W.M., Otten, R., Vermulst, A.A., Pez, O., Bitfoi, A., Carta, M., Goelitz, D., Keyes, K. M., Koc, C., Lesinskiene, S., Mihova, Z., Engels, E., and Kovess, V. (2014). Cross-country construct validity of the 'Dominic Interactive' Rowella Kuipers. *European Journal of Public Health, 24*(2). doi: 10.1093/eurpub/cku164.046.

Morris, A.S., Houltberg, B.J., Criss, M.M., & Bosler, C.D. (2017), Family context and psychopathology: The mediating role of children's emotion regulation. In Centifanti, L.C. and Williams, D.M. (Eds.)", *The Wiley handbook of developmental psychopathology* (pp.365-389). Wiley-Blackwell. doi: 10.1002/9781118554470.ch18.

Moskal, M., & Tyrrell, N. (2016), Family migration decision-making, step-migration and separation: Children's experiences in European migrant worker families. *Children's Geographies, 14*(4), 453-467. doi: 10.1080/14733285.2015.1116683.

Organisation for Economic Co-operation and Development (OECD) (2018). *The resilience of students with an immigrant background: Factors that shape well-being,* OECD Publishing, Paris, doi: 10.1787/9789264292093-en.

Patterson, J. M. (2002). Integrating family resilience and family stress theory. *Journal of Marriage and Family, 64* (2), 349–360. doi: 10.1111/j.1741-3737.2002.00349.x.

White, A., Laoire, C., Tyrrell, N., & Carpena-Méndez, F. (2011), Children's roles in transnational migration, *Journal of Ethnic and Migration Studies*, 37(8), 1159-1170. doi: 10.1080/1369183X.2011.590635.

555   Subjective configuration of the Dreamer youth as subjects with rights

Luz Maria Montelongo

The field of research developed in the last decade on migratory processes in the United States has been traversed by the political, social, and economic situation of the country of destination and origin. The literature on this topic is not part of a merely academic debate because, the agenda of migration public policy affects the configuration of the objectives and scope of the research.

In most of the investigations in which it is studied and problematized the right to higher education and its enforceability of young people who arrived in the United States at an early age, the approach is carried out from an impact perspective. The narrative of previous investigations mainly focus on contextualizing the Deferred Action Program (DACA) and distinguishing the benefits of its implementation by understanding it as a step towards social mobility mechanisms.

In this framework, two moments are observed. First, the production, socio-political, economic and cultural conditions which lead to the emergence of the program. Second, the impact that the program had on the life trajectory of young migrants.

In this presentation the results of a post-doctoral research, aiming to expand the DREAMers movement and the enforceability of their right to higher education through the young Americans' political-pedagogical fight to receive equal treatment. The objective is to analyze the articulation relationships and the impact of the political discourse of the alliances or antagonisms that young migrants in build with institutions such as civil organizations and government agencies, and other actors such as academics, researchers, or independent groups, and how such relationships affects the subjective configuration as subjects with rights, the enforceability of the right to education, and their participation in the DREAMER movement as an educational space.

The interest in the study of this movement is due to the capacity of immigrant youth who challenged the American social intellect. The methodology used in this study is inscribed in the principles of the interpretative paradigm and seeks the understanding of social phenomena. Therefore, it is an in-depth case study through in-depth interviews about the school and life trajectories of immigrant students who fight for the right to higher education in migratory contexts, in particular the DREAMers movement. Additionally, we analyzed the following empirical references: the biographical narrative, the DREAM Act, the DACA Program, the presidential speeches (Obama and Trump), and the narratives of key actors.

The present research project is supported by various tools of intellection of Political Discourse Analysis since it allows the use of various thinking logics and tools of Theoretical intellection. In turn, this enables the integration of the various theoretical inputs of the different research disciplines for the analysis of the constitution and functioning of social discursivities, specifically the conformation of immigrant Dreamer youth in the United States as subjects with rights. This leads us to other ways of studying and knowing the processes of development of the subject in society, and of the actions of social transformation. This work seeks to contribute to the debate and academic dialogue.

597   Bil-bunduqyia al-hurryia: Sahrawi students between pens and riffles

Rita dos Reis

Due to the non-decolonization of the Western Sahara and its subsequent invasion, since 1975 that Sahrawi youth is involved in a model of "transnational education" (Chatty et al. 2010), where thousands of young people leave annually the refugee camps (Tindouf, Algeria) to pursue their studies. That is a consequence of the priority given to education which led to the establishment of protocols between the exiled-Sahrawi Arab Democratic Republic and third countries (Algeria, Spain, Cuba, among others), developed during the liberation war period. Having been conceived as a national duty for the future independent country this became a transgenerational process (Fiddian-Qasmiyeh 2015).

For many years, youngsters were students and soldiers. After 1991's cease-fire, students became "peace messengers" and "ambassadors of the cause", raising awareness of the conflict in the host countries, converted into "home" in so many cases. In contrast with their parents that studied and *came back* – to the camps, cause and war – today's youth is permeated by transnational circular movements (Gómez 2010) between their study context and the refugee camps. That shape their perception of the exiled-SADR, the refugee camps (their birthplace), their homeland (the Western Sahara), and their individual desires, entangled between the wish for self-determination and, until very recently, a lack of hope.

The lives of Sahrawi students abroad were shaped by a time of neither peace nor war, which transformed these educational movements and the future perspectives and expectations (Koselleck 1979; Bryant and Knight 2019) of this second generation, who leaves the refugee camps to study and lives the cause from the outside. The rupture of the ceasefire (November 2020) changed the dynamics and conceptions of their present, shaping those of the future in an unknown way.

Having been raised amidst a peace building process and aiming a solution brokered by the UN, youth abroad tended to prefer a referendum of self-determination over war. However, slogans such as *"bil-bunduqyia al-hurryia"* (through guns, freedom) were present in official students/youth meetings, demonstrating that the return to armed struggle was somehow glimpsed. The same youngsters who mentioned preferring a peaceful solution, are the ones who today support the armed struggle and did not fail to drop college, return to the camps and join the army – amidst a global pandemic. If the educational experience and life abroad deeply differed from that of their parents, shaping future perspectives and opinions regarding the cause, the return to armed struggle seems to strengthen transgenerational perspectives, actions and relations, bringing together different generations, as well as all the communities in the diaspora.

Based on a long-term ethnographic research, this communication analyses how second generations of Sahrawi students shape their future between an (un)certain future and political activism, choosing between pens and riffles on a very unpredicted moment. How the transition from a status-quo to armed struggle is perceived? How does it change youngster's future perspectives?

6D   Families and Migration
Chair Irene Tuzi, Sapienza University of Rome, Italy
559   Family, friendship, and strength among LGBTQ+ migrants in Cape
       Town, South Africa: A qualitative understanding
       Brett Greenfield, Edward J Alessi, Melanie Yu, Sarilee Kahn, Shannon
       P Cheung, Sulaimon Giwa
508   Family Resources and Migration in Rural Senegal, West Africa
       Henri-Pierre Koubaka
790   Doing Family across Borders: Everyday Insecurities of Separated
       Syrian Households in Germany
       Irene Tuzi
859   Parental work migration and the children left behind in rural Romania. A
       qualitative perspective
       Gabriela Guiu, Georgiana Udrea, Malina Ciocea
728   Determinants of migration from rural households in India: An empirical
       investigation
       Shreya Nupur and Meghna Dutta

559   Family, friendship, and strength among LGBTQ+ migrants in Cape Town, South Africa: A qualitative understanding

Brett Greenfield, Edward J Alessi, Melanie Yu, Sarilee Kahn, Shannon P Cheung, Sulaimon Giwa

The purpose of this qualitative study was to explore how migrants in South Africa (SA) identifying as lesbian, gay, bisexual, transgender, queer, or with other diverse sexual orientations or gender identities (LGBTQ+) describe and understand their pre-migration family experiences and how family and other social relationships facilitated strength during post-migration.

Among the 4 million migrants living in SA, many are LGBTQ+ individuals fleeing persecution and violence in their countries of origin for constitutional guarantees of nondiscrimination in South Africa (Cock, 2003). While research on migrants has consistently shown that reliance on family members for support is essential to deal with resettlement challenges (Schweitzer et al., 2006), evidence suggests that LGBTQ+ migrants cannot always rely on family support due to homophobia and transphobia, requiring them to develop new family relationships, often consisting of friends and romantic partners (Cantú, 1999; Alessi et al., 2020). Although new relationships may provide a substitute for families of origin, offering financial and housing assistance, research shows that LGBTQ+ migrants sometimes maintain familial support post-migration (Chávez, 2011). In the South African context, however, studies have yet to examine how LGBTQ+ migrants navigate family relationships pre- and post-migration, as well as how they form new social relationships to facilitate their resettlement.

The study was guided by the following research questions: (a) How do LGBTQ+ migrants describe and understand their relationships with family members prior to migration? (b) How does support from family and other individuals facilitate LGBTQ+ migrants' strength following migration? We conducted six focus groups, consisting of both morning and afternoon sessions, with 30 LGBTQ+ migrants.

Four themes were identified using grounded theory: managing family responses during pre-migration: concealing, avoiding, disclosing; the power of (even) one: support during post-migration; 'love is a very big thing': drawing strength from chosen family; and 'pulling myself up': drawing strength from self-reliance. Participants reported experiencing negative responses from family, but some continued to rely on family support after arriving in South Africa. Further, participants often depended on newfound friendships for support, as well as their own internal resources. This self-reliance was, in part, facilitated by the participants' beliefs that they could not depend on their families because of the hostility faced in their countries of origin.

Findings highlighting the complexity of LGBTQ+ migrants' experiences across migration periods have implications for both research and practice. While LGBTQ+ migrants in SA may face abuse by family prior to migration, cut-offs do not necessarily occur following migration, and support from family may facilitate integration for LGBTQ+ migrants. Future studies may examine the psychosocial effects of concealing sexual orientation or gender identity from family among those who must rely on them for support. Mental health professionals and migrant assistance workers should harness LGBTQ+ migrants' support from their nuclear and extended family, if available, and chosen family, as this may ease resettlement. Last, it will be important to help LGBTQ+ migrants process the complex dynamics that may have existed prior to migration and how these dynamics unfold in the host country.

References

Alessi, E. J., Kahn, S., Greenfield, B., Woolner, L., & Manning, D. (2020). A qualitative exploration of the integration experiences of LGBTQ refugees who fled from the Middle East, North Africa, and Central and South Asia to Austria and the Netherlands. *Sexuality Research and Social Policy*, 17(1), 13-26. https://doi.org/10.1007/s13178-018-0364-7

Cantú, L., Jr. (1999). *Border crossings: Mexican men and the sexuality of migration* (Order No. 9942693). Available from ProQuest Dissertations & Theses Global. (304530831). https://login.proxy.libraries.rutgers.edu/login?url= ?url=https://www-proquest-com.proxy.libraries.rutgers.edu/dissertations-theses/border-crossings-mexican-men-sexuality-migration/docview/304530831/se-

Chávez, K. R. (2011). Identifying the needs of LGBTQ immigrants and refugees in southern Arizona, *Journal of Homosexuality, 58*(2), 189-218. https://doi.org/10.1080/00918369.2011.540175

Cock, J. (2003). Engendering gay and lesbian rights: The equality clause in the South African constitution. *Women's Studies International Forum*, 26(1), 35-45. https://doi.org/10.1016/S0277-5395(02)00353-9

Schweitzer, R., Melville, F., Steel, Z., & Lacherez, P. (2006). Trauma, post-migration living difficulties, and social support as predictors of psychological adjustment in resettled Sudanese refugees. *Australian and New Zealand Journal of Psychiatry, 40*(2), 179–187. http://dx.doi.org/10.1080/j.1440-1614.2006.01766.x

508   Family Resources and Migration in Rural Senegal, West Africa

Henri-Pierre Koubaka

For youths in rural Senegal, migration is a project that involves raising a considerable amount of money. Even though interviews with migrants reveal that there is a strong tendency nowadays for young migrants to raise their own money, family resources involvement in the migration project remains crucially important. In this presentation we look at:

- how family resources fund migration
- the types of resources family make available to migration
- where families get resources from
- how remittances are spent

Our presentation explores collective participation in organizing and supporting migrants' trips. We investigate the reasons and drivers behind youth migration, the expectations and the responsibilities to participate in the financial improvements of their original communities.

The presentation gives an understanding of the relationship between families' resources and migration. It analyses what family means in a Senegalese rural environment and looks at various ways migration is perceived in local communities, the effects of migration in dislocating families and communities while it studies the difference between families that benefit from remittances and those that do not, what remittances are spent on and the channels through which money is sent back into the communities.

790   Doing Family across Borders: Everyday Insecurities of Separated Syrian Households in Germany

Irene Tuzi

This research aims at investigating the challenges and everyday insecurities of separated Syrian families in Germany. During the so-called "refugee crisis", many families fled Syria or neighbouring countries at different stages and remained separated across borders. Those who made it to Germany were not all provided with the same status. Most Syrians were granted subsidiary protection, while only a minority received the full (political) refugee status. The main difference between the two lies in the right of family reunification. While the beneficiary of refugee status is granted the right to reunite with his/her family, the beneficiary of subsidiary protection does not have this privilege. For the latter category, family reunification is granted at the discretion of the authorities and only in cases of particular hardship. This means that the main challenge for separated Syrian families in Germany is not *when* they will be reunited, but *if* they ever will. Because of the hindrances of the family reunification system in Germany, these separations can last for a very long time and can change household structures and family dynamics fundamentally.

The interest in transnational families is long-standing in migration studies and a consistent number of studies have also focused on family reunification and the legal aspects of separation for refugees (Grote, 2017; Bick, 2018; Tometten, 2018; Sauer et al., 2018; Kraus et al., 2019). Significantly less is known about the different dimensions of separation in forced displacement, the challenges for both migrants and left-behind families, as well as the various ways people at both sides of international borders deal with separation.

This chapter aims at filling some of those gaps by answering these questions: What are the main challenges for separated Syrian families in German? What is the impact of separation on gender roles and relationships among Syrian families in Germany? How do separated Syrian men and women renegotiate these relationships and do family from afar? My findings indicate that separated families go through a series of everyday insecurities expressed through three main dimensions – a material, a relational, and an ethical dimension. Renegotiations to respond to the everyday insecurities engendered by separation occurred by establishing new networks and through the consolidation of family relations from afar. On the one hand, participants maintained the continuity of family in the transnational space of separation through what Anthropologist Suad Joseph called "family connectivity" (Joseph, 1993). On the other hand, coming to terms individually with separation as a condition to navigate instead of rejecting it was a preliminary step to renegotiate a new position on a relational level.

Primary data were collected in 2019 in different German states through individual semi-structured interviews carried out on the nature of the difficulties that separated family members experienced, their perception of those, and the coping strategies they employed to overcome those difficulties.

References

Bick, A. (2018). Right to family reunification in Germany. In Friedery, R., Manca, L. & Ros, R. (Eds.), *Family Reunification: International, European and National Perspectives* (pp. 95-118). Berlin: Berliner Wissenschafts-Verlag.

Grote, J. (2017). *Family Reunification of Third-country Nationals in Germany. Focus-Study by the German National Contact Point for the European Migration Network (EMN).* Federal Office for Migration and Refugees 2017. [Working Paper 73].

Joseph, S. (1993). Connectivity and patriarchy among urban working-class Arab families in Lebanon. *Ethos: Journal of the Society for Psychological Anthropology, 21*(4), 452-484.

Kraus, E. K. Sauer, L., Wenzel, L. (2019). Together or apart? Spousal migration and reunification practices of recent refugees to Germany. *ZfF – Zeitschrift für Familienforschung / Journal of Family Research 3*, 303-332.

Sauer, L., Diabaté, S., Gabel, S., Halfar, Y., Kraus, E. K., Wenzel, L. (2018). *Doing transnational family im Kontext von Flucht und Krisenmigration. Stand der Forschung.* Wiesbaden: Bundesinstitut für Bevölkerungsforschung. [BiB Working Paper 3/2018].

Tometten, C. (2018). Resettlement, humanitarian admission, and family reunion: The intricacies of Germany's legal entry regimes for Syrian refugees. *Refugee Survey Quarterly, 37*, 187-203.

859   Parental work migration and the children left behind in rural Romania. A qualitative perspective

Gabriela Guiu*, Georgiana Udrea, Malina Ciocea

* This work was supported by a grant of the Romanian Ministry of Research and Innovation, CNCS – UEFISCDI, project number PN-III-P1-1.1-BSH-2-2016-0005, within PNCDI III

This paper presents some major effects that parental work migration has on children's school performance, interpersonal communication networks and relationships' building with both their close and distant others. What we aim is to provide an image of the impact of the migratory phenomenon on the children that are left at home (from the latter's stance), as well as a better understanding of the consequences of parents' departure on their social, communication and educational behavior.

In Romanian society, labor migration stands as an active and continuous process causing important transformations at every level of our country's development. As somehow expected, the number of the Romanian people who decided to work abroad has considerably increased after 2007 (when Romania became an EU Member State and the borders were largely opened for its workers, goods and capital), and has totally exploded after 2014 when countries such as the UK or the Netherlands have also welcome the Romanian and Bulgarian workforce flow (Beciu et al., 2019; Bian, 2018). Accordingly, current unofficial statistics estimates the Romanian diaspora at over 5 million people, out of which many have left their children behind.

In this context, researches explore migratory trends and flows, causes and motivations of migrants' decision to leave their country and look for a job elsewhere, economic and demographic effects of the migration phenomenon (Bălan & Olteanu, 2017; Brock & Blake, 2015). However, there are fewer qualitative studies focusing on the challenges that parental emigration triggers for the children left at home. Thus, using in-depth interviews and hypothesizing that work migration inevitably leads to multiple and multi-layered changes that affect families in terms of lifestyle and life quality, communication, relationships, etc., our study discusses some of the main transformations generated by parental emigration (from those related to school performance to those raised by the day to day life provocations) from the children's own standpoint. Main attention is paid to the relationship between the 'missing' parent and the child who is usually thousands of kilometers apart and to how this personal, intimate relationship is reshaped by physical distance, new communication technologies/ platforms and all the new realities that the child has to confront alone.

In line with prior studies (Abrego, 2014; Madianou & Miller, 2012) and considering the long-term changes in its structure, dynamics and functionality, we argue that families are the first institutions affected by the labor migration phenomenon. The children who are in a situation where one or both their parents work abroad remain, however, the most vulnerable category in the whole process, and their cases should be carefully documented for a better understanding of this life-changing experience and of how the negative consequences emerging from it could be limited in the future. Even if most parents' decision to emigrate in search for better life prospects aims at creating a favorable environment for their children's development, the separation of families is often seen as one of the most negative effects of emigration, with tremendous impact on children's educational performance and personal wellbeing.

References

Abrego, L. J. (2014). Sacrificing Families. Navigation laws, labor, and love across borders. California: Stanford University Press.

Bălan, M., & Olteanu, C. (2017). Brain Drain In The Globalization Era: The Case Of Romania. Annals-Economy Series, 3, 26–35.

Beciu, C., Ciocea, M., Mădroane, I. D., & Cârlan, A. (2019). Introduction: Intra-EU Labor Migration and Transnationalism in Media Dicourses: A Public Problem Approach. In C. Beciu, M. Ciocea, I. D. Mădroane & A. Cârlan (Eds.), Debating migration as a Public Problem. National Publics and Transnational Fields (pp. 1–37). New-York: Peter Lang.

Bian, N. (2018). Harta diasporei. Campioni în UE la migrația internă. Câți români trăiesc în afara țării [The map of diaspora. EU champions in internal migration. How many Romanians live abroad.]. Retrieved at: https://www.g4media.ro/harta-diasporei-campioni-in-ue-la-imigratia-interna-cati-romani-traiesc-in-afara-tarii.html.

Brock, G., & Blake, M. (2015). Prosperity in developing countries, the effects departing individuals have on those left behind, and some policy options. Debating Brain Drain. May Governments Restrict Emigration?, Oxford University Press.

Madianou, M., & Miller, D. (2012). Migration and new media. Transnational families and polymedia. New York: Routledge.

728   Determinants of migration from rural households in India: An empirica investigation

Shreya Nupur and Meghna Dutta

Migration is an important livelihood diversification strategy to mitigate potential risks, such as crop failure, major illness, job loss etc., in rural areas (Katz and Stark, 1986). Migration and remittances acts as an insurance against these risks and save poor people from falling into extreme poverty. However, the literature dealing with migration in developing countries have devoted little attention to the particular group of 'rural poor population' while studying rural to urban streams (Tang, 2019). In India studies have mostly considered the individual's perspective and assumed migrant to be an individual actor while taking migration decision. Few scholars such as Stark (1991) and Chandrasekhar and sahoo (2018) emphasized the role of the entire household as a single decision making unit for migration. This perspective is salient especially for 'rural poor households' in developing world, despite knowing the fact that it is the rural poor who takes split migration decision and make household arrangements accordingly. Thus, this paper intends to study migration decision making strategy for 'rural poor households' by taking into account the household as a single decision making unit.

To examine the determinants of migration decision in 'rural poor households' in India considering household as a decision making unit.

The present study is based on the second round of India Human Development Survey data which is collected in between November 2011 to October 2012. We only consider a subset of 4,471 households of this survey to answer our research question. Since we want to examine the determinant of migration from 'rural poor households' we restricted our study sample to poor households of rural India. Thus, this data allows to study migration mechanism at household level. Here, the Logit model has been used to model the binary outcome that is whether the 'rural poor household' has sent at least one migrant or not.

The findings of this study indicates migration as an important livelihood strategy for rural poor households. It is likely to trigger migration in presence of debt in the household. Increasing household size having marginal irrigated landholding and belonging to forward caste group raises the probability of migration. In addition to that, households that have faced major shocks or events in form of illness and marriage are more likely to send out at least one of the member. However, welfare benefit distributions by the government dampens the odds of sending migrants from rural poor households.

This paper attempts to examine the probability of migration decision of a particular group 'poor rural household' from household perspective. The findings indicate migration as an important strategy to tackle poverty for poor households in rural India. At household level debt, shocks, dependent members, small landholding etc. increases, while welfare benefits and presence female elder head are likely to dampen the probability of migration. Moreover, it is important to understand the nexus between migration mechanism and poverty in rural poor households so that informed policy could be formulated for these vulnerable group.

References

Chandrasekhar, S., and Sahoo, S. (2018). "Short-term Migration in Rural India: The Impact of Nature and Extent of Participation in Agriculture". Working Paper No. 2018–016. Indira Gandhi Institute of Development Research. Available at: http://www.igidr.ac.in/igidr-working-paper-10/.

Katz, E., and Stark O. 1986. "Labor migration and risk aversion in less developed countries." *Journal of Labor Economics* 4: 131-149.

Stark, O. (1991). "The Migration of Labour". Cambridge: Basil Blackwell.

Tang S. (2019). "Determinants of migration and household member arrangement among poor rural households in China: The case of North Jiangsu". *Population Space Place*.

6E   Migration Governance

802   The Efficiency of the International Organizations to Preserve the Refugee Protection Regime during International Crisis

Nihal Eminoğlu

The international organizations (IOs) play a dominant and crucial role in protection of norms related to Global Refugee Protection Regime (GRPR) during times of crisis. However, the success and capacity of the IOs to preserve the standards of the Regime has always been a controversial issue. In this regard, Covid-19 pandemic, as one of the most global crises that the world faces in recent history, has been unique experience for testing their effectiveness on the protection of international standards for refugees.

The main objective of the IOs is to balance the needs and interests of states and needs and interests of the humankind which are generally in conflict especially during the times of crisis.
In this context, the question on how adequately the 'balance of power' contributed to guarantee the norms of international society on refugee protection during COVID-19 crisis will be questioned in this study and we will seek the answer through the effectiveness of international organizations since they undertook a more active role within this process. To do so, the study will conduct an analysis through the policies and practices of three major organizations and their agencies, namely, European Union (EU), United Nations (UN), and the Council of Europe (CoE), particularly in relation to their interactions with states to protect the 'balance' for the GRPR.

The study will be based on the theorical framework of the English School which prioritized the 'balance of power' as one of the mechanisms of the international society. In this framework the study will analyze the efforts of IOs, under the concept of balance of power, in terms of safeguarding the fundamental principles of global refugee protection regime in crisis periods.

References

Barry Buzan, "The English School: an underexploited resource in IR", *Review of international Studies*, 2001

Hedley Bull, *The Anarchical Society: A Study of Order in World Politics*, PALGRAVE, 2002

644   At the Borders of the European Union: Irregular Migrants as a New Problem Area in Turkish-Greek Relations

Pınar Çağlayan

While forced migration has mostly emerged as an internal problem of countries due to the fact that it takes place as a practice of internal displacement, it shapes inter-state relations as well by causing border security problem for relevant states. In this context, the human mobility across international borders not only affects sociological, economic and political relations between the victims of forced migration and the destination country but also changes the trend of the relations between those states who are mostly-affected from these flows. Moreover, it has effects on reproducing the current problems of neighboring countries and so it serves as a catalyst in this reproduction process.

In this regard, it is seen that the undocumented migration which has begun to increase since the 1990s, has become another problem area between Turkey and Greece since these states have become the main targets of irregular migration movements. However, this new problem area not only needs to be analyzed within the framework of a border security problem but also an ideological layer that historically determines the characteristic of Turkish-Greek relations.

In general, both Turkey and Greece, rather than addressing their problems, approached each other within the framework of "otherization" and have used this as an ideological tool in their -domestic politics. In particular, this practice of "otherization", which began in 1950s with Cyprus issue between the parties, has been gradually reproduced with additional problems such as determination of the maritime sovereignty areas in the Aegean Sea and the borders of the airspace. Although the discourse of "otherization" in Turkish-Greek relations has been less prevailing in political area and mass media thanks to the optimistic atmosphere emerged after the 1999 Marmara Earthquake in Turkey, it is analyzed in this paper that the irregular migration flow between the parties' borders, changed this peaceful tone and revealed this discourse in a populist manner.

In this study, firstly, I will show how both Turkey and Greece have used forced migrants as an ideological and political tool to resurrect their pre-existing issues. Secondly, I will discuss how Turkey's opening its borders to asylum-seekers - who were willing to reach EU countries- between 28th February-6th March 2020 increased the tension between the parties. In this scope, how Turkish and Greek politicians and mass media dealt with the subject will be examined by employing discourse analysis. The ideological approaches of both countries to each other and what type of discourses are produced within this period will be the main focus of this study.

858   The Prohibition of Collective Expulsions in EU

Aikaterini Togia

The purpose of the present paper is to provide a full scope of the prohibition of collective expulsions in EU, taking into consideration the current International, European and EU law as well as case law of the European Court of Human Rights, in the context of migration flows, which attempt to cross the EU external borders.

Even though it is accepted that collective expulsions are prohibited, some EU member states have been alleged that the practices that they follow in order to manage their external borders, and prevent migratory flows from entering the EU area, equal to collective expulsions, violating directly the fundamental rights of the expelled persons, as provided in International, European and EU law. The European Court of Human Rights has repeatedly found that collective expulsions are unlawful under International and European human rights law, however there are cases in which the elements presented did not amount to a violation of the art. 4 of Protocol 4 of the ECHR[21].

Taking the above into consideration, the present paper will present the current international, European and EU law according to which the collective expulsions are prohibited[22] and provide an explanation of the terms 'expulsion' and 'collective'. Moreover, this paper will refer to key judgments of the European Court of Human Rights concerning the collective expulsion, presenting the situations and elements that the ECtHR found that amount to a violation or not of the art. 4 of Protocol 4 of the ECHR. The topic of collective expulsions is extremely interesting, when assessing the measures that the EU member states take in order to manage their external borders which in some cases are also the external borders EU and the potential violation of fundamental rights of the persons expelled.

713   What is the Value of Diplomacy for International Refugee Protection during Times of Crisis?

M. Gökay Özerim

The international regime for the protection of refugees lays down a structure based on the legal instruments and structures not only designed to provide

---

[21] ECtHR, Hirsi Jamaa and Others v. Italy [GC], No. 27765/09, 23 February 2012, ECtHR, N.D. and N.T. v. Spain [GC], Nos. 8675/15 and 8697/15, 13 February 2020, paras. 185 and 187, ECtHR, Moustahi v. France, No. 9347/14, 25 June 2020, paras. 133–137. ECtHR, Čonka v. Belgium, No. 51564/99, 5 February 2002. ECtHR, M.A. v. Cyprus, No. 41872/10, 23 July 2013, ECtHR, Khlaifia and Others v. Italy [GC], No. 16483/12, 15 December 2016, paras. 237–254.
[22] art. 13 of the ICCPR, art. 5 (a), 6 of the CERD, art. 19 of EU Charter, art. 4 of Protocol 4 of the ECHR, art. 19 (8) of the ESC.

international protection for individuals but also to clarify the obligations of states and other stakeholders for sustaining this system. However, endurance and the efficacy of this regime during the periods of international crisis is still questionable. The economic and social crisis in recent decades caused one more time to question the vulnerability of this regime and the possible tools to prevent its' fragility.

This study aims to discuss, whether diplomacy might be a reliable tool to provide endurance of the international refugee protection system by the times of crisis. As to achieve this analysis, the study theoretically examines the "power of diplomacy" and it focuses on the case of diplomatic relations at global level for providing the sustainability of the international protection system during the COVID-19 pandemic. The analysis is based on the theoretical framework of the English School, which claims that diplomacy is one of the prominent institutions of the international society for defining common interests or negotiating them. Accordingly, diplomacy is considered as a tool and institution of the international society to explain the functioning of relations between states and the establishment of order in world politics.

Diplomacy has played a vital role in the emergence of the international refugee protection system, as states agreed on and encoded the norms and rules of this regime. In this vein, we might expect the intensive functionality of diplomacy to protect this system when international society experiences a crisis. This study will discuss whether this expectation about diplomacy has a certainty and the possible factors that might influence the functionality of it.

References

Barry Buzan, "The Primary Institutions of International Society", Barry Buzan (ed.), *From International to World Society? English School Theory And The Social Structure of Globalization,* Cambridge, Cambridge University Press, 2004, p. 161-204

UNHCR, "Key Legal Considerations on access to territory for persons in need of international protection in the context of Covid-19 response", 16 March 2020, https://www.refworld.org/docid/5e7132834.html

Andrew Linklater, "Prudence and Principle in International Society: Reflections on Vincent's Approach to Human Rights", *International Affairs,* Vol. 87, No. 5, 2011, p. 1191.

6F   Health and Migration
Chair: Gul Ince-Beqo, University of Bari, Italy

775   Migrants and asylum seekers health right: Italian (and Apulian) legislation in the European contest
Alda Kushi, Michela Camilla Pellicani, Rosa Venisti

705   Investigating the Impact of Lack of Social Support on the Mental Wellbeing among LGBTQ+ Asylum Seekers and Refugees during Post-Migration in the UK
Ahmad Riaz, Faridah Nabagereka, Pearlgin Lindiwe Goba

793   Do immigrants from high-fertility countries adapt their fertility behaviour to Spain's lowest-low and latest-late fertility regime?

Jesus Garcia-Gomez, Chiara Dello Iacono, Mikolaj Stanek

775   Migrants and asylum seekers health right: Italian (and Apulian) legislation in the European contest

Alda Kushi, Michela Camilla Pellicani, Rosa Venisti

Analysing European Union regulation on public health, particularly that concerning refugees and asylum seekers, this study aims to examine how the Italian legislation and the legislation of the Apulia region are placed in the European context.

The 2019 WHO Europe report states the importance to protect the health of refugees and migrants for several reasons: right to health is a basic human right, under the 1966 *International Covenant on Economic, Social and Cultural Rights*; refugees and migrants contribute actively to development of the host society and country of origin; the existence of clusters of population with lower health coverage can have negative health outcomes for the whole community; early diagnosis and treatment save lives and cut treatment costs; prioritizing vulnerable populations and individuals most at need in societies is a sound public health strategy.

Restricted health care coverage for migrants and asylum seekers can have negative repercussions on public health and can hinder the achievement of national and international health goals.

However, at European level, the legislation that guarantees health protection to migrants and asylum seekers is still weak and fragmented. Indeed, this legislation is scattered across different areas of the European Union's competences and actions. That's why it is necessary to analyse several documents adopted at European level such as: public health legislation, focusing on migrants and asylum seekers; documents relating to the integration process focusing on health protection; European Charter of Human Rights and the jurisprudence of the Court of Justice.

Within the EU member state in Italy the right to health is particularly relevant. In fact, the health protection is provided into Constitutional Charter (art. 32). The Apulian context represents an exception in the national territory since it extends the medical treatments and services provided for Italians and regular migrants to those irregular ones as well (regional law n.32/2009).

The Apulian case demonstrate that A closer look at regional context and an inclusive policy make the legislation on the protection of the health of migrants and asylum seekers more effective.

705   Investigating the Impact of Lack of Social Support on the Mental Wellbeing among LGBTQ+ Asylum Seekers and Refugees during Post-Migration in the UK

Ahmad Riaz, Faridah Nabagereka, Pearlgin Lindiwe Goba

Past research has identified high levels of mental distress among LGBTQ+ asylum seekers, including depression, anxiety and post-traumatic stress disorder (Piwowarczyk, Fernandez & Sharma, 2016). Others (Chu, Keller, & Rasmussen, 2013; Porter & Haslam, 2005) have indicated that stressors (financial, social and interpersonal) resulting from post-migration play a significant role in mental distress, highlighting the importance of viewing the mental wellbeing of refugees as a more nuanced issue than simply a post-traumatic consequence of trauma. The above reveals the impact of the precarious life conditions on the LGBTQ+ migrants' mental health, resulting from the combination of pre-migration/migration traumas and post-migration barriers. As a result, the study aims at exploring whether the combination of stressors experienced by LGBTQ+ migrants during their post-migration phase in the UK prevents opportunities for social connectivity and support, consequently affecting their mental wellbeing. This phenomenon has been under-researched in the UK.

The study applies the social-cognitive processing (SCP) model (Lepore, 2001) on adjustment to traumatic event as a framework to further examine the impact of social constraints on the mental wellbeing in the sample. In presence of social constraints, individuals are reluctant to express trauma-related feelings due to critical, invalidating or alienating responses from others, delaying recovery following a traumatic event. Accordingly, social constraints experienced by LGBTQ+ migrants on arriving to the UK (in terms of lack of social support and a *culture of disbelief* within the asylum system; Connely, 2013) could contribute to prolonged and increased distress following pre-migration and migration trauma, via negative cognitions that the individual holds about themselves, others and the world. It is believed that these population groups are victims of the intersection of multiple discrimination (sexual, racial, ethnic, etc.), often leading to expectations of negative reactions from others and perceived unreceptive social support. In this study, the lack of appropriate government's systematic psycho-social support is perceived to be a level of social constraints, capable of impacting UK-based LGBTQ+ migrants' mental wellbeing.

It is hypothesised that having less supportive system may reduce participants' opportunities to process thoughts pertaining to personal distressing traumatising events, thus reinforcing conditions of negative cognitions (negative appraisals) that would indirectly affect mental wellbeing. The sample recruitment follows a non-probability purposive critical case sampling method, and selection criteria includes individuals who have been granted or are seeking asylum in the UK due to their identity as being LGBTQ+. The data is still at its collection stage and will be analysed using SPSS software. This research aims to test specific hypotheses by measuring the relationships between social constraints, negative cognitions, and mental wellbeing among this group. Correlational analyses will be conducted in order to determine potential significant relationships. Mediation analysis regression will be conducted in order to test whether negative cognitions would mediate the relationship between social constraints (predictor) with the mental wellbeing (outcome).

By demonstrating that the social-cognitive model of processing trauma reflects the experiences of LGBTQ+ refugees, there are implications for mental healthcare, provision of social support, and re-design of the asylum-seeking process for this group.

Connely, E. (2013). Queer, beyond a reasonable doubt: refugee experiences of 'passing' into 'membership of a particular social group'. UCL Migration Research Unit Working Papers, No. 2014/3

Chu, T., Keller, A. S., & Rasmussen, A. (2013). Effects of post-migration factors on PTSD outcomes among immigrant survivors of political violence. *Journal of immigrant and minority health, 15*, 890-897.

Lepore, S. J. (2001). A social-cognitive processing model of emotional adjustment to cancer. In A. Baum & B. Andersen (Eds.), *Psychosocial interventions for cancer* (pp. 99-118). Washington, DC: APA.

Piwowarczyk, L., Fernandez, P., & Sharma, A. (2016). Seeking Asylum: Challenges Faced by the LGB Community. *Journal of Immigrant and Minority Health, 19*, 723-732. doi:10.1007/s10903-016-0363-9

Porter, M., & Haslam, N. (2005). Predisplacement and postdisplacement factors associated with mental health of refugees and internally displaced persons. *JAMA, 294*(5), 602. doi.org/10.1001/jama.294.5.602

793   Do immigrants from high-fertility countries adapt their fertility behaviour to Spain's lowest-low and latest-late fertility regime?

Chiara Dello Iacono, Jesus Garcia-Gomez, Mikolaj Stanek

During the first decade of this century Spain experienced a rapid increase of the immigrant population: it is now the European country with the highest number of Latin American immigrants and the second highest number of Maghrebi immigrants. The fertility regime of an immigrant group is a relevant indicator of integration with respect to the receiving society. However, the fertility regime of the descendants of immigrants have been little studied in Southern European countries. Immigrants from Latin America and the Maghreb in Spain have similarities and differences. Both come from countries with an earlier fertility regime and higher fertility. However, the motivation for migration is different. Immigrant women from Latin America come to Spain mainly with the aim of improving their labour market prospects and display high activity rates in the Spanish labour market. Immigrant women coming from the Maghreb mainly arrive with the aim of regrouping with their male partner and forming a family, and display low activity rates. Therefore, the level of integration of these two immigrant groups with respect to the fertility patterns of the native population may be different both in 1st generation Immigrants and in their descendants. Previous studies have found that Latin American 1st generation immigrants, in their effort to achieve a high participation in the labour market, opt to have fewer children than immigrants from the Maghreb, who tend to follow the fertility patterns of their countries of origin. However, due to the lack of adequate databases, the fertility regime adopted by the descendants of these immigrant groups in Spain remain unknown. This study takes advantage of the opportunity to investigate the fertility regime of the 1st, 1.5 and 2nd generation of immigrants in Spain between 2011-2015. A novel database which links Natural Movement of the Population Records to the 2011 Spanish Census is used. By means of Negative Binomial Regression Models and the construction of a set of interaction terms the fertility patterns of Latin American and Maghrebi immigrants and their descendants in Spain are investigated. The results show that the level of integration of Latin American immigrant women is much higher than that of Maghrebi immigrant women, both in the 1st generation and in the 1.5 and 2nd generations. These findings confirm the Segmented Assimilation Theory, the level of integration of different immigrant groups depends on issues related to their origin such as the motivation to migrate. Interestingly, we conclude that a high level of education and high labour market participation operate as factors that promote the integration of immigrant women and their descendants with respect to the fertility regime of native women.

6G   Migration Theory and Research: New Debates

Chair: Ruchi Singh, Prin. L. N. Welingkar Institute of Management
Development & Research, India

565   Reframing migrancy through intersectional analysis: conceptualizing the embodiment of the migration experience from the Mexican-United States migration field framework
Renato de Almeida Arao Galhardi

628   Between work and "invitation to travel". In the Syrians refugees' kitchens in Burgundy (France)
Jeremy Sauvineau

843   Practical Insight from a First-Timer's Fieldwork
Elif Demirbas

884   Home' and 'homeland' as mobile places: Re-examining the term country of origin in migration studies
Maria Panteleou

565   Reframing migrancy through intersectional analysis: conceptualizing the embodiment of the migration experience from the Mexican-United States migration field framework

Renato de Almeida Arao Galhardi

One of the historical consequences of Mexican immigration to the United States is not only the creation and consolidation of transnational social migration fields (Basch, Glick Schiller & Szanton Blanc, 1994), but the entrenchment of the experience of migration as more than just a cultural repertoire or social capital. These experiences highlight the penetration of the network-society (Castells, 2001), the connective turn (Hoskins, 2011) and the relational self (Chen, Boucher and Tapias, 2006) of the Mexico-United States migrational field. How, then, do migrants negotiate their *migrancy* among themselves? The overview of research on Mexican migration to the United States, constructed in the 20th century within, mostly, the boundaries of the migratory field of each nation, has discussed, at length, Mexican migration from a plethora of perspectives that seek to capture migrancy (Brettell & Hollifield, 2015). The literature seems to indicate that the experience of migration is a structuring aspect of the ontological construction of social reality. Migrancy, then, seems to indicate something more than displacements and movements in space-time. The experience of migrancy suggests a with anthropologist Arjun Appadurai's "scapes" of cultural engagement within the "work of the imagination" (Appadurai, 2001). The migrational experience, deposited in the concept of migrancy, positions the relational Self within a structural, ideological, cultural, economic, and social valences constructing an additional "scape": a "migrancy-scape". By framing migrancy as a Durkheiman "social fact", and applying to it the particularities of Bourdieu's *habitus*, the concept of migrancy becomes a powerful tool that adds a necessary analytical dimension to migration analysis. Within this working framework of migrancy, intersectional feminist theory provides a sharp and useful resource to reengage with the concept of migrancy in a meaningful way. Articulating migrancy -migrancia in Spanish- within Mexican-United States migration analysis allows for a more comprehensive, historically situated and embodied, construction of the migration experience within a macro-micro analytical framework. By articulating, at least, the three variables of the most basic intersectional composition -gender, race, and ethnicity- migrancy can provide an essential and important baseline for migration analysis, especially in the context of Mexican-United States migration relations. With this, I propose a reengagement with a more substantiated concept of migrancy that brings the scope of intersectional theory to migration analysis, recuperating the *habitus* of migration experience to the forefront of migration analysis allowing for visibility of the embodiment of migration. I argued that this approach adds a "body" to the migration analysis and expands its scope by adding a new "scape" to the dimension of the perception of migration experience. By framing migrancy through intersectional theory, as a social fact, articulated through habitus and within a "scape", migrancy can be better articulated within migrational analysis and effectively articulate the experience of migration.

628   Between work and "invitation to travel". In the Syrians refugees' kitchens in Burgundy (France)

Jeremy Sauvineau

Contemporary, anthropological research is mainly interested in "what city make to migrants"; unfortunately, just a few of them are interested in "what migrants make to the city" (Agier, 2016). This is the question we would like to focus on, by investigating the Syrian culinary entrepreneurship in Burgundy (France). Indeed, the presence of syrian diaspora, since the so-called "refugee crisis" (2015-2016), has manifested by the opening of syrians' restaurants and grocery shops. Far from being a strictly economic issue, the study of Syrian shops (groceries and restaurants) leads us to analyze the complex interweaving of Syrian chefs' objectives. What are they?

First and foremost, the opening of one's own restaurant is linked to the problem of work. The use of "cultural resources" (Jullien, 2016), seems to be a "tactic" (Certeau, 1980) to avoid the multiple difficulties that foreigners have to face in the French context. Thus, starting from biographical interviews, we would like to highlight the difficulties raised by migrants in their professional careers: how the experience of unemployment and discriminations lead Syrians to think about ethnic entrepreneurship (Ray, 2011; Ibrahim & Galt, 2011) and then, "cooking up their own status" (Katz, 2011)? How do they build their shops in a strained context?

At least two other related objectives must be added to the economic question. On the one hand an "experiential" concern. Through a "Syrian" decor, a different culinary aesthetic or through discussions about Syria, the aim of the chefs is to provide an "experience" (in the sense of Dewey (2016)) to the customers. How, in practical terms, do they provide this experience? How do they make it happen? What are the customers reactions? Do they feel the experience in the same way the chefs wanted them to live? On the other hand, a fully political component – but related to the question of "experience". Whether they are former opponents of Bashar al-Assad's regime or not, the Syrian chefs suggest a double political objective. First, because they wish to put forward a different "destroyed country's" story as proposed by the French medias. What picture of Syria do they present in their shops? What do they tell the customers to make these differences? On the other hand, the chefs' *"invitation to travel"* is an invitation to the composition of a common world, beyond the differences (often naturalized) between French and Syrians. Is it a way to keep away the "communitarian" critic?

This paper is based on an ongoing thesis work, which bear interest in the affordances allowed by the "cultural resources" (Jullien, 2016) of migrants and refugees (including cooking). More specifically, the ethnographic material mobilized comes from participating observations in restaurants and cookery workshops as well as six interviews conducted in Syrian restaurants and grocery shops.

References

Certeau M. (de), *L'invention du quotidien t. 1. arts de faire*, Paris, Gallimard, coll. « Folio-essais », 2017 [1980].

Dewey J., *L'Art comme expérience*, Paris, Gallimard, coll. « folio essai », 2016 [1934].

Ibrahim G., Galt V., « Explaining ethnic entrepreneurship: An evolutionary economics approach", *International Business Review*, 20, 2011, pp. 607-613.

Jullien F., *Il n'y a pas d'identité culturelle. Mais nous défendons les ressources d'une culture*, Éditions de L'Herne, Paris, 2016.

Katz J., « Se cuisiner un statut. Des noms aux verbes dans l'étude de la stratification sociale », *ethnographiques.org*, 23, 2011.

Ray K., « Dreams of Pakistani Grill and Vada Pao In Manhattan », *Food, Culture & Society*, 14:2, 2011, pp. 243-273.

843   Practical Insight from a First-Timer's Fieldwork

Elif Demirbas

Research methods is a critical, but often an overlooked, part of any research that involves some form of data collection. Every PhD thesis that deals with empirical data needs to have a methods chapter that would ideally bring together the literature on the particular method(s) used and the actual fieldwork experience. These chapters are important both to legitimise the study and to guide people who are interested in doing a similar research. However, the actual experience of fieldwork often turns out to be quite different from the one written on paper, with many pitfalls, failures, frustrations glossed over or completely omitted. This is a great disservice to other PhD students or early career researchers who are about to embark on their first fieldwork and who would want to know what exactly they are getting themselves into.

When studying migration, researchers often come into contact with vulnerable people, try to gain their trust, talk about illegal activities, go to refugee camps, cross nation borders in search of people, and do many other activities that the first-time researcher may have never done before. Researchers often feel like a fish out of water during their first fieldwork, although, detailed accounts of fieldwork experiences could help in giving ideas to other researchers, whether they are experienced or inexperienced. In this presentation, I propose to talk about my fieldwork experience, highlighting both its successes and failures. My research is on Syrian refugees living in Turkey, their integration into the labour market and the ensuing precarity they live in. I conducted 31 semi-structured interviews with Syrian refugees in two cities in Turkey over the course of summer 2020. My fieldwork was laden with difficulties, not just because of the restrictions relating to Covid-19, but also resulting from my inexperience, my lack of contacts and the unwillingness or incapacity of all the NGOs and key workers that I contacted to help me.

The way in which empirical data is collected can be as important as the data collected or the theoretical concepts used to make sense of them. There is a disdain in academia, especially in social sciences, towards technical knowledge, or at best an avoidance of technical issues. Theory always reigns supreme in social sciences; but, we all can benefit from each other's experience. To that end, I propose to talk about the practical aspects of my fieldwork, rather than going into a theoretical discussion on research methods. Specifically, I want to emphasise the difficulties of doing fieldwork as a lone PhD student, such as lack of contacts, funds, and the legal restrictions surrounding doing research with refugees. Then, I will go on to recount how hard it was to find people to participate in my research and the mistakes I made during the interviews. This account will be supported by excerpts from my fieldnotes and field diary along with anecdotes from the fieldwork itself.

Thank you for your consideration.

Elif Demirbas

884   Home' and 'homeland' as mobile places: Re-examining the term country of origin in migration studies

Maria Panteleou

In the modern globalized world, the identifications and the relationships, that migrants construct on the "home" and "homeland" are so complicated that they cannot simply interpreted either as "rooted belonging" or "rootless mobility" (Baker, 2012, p.26). Anthropological studies have examined critically the "home", away from the sedentarism, emotional approach, where it is understood as "a unique, stable location, a place of birth, connected with parents, childhood and the past" (Van Boeschoten & Danforth, 2015, p.290), claiming that if we consider not only the spatial but also the temporal dimension, the cultural notion, that is attributed to specific places, changes over time. At the same specter, the notion of the one and unique homeland, which is to some extend invented by the imaginaries of deterritorialized groups (Appadurai, 2014, p.78), has been questioned and replaced by the viewpoint of a "mobile" homeland, that permit people to "feel like home in more than one places" (Van Boeschoten & Danforth, 2015, p.290-291). This presentation, using material from triennial anthropological fieldwork (2015-2017) with Albanian migrants, who live and work in Corinth since 1998, moving temporally, especially during holidays, to their "home" and "homeland" in Albania, demonstrates that they experience there the sense of foreignness. Wherefore apart from their family, the wider social context in post-socialist Albania is unfamiliar because their relatives or/and their family are scattered across different countries, capable condition to convert "homeland" and "home" to "empty" and "meaningless" notions. Furthermore, examining the temporal familial visits that Albanian migrants welcome in Greece, it seems that the temporal mobility of their relatives brings the sense of "home" itself together in Greece. The presentation concludes that in the case of Albanian migrants in Corinth, the adaption of the term country of origin, which is widely used for analytical purposes in migration studies, defines them in advance by a spatial notion, whereas the subjective conceptualizations of the "home" and "homeland" show primarily that they are mobile, secondly that they make sense for Albanians only through the symbolic, relational and experiential dimension of the place.

References

Appadurai, A., (2014), Modernity at large: Cultural dimensions of globalization. Athens: Alexandria.

Baker, K., (2012), "Identity, Memory and Place". The Word Hoard 1 (1): 23-33. http://ir.lib.uwo.ca/wordhoard/vol1/iss1/4 Accessed: 25.2.2021.

Van Boeschoten, R. and L. M. Danforth, (2015), Children of the Greek Civil War: Refugees and the politics of memory. Athens: Alexandria.

12:15-12:45 BREAK

Day Three 8 July 2021 Thursday

Day Three 8 July 2021 - 12:45-14:15
Institute for Mobile Studies Special Roundtable [Click here to Join]
Moderator: Eugene Ch'ng, Professor of Cultural Computing, School of International Communications, University of Nottingham Ningbo China
Panellists:

Antonio Lam, Managing Director of Shores and Legal, London, UK: **"How technology has transformed my job as an immigration practitioner"**

Dr Xiaoge Xu, Associate Professor in Media and Communication Studies, UNNC: **"Mapping, measuring and modelling mobility: initial thoughts for global collaboration"**

Amira Halperin, Deputy Director of Institute for Mobile Studies, UNNC: **"Mobile Phones and Forced Migration"**

Lei Hao, Teaching Fellow at School of International Communications; Research Fellow at Institute of Asia and Pacific Studies; Research Fellow at Institute for Mobile Studies, UNNC: **"The Concretisation of Blockchain Technology in Chinese Technoliberalist Crypto Space"**

Troy Chen, Director of Teaching, Assistant Professor in Media, Communication and Cultural Studies, UNNC: **"Mobile Self-portrayal of Chinese maid A reflection of the social tensions between female domestic workers and the rising middle class in China"**

7A   Work, Employment and Migration

Chair: Joao Peixoto, Universidade de Lisboa, Portugal

865   Departure from Brazil, arrival in Portugal and England: work and career for Brazilian migrants
Andrea Oltramari, Duval Fernandes, Joao Peixoto

866   Out of sight, out of mind: Impact of COVID-19 pandemic in hidden unemployment on migrants' collectives in European Southern countries
Andres Coco-Prieto, Laura Suarez-Grimalt, Montserrat Simo-Solsona

889   Employment Subsidise, Capacity Reinforcement, and Sanction: In Government's activation governance for work promotion
Esien Eddy Bruno

875   Social and Economic Contexts of Migration: Why Turkey is Attracting Georgian Women Labour Migrants?
Meryem Ayşe Göktaş

865   Departure from Brazil, arrival in Portugal and England: work and career for Brazilian migrants

Andrea Oltramari, Duval Fernandes, Joao Peixoto

The migratory project can present itself in a different way when analyzing different nationalities and different genders. Some studies have already pointed out that the insertion of work and the resumption of careers for women, for example, can be quite traumatic. As Hirata (2009, p. 31) points out "international female migrations represent one of the factors that strengthen this movement of precarious work for women". Violence seems to be aggravated by nationality, due to the stereotype of sensuality linked to the image of the Brazilian (Fraga, Antunes & Rocha-de-Oliveira, 2020). Thus, it is important to associate gender discussions with migration, as the possibilities of insertion and permanence in the labor market depend on socio-historical contexts. In general, women end up being neglected in international opportunities, even with high qualifications, considering that some countries are still restricted when it comes to the presence of women in organizational and power spaces (Fraga, Antunes & Rocha-de-Oliveira, 2020; Wasserman & Frenkel, 2015). The objective of this research was to identify the reasons, differences and difficulties faced by Brazilians to (re) build their careers due to migration reasons. The research included a semi-structured script that concerned questions about work and family in Brazil, migration process and project, work in Portugal and England, life and family in England and Portugal. 69 people were interviewed in Portugal and 16 people in England. The interviews in Portugal started before the pandemic period and in England during the pandemic period, a fact that made them all be carried out remotely. It was possible to identify three groups for Brazilian migration in England: a first group, quite precarious, with informal work; a second group, qualified and trying to cross from the ingenuity of immaterial work and entrepreneurship, to less precarious and meaningful activities, composed predominantly of women; and a third group, qualified and who immediately managed to fit into their area of activity, being mostly men. For the case of Portugal, we observe two large groups 1) qualified who work in their area of training, being predominantly men; 2) qualified at departure and disqualified at destination, being predominantly women. Women have their lifestyle changed more intensely, despite the efforts they make to insert themselves in the new culture and new work spaces, since they face prejudice in duplicity: for nationality and gender. In general, the motive of the migratory project was to seek better quality of life and work, driven by the romanticization and illusion built by migrants.

References

Fraga, A. M., Antunes, E. D. D., & Rocha-de-Oliveira, S. (2020). O/A Profissional: As Interfaces de Gênero, Carreira e Expatriação na Construção de Trajetórias de Mulheres Expatriadas. *Brazilian Business Review*, *17*(2), 193-210.

Hirata, Helena. (2009). A precarização e a divisão internacional e sexual do trabalho. *Sociologias*, (21), 24-41.

Hirata, H. (2018). Gênero, patriarcado, trabalho e classe. *Revista Trabalho Necessário*, *16*(29).

King, Russell; LULLE, Aija. Research on Migration: Facing Realities and Maximising Opportunities. Luxembourg: Publications Office of the European Union, 2016.

Wasserman, V., & Frenkel, M. (2015). Spatial work in between glass ceilings and glass walls: Gender-class intersectionality and organizational aesthetics. *Organization Studies*, *36*(11), 1485-1505.

866   Out of sight, out of mind: Impact of COVID-19 pandemic in hidden unemployment on migrants' collectives in European Southern countries

Andres Coco-Prieto, Laura Suarez-Grimalt, Montserrat Simo-Solsona

One of the most relevant effects of the COVID-19 pandemic period in European Southern countries is the increase of fragility and insecurity in the labor market. In recent years, there has been considerable research on the impact of economic crisis on employment and working conditions. Importantly, many studies have focused on migrant population groups (Carrasco and García Serrano, 2015; Gil-Alonso and Vidal-Coso 2015) due to their greater vulnerability to economic instability (Gröger, 2021; Llorente Heras, 2020). During the COVID-19 pandemic, official data provided by different countries (expect Spain) did not show a relevant increase of unemployment in their native or migrant populations. These values might be misleading, since the measurement of unemployment rate based on ILO criteria do not properly reflect the real range of unemployment in migrant populations. As a result, a part of this unemployment remains 'hidden' in inactivity situations and other part in occupation. In this context, we consider that hidden unemployment can reflect more accurately the effects of the pandemic on migrant population than other unemployment estimations.

Here, we aim at analyzing the hidden unemployment rates and their impact on migrant collectives during the COVID-19 pandemic, considering variables such as nationality, years of residence in the country of destination, country of origin and level of education. We focused this analysis on Spain, Portugal and Italy, three European Southern countries sharing similarities in welfare state and economic situation while differing in the evolution of the pandemic and migratory policies implemented by their national governments. Using secondary data from Labour Force Survey (Eurostat), we enlarge the operationalization of unemployment including discouraged workers who are assigned to inactivity situation because they don't look actively for a job and involuntary underemployment people, according to Araujo-Guimarães (2012); Reta and Toler (2006) and Pérez Infante (2000) contributions.

Taken together, our results suggest that the impact of unemployment in migrant population can be more accurately measured using alternative indicators to reveal hidden unemployment caused by COVID-19 pandemic. The estimation of hidden unemployment using our analysis model revealed a very significant increase of unemployment in migrant population. Despite native populations also differed in their official and hidden unemployment rates, these differences were greater in the migrant populations. Differences between both groups and their unemployment rates are reduced as the years of residence of the migrant population in the country of destination increase. Since labor market is a key axis for analyzing the integration of the migrant population (Portes and Böröcz, 1998), our data reflect how hidden unemployment can also serve as a more accurate indicator for the analysis of the assimilation of these groups than traditional employment values and give visibility to those that have more chances to be in the darkness.

References

Araujo Guimarães, N. (2012). ¿Cómo salir del desempleo? Lazos fuertes y lazos débiles en la búsqueda de trabajo en São Paulo, Brasil. *Sociología del Trabajo*, 74, pp. 69-92

Carrasco, C; García Serrano, C. (2015). Efectos de la crisis en la estructura ocupacional y la biografía laboral de la población migrante. Migraciones, 37, pp.75-96.

Gil-Alonso, F; Vidal-Coso, E. (2015). Inmigrantes extranjeros en el mercado de trabajo español. ¿Más resilientes o más vulnerables al impacto de la crisis?, Migraciones,

37, pp.97-123.

Gröger, A. (2021). Easy come, easy go? Economic shocks, labor migration and the family left behind. Journal of International Economics, 128.

Llorente Heras, R. (2020). Impacto del COVID-19 en el mercado de trabajo: un análisis de los colectivos vulnerables. Instituto Universitario de Análisis Económico y Social, Documento de Trabajo 02/2020

Pérez Infante, J. I. (2000). La medición del desempleo en España: la EPA y el paro registrado. Revista del Ministerio de Trabajo y Asuntos Sociales, 21, pp. 15-57.

Portes, A; Böröcz, J. (1998). Contemporary immigration: Theoretical perspectives on its determinants and modes of incorporation". International Migration Review: Special Silver Anniversary Issue: International Migration an Assessment for the 90's, 23 (3), pp. 606-630.

Reta, M; Toler, S. M. (2006) Desempleo oculto. Su medición y representatividad. Ciencia Docencia y Tecnología, 17 (32), pp. 131-150.

889   Employment Subsidise, Capacity Reinforcement, and Sanction: In Government's activation governance for work promotion

Esien Eddy Bruno

Purpose: Research on OECD countries indicates a demographic and fiscal constraint that has prompted a shift from income maintenance to activation governance, which enables unemployed people to enter work, but the workfare policy measures do not always comport with its intension. This paper analyses employment subsidizes, capacity reinforcement, and sanctions under work-related activation governance to enable young third-country immigrant's (TCIs) transition from welfare to all types of work in Austria, Finland, and Czech Republic

Design/methodology/approach: Regarding the research methodology, qualitative date was collected from the case study authorized Employment Acts, official reports, published and unpublished scholarly text for analysis. The data were analysed through qualitative content analysis and document's analysis techniques to generate an insight and in-depth theory generating study with multidimensional data to interpret and understand the real-life phenomenon.

Findings: This study has shown that hiring subsidies, targeted education and training, and heightening cost of noncompliance formal rules were a major perceived influence in activation governance to administer young TCIs transition from welfare to all types of work in Austria, Finland, and Czech Republic. However, Czech Republic work-related activation governance is dissimilar to Austria and Finland with the focus on investment incentive governance to encourage employers and/or registered unemployed job's creation, whereas Finland and Austria prefer to grant employers wage subsidies when they employ multiple disadvantaged registered out-of-placed people. This paper suggests that more emphasis on transparency, efficiency, feasibility, and equal opportunity may be more beneficial than continuing to focus on purely work-related reform with stringent limit and social control on eligibility for further reform.

Research limitation/implications: The research was limited in several ways. For instance, it primarily concerned the case study of Austria, Finland and Czech Republic and cannot be generalized to explain other countries leading to low external validity (Ragin, 1987). Nevertheless, it may be generalized to a theory in the way scholars' theory-generate findings from one case study to the other. Moreover, to some extent, the researcher faced a language barrier, as some of the documents were in Czech language, but could use several authorized English translation's version and support from colleagues.

Practical implication: The result contributes to TCN research possibilities to refine social and/or public assistance policy programs and implementation of quality service delivery, especially to support heterogeneous young TCNs' subgroups and socio-economically disadvantaged people's participation in employment systems. The diagnostic model may be used for further studies analysis in the realm of labour market performance and third-country national employment-related transition in comparative entities and other countries.

Originality/Value: The study draws on existing literature and information on the governance and implementation of work-related activation incentives to develop a diagnostic framework and analyses young third-country immigrants' transition from welfare to all types of work in Austria, Finland, and Czech Republic. It identifies a pattern that if discretion during implementation and regulation on who crosses the benefits threshold persists, problems of transparency, efficiency, and equal opportunity may prevail not only, to hinder minority groups labour market upward mobility, but jeopardizes belongings, economic prosperity, and participatory democratic values.

875   Social and Economic Contexts of Migration: Why Turkey is Attracting Georgian Women Labour Migrants?

Meryem Ayşe Göktaş

Georgia is an emigration country with emigrants dispersed among the world as labour migrants supporting their families with remittances. There are several reasons and processes for choosing a country for immigration and Turkey is one of the countries Georgian women is migrating. Because of the Neoliberal economic system in Turkey and the devastation created by the collapse of the Soviet Union, most of the migrants are women migrating through gendered paths to gendered works as entertainment, domestic or care workers. There are many anthropological or quantitative work on the issue but, Georgian women is either studied based on returned migrants in Georgia nor studied based on their gendered work market. However, in between of Turkey and Georgia, there is a need for clarifying the migration routes by examining reasons and processes. Therefore, study had conducted with Georgian middle- aged women who had been working in Maltepe, Ankara either as domestic workers or care-givers. Qualitative method had selected for this study in order to reveal the reasons of migration with in-depth semi-structured interviews. Because of COVID-19 pandemic, interviews had been realized from online meeting applications. As a result of the study, there are two revealing contexts decisive in the migration route and process. First one is social context shaped by social networks and gendered and cultural closeness. Second one is economic context shaped by low financial costs and wage differentials. Despite the different reasons and contexts, there is one commonality that these women are carrying economic and psychological burden of their families and children by excepting the challenges of migration to Turkey and the world.

7B   Space and Migration
Chair: Fethiye Tilbe, Tekirdag Namik Kemal University, Turkey
509   Linking Urban Public Space and Migrant Integration: The Struggle for and the Magic of Time
Chen Qu
518   The Reception Assemblage: Rethinking the Relationship between Informal Settlements and Formal Reception Practices
Eleanor Paynter
521   Giving voice to the immigrants. Tensions and paradoxes in Participatory Theatre (Turin, Italy)
Francesca Quercia
822   Walking and Talking: Connecting Turkish/Kurdish Women's Activist Memories with London's Changing Landscape
Feride Kumbasar

509   Linking Urban Public Space and Migrant Integration: The Struggle for and the Magic of Time

Chen Qu

Chinese post-migratory urban lives seem to be discussed merely from a sociological perspective in most current studies with the dynamics of urban public space seldom considered. My research explores the role of public space in the integration process by both expanding the concept of integration and examining migrant uses and senses of place, based on fieldwork in a Chinese megacity. The evidence suggests that urban public space can promote integration in various ways, and this presentation focuses on how migrants' use of such space, arguably linked to migrant citizenship, is influenced by temporal factors, alongside the interplay of migrants' financial burdens and institutional restrictions. One the other hand, lengthy residence in the host city may promote migrants' acculturation, local socialisation and identity-building as 'insiders', which indicates migrant integration's different dimensions can be connected through 'time'. Recommendations oriented to migrant routine, citizenship and cultural implications of urban public space are discussed at the end of the presentation.

518 The Reception Assemblage: Rethinking the Relationship between Informal Settlements and Formal Reception Practices

Eleanor Paynter

Scholarship on migrant reception sites has generally focused *either* on official centers regulated by local and national authorities,[23] *or* on informal settlements that emerge through migrants' collective occupation of a space and collaboration with grassroots organizations.[24] With this epistemic separation, informal settlements have not only been studied for their representation of the state of exception,[25] they have been exceptionalized through their treatment as wholly separate from formal systems of reception and asylum.

This article reconceptualizes informal settlements occupied by recently arrived migrants as a critical part of reception processes and experiences, in particular in destination countries experiencing so-called border crises. Drawing on fieldwork conducted at reception sites in Italy during Europe's recent "refugee crisis," I propose a theoretical framework to understand formal and informal reception sites as co-constitutive of a larger governing structure that I term the "reception assemblage," or the web of sites and practices through which migrants initially enter a country and navigate its legal and social systems. I argue that, as reception sites grow in number and exceed capacity, asylum governance relies on the existence of both centers and informal settlements, and these sites should be studied not only for their differences, but for their congruities, including the forms of violence and agency that shape both types.

This article is organized into two main sections, one focused on theories of the camp and reception, and the other informed by empirical study. In the latter section I present excerpts from oral history interviews I conducted between 2017 – 2019 with West African asylum seekers and Italian staff and volunteers at an official reception center in the Molise region and an informal settlement in Rome. In these interviews, analyzed with the methods of folklore and linguistic anthropological narrative studies,[26] narrators recounted their experiences of displacement and described their movements between formal and informal sites in nonlinear terms, and their accounts also demonstrated that the forms of violence and agency often studied in informal settlements also shape experiences in official centers. Discussing these interviews in the context of local and national policy changes, I demonstrate how the reception assemblage that is produced through the coexistence of these sites not only shapes

[23] Campesi, Giuseppe. 2018. "Between Containment, Confinement and Dispersal: The Evolution of the Italian Reception System before and after the 'Refugee Crisis.'" *Journal of Modern Italian Studies* 23 (4): 490–506.

[24] Belloni, Milena. 2016. "Learning How to Squat: Cooperation and Conflict between Refugees and Natives in Rome." *Journal of Refugee Studies* 29 (4): 506–27.
Isakjee, Arshad, Thom Davies, Jelena Obradović-Wochnik, and Karolína Augustová. 2020. "Liberal Violence and the Racial Borders of the European Union." *Antipode* 52 (6): 1751–1773.

[25] Agamben, Giorgio. 1998. *Homo Sacer: Sovereign Power and Bare Life*. Stanford University Press.
Dines, Nick, Nicola Montagna, and Vincenzo Ruggiero. 2015. "Thinking Lampedusa: Border Construction, the Spectacle of Bare Life and the Productivity of Migrants." *Ethnic and Racial Studies* 38 (3).

[26] Shuman, Amy. 2012. "Exploring Narrative Interaction in Multiple Contexts." In *Varieties of Narrative Analysis*, edited by James Holstein and Jaber Gubrium, 125–50. Los Angeles: Sage.

migrants' experiences of reception, but is critical to the functioning of the asylum regime during crisis, in processing claims and in managing migrant subjects.

521   Giving voice to the immigrants. Tensions and paradoxes in Participatory Theatre (Turin, Italy)

Francesca Quercia

For the past thirty years, with the redefinition of cultural and urban policies, artists have been assigned to social missions: strengthening social ties, contributing to overcoming working-class neighbourhoods and to integrate immigrants (Blondel 2001; Briata, Bricocoli, et Tedesco 2009; Bureau, Perrenoud, et Shapiro 2009). That process has been taking hold in many European countries, including Italy. As part of urban renewal programmes, a large number of theatre artists have taken over working-class neighbourhoods. They have proposed artistic projects with immigrants and have been displaying a dual objective of "integration" and of "empowerment" of projects' participants (Pontremoli 2005). They usually show their determination in giving voice to minorities. However, these artists most often belong to the majority group in the host society (in terms of nationality and ethnicity). This opens a set of questions: how can they represent groups which they don't belong ? How can they represent groups agaist which they have a dominant position ? How can they guarantee free expression and visibility in public space of minorities, if they embody unwittingly the « standard and universality »(Kebabza 2006, 12) ?

This paper is based on a four-year ethnographic survey carried out within a theatre association[27]. It questions how her director succeeds in forging a recongnized professionnal role, by self-designating as en intermediary between immigrants and Italian society. She tries to emancipate immigrants, but she faces many contradictions during the implementation of projects. Despite her antiracist believes, she ends up producing minorization of immigrants (Guillaumin 2002). Based on a triple dynamics – of « racialization » (Guillaumin 2002; 2016), « ethnicization »(Jounin, Palomares, et Rabaud 2008) and « culturalization » (De Rudder, Poiret, et Vourc'h 2000) - this process assigns minorities to radical otherness, over which they have little power.

Selected Bibliography

Blondel, Alice. 2001. « Poser le Tricostéril sur la fracture sociale. L'inscription des établissements de la décentralisation théâtrale dans des projets relevant de la politique de la ville ». *Sociétés et représentations* 1 (11).

Briata, Paola, Massimo Bricocoli, et Carla Tedesco. 2009. *Città in periferia*. Roma: Carocci.

Bureau, Marie-Christine, Marc Perrenoud, et Roberta Shapiro, éd. 2009. *L'artiste pluriel:*

---

[27] This doctoral research is based on a comparative survey between six theatre associations in France and Italy. This paper is focused on an italian association named "Lotros" in which I conducted biographical interviewes with her director (3), interviwes with trainees (8) and participants (8). I also had a lot of informal discussions with immigrant participants, and a number of interviews with elective representatives et local public servants (10). Participant observation took place in different situations (rehearsals, performances, meetings, etc.).

démultiplier l'activité pour vivre de son art. Villeneuve-d'Ascq: Presses universitaires du Septentrion.

De Rudder, Véronique, Christian Poiret, et François Vourc'h. 2000. *L'inégalité raciste*. Paris: Presses Universitaires de France.

Guillaumin, Colette. 2002. *L'idéologie raciste. Genèse et langage actuel*. Paris: Gallimard.

———. 2016. *Sexe, race et pratique du pouvoir*. Donnemarie-Dontilly: Editions iXe.

Jounin, Nicolas, Élise Palomares, et Aude Rabaud. 2008. « Ethnicisations ordinaires, voix minoritaires ». *Societes contemporaines* n° 70 (2): 7-23.

Kebabza, Horia. 2006. « "L'universel lave-t-il plus blanc ?" : "Race", racisme et système de privilèges ». *Les cahiers du CEDREF. Centre d'enseignement, d'études et de recherches pour les études féministes*, n° 14 (janvier): 145-72.

Pontremoli, Alessandro. 2005. *Teoria e tecniche di teatro educativo e sociale*. Torino: UTET Libreria.

822 Walking and Talking: Connecting Turkish/Kurdish Women's Activist Memories with London's Changing Landscape

Feride Kumbasar

The London Borough of Hackney is defined to be a 'superdiverse' borough which provided 'home' for many migrant and refugee communities including the Irish, the Caribbean Community, the Cypriot Turkish, the Jews, the Turks and the Kurds, the Vietnamese, the Somali's, other Africans and Polish over the centuries. *"The long history of diversification in Hackney suggests that its residents experience ethnic, religious and linguistic diversity 'as a normal part of everyday life"* (Wessendorf, 2014*)*.

This paper addresses a question largely ignored in the literature on migration and "transnational community": in what way super-diverse landscapes are effective to facilitate resettlement and reproduction of multiple identities of newly arrived communities? By focusing on the 'everyday life' experiences of Turkish and Kurdish (T/K) women migrants from Turkey who arrived in 1980s and worked in garment making workshops in Hackney, I examine the process of inbuilding subjectivity, agency and 'diaspora space' in the context of super-diverse landscape.

I study the construction of migrant women's memory and identity through a "go-along interview conducted with a Kurdish refugee woman, who was involved in organising campaigns against violence against women among Turkish and Kurdish women garment workers.

The go-along interview is an innovative ethnographic method used to collect data about the role of place in 'everyday life'. It involves walking or riding along with the participants in a quest to map their engagement with place and space. In my go-along interview I follow the traces of T/K women's everyday interactions in Hackney to explore the past (as it offered them employment in garment making industry and as it is once defined as a Turkish neighbourhood), present (as many community places disappeared as part of urban development/gentrification) and future (as women's activism is being diluted/evolved since shared ethnic, religious or township identity is becoming ground for community places).

I focus on the participant's memory and articulation of Dalston Kingsland Road, Ridley Road Market and Halkevi (People's Home), one of the biggest and most diverse community centres in Hackney in 1980s, in forming imagined Turkish and Kurdish communities. By doing this I explore the importance of super-diverse neighbourhoods for migrant women to claim and exercise their cultural, ethnic, religious and gender rights. I also investigate how community centres play a contradictory role in shaping women's subjectivity: as on the one hand, they offer social and political participation opportunities; on the other, they prevent women to claim their gender identity and gender rights.

Indicative bibliography

Brah, A. (2005) Cartographies of Diaspora: Contesting Identities (Gender, Racism, Ethnicity). London: Routledge

Erel, U. (2009) Migrant Women transforming Citizenship- Life-stories from Britain and Germany. London: Ashgate Publishing

Gilroy, P. (2004) After Empire: Melancholia or convivial Culture? London: Routledge

Gluck. B.S. & Patai, D. (1991) Women's Words: The Feminist Practice of Oral History. London: Routledge

Kusenbach, M. (2003) 'Street phenomenology, The go-along as ethnographic research tool', Ethnography. Vol. 4(3): 455-485. London: Sage publication

Vervotec, S. (2007) Super-diversity and its implications. Ethnic and Racial Studies, 30, pp1024-1054

Wessendorf, S. (2014) 'Being open, but sometimes closed'. Conviviality in a super-diverse London Neighbourhood. European Journal of Cultural Studies, 17(4), pp.392-405. Sage Publishing

7C   Youth Migration
Chair: Ana Vila Freyer, Universidad Latina de México, Mexico
873   Challenges and reconfigurations on Global South initiatives for Higher Education: Habesha Project, a Mexican project for displaced Syrian youth
Ared Alejandra Garcia
874   Migrants Teen at School: The State Against Migration
Paula Alonso
877   A Spatial Appraisal of Education and the Vulnerability of Internally Displaced Children in Abuja: Durumi Camp
Stephen Ajadi

873 Challenges and reconfigurations on Global South initiatives for Higher Education: Habesha Project, a Mexican project for displaced Syrian youth

Ared Alejandra Garcia

By the end of 2018, 70.9 million individuals were forcibly displaced worldwide due to conflict, persecution and human rights violation: 41.3 million internally displaced people, followed by 25.9 million refugees and 3.5 million asylum seekers (UNHCR 2018, 2). As one of the main consequences these massive forced movements is the limitation for host countries to provide basic humanitarian rights to displaced population. In addition to food, shelter and health, there has been a noticeable increase from governments and civil organizations to recognize education as part of a crucial humanitarian right (Sinclair 2001, 2; Zeus 2011, 257). However, the main efforts and projects for education are focused in primary and secondary levels (Rahseed & Munoz 2016, 174).

Concerning higher education, only 3% of the refugee sector around the world are registered in university programs, an alarming gap contrasted with the 36% of the global population enrolled (UNHCR, 2019), not including the number of displaced and asylum seekers who are also left out from higher education access. Due to the continuous loss of several young generations and the latest focus on the Syrian conflict, diverse initiatives have been created with the aim to provide higher education for refugees and asylum seekers. Most of these international organizations, governments and civil associations are positioned in the Global North, thus there is few academic discussion concerning Global South initiatives.

In 2015, the Mexican civil organization Habesha Project started providing scholarships for young Syrians to continue or start their tertiary education in private universities across the country. Habesha Project is run by a young and small team that so far has been able to bring up to 17 Syrian students to Mexico. The initiative includes a full university scholarship, a monthly stipend and ensure Spanish classes. This is the first project of its type in the country and in the Latin American region. Therefore, in depth research about the functioning, accomplishments and failures through the lenses of the Syrian beneficiaries and staff are necessary to analyze the challenges higher education projects through civil organizations in the Global South. This research is based on thematic analysis with recollection of interviews and fieldwork in 2019 in Mexico, as well as an online continuation in 2021. This proposal intends to demonstrate the power relations between beneficiaries (Syrian students) and its consequences on the improvements and challenges for Syrians to continue their educational journey.

874   Migrants Teen at School: The State Against Migration

Paula Alonso

This paper analyses the influence on the schoolar migrants experiences by the educational institution. The main goal is to address how the Spanish educational policy is applied in Galicia, from the point of view of educational professionals

Education is the instrument that positions the individual as an actor, self-reflective, who thinks of himself and thinks towards others, and inserts him into the social scene, discarding his role as a spectator. The State has a lot to say in this matter. If we focus on the the educational system, this helps to understand the rol of the State in respect of equal opportunities or equity, that should be protected for the sustainable development of citizenship and democratic quality.

In post-industrial societies, the implementation of those idyllic principles dependent on the political power of the State. If it is true that "education constitutes, since the second half of the 20th century, the institution that represents the equalization of opportunities for all individuals in the face of their life trajectories" (Larios Paterna, 2009: 57), it should be the responsibility of the State to defend of the right to education, creating welcoming and non-exclusive structures.

Our hypothesis is that there are structural factors - educational policy - that influence the school experience of migrants and bring them an educational disadvantage. It is based on the idea that the educational context, delimited by unstable educational laws, fully affects their experiences and rhythms, through mechanisms that operate in the centers.

The methodology used is qualitative, based on conducting 19 in-depth interviews with professionals in the educational field in Galicia (Spain). Through their diagnosis, we show what is happening with the educational diversity. The results offer a vision of the educational institution that reveals a negative picture validating the initial hypothesis.

References

Larios Paterna, M. J. (2009). El derecho a la educación de los inmigrantes: la concentración como límite a su pleno ejercicio. In Inmigración y educación (pp. 57-88). Centro de Estudios Políticos y Constitucionales (España).

877   A Spatial Appraisal of Education and the Vulnerability of Internally Displaced Children in Abuja: Durumi Camp

Stephen Ajadi

Conflict in Nigeria continues to expand with the proliferation of newer agencies and displacement reaching new heights. The Global Terrorism index places Nigeria as the most terrorised country in Africa and the third in the world (IEP, 2020). Insurgency, banditry, militancy and herdsmen conflict over land and grazing rights have spread from the north all the way to the south of the country. There have also been specialised attacks on public schools. Internal displacement has increased steadily from 2018 (IDMC, 2020). Abuja is the capital of the country and it is home to a growing number of IDP. What used to be a small, localised footprint of IDP in Abuja has now extended noticeably since 2014. Currently in Abuja, there are a number of formal and semi-formal IDP settlements in New Kuchingoro camp, Kuje area (including Pegi), Lugbe camp, Durumi (Area 1) camp, Wassa settlement, Jikwoyi (including Karu, Orozo and Mararaba Loko host communities),Waru, Yimitu and Zhindyina host communities. There are also camps in Karamajiji and Wuye. The children in Abuja IDP camps have significant difficulty in accessing proper education given the integration barriers of the city as well as the high cost of living which in turn means that education is very expensive. Using Durumi camp as a case study, this study employs a mixed method approach of ethnographic survey and GIS analysis to investigate the vulnerability of IDP children in Abuja with respect to education. Though the cost of education is an obvious barrier towards integration and inclusion, this research shows that more social problems and dynamics are at play. These issues overlap each other and contribute to the accessibility and inclusivity of IDP children in Abuja with respect to education. There is also evidence of resilience to the vulnerabilities shown at varying levels of space within the camp. The study goes beyond highlighting problems of a demography to understanding of how spatial factors of displacement and urbanity may contribute to prospects and frameworks of pragmatic integration and in turn, sustainable development.

References

IEP, (2020), *'Global terrorism Index', Measuring the Impact of Terrorism'*. Institute for Economics and Peace, Accessed 20-01-2021 from: https://reliefweb.int/sites/reliefweb.int/files/resources/GPI_2020_web.pdf

IDMC (2020), *'Global Report on Internal Displacement: 2020'*, Internal Displacement Monitoring Centre; Norwegian Refugee Council, accessed 15-01-2021 from: https://www.internal-displacement.org/sites/default/files/publications/documents/2020-IDMC-GRID.pdf

7D Migration and Identity

Chair: Liat Yakhnich, Beit Berl College, Israel

495 "I have an identity, I have roots": Identity experiences among young adult Ethiopian immigrants in Israel

Liat Yakhnich and Sophie D. Walsh

Abundant theory and empirical research have examined identity processes following immigration; however, scarce literature has examined how immigrants themselves identify and experience issues related to their identity. Taking a phenomenological approach, we examined a unique group of young Israelis who immigrated from Ethiopia to understand how they themselves relate to their identity and what, for them, are the salient issues involved in their identity negotiations. Ethiopian immigrants are a black Jewish minority in a predominantly white Israeli society. Their immigration and absorption were characterized by a move from a mainly rural to an urban society, discrimination, low SES, weakening of traditional community and familial structures, and erosion of the Amharic language and Ethiopian culture. As such, the Ethiopian immigrants' story provides a unique opportunity to understand how individuals make sense of their own identities and identity processes, when bridging multiple cultural realities and minority status.

Nineteen (19) participants, who immigrated to Israel from Ethiopia as children and adolescents, were interviewed for this study. The findings point to a number of identity related issues, most of which highlight the interplay between society and personal identity negotiation: 1) the role of context/ society in making identity negotiation inherent (grappling with identity as an event necessitated for the individual); 2) the strive for a flexible, integrated identity in which different elements can take to the forefront in different contexts; 3) a narrative of "turning points" as a catalyst to identity negotiation; 4) society as prioritizing a collective identity over the personal and demanding from the individual to represent the collective. We suggest that these four elements may be characteristic of minority groups for whom stigma and discrimination, visibility, and minority status make identity negotiation a crucial part of the individuals experience.

503 The future of differences in a world of migration

Orazio Maria Gnerre

Human migrations are now a constitutive element of the world social panorama and their causes are notoriously multiple. Although the human migration phenomenon has always existed, and that it has been an essential element in the birth and development of civilizations, it takes on a completely different face in this historical contingency thanks to the notable advances in technology and the abbreviation of real or perceived distance.

The question that arises in this sense is what is the future of the concept of "difference" in a world where the encounter between peoples is increasingly immediate and apparently chaotic. There are different ways of approaching the problem, and they constitute the context of ideological conflicts regarding the subject in the contemporary world.

The question about the future of difference in a world as globalized as ours, followed by those of coexistence, the meaning of multiculturalism and the possible governance of these differences, questions us all and needs innovative and convincing answers.

593   Predominance of Kerala Muslims' Gulf Migration; Trends, Pattern and Impact

Afsal K

India is the largest sending country of migrants globally and holding the top place in receiving of remittances. Major migration corridors of Indians are Middle-east Asia, South-east Asia, North America and Europe. Gulf Cooperation Council (GCC) Countries has been a significant destination of Indian since the 1970s. In the early 1970s, oil price increased and resulted in unexpected wealth accumulation in the Gulf countries. Economic boom resulted in different developmental activities in this region and increased demand for various types of workers, especially for construction, transportation, trade, commerce, health and education (Sekhar, 1997). Lack of human resources in gulf countries caused labour shortage and attracted salary caused the massive flow of semi-skilled and unskilled labour migrants to gulf countries especially from India, Bangladesh, Pakistan and other Southeast Asian countries (Odengaden, 2009). Since then, the number of Indian diasporas quadrupled in the gulf region.

Among migrants toward the Gulf region, most of them were from southern parts of India, mainly from Kerala, the state dominated by sending a large number of migrants to the Gulf countries. Gulf migration and remittances resulted in Kerala's unexpected socio-economic developments, especially for backward communities like Muslims and Ezhava Hindus and other backward regions of Kerala's northern part (Zachariah et al. 2000). Currently, 90 percent of international migrants are working in six gulf countries: UAE, Saudi Arabia, Oman, Qatar, Kuwait, and Bahrain and most of them are low skilled and semi-skilled labourers. Furthermore, in Kerala, though Hindus are the majority in population, Muslims are 42 percent of total international migrants followed by Hindus (35 percent) and Christians (24 percent) (Rajan, 2019). In terms of receiving remittances, Muslim community holding the top position followed by Hindus and Christians. International migration from Kerala and its remittance resulted in socio-economic changes, mainly in education, health, demography, employment, per capita income, especially for the Muslim community. In this context, the present study exploring the levels, trends, and pattern of Kerala Muslim migration towards the Gulf region and its impact in community based on data collected from Kerala Migration Survey 2018 and other literatures.

619   Migration and Identity politics in Jordan

Nur Köprülü

Jordan epitomizes one of the few countries not only in the Middle East region, but also in the international system which has the highest ratio of refugees to native population of any country. Despite the fact that Jordan is not a party to the Geneva Convention signed in 1951, it hosts the largest number of Palestinian refugees in any single country in the world. Jordan's decision to annex the West Bank territories and East Jerusalem in 1950 and the subsequent influx of Palestinians into country's borders allowed the Palestinians to outnumber the native Jordanians. What is more, the Kingdom has become the only Arab country granting Palestinians the right to citizenship. Following the incorporation of the West Bank, Jordan's identity politics as well as regime type has become to be determined by the existence of Palestinians and the ramifications of the Palestine Question. Besides the Palestinians, following the US strike against Iraq in 2003 Jordan also opened its borders to the Iraqi refugees. Recently with the outbreak of the war in Syria, Jordan represents one of the three key hosting countries in the region that shouldered Syrian refugees after Turkey and Lebanon.

Nevertheless, Jordan is a home for millions of migrants, it lacks economic resilience to cope with the influx of refugees. In addition, the political stability of monarchy is at risk since the 2011 Arab Uprisings when the large-scale protests have taken to the streets. The resurgence of the opposition since 2018 also alarms the Kingdom of a potential internal unrest. It is apparent that the Kingdom lacks the resources to absorb the migrants either as labour migrants or as refugees; and utterly seeks for a two-state solution to the Palestine Question that would enable Palestinians the right of return.

In light of these challenges that Jordan faces within and across its borders, this paper will examine the responses of the Kingdom of Jordan governing the issue of migration and the challenges of the integration of the migrants and refugees in the country. The paper, thus, aims to re/address the identity politics that the monarchy pursues and the policies of social cohesion of the different segments of society.

7E   Migration, Politics and Law

Chair: Sevim Atilla Demir, Sakarya University, Turkey

857   Migration Diplomacy: A New Way To Bargain
       Melek Özlem Ayas
625   The Impact of EU's New Pact on Migration Diplomacy
       Nur Seda Temur
834   Diplomacy of Diaspora: Analysis of Turkish Diaspora
       Durmuş Çakır
631   The Problem of Immigrant Workers Who Later Acquired Citizenship to
       Borrow Their Service Period Before Being a Citizen
       Nihan Gizem Kantarci

857   Migration Diplomacy: A New Way To Bargain

Melek Özlem Ayas

The concepts of migration and power are always in relation with each other. The communication between the concepts affects both domestic and foreign policies of international actors and states at different levels. The combination of migration and diplomacy can be explained by the importance of migration and asylum policies in states' diplomatic practices. Those two terms create an important tool to make sense of some of the bargains between international actors related to migration and the various goals and demands to be achieved.

Migration diplomacy has emerged with the reshaping of migration policies for different purposes, which emerged with the roles that states assume due to migration movements and their duties arising from these roles. In other words, migration and migration policies, which are always a bargain issue, changed shape over time and laid the foundations of migration diplomacy (Seeberg, 2020). In this bargaining process, migration diplomacy has been modelized by using migration movements strategically, depending on the negotiation and communication powers of the states and turned them into a tool.

Both notions, diplomacy and migration diplomacy, emphasize the negotiation and communication of the states, are related to the persuasion and influence capacity of the states. Migration diplomacy can involve the use of diplomatic methods to achieve various goals and have provided a suitable space for the use of migration policies linked to political and economic interests as a strategic tool for states to realize their different interests.

There has not been much study in the field regarding migration diplomacy, nevertheless, it's always possible to talk about studies on diplomatic interactions linked to migration. Nazlı Choucri (1977), Michael S. Teitelbaum (1984), Myron Weiner (1992), Kelly M. Greenhill (2010), Helene Thiollet (2011), Donna R. Gabaccia (2012) and Meredith Oyen (2015) has been conducting various studies on the linkage between migration and diplomacy. Those studies enabled Adamson and Tsourapas to theorize the concept of migration diplomacy.

This study, which focuses on the concepts of diplomacy and migration diplomacy, has been prepared primarily to reveal the relationship between the concepts. In order to properly address the relationship and interaction in between, firstly, following questions were asked: "What is migration diplomacy?" and "Is migration diplomacy useful as a tool in international relations?" A comprehensive literature review was conducted to answer these questions. It is aimed first to define the concept in question and then to determine its place through the examples presented to be made on the subject. It is possible to say that the novelty of the concept of migration diplomacy makes it difficult to scan the literature, but it gives the work freedom by providing originality.

625   The Impact of EU's New Pact on Migration Diplomacy

Nur Seda Temur

As the European Union launched its New Pact on Migration and Asylum on 23 September 2020, many anticipated certain changes in foreign policies of EU member states. Within this context, migration diplomacy was not the exception. With regard to this inference, this article will examine the following question: How will the EU's New Pact on Migration and Asylum impact migration diplomacy? Concerning this question, in this article, I will try to defend the idea that although the New Pact strengthens the interdependency between EU member states, immigration towards EU member states will be complicated, which will raise the importance of migration diplomacy among migration-receiving, migration-sending, or transit states. With respect to this claim, after the introduction part, this research paper will first focus on the concept of migration diplomacy, and the discussion of the term from realist theoretical framework. After this, the EU's New Pact on Migration and Asylum will be examined, and its comparison with the 2008 EU's Pact on Migration and Asylum will be made. Before the concluding remark, the impact of the New Pact on migration diplomacy will be discussed. In the conclusion part, an overall evaluation will be made. This research paper will be a qualitative study. In particular, the data about decision taken in the New Pact on Migration and Asylum will be gathered from both primary and secondary resources through document analysis. Indeed, primary sources will be composed of official documents about the New Pact. These documents will be used mostly for the comparison between the New Pact (2020), and the previous pact (2008). Secondary sources will be composed of relevant books, articles, academic journals, research papers, and newspapers. These sources will be used for the discussion on migration diplomacy and the impact of the New Pact on it.

References

Adamson, F. B., &Tsourapas, G. (2019). Migration Diplomacy in World Politics. *International Studies Perspectives*, 20(2), 113-128. doi:10.1093/isp/eky015

Cooper, A. F., Jorge H., & Ramesh T. (2013). "Introduction: The Challenges of 21st-Century Diplomacy." In *the Oxford Handbook of Modern Diplomacy*, edited by Andrew F. Cooper, Jorge Heine and Ramesh Thakur, 1-31. Oxford: Oxford University Press.

European Commission, Communication from the Commission to the European Parliament, the Council, the European Economic and Social Committee and the Committee of the Regions on a New Pact on Migration and Asylum, COM (2020) 609 final, Brussels, 23.9.2020, https://ec.europa.eu/info/sites/info/files/1_en_act_part1_v7_1.pdf.

European Commission, Communication from the Commission to the European Parliament, the Council, the European Economic and Social Committee and the Committee of the Regions on a New Pact on Migration and Asylum, COM (2008) 13440/08 ASIM 68, Brussels, 24.9.2008, https://data.consilium.europa.eu/doc/document/ST-13440-2008-INIT/en/pdf

Greenhill, K. M. (2010). *Weapons of Mass Migration: Forced Displacement, Coercion, and Foreign Policy*. Cornell Studies in Security Affairs. Ithaca, NY: Cornell University Press.

Hamilton, K., & Langhorne Richard. (2011). *The Practice of Diplomacy. Its Evolution, Theory and Administration*. Second edition. Abingdon: Routledge.

İçduygu, A., & Üstübici A. (2014). "Negotiating Mobility, Debating Borders: Migration Diplomacy in Turkey–EU Relations." *New Border and Citizenship Politics*, edited by Helen Schwenken and Sabine Ruß-Sattar, 1st ed., Palgrave Macmillan, 44–60.

İçduygu, A., & Aksel, D. B. (2014). Two-to-Tango in Migration Diplomacy: Negotiating Readmission Agreement between the EU and Turkey. *European Journal of Migration* and Law, 16: 336-362.

Jegen, L., Claes, J., & Cham, O. N. (2020). Towards Mutually Beneficial EU-West African Migration Cooperation?: Assessing EU Policy Trends and Their Implications for Migration Cooperation. *Clingendael Institute*, 1-12. doi:10.2307/resrep27539

Keohane, R. O., & Nye, J. S. (1977). *Power and Interdependence*. 4th ed. London: Longman.

Koinova, M. (2011). Diasporas and Secessionist Conflicts: The Mobilization of the Armenian, Albanian and Chechen Diasporas. *Ethnic and Racial Studies* 34: 333–56.

Koinova, M. (2018). Sending States and Diaspora Positionality in International Relations. *International Political Sociology* 12: 190–210.

Koinova, M., & Tsourapas, G. (2018). How Do Countries of Origin Engage Migrants and Diasporas? Multiple Actors and Comparative Perspectives. *International Political Science Review* 39: 311– 21.

Norman, K. P. (2020). Migration Diplomacy and Policy Liberalization in Morocco and Turkey. *International Migration Review*, 54(4), 1158–1183.

Norman, K. P. (2020). Migration Diplomacy and Policy Liberalization in Morocco and Turkey. *International Migration Review*, 54(4), 1158-1183. doi:10.1177/0197918319895271

Nye, J. S. (2004). *Soft Power: The Means to Success in World Politics*. New York: PublicAffairs.

Oyen, M. (2015). *The Diplomacy of Migration: Transnational Lives and the Making of US- Chinese Relations in the Cold War*. Ithaca: Cornell University Press.

Powell, R. (1991). Absolute and Relative Gains in International Relations Theory. *American Political Science Review* 85: 1303–20.

Schwenken, H., & Russ-Sattar, S. (Eds.). (2014). *New Border and Citizenship Politics* (1st ed.). Basingstoke: Palgrave Macmillan.

Teitelbaum, M. S. (1984). Immigration, Refugees, and Foreign Policy. 1984. *International Organization*, 38 (3): 429-450.

Thiollet, H. (2011). Migration as Diplomacy: Labor Migrants, Refugees, and Arab Regional Politics in the Oil-Rich Countries. *International Labor and Working-Class History*, 79(1), 103-121.

Thiollet, H. (2011). Migration as Diplomacy: Labor Migrants, Refugees, and Arab Regional Politics in the Oil-Rich Countries. *International Labor and Working-Class History*, 79(1), 103-121. doi:10.1017/s0147547910000293

Tollison, R. D., & Thomas D. W. (1979). An Economic Theory of Mutually Advantageous Issue Linkages in International Negotiations. *International Organization* 33: 425–49.

Tsourapas, G. (2017). Migration diplomacy in the Global South: Cooperation, coercion and issue linkage in Gaddafi's Libya. *Third World Quarterly*, 38(10), 1-20. doi:10.1080/01436597.2017.1350102

Weiner, M. (1992). Security, Stability and International Migration. *International Security* 17(3): 91-126.

834   Diplomacy of Diaspora: Analysis of Turkish Diaspora

Durmuş Çakır

In international relations studies, the increasing interest in migration phenomenon along with migration mobility enables some concepts to come back to the agenda and to be discussed again. The concept of diaspora has also been a concept that draws the attention of the international community along with immigration mobility and has been focused on recent studies (Riordan, 2003; Rana, 2011; Birka & Klavis, 2020). In the process of foreign policy making, the importance of diasporas is increasing in global politics (Tellander & Horst, 2017, 7). In addition, the diversification of diplomatic practices as a result of the change and transformation process in diplomacy has increased the role of diasporas in the field of international relations and diplomacy (Brinkerkoff, 2019,53).

With the end of the Cold War, the qualitative and quantitative increase in non-state actors ended the understanding that the state is the only dominant actor in diplomacy activities (Cull, 2010, 15). The apparency of non-traditional actors has started to gain importance in the new public diplomacy understanding (Stanzel, 2018, 6). Because the need for diplomacy has turned into a form that includes commercial and social relations beyond wars, land and colonial races and searches. In fact, this form is built on seeking solutions to other types of conflicts and pursuits in an age where land disputes have been reduced relatively dramatically without total wars. This transformation has led to the discussion in the literature that diasporas, who are not traditional players in diplomacy, are a potential diplomatic actor that can fulfil the basic functions of diplomacy such as communication, representation and negotiation (Ho & McConnell, 2017, 1). Undoubtedly, the existence of diasporas within the public opinion of the target country contributes to the diplomatic agency of these human communities in the new public diplomacy approach.

Rethinking Diaspora Diplomacy

Although the concept of diaspora diplomacy is discussed in the context of public diplomacy, it is a concept that has not been fully filled yet (Dickinson, 2020, 753). Therefore, the conceptual contradiction in diaspora diplomacy continues. Current studies in the literature use diaspora diplomacy together with the diaspora politics of states and cause the confusion to continue by expanding the area of use of the concept (Uysal, 2019, 273).

Since the diaspora policies of states are evaluated through public diplomacy, the literature focuses only on state policies. Diaspora diplomacy is not only a situation in which states are effective in foreign policy by using diasporas, but also a process in which diasporas affect homelands (Rana, 2011).

In recent years, the relationship between the state and the diaspora has begun to be discussed among the complexities of the transnational age. The reason for this is that diasporas become permanent in their host countries and continue their activities with networks that go beyond borders. This power gained by the diasporas has made it necessary for the homeland to follow their diaspora and develop policies towards them. The return of their diaspora is no longer required by the homelands. Instead, diasporas have evolved into a community of people where they are asked to achieve safe and effective status in their countries. Homelands have also started to adopt various policies in order to benefit from these diaspora groups. In addition, Homelands try to redefine their roles outside of their regional borders through the policies they implement (Ragazzi, 2014). These developments eliminate the domestic-foreign policy distinction in the relationship between the diaspora and the homelands. Diaspora communities whose roles have increased in the fields of culture and international relations, especially in economic development, are instrumentalized in public diplomacy during the active implementation of national strategies (Stone & Douglas, 2018, 1).

References

Riordan, S. (2003). The New Diplomacy. Cambridge: Polity Press

Rana, Kishan S.(2011).21st Century Diplomacy: A Practitioner's Guide. London: Continuum

Birka, I., & Klavins, D. (2020). Diaspora diplomacy: Nordic and Baltic perspective. Diaspora Studies, 13, 115- 132.

Brinkerhoff, J.M. (2019). Diasporas and Public Diplomacy: Distinctions and Future Prospects. The Hague Journal of Diplomacy, 14, 51-64.

Cull, N. (2010). Public diplomacy: Seven lessons for its future from its past. Place Branding and Public Diplomacy, 6, 11-17.

Stanzel, V. (2018). New realities in foreign affairs: diplomacy in the 21st century.

Ho, E. L. E., & McConnell, F. (2017). Conceptualizing 'diaspora diplomacy': Territory and populations betwixt the domestic and foreign". Progress in Human Geography, 43(2), 235–255.

Dickinson, J. (2020). Visualising the foreign and the domestic in diaspora diplomacy: images and the online politics of recognition in #givingtoindia. Cambridge Review of International Affairs, 33, 752- 777.

Uysal, N. (2019). The Rise of Diasporas as Adversarial Non-State Actors in Public Diplomacy: The Turkish Case. The Hague Journal of Diplomacy, 14, 272-292.

Ragazzi, F. (2014). A comparative analysis of diaspora policies. Political Geography,41,74-89.

Stone, D., & Douglas, E. (2018). Advance diaspora diplomacy in a networked world. International Journal of Cultural Policy, 24, 710- 723.

631   The Problem of Immigrant Workers Who Later Acquired Citizenship to Borrow Their Service Period Before Being a Citizen

Nihan Gizem Kantarci

Sosyal güvenlik hakkı, temel haklardan olup Anayasa ile güvence altına alınmıştır. Anayasa'nın 60. maddesinde bu husus açıkça belirtilmiştir. Maddenin kapsamından salt vatandaşların değil, göçmen işçilerin, mültecilerin, geçici koruma altındakilerin de yer aldığı sonucuna ulaşırız. Anayasa'nın 16.

maddesinde ise, yabancılar için temel hak ve özgürlere ilişkin kısıtlama sadece kanunla yapılabilecektir.

Bir Türk vatandaşının yabancı ülkede çalışmasına ilişkin sosyal güvenlik hakları konusunda, özellikle yurda dönüşte gerekli desteğin sağlanması için 3201sayılı kanunda özel düzenleme yapılmıştır[28]. Kanun metninde açıkça *"bir Türk vatandaşının"* ifadesi bulunmakla birlikte, *sonradan idari işlemle Türk vatandaşlığına geçen bir göçmen aynı hakka sahip midir?* sorusunu gündeme getirtmektedir. Sorunun yanıtında sosyal güvenlik hakları açısından ilk olarak doğuştan Türk vatandaşı olan ile sonradan yani idari işlemle vatandaş olan kişinin temel özelliklerinin aynı olduğu kabul edilmelidir. Sosyal güvenlik hakları ile ilgili, sonradan yurda dönen Türk vatandaşlarına gerekli desteğin sağlanması için yapılan düzenlemede kanun koyucu takdir yetkisi vermiştir. Eğer metni dar yorumlarsak sadece doğuştan Türk vatandaşlarına bu hakkı tanımamız gerekecektir. Hukukun temel ilkelerinde yer alan yorum kavramını kullanırken, eşitlik ilkesi, mülkiyet hakkı, ayrımcılık yasağı gibi objektif kıstaslar dikkate alınmalıdır. Bu doğrultuda sonradan Türk vatandaşı olan bir göçmen işçiye, yurt dışında geçirdiği hizmet sürelerine ilişkin farklı muamele yapılması için makul bir gerekçe bulunmalıdır. Her iki gruptaki kişi de benzer şekilde sigorta primi ödeyecek olup devlete mali bir ek yük getirmeyecektir. Kanunun temel amaca sosyal devlet ilkesinin gereği, Türk vatandaşının yurt dışında geçirdiği çalışma süreleri yönünden mağdur olmamasıdır. Konu hakkında 2005 yılında Yargıtay Hukuk Genel Kurulu[29] aksi yönde karar vermiş, 2020 yılında ise Anayasa Mahkemesi oyçokluğu ile olumlu karar vermiştir[30]. Yargı kararlarının karşı görüşü özellikle devletlerin ikili sosyal güvenlik anlaşmalarının bulunması, mütekabiliyet ilkesine göre değerlendirme yapılması yönündedir. 6458 sayılı YUKK. 88.[31] maddesinde ise uluslararası korumadan faydalanan kişilerin mütekabiliyet ilkesinden bağımsız tutulduğu yönündedir.

Örneğin Suriye'den gelen ve geçici koruma altında olan, çalışma izni alan bir işçi, sonradan Türk vatandaşlığını kazanırsa, Suriye'de çalışarak geçirdiği hizmet süreleri ne olacaktır? İki ülke arasında sosyal güvenlik anlaşması bulunmamaktadır. Mütekabiliyet ilkesini öncelikli kabul edersek bu kişinin vatandaş olmadan önceki çalışma süreleri yok hükmünde kabul edilecek, dolayısıyla hiçbir zaman değerlendirmeye tabi tutulamayacaktır. Oysa doğuştan Türk vatandaşı olan bir kişinin, örneğin Almanya'da çalıştığı hizmet sürelerini Türkiye'de borçlanabilmesine hem mütekabiliyet ilkesi hem de 3201 sayılı kanun gereği izin verilirken, sonradan Türk vatandaşı olan Suriye'den gelen kişiye aynı hakkın verilmemesi hem eşitlik ilkesine hem de sosyal devlet ilkesinin temel yapısına aykırı olacaktır.

Temel insan hakkı olan sosyal güvenlik hakkı, işçi lehine yorum ilkesi, ayrımcılık yasağı birlikte değerlendirilerek, borçlanmanın aktüeryal bir farkı bulunmaması

---

[28] RG., 22.5.1985, S. 18761, 3201 sayılı Yurt Dışında Bulunan Türk Vatandaşlarının Yurt Dışında Geçen Sürelerinin Sosyal Güvenlikleri Bakımından Değerlendirilmesi Hakkında Kanun,
[29] HGK., E. 2005/21-682, K. 2005/618
[30] Anayasa Mahkemesi Kararı, 2017/40089, RG., 1.7.2020, S. 31172
https://kararlarbilgibankasi.anayasa.gov.tr/BB/2017/40089
[31] RG., 11.4.2013, S. 28615, 6458 sayılı Yabancılar Uluslararası Koruma Kanunu

ve her iki grubun da eşit prim ödemesi doğrultusunda vatandaşlığın kazanılması konusunda ayrım yapılmadan yurt dışında geçirilen süreler borçlanılabilmelidir.

7F   Remittances

Chair: Farid Makhlouf, ESC Pau Business School, France

624   Remittances, Agriculture Investment and Cropping Patterns
       Ubaid Ali
640   The Path of Remittances to Consumption or Saving! Albania case
       study
       Nevila Mehmetaj
666   Literature review on remittances' utilization in migrants home countries
       Eugene Terungwa Agoh and Vilmante Kumpikaite-Valiuniene
675   Migration, Income and Remittances: Does The Host Country Matter?
       Farid Makhlouf

624   Remittances, Agriculture Investment and Cropping Patterns

Ubaid Ali

This paper compares the behavior of migrant and non-migrant farm household towards agriculture by examining how being a migrant and recipient of remittances influence household decisions regarding agriculture investment and selection of capital and labor-intensive crops. We investigate overall as well as separate effect of domestic and foreign remittance reception. We construct a model to show that migrant households receiving remittance income have the possibility to employ this additional income to raise their investment in agriculture. However, in short run an opposite reaction may appear if labor constraint due to the absence of migrant member is binding and lack of capital accumulation. We hypothesis that due to labor loss to the migration, household will decrease their production of labor-intensive crops like vegetables, fruits and rice and will increase capital intensive high input requiring cash crops like sugarcane and cotton. Controlling for endogeneity of remittances through instrumental variable strategy, we analyze data on 5,647 rural households from the eleventh round of the Pakistan Social and Living standards Measurements (PSLM) survey carried out in 2018-19. Our findings show a substantial negative effect of being a migrant household on investing in agriculture. Migrant household who receives remittances, has an 81.41% less in agricultural investment compare to non-migrant household. Probing source of remittances, the impact is high for domestic remittances recipient households having 83.64% less agricultural investment than non-migrant household migrant household. For foreign migrant households, this difference is 61%. The households' cropping patterns also become negative showing less agricultural production not only of capital-intensive cash crops i.e., sugarcane and cotton, but also less production of moderately capital-intensive subsistence wheat. Similarly, production of labor-intensive crop (vegetables, fruits, and rice) and moderately labor-intensive crops (pulses, maize, and fodder) also remain low than non-migrant member households. The production of cash crops and wheat crop are low by 89% and 77.78%, whereas that of labor-intensive crops and moderately labor-intensive crops are low by 81% and 61% in contrast to the non-migrant households.

We dissect migrant households in to domestically and internationally migrant households and tried to estimate the impact on cropping patterns. Based on the estimates, both domestic and international members migrant households are characterized by low agriculture production, except for international migrant member households where the production of labor-intensive crops is insignificantly negative. Between domestic and international where the impact is found to be significant, is more obvious for low remittance domestic migration. These findings highlight a detrimental impact on agricultural output and food security of short duration and annual crops arising from the absence of migrants, which should be addressed in future policies related to food security and rural development.

640   The Path of Remittances to Consumption or Saving! Albania case study

Nevila Mehmetaj

Since the change of the political systems in 1990-s in Albania, massive migration have been a continuous phenomenon of different scales in Albania. Meantime the phenomenon is associated with international inflows of financial resources from the expatriates. Remittances have been a vital financial source of living for a considerable number of population. Therefore they constitute an important financial mechanism to the funding of the country economy. Based on this how far may remittances have impact on the country macroeconomic gears. Therefore it is the purpose of this paper to analyze the effect of the remittances on the macroeconomic variables such as the aggregate consumption, aggregate saving and economic growth rate.

Many studies are performed in different developing countries presenting different results. Some studies show a positive impact of remittances on economic growth (Fayissa & Nsiah, 2010; Shera & Meyer, 2013). While other empirical regression analysis of emerging countries with long period data confirm a negative relation effect of remittances to the country's economic growth or development (Sutradhar, 2020). Empirical evidence analyzed the yearly data of 22 developing countries for the period 1960 - 2010, showing that remittances do not have uniform macroeconomic effects through countries or across time. The results suggested that remittances diminish macroeconomic volatility mainly through smoothening aggregate consumption (Mishi & Kapingura, 2013).

In this study a qualitative and quantitative analysis is presented. Three simple regressions analyses (OLS) are performed, on the effect of remittances on economic growth rate (first model); on the effect of remittances on the country aggregate consumption rate (second model); and on the effect of remittances on the country aggregate saving rate (third model). All variables are expressed in percentages of GDP. Country national indicators of Albania are used from the World Bank database for the period 1992-2019. The model results of the study show that the majority of remittance income is consumed from the recipient families adding to the aggregate demand. As a multiplier effect of the consumption in the economy, 1 percentage increase of remittances contributes to 3.2336 percent increase in aggregate consumption in economy. Although it is supposed that the multiplier effect of consumption can lead to a boost of economic growth, but the model results show that there is a positive relationship but it is not significant. While there is a positive relation of remittances to the national savings, but also it is not significant to the model.

666 Literature review on remittances' utilization in migrants home countries

Eugene Terungwa Agoh and Vilmante Kumpikaite-Valiuniene

According to world bank report of 2019 suggest low- and middle-income countries (LMICs) received $554 billion in remittances (World Bank, 2019). In sub-Saharan African countries, studies proved that remittances are a significant livelihood for majority of remittances receiving homes as it improves nutritional outcomes, associated with higher spending's in education by remittances (REM) recipients' families (Ajaero et al, 2018; Odipo, Olungah, and Omia, 2015).

In central and eastern European countries, REM are mostly used for consumption purposes such food. REM study in Mexico show coloration between REM and education expenditure. In Argentina, remittances where found to contribute investments in businesses and stock market between 1956 – 1996. These variations are many and vary from geographical regions and per countries of migrants sending countries.

Given the importance's of remittances, the purpose of this study is to present systematic literature review of utilization of remittances in various migrant home countries and to group those countries according to REM utilization.

This study focuses on scientific articles analyzes of utilization of remittances and their social-economic impact on 156 countries and regions spanning over 35 years. A combination of theoretical and empirical studies were analyzed to present various ways remittances are utilized in various countries and regions. MAXDQA software program was used for analysis and to elaborate map of remittances utilization and their impact and various impact variations across the countries.

According to Durand's (1994) (cited by Goldring, 2004), REM could be classified into four groups according to their utilization: 1) remittances as source of investment (ICT, Housing, Agriculture, Crisis management, Financial investments and Savings), 2) remittances as source of capita (productive investment, Democratic purposes and energy) and 3) remittances as wages and compensation (Self-utilization, Education, Health care and Food consumption).

Though inclusive, this ongoing literature review/research paper shows that remittances are utilized differently, depending on a given country's specific social-economic factors. Certain factors are known to influence the amount of remittances sent periodically to help families in home countries coupe under challenging times while, on the other hand, conflicts, politics, and natural disasters affect remittances amounts received in certain countries.

Furthermore, a grouping of countries based on remittances utilization under the above listed remittances utilization classification was shown to present a pictorial and easier understanding of remittances utilization in receiving migrant countries.

Evidently, we suggest remittances are utilized in various ways which are influence by the social economic status of the receiving household and the country at large. All analyzed studies were grouped according to remittances utilization in different studied countries.

Studies on remittances utilization in different countries demonstrate variety on REM utilization. We provide a map of REM utilization and groups of countries based on exiting studies. We cannot state that REM are utilized just for highlighted purposes in analyzed countries and are not used for other purposes. However, we provide a picture of REM utilization purposes in grouped countries according to analyzed studies.

References

Ajaero, C. K., Nzeadibe, C. T., Obisie-Nmehielle, N., & Ike, C. C. (2018). The linkages between international migration, remittances and household welfare in Nigeria. *Migration and Development, 7*(1), 40-54.

Goldring, L. (2004). Family and collective remittances to Mexico: A multi-dimensional typology. *Development and change, 35*(4), 799-840

Khatri, B. B. (2017). Utilization of remittance at household level: A case of Khanigaun Village of Resunga Municipality, Gulmi District. *Nepalese Journal of Development and Rural Studies, 14*(1-2), 12-20.

Mabrouk, F., & Mekni, M. M. (2018). Remittances and food security in African countries. *African Development Review, 30*(3), 252-263.

Odipo, G., Olungah, C. O., & Omia, D. O. (2015). Emigration and remittances utilization in Kenya. *Journal of Research on Humanities and Social Sciences, 5*(14), 163-172.

Pant, B. (2011). Harnessing remittances for productive use in Nepal. *Nepal Rastra Bank Economic Review, 23*, 1-20.

675   Migration, Income and Remittances: Does The Host Country Matter?

Farid Makhlouf

This paper aims to explain the dierence in growth rates of remittances to Morocco from 12 host countries. Two main insights of this paper are: 1) in the traditional host countries for Moroccan migrants such as France, the growth of remittances is mainly due to the increase in migrants income; 2) in the new host countries for Moroccan migrants such as the USA, the growth of remittances is due for a large part to the increase in the number of migrants.

7G   Insecurity, Conflict, Migration

Chair: Olgu Karan, Baskent University, Turkey

527   Division and Unity, Conflict and Cooperation: Sudanese Strive to Create Political Change in the Homeland
Lisa Richlen

685   Rohingya Refugee in Aceh Indonesia: Religious Solidarity or Human Solidarity?
Manotar Tampubolon

722   The carry-over effect of perceived threat from asylum seekers in Europe to Israeli local outgroups
Nonna Kushnirovich and Sabina Lissitsa

526   Racism on the Web: A Case Study on Representation of Syrian Hookah Smoking in Turkey
Olgu Karan and Banu Erşanlı Taş

527   Division and Unity, Conflict and Cooperation: Sudanese Strive to Create Political Change in the Homeland

Lisa Richlen

Transnational groups often organize politically to generate change in the homeland. This is widely understood to generate conflict however factors that promote cooperation around political issues are poorly theorized (Griffiths, 2000). This paper will compare the activities of a small group of Sudanese political activists who are members of Israeli branches of Sudanese political movements with the community at large which engaged in supporting regime change in Sudan in early 2019 through participation in a series of events. While the political movements, and Sudanese politics in general, is contentious and conflict inducing, regime change events were characterized by unity and cooperation around political issues. As such, the research enhances understanding of factors that promote political mobilization amongst the wider communities of asylum seekers and which help such communities to overcome political fractures. The findings, further, reinforce the notion that diaspora politics is contentious (Ostergaard-Nielsen, 2001, 2003), that a small group of individuals are actively engaged in on-going political activities (Shain & Barth, 2003) and that diaspora politics constitutes a unified transnational space (Turner, 2008). The paper is based on ethnographic research including semi-structured interviews with 48 young males and attendance at five regime change events.

Bibliography

Griffiths, D. (2000). Fragmentation and consolidation: The contrasting cases of Somali and Kurdish refugees in London. *Journal of Refugee Studies*, 13(3), 281–302. https://doi.org/10.1093/jrs/13.3.281

Ostergaard-Nielsen, E. K. (2001). Transnational political practices and the receiving state: Turks and Kurds in Germany and the Netherlands. *Global Networks*, 1(3), 261–282. https://doi.org/10.1111/1471-0374.00016

Ostergaard-Nielsen, E. K. (2003). *Transnational politics: The case of Turks and Kurds in Germany*. Routledge.

Shain, Y., & Barth, A. (2003). Diasporas and International Relations Theory. *International Organization, 57*(3), 449–479. https://doi.org/10.1017/s0020818303573015

Turner, S. (2008). The waxing and waning of the political field in Burundi and its diaspora. *Ethnic and Racial Studies, 31*(4), 742–765. https://doi.org/10.1080/01419870701784505

685   Rohingya Refugee in Aceh Indonesia: Religious Solidarity or Human Solidarity?

Manotar Tampubolon

The Rohingya are the most discriminated ethnic group in the world today. Rohingya refugees are again facing widespread resistance. Even Bangladesh, the origin of the Rohingya, has also refused their arrival to protect the spread of the COVID-19 pandemic. The same is done by Malaysia, which previously tolerated thousands of Rohingya asylum seekers and criticized Myanmar's persecution of its predominantly Muslim minority, now claims that there are "unfair hopes" for Malaysia to help Rohingya refugees in this climate. Xenophobia triggered by the COVID-19 pandemic. Indonesia has a different attitude, accepting with open arms that 99 Rohingya asylum seekers arrive on the coast of Aceh by boat after being tossed about in the ocean for over 120 days (Walden & Jones 2020). When other countries reject Rohingya refugees, Indonesia accepts them. This study aims to determine whether acceptance is purely humanist reasons or just solidarity. It also investigates whether the perceived religious sameness between victim and recipient affects the intention to change the Rohingya refugee's fate. In this context, I define social solidarity (Straehle 2020) as to how the Acehnese people in Indonesia feel they belong to the same religion as Rohingya refugees. Inspired by the concept of solidarity for refugees (Bauder & Juffs, 2019), this paper examines the idea of solidarity for refugees based on the same religion. I will discuss the relationship between the problems faced by Rohingya refugees and religious solidarity in this paper. This paper shows that the Acehnese people in Indonesia accept Rohingya refugees on the grounds of the same religion and not because of their fundamental human responsibility. These results show that the receiving community considers Rohingya refugees as victims whom they perceive as identically the same as themselves. On this basis, I should consider the concept of human solidarity more crucial than religious solidarity when accepting refugees.

722   The carry-over effect of perceived threat from asylum seekers in Europe to Israeli local outgroups

Nonna Kushnirovich and Sabina Lissitsa

The increased numbers of recent immigrants and asylum seekers who arrived in the European Union (EU) from African, Middle Eastern and Asian countries has come to dominate political and media discourse. The media has reported this phenomenon as a so-called "refugee crises", suggesting an allegedly unmanageable influx of foreigners. Even though they offer opportunities for economic growth, cultural enrichment, and a solution to declining native birth rates, their presence is mainly accompanied by perceptions of threat. Many studies have corroborated that perceived threat is an important mechanism explaining exclusionary attitudes to immigrants. Furthermore, attitudes toward one object can be generalized toward other objects, and this process also applies to groups. Following this generalization logic, studies examined the effect of a *distant* threat and found that people become more prejudiced toward local outgroups when distant threats carry over into local intolerance.

Our research objectives are: 1) to investigate the effect of distant perceived threat from European Union asylum seekers (hereafter EUAS) on attitudes toward local outgroups: Israeli Palestinians (hereafter IP), Non-Israeli Palestinians (hereafter NIP), and asylum seekers in Israel (hereafter IAS), controlling for face to face interaction with these minorities; and 2) to compare between the effects of perceived threat from distant outgroup and face-to-face interaction with local outgroups on attitudes toward local outgroups.

The study was conducted using an online survey of 1311 Israeli Jews.

Findings. The findings show perception of a medium-high level of realistic and symbolic threat from EUAS. The attitudes of Israeli Jews toward local outgroups range from slightly negative (toward IP), moderately negative (toward IAS), to extremely negative (toward NIP). Such attitudes indicate a great deal of subtle (or even blatant) prejudice in Israeli society. Face-to-face contacts with all minority groups was relatively rare and ranged from less than once a month for NIP and IAS to a few times per month for IP. Realistic threat from EUAS was negatively related to positive attitudes toward three local outgroups, while the association between symbolic threat from EUAS and attitudes toward the local outgroups was insignificant. The effect of distant realistic threat was more pronounced than the effect of symbolic threat and the effect of face-to-face contact.

This research revealed distant threat as a potential source of intolerance toward local "others" and conflict escalation. In line with our findings, policy makers should consider the escalation of distant crime, terrorist activities and economic crises attributed by the media to Muslim asylum seekers in Europe, as a potential trigger for local conflict escalation, and formulate a policy which may prevent or moderate it. Based on the suggestion that perceived distant threats from EUAS originated predominantly from negative Israeli media coverage of the EU asylum seeker crisis, we may assume that the manner in which migrants and immigration are described, categorized, and represented does matter. If this assumption corresponds to reality, framing refugees and asylum seekers in a more positive light may reduce xenophobic attitudes and, together with intergroup encounters, moderate intergroup conflict.

526   Racism on the Web: A Case Study on Representation of Syrian Hookah Smoking in Turkey

Olgu Karan and Banu Erşanlı Taş

This study focuses on the web representations of Syrian refugee hookah smoking leisure activity at public spaces in Turkey. The research question of this study is that how majority members of the society represent Syrian hoojah smoking leisure activity on the web pages. The research employs critical discourse analysis as a methodology. In so doing, the study aims to reveal the reproduction of racism through discourse and communication as well as the function of ideology that conceals inequalities and legitimises them as natural.

7H   Health and Migration

Chair: Sadhana Manik, University of KwaZulu, South Africa

903   No recourse to public funds and the necessity of social reproduction: the transnational dimensions of COVID-19
Michael Boampong

905   Interpreting with refugees in COVID times: increasing the vulnerability of beneficiaries and professionals
Daniela Herrera Rubalcaba, Maria Jesus Cabezon Fernandez, Pablo Pumares Fernandez, Ruben Rodriguez Puertas

1030   Challenges for asylum-seekers and refugees to become independent in times of COVID19 in Spain
Alberto García Martín, Elena Martínez Goytre, Pierina Cáceres Arévalo

1047   The Impact of the COVID-19 pandemic on South African Migrant teachers
Sadhana Manik

903   No recourse to public funds and the necessity of social reproduction: the transnational dimensions of COVID-19

Michael Boampong

COVID-19 pandemic has put questions around the rights of migrants to access public funds into the light of the negative impact of the 'no recourse to public funds' (NRPF) policy. Drawing on multi-sited ethnographic research with British-Ghanaians families, this paper focuses on the everyday material social practices of parenting, care and transnational practices through which people reproduce themselves, and the havoc wreaked on them by immigration control and lockdown from mobility. It further explores transnational families exchange of ideas about care, the flows of healthcare information, restricted transnational flows of grandparents and parents as carers and the differentiated impacts on children and social relations.

To conclude, the paper will draw on three dimensions of social reproduction (i.e. finance, production and reproduction) to discuss the impact of COVID-19 on British-Ghanaian migrant healthcare workers working conditions, transnational care practices and their access to public resources. Majority of the research participants are women carers whose children are in care. With vulnerabilities to employment and restrictions in mobility, this paper goes further to offer a transnational social protection strategy, based on feminist political economy and 'reproductive bargain'. In particular, It argues for policy consideration of transnational reproductive care in times of crisis. Such a social protection strategy much be linked to migration, employment, wages and social security payments and the provision of transnational care across generations and space.

905 Interpreting with refugees in COVID times: increasing the vulnerability of beneficiaries and professionals

Daniela Herrera Rubalcaba, Maria Jesus Cabezon Fernandez, Pablo Pumares Fernandez, Ruben Rodriguez Puertas

In the last decade, the international protection and asylum system in Spain has evolved within a context of precariousness, which has determined the resources allocated to the services associated with the asylum program. Such precariousness together with the "rigidity of the integration itineraries" (Garcés y Pasetti, 2019) increases the vulnerability of asylum seekers. Humanitarian interpretation is a key service on the refusal or acceptance of the asylum application due to the relevance of the interviews conducted during the asylum procedure. As a result, it could influence to some extent the well-being and the vulnerability of the asylum seekers (León-Padilla *et al.*, 2016). The traditional weakness of the Spanish asylum system faces today new challenges due to the increase of the asylum applications received in 2019 and the pandemic context that emerged from the Covid-19 in 2020.

In this paper, from 25 in-depth interviews conducted with experts and humanitarian interpreters, we analyse to which extent the pandemic has influenced the situation of the interpreters and the asylum seekers, and which strategies have been implemented to guarantee asylum seekers' rights. First, the most common challenges on the humanitarian interpretation with refugees are the increase of the de-professionalisation on volunteers with no specific knowledge acquired on ethic codes, interpretation techniques, or sociocultural aspects regarding asylum seekers. The cause is the increase in the interpretation demand and the inadequacy of funding for this service. A usual strategy is to hire external companies to carry out interpretation and translation tasks that are not particularly trained to work in a humanitarian context and, in extent, to understand the beneficiaries' needs. As a result, a lack of congruence takes place between beneficiaries' narratives and interpreter reports.

Nevertheless, due to the pandemic context, these difficulties have been constrained. The narratives highlight that the face-to-face interpretation loses effectivity due to the requirement to wear the masks that make more difficult the interpretation of non-verbal language. One of the biggest obstacles was found in telephone interpreting because of the barriers in generating bonds and trust between interpreters and users. In this line, COVID-19 lockdown increased digital divide which is causing many difficulties in the interpretation and the access to the resources in general. Furthermore, the pandemic context has constrained other services associated to the assistance of the asylum seekers, for instance, Spanish courses were cancelled, delays on the the psychological and health assistance or the increase of domestic conflicts within the families sharing same housing spaces. These challenges compromise the accomplishment of the rights of asylum seekers.

References

Garcés-Mascareñas, Blanca y Pasetti, Francesco. ¿A más solicitudes de asilo igual recepción? El sistema de acogida en España desde 2015. *Anuario CIDOB de la Inmigración 2019* (noviembre de 2019), p. 114-126.

León-Padilla, J., Jordá-Mathiasen, E., & Prado-Gascó, V. (2016). La interpretación en el contexto de los refugiados: valoración por los agentes implicados. *Sendebar*, 27, 25-49.

1030   Challenges for asylum-seekers and refugees to become independent in times of COVID19 in Spain

Alberto García Martín, Elena Martínez Goytre, Pierina Cáceres Arévalo

The aim of this proposal is to provide elements in response to the question: How the pandemic has influenced on the asylum seekers flows and their living conditions in Spain? More precisely, we have analyzed the process through which asylum-seekers and refugees win independence (autonomía) within and once they leave the Reception System for International Protection (Sistema de Acogida de Protección Internacional, SAPI), in relation to different factors, such as: administrative and legal procedures, language learning, training, labor inclusion and housing.

Among those different elements which have an influence on the experiences of people with access to the SAPI (about 30% of asylum-seekers in Spain), we have paid special attention to the role of housing as a safe space from which a new life in the receiving country can begin. According to the FOESSA Foundation (2019: 39), the lack of residential integration reinforces different social problems. In other words, residential exclusion is often the cause and not just the consequence of other exclusion processes. The emergence of COVID reveals housing is a fundamental protection element in the health crisis. The impact of this crisis in Spain, since March 2020, offers a different scenario and new challenges. For this reason, we have analyzed the impact of the crisis on the International Protection System and the lives of asylum-seekers.

To achieve the goals previously defined, this study has been carried out through an initial documentary analysis to better understand the reality of asylum-seekers and an analysis of quantitative data from secondary sources to characterize the context and their main profiles. Up to 61 in-depth interviews have been conducted, distributed as follows: 35 with key informants from the public administration, third sector entities, universities and the real estate sector; and 26 with participants of the Program for International Protection implemented by Provivienda Association, in Madrid and Granada. The participants interviewed came from 15 different countries, within and once they have left the Program.

At the beginning of the health crisis, the first state of alarm in Spain had an impact on administrative and legal procedures, blocking processes in some key cases such as registration, access to accommodation at the entrance to the SAPI, problems to have access to an independent house without social intermediation, or the renewal of work contracts. Although measures were taken to limit those effects, in many cases the negative impact could not be avoided because many of the stakeholders involved (the administration itself, banking and financial entities, employers' organizations and companies, etc.) did not know about these "extraordinary measures".

In addition to administrative difficulties, the health crisis caused other social and economic problems, in cases of coexistence in shared housing or the loss of jobs or income, for example. The aim of our report was to detect key elements for the independence and integration of asylum-seekers and refugees, in a very special context, defined by the COVID crisis, during which social entities in charge of the SAPI had to offer innovative solutions to unforeseen situations, in a very short time.

References

Asociación Provivienda (2019). Una casa como refugio: itinerarios residenciales de las personas solicitantes de Protección Internacional en Madrid y Vigo. Madrid:

Asociación Provivienda. Asociación Provivienda (2020). ¿Se alquila? Racismo y xenofobia en el mercado del alquiler. Madrid: Asociación Provivienda. Asociación Provivienda (2021). Una casa como refugio 2. Retos para la autonomía de las personas solicitantes y beneficiarias de protección internacional. Madrid:

Asociación Provivienda. Fundación FOESSA (2019). VIII Informe FOESSA: La exclusión social se enquista en una sociedad cada vez más desvinculada. Madrid:

Fundación FOESSA and Caritas Española Editores.

Garcés-Mascareñas, B. and Ribera Almandoz, O. (2020). Políticas de la indigencia. Solicitantes de asilo sin casa en Europa, CIDOB Notes Internacionals, no 237.

Iglesias Martínez, J. Á., Urrutia, G. Buades, J., and Vicente. T. (2016). ¿Acoger sin integrar?. Universidad Pontificia Comillas ICAI-ICADE.

Ribera Almandoz, O.; Delclós, C.; and Garcés Mascareñas, B. (2020). ¿"Casa nostra, casa vostra"? Condicions i trajectòries d'accés a l'habitatge de sol·licitants d'asil i refugiats a Catalunya. Enquesta CASASIL 2019: Informe de resultats, Monografias CIDOB no. 77.

1047   The Impact of the COVID-19 pandemic on South African Migrant teachers

Sadhana Manik

Highly skilled professionals have always been an attractive resource for countries to achieve their development goals. Teaching comprising highly skilled professionals, is now widely recognized as a mobile profession (Bense, 2016). South African migrant teachers can be now be found plying their skills in numerous countries developing and developed countries. The doors for qualified South African teachers post- apartheid, to emigrate to destinations abroad to teach have continued to open until the onset of the COVID-19 pandemic which brought the world to a standstill for more than a year. This paper delves deeply into the impact of the pandemic on five South African migrant teachers in different countries, who have been affected by the nuances of the corona virus. The data is from a qualitative longitudinal study on South African migrant teachers. The theoretical insights are sourced from natural disaster scholarship coupled with Lefebvre's rhythm analysis (2004) and Thorpe's (2015) use of 'arrhythmic experiences'.

14:15-14:45 BREAK

Day Three 8 July 2021 Thursday

Day Three 8 July 2021 - 14:45-16:15
8A   Work, Employment and Migration
Chair: Fethiye Tilbe, Tekirdag Namik Kemal University, Turkey
504   The Reflection of Discrimination And Gender on Labour Rights: Syrian
       Women in Turkey- A Comparative Analysis
       Aysel Ebru Ökten and Itır Aladağ Görentas
543   Undocumented migrants and the labour market in Chile
       Marcela Gonzalez and Oana Burcu
548   Assessing the risks to labour exploitation among migrant workers in the
       UK
       Alison Garnder and Oana Burcu
716   What attracts young talents to first-tier cities? Evidence from China
       Chi Jin

504   The Reflection of Discrimination And Gender on Labour Rights: Syrian Women in Turkey- A Comparative Analysis

Aysel Ebru Ökten and Itır Aladağ Görentas

Turkey has been home to displaced Syrians since April 2011. Today Syrian community in Turkey is close to 4 million and women generate 45 % of it. In time, expected temporariness has begun to evolve to permanency and each individual has to find their way through the crisis. Though legal regulations such as Law on Foreigners and International Protection and its Temporary Protection Regulation, European Convention on Human Rights and dubious EU- Turkey Statement of 2016 confer labour rights to some extent, it is of common knowledge that Syrians generally work undocumented and this situation make them even more vulnerable.

This study focuses on lived experiences of Syrian women in Turkey regarding working rights. First, the research will focus on legal regulations in Turkey on foreigners' labour rights and discrimination. Afterwards, by in-depth interviews and surveys in Kocaeli, İstanbul, İzmir and Gaziantep we will analyze possible discriminative experiences Syrian women might come across, comparatively. The current research shows Syrian women face difficulties in accessing

238

employment opportunities. Only 15 % of women are employed (Yucel et al., 2018). Yet once they are employed (or the ones employed), they go through other kinds of obstacles. The aim is to evaluate if legal rights reflect in real life experiences. The study also proposes a gendered analyse of changing roles in Syrian families and its sociological effects.

543   Undocumented migrants and the labour market in Chile

Marcela Gonzalez and Oana Burcu

During the last decade, Chile has for the first time in its history experienced a rapid increase in international immigration. Today, migrants make up 8% of the total population and most of them are from Venezuela (ref). As in other countries, a significant proportion of migrants experience vulnerable living conditions after their arrival, but has accentuated since 2018, when the Chilean government has imposed new "regulations" on granting visas to Venezuelans with the aim of disincentivizing migration. However, as the literature shows, border restrictions do not necessarily deter migration (ref) they just accentuate migrants' vulnerabilities at arrival. The number of undocumented migrants in Chile increased and they were driven into the underground economy, in industries such as the agriculture, constructions and hospitality, prone to exploitation through underpayment, long working hours and discrimination, or into the unregulated gig economy. In either case, migrants do not benefit from any legal protection and they cannot access state support. In other words, through visa restrictions and bureaucracy, Chile has limited people's access to fair and decent work, which goes against the UN sustainable development goals, which promote sustainable economic growth and decent work for all.

This research therefore raises a timely question that requires immediate action: What is the vulnerability to modern slavery that Venezuelan undocumented migrants face in Chile? Unlike other studies (ref), we focus particularly on migrants who entered the unregulated labour market, and have started microenterprises to support their families. This has helped them build independence and a higher income, but has also increased their vulnerability to Covid due to direct customer contact, and increased their risk to criminalization by police, the right-wing media and the populist government. We explore undocumented entrepreneurs' vulnerability to modern slavery through an interdisciplinary framework based on the intersection between an infectious disease, undocumented migration and an unregulated labour market. We capture the experiences of undocumented small "entrepreneurs" through 10 photo-elicitation interviews conducted online or via telephone. This strategy involves asking participants to take photographs of their daily life in relation to the topic of the study. Their images are used as props to guide the individual interview. We complement these interviews by collecting more data from Chilean NGOs that work directly with migrants.

This research explores the undocumented migrants' vulnerabilities to modern slavery, assesses the benefits of microenterprises as a way of minimising these vulnerabilities, and overall aims to contribute to raising awareness and putting this issue on the political agenda in Chile.

548   Assessing the risks to labour exploitation among migrant workers in the UK

Alison Garnder and Oana Burcu

Covid-19 has triggered a global crisis with severe economic and health consequences, particularly for vulnerable individuals that rely on seasonal work in the British agri-food industry. The impact on the UK food supply chains caught both government and businesses off-guard, with consumers worried about food shortages and agricultural producers concerned that a shortage of seasonal workers would lead to wastage of food harvest and irrecuperable financial loss. Consequently, the pandemic triggered a rapid labour recruitment process, with diminished attention to ensuring that employment agencies and gangmasters were meeting appropriate standards. For a short period labour inspections were also suspended, potentially resulting in a higher risk of exploitation.

This paper tackles the following inter-related questions: What risks and challenges did COVID-19 bring for workers? What understanding do workers have of their labour rights under UK law? Do workers consciously expect and accept poor or exploitative conditions? Through the use of electronic surveys, key informant interviews and policy review this research will provide the first large N study of the impact Covid-19 had on the labour conditions. We draw on the concept of "subjective legal empowerment" (Porter, 2014; van Waas, 2014) in order to focus on whether there is suitable opportunity and possibility for Romanian workers to use the law to improve their lives. Specifically, we will look at four sources of self-efficacy (Porter, 2014) to explain the lack of reporting of exploitative labour conditions: negative personal experience, seeing others failing in this task, emotional state induced by attempts to tackle the task, and the lack of information given to an individual about tools with which to tackle the task. In line with the literature, we believe that legal empowerment is a tool that can improve the socio-economic situation of disadvantaged groups (Golub, 2010) and in the context of this project it could minimise future exploitative conditions for seasonal labourers. We focus on Romanian workers, one of the largest seasonal workforces in the UK, and also one of the groups most susceptible to labour exploitation. We also pay particular attention to Roma groups from Romania, which are traditionally more economically deprived, discriminated against and hence more vulnerable. Romanian nationals are also consistently among the top 10 nationalities and the largest group of European Union citizens accepted as potential victims of exploitation within the National Referral Mechanism (NRM), based on which, labour exploitation is by a large margin the most commonly-observed type of modern slavery within the Romanian group,

These findings map the labour exploitation situation of Romanian migrants in the UK. They also inform practical policy recommendations on how to improve current practices and policies, and how to prevent exploitation within one of the most vulnerable industries and labour segments in the UK.

716 What attracts young talents to first-tier cities? Evidence from China

Chi Jin

With the increasing mobility of the population, how to attract and retain talent has recently become a key issue for city administrators. The ability to attract talent is what creates regional advantage: those that have the talent win, whereas those that do not lose (Florida 2005). Over the past few decades, China has experienced remarkable economic growth, gradually transforming from a global labor-intensive manufacturing base to a more technology /knowledge-based economy, which has resulted in a profound change in the composition of employment towards skilled labor and highly educated professionals(William 2014). Against this background, many Chinese cities have been engaging in a fierce "battle for talents" (CICC 2018). Cities offer discounts on housing purchases, favorable treatment on housing rentals, plus cash incentives and business start-up subsidies, etc. to attract talents to settle down and work in the city. Previous research indicated that talents tend to flow into first-tier cities[32] for higher salaries and better quality infrastructure (Liu et al. 2017). However, with the increasingly unaffordable prices in first-tier cities and the catching up of second-tier cities, the inflow of talent into first-tier cities seems to slow down (Chen, Hu, and Lin 2019). Whether first-tier cities are attractive to young talent nowadays has rarely been studied. This research aims to examine the drivers of university students' intention to migrate to China's first-tier cities in China after graduation from a behavioral perspective. Using the Theory of Planned Behavior (TPB) (Ajzen 1991), we conducted a two-stage investigation. In the first stage, an open-ended questionnaire was used and 18 salient beliefs affecting the mobility of university students to first-tier cities were elicited. In the second stage, we collected online questionnaires from 1242 university students across China about their intentions to migrate to first-tier cities. Structural equation modeling (SEM) was adopted to analyze the influence of attitudes, subjective norms, and perceived behavioral control of university students on their intention to develop in first-tier cities. The results showed that over 60% of university students expressed a strong intention to migrate to a first-tier city after graduation. Furthermore, behavioral beliefs such as fulfilling one's future dreams, better job opportunities, and higher income have a positive effect on students' intention to move to a first-tier city. Social pressures from family, friends, and peers also have a positive effect. However, the high housing prices in first-tier cities and the talents' family attachments discourage students' migration intention to first-tier cities. Our research not only confirms the applicability of the TPB in the study of population migration but also presents the behavioral drivers of young talents' migration intention.

Reference

Ajzen, I. 1991. 'THE THEORY OF PLANNED BEHAVIOR', *Organizational Behavior and Human Decision Processes*, 50: 179-211.

Chen, Jie, Mingzhi Hu, and Zhenguo Lin. 2019. 'Does housing unaffordability crowd out elites in Chinese superstar cities?', *Journal of Housing Economics*, 45: 101571.

CICC, China Internet Information Center. 2018. "Why are Chinese cities fighting for talent?" In, https://www.prnewswire.com/news-releases/why-are-chinese-cities-fighting-for-talent-300657261 . html.

Florida, Richard L. 2005. *Cities and the creative class* (Psychology Press).

Liu, Ye, Jianfa Shen, Wei Xu, and Guixin Wang. 2017. 'From school to university to work: migration of highly educated youths in China', *The Annals of Regional Science*, 59: 651-76.

William, S. Harvey. 2014. 'Winning the global talent war: A policy perspective', *Journal of Chinese Human Resource Management*, 5: 62-74.

8B Space and Migration

Chair: Pinar Yazgan, Sakarya University, United Kingdom

762 Communal space in community housing for Refugees in Transit

Akino Midhany Tahir and Febrianty Hasanah

Home is one of the important indicators in someone's life that is connected to social and emotional aspects. Home is more than just physical elements inside the house, but also the cultural values, social relations, security, identity, and immaterial ideas (Kim and Smets, 2020; Willem at al, 2020). Living in a transit country for years leads refugees to face insecurity and uncertainty about their present and future life. They also encounter temporal, emotional, and spatial shifts of home. In Makassar, a refugee-hosting city in Indonesia, there are 22 community housings provided by IOM for refugees. A community housing can accommodate more than 100 refugees, both single and family. In this type of housing, communal space and activities are vital to the process and spatial transition of 'home' from the previous location in their country of origin to the current in-transit location in Indonesia.

This study aims to identify the characteristic of communal space in shared accommodation for refugees in transit, using three different community housings located in different neighborhoods as case studies. The analysis focuses on the spatial structure and activities in the accommodations, particularly in the communal spaces, to illustrate the diversity of refugees' lived experience. Preliminary conclusion shows that space-making, shared activities, and connectedness are important factors in creating the sense of community. Attributes in a space affects the meaning of space and experience inherent in the space itself. Space is expected not only to be related to the physical elements, but also to be able to provide shared functions that allow shared activities. From these two things, a space can create connectedness to both space and the users of the space. Furthermore, social support developed from communal activities and the use of communal space adds to the strength of bonds between residents in the community housing.

References

Kim, K., & Smets, P. (2020). Home experiences and homemaking practices of single Syrian refugees in an innovative housing project in Amsterdam. *Current Sociology*, 1-21.

Willems, S., Smet, H. D., & Heylighen, A. (2020). Seeking a balance between privacy and connectedness in housing for refugees. *Journal of Housing and the Built Environment*, 35, 45-46.

766   Identifying gaps in refugee management in Indonesia

Akino Midhany Tahir, Jean Sonia Pantouw Langi, Nino Viartasiwi

Since Indonesia has not ratified the 1951 Refugee Convention and its 1967 Protocol, refugees and asylum seekers cannot settle permanently and are now trapped in a protracted situation. Despite its status as a non-signatory to the international instruments, Indonesia and other ASEAN member states, such as Malaysia and Thailand, abide by the principle of non-refoulement. In Indonesia, the refugees and asylum seekers live dispersedly across several locations. For instance, Greater Jakarta, Medan, Bogor, Makassar and Pekanbaru are each home to more than 1,000 urban refugees, with the remaining refugees are scattered in other regions such as Kupang, Lombok, and Aceh. Municipalities and regions in Indonesia are facing various challenges, which are also exacerbated by limited experiences and capacity in dealing with refugees. As a result, each municipality or region implements a different mechanism in handling refugees, which may involve different sets of stakeholders.

Based on the situation described, this research aims to identify overlaps, key challenges and analyze gaps of roles in refugee management at the national and municipal level in Indonesia, and also to unfold how transit countries, such as Indonesia along with its cities, respond to the trend of forced migration and the global refugee crisis. The methodology underpinning this research is literature reviews on refugee management and stakeholder mapping workshop focusing on Makassar and Bogor as cities of case studies. This research concludes that Indonesia's refugee management is still on an ad-hoc basis and relies heavily on the role of NGOs and other non-state actors. Nevertheless, there are some understudied stakeholders who may play an important role or have a strong influence on refugee management at the municipal level. Moreover, having a primary goal in refugee advocacy is also important to determine which stakeholders are suitable for each refugee management activity. The conclusions could be formulated as a set of recommendations to enhance Indonesia's currently available refugee policies.

659   When Do Workers Prefer Open Borders?

Kristina Sargent

When making the decision to move to another country for work, people take into consideration the likelihood of obtaining work, the value of that work (often relative to work at home), and the costs they face when moving and living away from home. Workers' migration decision additionally imposes externalities on the market they leave as well as the market they join. With this in mind, I build a two-country search and matching model with costs of migration for workers. I focus on fixed move costs as well as a flow cost faced anytime a worker is away from his/her country of origin. Next, I conduct a welfare analysis with varying objective functions for workers to evaluate how workers would choose between a world of open compared to closed borders. Workers typically prefer open borders to closed, with some exceptions depending on particular parameterizations and definitions of welfare, as well as they structure of government funding for unemployment benefits. Overall, all workers are usually better off in a world of open migration with migration costs and frictional labor markets. While migrants have a revealed preference for open borders, even workers who choose not to move are better off when such movement is allowed.

522   Immigrants and Sao Paulo city (Brazil): interaction and sociability ways

Camila Escudero

The main objective of this article is to investigate the modes of interaction and sociability of Latin American immigrants with the São Paulo city, the greatest context of international migratory presence in Brazil. The latest dates, from 2019, shows that 361,201 foreigners live in the city, which represents about 3% of the local population. The nationalities of origin are quite diverse, with emphasis on Peruvian, Bolivian, Venezuelan and Haitian (IOM, 2019).

This study is part of a larger investigation, which has been started in 2019, in the Social Communication field. Our intention is to design a referential framework organized in two levels: the first one contemplates interaction and sociability ways based on the immigrant's local networks and connections, composed, mainly, from their participation in different collective spaces in the city; the second one is to understand these forms from the permanent contact of this foreigner with the city and his/her experience with the São Paulo rhythm and its daily life. For this, we used the Participant Observation research technique – working with six groups, collectives and immigrant organizations, for about one year, in their own communication vehicles (newspapers, websites, blogs, virtual social networks, videos etc.), help them to produced their contents.

As a theoretical-conceptual resource, we used an interdisciplinary suggestion that links concepts from Communication and Anthropology fields. We emphasized the idea of communication as a tie/bond, according to Muniz Sodré

(2014), in dialogue with the mediator concept, according to Velho (2010), both Brazilian intellectuals. For the first author, communication is not only the information transmission or speeches, but rather a modeling way (organization of real exchanges) and a process (action) of putting differences in common, of establishing bonds on the part of individuals. On the other hand, Velho discusses the potential for dialogue of the subject-mediator in face of a cosmopolitan experience, at the level of objective culture and material relations, or at the level of relations between different groups or people, negotiating reality and building it in an uninterrupted process.

As main results, we try to demonstrate that the immigrant's sociability and interaction ways with the São Paulo city indicates the constitution of the social relations forms through living in the common space – with local habitants and/or with others immigrant groups – besides the composition of meanings shared at a socio-cultural level. It is a complex process, which involves knowledge, recognition, actions and relationships and shows that, in the case of migratory processes, the characteristics of the city – geographic, climatic, infrastructure etc. – are not empty meanings for external person, but they produce effect and demand tension and conflict with cultural matrices composed of identities and histories.

References

OIM – Organização Internacional para as migrações (2019). A cidade de São Paulo: Perfil 2019 – Indicadores da governança migratória local. Genebra: OIM.

SODRÉ, M. (2014). A ciência do comum – Notas para o método comunicacional. Petrópolis: Vozes.

VELHO, G. (2010). Metrópole, cosmopolitismo e mediação. Horizontes Antropológicos, Porto Alegre, Ano 16, N. 33, p. 15-23.

8C	Migración y futuro de la arquitectura

Chair: Emanuele Giorgi, Tecnológico de Monterrey in Chihuahua, México

1015 Sociedades receptoras: la arquitectura hospitalaria como inclusiva del migrante
Ana Laura García Hernández

1016 Principios de una arquitectura acertada a las necesidades de los migrantes
Estefany Hernández Gutiérrez

1017 La influencia del diseño arquitectónico en el bienestar de los migrantes refugiados
Laura Sofia Martínez

1018 La arquitectura bioclimática como aliada para el bienestar de migrantes: estudio en climas áridos y fronterizos (Chihuahua, México).
Jacqueline Beltrán Palomares

1014 ¿Cómo la migración definirá el futuro de la arquitectura?
Paulina Elizabeth Martínez Gámez

1015   Sociedades receptoras: la arquitectura hospitalaria como inclusiva del migrante

Ana Laura García Hernández

Las ciudades y su arquitectura cada vez se interesan más en la inclusión de los migrantes debido al potencial que estos pueden aportar para su desarrollo. La arquitectura tiene como reto entender la manera en la que debe evolucionar para permitir un desarrollo siempre más necesario, el cual refleje conceptos de bienvenida, recepción y colectividad para el migrante. De este modo, surge la interrogante de la manera en que la ciudad y su arquitectura pueden llegar a ofrecer hospitalidad al migrante que se instala. Para entender cuáles son estos retos y evoluciones necesarias, esta investigación analiza cuatro casos de estudio internacionales en donde ciudades de distintas culturas emplean la arquitectura para ofrecer algo más que un refugio efímero al migrante. La ciudad de Calgary cuenta con el edificio de CIES, en el cual se busca ayudar a los inmigrantes y a las personas en desventaja económica a encontrar su lugar en la sociedad canadiense ofreciéndoles educación, una bolsa de trabajo y capacitación laboral. CAFEMIN, en la Ciudad de México, promueve el desarrollo integral de mujeres y familias migrantes brindándoles conocimiento para poder adquirir un empleo. En Shanghai, el Centro Shanghai Gucun, brinda un espacio arquitectónico seguro, sostenible y digno para niños y familias migrantes marginadas en donde estos pueden aprender y formar comunidad. Ámsterdam alberga el proyecto urbanístico denominado Zona Social Especial de Wittenburg que busca conformar un espacio de llegada para los migrantes con la construcción de edificaciones de vivienda colectiva, trabajo, educación y recreación; complementarias a la arquitectura existente de la zona. Esta diversificación de proyectos permite ampliar el estudio y observar las diferencias y similitudes que existen alrededor del mundo en torno al recibimiento del migrante que se instala. La investigación arroja la necesaria existencia de una arquitectura hospitalaria con el migrante, en donde la inclusión a la vida social y económica, la conformación de una comunidad y la coexistencia con los residentes originales son necesarias. En particular, se demuestra cómo la educación y los espacios para impartirla junto con la generación de un sentimiento de comunidad son imprescindibles para el desarrollo tanto del migrante como de la comunidad local.

1016   Principios de una arquitectura acertada a las necesidades de los migrantes

Estefany Hernández Gutiérrez

La arquitectura se considera como una de las disciplinas más completas, ya que se abordan en ella aspectos de arte, ciencias y humanidades. Esta última, la convierte en algo sumamente empático (García, 2018, p.11). Es por ello que suele tomarse en cuenta al cliente, con la finalidad de que sus peticiones sean atendidas y acertadas. El término acertado, en la arquitectura, implica realizar el diseño y construcción de manera adecuada para que este tenga un buen efecto hacia el usuario, además, de ser conscientes de que el ser humano tiene necesidades personales. Sin embargo, este conocimiento, que se considera como "default" en la arquitectura, parece ser ignorado o irrelevante en algunos casos, específicamente, en los módulos de emergencia. La arquitectura efímera por emergencia, debe garantizar calidad y capacidad de proporcionar refugio en el menor tiempo posible. En particular, estas soluciones arquitectónicas, están destinadas a albergar, durante un tiempo limitado, a una masa de personas que han migrado debido a una crisis humanitaria o ambiental(Consuegra, 2020). Dicho lo anterior, es relevante cuestionar sobre la existencia de módulos de emergencias que hayan considerado en el proceso de diseño al usuario y su relación con el entorno,y que respetaran la premisa de la arquitectura (sobre cubrir las necesidades personales) junto con la rapidez y urgencia que se le debe dar al mismo.

Ahora bien, se plantea una interrogante: ¿Cuáles fueron las experiencias de diseño más acertadas de los módulos de emergencia?

Para responder esta pregunta, se llevó a cabo una recolección de datos en la que se investigaron como casos de estudios varios proyectos de arquitectura modular por contextos de emergencia. Posteriormente, se clasificaron y analizaron los datos según indicadores clave que deben tener por ser arquitectura efímera por emergencia (Equipo Editorial, 2017). Para corroborar estos indicadores, se realizaron dos entrevistas, acerca de la migración, sus razones y posibles alternativas, a expertos que han presenciado el fenómeno de la migración desde el puesto de director de una Casa del Migrante en Ciudad Juárez, y una arquitecta y cofundadora de un taller donde son partícipes migrantes, en su mayoría africanos, en Berlín. En conclusión, la arquitectura, además de poder ofrecer un módulo efímero funcional y seguro, tiene la capacidad de aportar a la restauración de la dignidad y bienestar físico-emocional de refugiados y migrantes. Por esto, es indispensable desarrollar proyectos que cumplan con los principios de protección, que atiendan las necesidades básicas de manera higiénica, que respeten la diversidad cultural y que establezcan un diálogo tanto con la población refugiada y migrante, como con el lugar.

1017   La influencia del diseño arquitectónico en el bienestar de los migrantes refugiados

Laura Sofia Martínez

La migración es un fenómeno que experimentan las personas por múltiples razones, entre estas políticas, sociales, económicas o ambientales. Lamentablemente, la migración de refugiados es considerada una crisis, pues la combinación de desastres naturales y conflictos armados han desplazado a millones de personas a lo largo de la historia, para las que los países receptores no estaban preparados (Naciones Unidas, 2017). El bienestar tanto físico como psicológico de los migrantes está directamente asociado con el diseño arquitectónico de los campos y, a pesar de que la migración no sea un fenómeno para nada reciente, siguen existiendo múltiples problemáticas de diseño que afectan a los involucrados en este fenómeno.

A lo largo de los años, se han buscado soluciones de viviendas y sistemas espaciales para estos campos. Sin embargo, ninguna ha resultado del todo exitosa, en particular porqué muchos de los campos que iban a ser supuestamente temporales llevan décadas expandiéndose. Lo que lleva a cuestionar cuáles son los factores que contribuyen a que los migrantes pasen de sentir incertidumbre sobre sus futuros, a sentir pertenencia de sus alrededores, llegando a una pregunta aún más específica, ¿cómo el diseño arquitectónico influye en el bienestar de los migrantes en estos contextos de "temporalidad eterna"?

Para esto, se realizó una investigación basada en dos casos de estudio de los campos más grandes del mundo, el campo de la Ciudad de Kakuma en Kenia, que alberga a 182,000 refugiados y existe desde 1992; y el campo de refugiados en Zataari, Jordania, que alberga a 80,000 migrantes desde el 2012. Estos campos serán calificados según los indicadores establecidos por la Organización para la Cooperación y Desarrollo Económicos (OECD), evaluando el estado del bienestar de los migrantes residentes. Estos factores consisten de dos categorías: Calidad de Vida y Condiciones Materiales. Estas categorías agrupan los indicadores usados: en la primera categoría se tomarán en cuenta Estatus de la Salud, Educación y Habilidades, Conexiones Sociales, Calidad del Medio Ambiente y Seguridad Personal. Para la segunda categoría se tomarán en cuenta Ingreso y Riqueza, Trabajos y Ganancias, y Alojamiento. No se encontró información relevante para la investigación sobre los indicadores de Balance Trabajo-Vida, Compromiso Cívico y Gobernanza, y Bienestar Subjetivo, por lo que no serán tomados en cuenta (OECD, 2018).

Los resultados de este análisis evidenciaron que los ámbitos urbanos, económicos y sociales son de gran valor para el bienestar de los migrantes. En los campos de larga permanencia, el diseño es responsable de establecer las conexiones sociales entre los migrantes y la vivienda, y que es el lugar en el que pasan la mayor parte de su tiempo. Además se evidencia como en los campos de larga permanencia, sea importante brindar oportunidades de diseño participativo, pues permite expresar su individualidad y cultura. En particular, porqué así los migrantes pueden resaltar sus necesidades y deseos, involucrarse con sus alrededores y seguir sintiéndose conectados a las tierras que fueron obligados a abandonar.

1018   La arquitectura bioclimática como aliada para el bienestar de migrantes: estudio en climas áridos y fronterizos (Chihuahua, México).

Jacqueline Beltrán Palomares

Cada año, miles de migrantes de Centroamérica cruzan México intentando entrar a Estados Unidos de América. Según el INEGI, de 100 personas que llegan al estado de Chihuahua, 93 de ellas pretenden cruzar la frontera. Debido al clima extremoso y árido del estado de Chihuahua, los migrantes sufren de un significativo desgaste físico y emocional. Por ello, nacieron varias asociaciones que gestionan casas de migrantes para apoyar a quienes cruzan por este estado. Esto evidencia la importancia del papel de la arquitectura para (1) desarrollar espacios que contribuyan al bienestar físico y emocional en el camino del migrante y (2) permitir a las asociaciones proporcionar espacios dignos y acogedores aprovechando los recursos que el ambiente de Chihuahua ofrece. Dicha información dirige a la pregunta de investigación: *¿Cómo puede la arquitectura bioclimática ayudar a las casas de migrantes y albergues en el estado de Chihuahua a ofrecer mejores soluciones de hospedaje?*

Se realizó el análisis de dos edificaciones en el estado de Chihuahua desde un punto de vista bioclimático: de los 67 municipios que conforman el estado, se eligieron dos, siendo estos de las ciudades principales, para el análisis de dos casas de migrante. La primera recibe el nombre de "Casa del Migrante San Agustín", la cual tiene una capacidad de ochenta personas, presenta un área de terreno construido de 711 m² y el área exterior es de 800 m². Lleva laborando desde mediados de abril 2020 y se encuentra ubicada al sureste de la ciudad de Chihuahua, capital del estado. La segunda casa se localiza en Ciudad Juárez, específicamente al noroeste, colindando con la frontera hacia Estados Unidos de América; recibe el nombre de "Casa del Migrante" y gestiona desde 1986, tiene una capacidad de 600 personas y cuenta con áreas verdes que ocupan un área de 2,570 m² y un área ocupada en el edificio principal de 512 m².

Estos dos casos se analizaron bajo los parámetros de:(1) aprovechamiento solar de los edificios con respecto a su orientación y posicionamiento en el predio, (2) la cantidad de dinero que se aporta a la casa para cubrir los servicios de electricidad y (3) los termopreferendums de los migrantes que llegan a hospedarse.

Los resultados evidenciaron las pocas o nulas estrategias bioclimáticas empleadas en ambas edificaciones. A pesar de la gran labor de los administradores en ofrecer soluciones para el bienestar de los migrantes, se expone rápidamente el por qué (1) se logran parcialmente los niveles de confort de los migrantes que atienden a dichas casas y (2) que la gestión de la casa en cuestión de finanzas se ve afectada intentando alcanzar los mismos.

La arquitectura bioclimática maneja múltiples estrategias para aprovechar los recursos del medio, convirtiéndola en la clave para brindar un espacio incluyente, digno y acogedor.

El papel principal del arquitecto es garantizar el bienestar de los usuarios por medio del diseño de la estructura. Es imprescindible que nuestros proyectos (1) sean de ayuda para las comunidades vulnerables y (2) que favorezcan y aporten valores a nuestra sociedad.

1014   ¿Cómo la migración definirá el futuro de la arquitectura?

Paulina Elizabeth Martínez Gámez

El cambio climático presenta grandes consecuencias en la migración (IOM, 2008). En los últimos 30 años tormentas, sequías e inundaciones han aumentado de manera considerable, impactando en particular las poblaciones más vulnerables, con consecuencias en múltiples ámbitos (físico, económico y de salud) y originando importantes fenómenos de desplazamientos (United Nations, 2012).

Los desastres naturales, siempre más extremosos y frecuentes, son provocados evidentemente por el cambio climático y generan una vulnerabilidad física por la destrucción o pérdida de bienes de comunidades locales (IOM, 2008). Así mismo, se espera que para el 2050 haya espacios más áridos y lugares con sequías constantes, con consecuentes disminuciones de productividad en muchos aspectos, y afectando la economía (IOM, 2008). También, los cambios climáticos afectarán aspectos ambientales relacionados a la salud, como contaminación del aire y de las reservas hídricas, calidad de los alimentos y contribución a las enfermedades cardiovasculares y respiratorias que tienen las temperaturas extremas en la población vulnerable (United Nations, 2018). Aunque escenarios catastróficos se están delineando por el futuro, muchos cambios ya impactaron un porcentaje relevante de la población mundial.

Los arquitectos y diseñadores urbanos tienen un rol importante en interpretar estos fenómenos, para poder ofrecer propuestas óptimas a los nuevos fenómenos sociales que se generan. Por la capacidad de la arquitectura de lograr impactos positivos si es pensada correctamente, la pregunta de esta investigación es ¿Cómo la migración definirá el futuro de la arquitectura?, la cual surgió con la intención de entender cuáles características debería tener la arquitectura para ser sensible a las necesidades de los seres humanos que migran por el cambio climático.

Para responder dicha pregunta se analizaron, bajo indicadores de carácter físico, económico y de salud, las necesidades que caracterizan las poblaciones de los "migrantes climáticos" en el mundo. Con comparaciones con proyectos de éxito, se asociaron estas necesidades sociales específicas, con las necesidades espaciales que una "buena" arquitectura tiene que proponer para (1) solucionar las necesidades particulares de las personas desplazadas que llegan a su nuevo destino, (2) actuar sensiblemente al contexto social y medioambiental y (3), al mismo tiempo, aportar de manera significativa a la reducción del cambio climático. Los resultados generaron suficientes características para así redactar líneas guías de intervención en dichos contextos de migración climática, que se pueden categorizar en: atención al medio ambiente; consideraciones universales para la persona; calidez y comodidad de los espacios; relaciones con el contexto social y productivo; Esto significa definir principios bases para proyectos de arquitectura enfocados en propuestas para "migrantes climáticos".

Gracias a los resultados, se concluyó que los espacios necesarios para los migrantes climáticos, son principalmente arquitectura consciente y amigable al medio ambiente, además de consideraciones universales para la persona que llegue a dichos lugares, y así, crear un espacio cómodo y cálido.

Referencias bibliográficas

United Nations. (2012). *Migration, Environment and Climate Change: Assessing the Evidence*. United Nations.

International Organization for Migration (IOM). (2008). *MRS N°33 - Climate Change and Migration: Improving Methodologies to Estimate Flows*. International Organization for

Migration (IOM).

United Nations. (2018) *Cambio climático y salud.* https://www.who.int/es/news-room/fact-sheets/detail/climate-change-and-health

8D   Migration and Identity

Chair: Inci Aksu Kargin, Usak University, Turkey

828   Claiming the Power of Un/Gratefulness: Refugees' Narratives of Self
        Irina Kyulanova
830   Production Perspectives in Central American Migrant Life Stories While
        in Transit at the U.S.-Mexico Border
        Stephanie Kaczynski
831   Challenges in the Preservation of Cultural Identity: The Case of
        Romanian Immigrants in Belgium
        Anca-Diana Bibiri and Mihaela Mocanu
768   Brazilian women in Portugal, Colombian women in Spain. Illegality as a
        resistance strategy against the neoliberalization of life.
        Andrea Souto Garcia and Nazaret Abalde Bastero

828   Claiming the Power of Un/Gratefulness: Refugees' Narratives of Self

Irina Kyulanova

In her memoir *The Ungrateful Refugee* (2019), Dina Nayeri questions the ethics of host societies expecting gratefulness from refugees. Nayeri challenges the host countries' tacit perception of the need for those who have been granted refugee status to denounce their previous identity in appreciation for a supposedly gratuitous act of rescue. In this paper, I will employ Nayeri's work as a metatextual lens through which to explore the theme of gratefulness in a selection of other contemporary autobiographical accounts of escape from war and becoming a refugee. I will trace the Western notion of gratitude to dominant political, religious, and psychological discourses, focusing specifically on its role in conceptualising social inequality and state welfare on the one hand, and on the other – the politicised imperative of positive psychology to pursue individual happiness (e.g. through practices such as mindfulness and gratefulness diaries). Considering the refugees' memoirs as performances of selfhood, I will discuss how expressions of gratefulness in them are attuned to host societies' expectations; whether they might be interpreted as what Nayeri refers to as "pandering", due to the position of these memoirs as a sort of currency for purchasing the recipient society's welcome and support, but also whether such sentiments may be grounded in the framework of the refugees' inherited culture and hybrid identity. Further, I will examine the possibilities afforded in the refugee memoir genre displays of ungratefulness, for resistance to the stereotypical linear narrative patterns of trials and triumph, persecution and rescue. Drawing on debates on the reciprocity implicitly involved in gift exchanges, as expounded in Terry Eagleton's *Radical Sacrifice*, I discuss whether the memoirs offer any space for liberation from the perceived indebtedness brought about by the act of receiving asylum. I will discuss the degree to which writing about lack of thankfulness, rejection of charity, impatience or assertion of the right of choice tests the limits of palatability of refugees' honesty for the reader. In my analysis, I will attempt to draw conclusions on the connection between expressing gratefulness or ungratefulness and the dynamics of conceding or gaining narrative power in the process of producing new immigrant selves.

Works Cited

Cerew, Bruce. *War Child: A Memoir.* Amara Books, 2008.

Eagleton, Terry. *Radical Sacrifice.* Yale UP, 2018.

Eakin, Paul John. *Living Autobiographically: How We Create Identity in Narrative.* Cornell UP, 2008.

Kamara, Mariatu, with Susan McClelland. *Bite of the Mango.* Annick Press, 2008.

Nayeri, Dina. *The Ungrateful Refugee: What Immigrants Never Tell You.* Canongate, 2019.

830 Production Perspectives in Central American Migrant Life Stories While in Transit at the U.S.-Mexico Border

Stephanie Kaczynski

Implemented in January 2019, the United States' Migrant Protection Protocols (MPP) forces migrants to remain in a liminal space of perpetual transit (Frank-Vitale, 2020) and renders them even more vulnerable to exploitation, trafficking, violence, and murder (Garrett, 2020) while they wait indefinitely to proceed through the U.S. migration legal process. Countless media sources covered the caravans and their arrival in Mexican northern border cities; however, very few extended firsthand accounts are publicly available from Central American migrants living on the U.S.-Mexico border while seeking asylum in the U.S.

This analysis responds to calls to study migration in ways that normalize neither mobility nor stasis (Glick Schiller & Salazar, 2013) and to analyze migrant life stories shared in transit, as opposed to experiences recounted in the "sending" country or after arriving at the "receiving" country (Frank-Vitale, 2020). I analyze two extended accounts of migrant life stories in transit: Alejandra, in an interview produced for a mainstream radio news show, and Douglas, through his own poetry on public social media platforms. Autoethnographic performance yields myriad benefits, including critical reflection and self-expression (Alexandra, 2014) and personal and social identity transformation (Price & Ogden, 2019). In examining how Central American migrants perform autoethnography through recounting experiences of violence, living in liminal transit, and envisioning a future, I explore tensions between production perspectives in migrant life stories of Central Americans living on the U.S.-Mexico border. Specifically, I argue divergent perspectives of mainstream media production versus self-production of migrant life stories structure subjects' performance of their identity as well as specific visions of migrants' future horizons.

Tensions between the mainstream media and self-produced accounts offer crucial insights into migrants' perceived horizons in their own life stories. In Alejandra's heavily mediated account, the migrant experience comprises predominantly suffering, with minimal hope for a future not in transit. Standards of objectivity dissuade mainstream journalists from advocating for more humane migration policies; as a result, the journalist constructs an "objective" narrative of Alejandra's horizon as bleak and entirely outside of her control. In contrast, Douglas articulates his continuous occupation of a space of transit, with the fear and dangers that accompany such a space, while also sharing his vision of a horizon in which he will no longer be in a space of constant motion. In his self-produced performance, Douglas details multiple overlapping perspectives regarding his identity as a Honduran migrant, speaking to his liminal, transitory status. For Oviedo, this shifting identity underscores Tijuana as a site of "forced immobility," in which he can neither cross the border nor return home, rendering him vulnerable to discrimination and violence without community support for protection (Fernández Casanueva & Juárez Paulín, 2019, p. 157).

Engaging in autoethnographic performance enables Alejandra and Douglas to process experiences and build connection with other migrants, suggesting transformative potential for migrant horizons. Nonetheless, lack of agency over production inhibited Alejandra's ability to fully construct her identity and future goals. This analysis thereby offers implications for engaging migrants in production and discursive control over their performed autoethnographies.

References

Alexandra, D. (2014). Digital storytelling as transformative practice: Critical analysis and creative expression in the representation of migration in Ireland. *Journal of Media Practice, 9*(2), 101–112. https://doi.org/10.1386/jmpr.9.2.101_1

Fernández Casanueva, C., & Juárez Paulín, A. (2019). El punto más al sur y el punto más al norte: Tapachula y Tijuana como ciudades fronterizas escenarios de inmovilidades forzadas de migrantes, desplazados internos, solicitantes de refugio y deportados. *Península,* *14*(2), 155–174. http://www.scielo.org.mx/pdf/peni/v14n2/1870-5766-peni-14-02-155.pdf

Frank-Vitale, A. (2020). Stuck in motion: Inhabiting the space of transit in Central American migration. *The Journal of Latin American and Caribbean Anthropology, 0*(0), 1–17. https://doi.org/10.1111/jlca.12465

Garrett, T. M. (2020). COVID-19, wall building, and the effects on Migrant Protection Protocols by the Trump administration: The spectacle of the worsening human rights disaster on the Mexico-U.S. border. *Administrative Theory & Praxis, 42*(2), 240–248. https://doi.org/10.1080/10841806.2020.1750212

Glick Schiller, N., & Salazar, N. B. (2013). Regimes of mobility across the globe. *Journal of Ethnic and Migration Studies, 39*(2), 183–200. https://doi.org/10.1080/1369183X.2013.723253

Price, M. L., & Ogden, M. R. (2019). Interactive/transmedia storytelling as cultural narrative: Stories of family, place and identity. In T. A. Hayes, T. Edlmann, & L. Brown (Eds.), *Storytelling: Global reflections on narrative* (pp. 205-215). Brill.

831   Challenges in the Preservation of Cultural Identity: The Case of Romanian Immigrants in Belgium

Anca-Diana Bibiri and Mihaela Mocanu

Identity ia a fluid concept, constantly changing and defined depending on "the other". In this sense, considered an individual construct (Easthope, 2009), identity is understood as a spatial category since the ideas of territory, self and "us" all require symbolic, socio-cultural and/or physical dividing lines with the *Other* (Paasi, 2001). Assuming that identity is a dynamic process, this research pursues the mutations suffered by the social and cultural identity of immigrants after they left the country of origin. The Romanians identities migrate with them, but are also rearticulated in the process. So are the territories and borders across which they migrate. That is, not only the identity of the migrant, but also the identity of the 'host' country or city is rearticulated when people move from one place to another (La Barbera, 2015).

Our study is methodologically based on a qualitative research about the migration impact upon the social and cultural identity of Romanians immigrants in Belgium within the project *Sociocultural challenges of the migration phenomenon in the EU. The case of Romanian immigrants in Belgium* (MIG Ro-Be).. This study is relevant given the fact that, since 2007, the year when Romanian joined the European Union, and, so far, our country has the highest growth rate of migration in Belgium: according to the Belgium statistics (www.myria.be), Romania provided the largest number of immigrants in the country.

This research focuses on two fundamental elements that constitute the individual and group identity: language and religion, and have the following assumptions: language remains one of the main identity factor among immigrants, seen as a means of preservation and cultivation of national identity; and migration strengthens the spiritual dimension, leading to an increase in religious practice in the immigrants host country. This perspective is enhanced by the objective and external identity, generated by the perceptions and attitudes of the others to Romanian immigrants in Belgium.

As a results of this study, Romanian immigrants in Belgium make efforts to preserve their identity by participating to religious services as well as by keeping and cultivating Romanian traditions and customs; also, they preserve their maternal language in the family, in the relation with connational people, even in the case when they work together, perform different activities in the Romanian communities.

One the one hand, the Romanian immigrants have to face a constant struggle for the process of integration, but, on the other hand, they want to preserve their cultural, linguistic and religious identity.

The preservation of the national identity is intensified in the communities of Romanian immigrants from abroad: language, culture, and history are defining elements of national identity that define an individual. What are the changes that have taken place in the cultural horizon of Romanians in Belgium? What is the socio-linguistic impact they have experienced in the acculturation process? What role does religion play in preserving ethnic identity? How is Romanians identity modeled when confronted with the tow different/contradictory cultural forces? How do all these factors influence the construction of Romanian immigrants new identity(s)?

References

Easthope, H. (2009) 'Fixed Identities in a Mobile World? The Relationship Between Mobility, Place and Identity', *Identities* (16)1: 61-82.

La Barbera, Maria Caterina (ed.), *Identity and Migration in Europe: Multidiciplinary Perspective*, International Perspectives on Migration 13, Springer International Publishing Switzerland, 2015.

Paasi, A. (2001) 'Europe as a Social Process and Discourse: Considerations of Place, Boundaries and Identity', *European Urban and Regional Studies* 8(1): 7-28. www.myria.be

768   Brazilian women in Portugal, Colombian women in Spain. Illegality as a resistance strategy against the neoliberalization of life.

Andrea Souto Garcia and Nazaret Abalde Bastero

During three decades, the migrations of Colombian and Brazilian single women to Spain and Portugal, have attested to the impossibility of living in Latin America under the Neoliberal regime. From an intersectional approach located in coloniality, we analyse the complex character of both fluxes where, the colonial history, which links the territories of origin and destination, and neoliberalism, come together as main conditioners of the entry of southern women to globalized labour circuits.

Departing from a multi-situated fieldwork carried out between the urban peripheries of São Paulo, Porto and Madrid, consisting of 40 in-depth interviews conducted with Brazilian and Colombian women; this work furthers the concept of 'autonomy of migrations' and `border´ (Cordero, Mezzadra and Varela, 2019). We track the causality that makes Colombian and Brazilian migrant women travel alone. Through the hybrid narratives that they deploy to make sense of their migratory and vital trajectories, we discover these women as transnational emerging figures captive between macro structural powers and an unwavering will. We understand the feminized migrations as a response to the transformation of temporal and spatial parameters derived from the neoliberalisation of life in Latin America. In doing so, we reveal women´s trajectories in the transnational social space as a main location for economic and political violence to be exerted, but also as a place where a culture of insubordination may grow. In this sense, the lonely migrations of Colombian and Brazilian women can be read as a strategy of political and daily resistance against the expansion of capital and borders, in which *illegality* become not only a survival device but also an ethic claim.

615   The 217 Brazilian Migration Law: innovations, gaps and political turmoil

Tatiana Waisberg

The new Brazilian migration law was sanctioned in the middle of political turmoil in a time when Brasilia was stormed by violent protests. On May 24th, 2016, President Temer, the former-vice-president of President Rousseff impeached few months before, authorized the army forces to restore the order, and signed a humanitarian legislation on migration law. The new migration law replaced the Brazilian Foreign Statute from 1980, moving from the backward national security concerns to a human rights-oriented legislation, abolishing the very concept of "foreign nationals". To protect the most vulnerable migrants, different legal responses were designed to special situations, such as human trafficking victims, statelessness and humanitarian visas, including environmental induced-migration. The most vulnerable are the most benefited by the new law, entitled to more state protection, including the possibility to choose the Brazilian nationality. Despite the fact that these pro-human rights narratives may be associated with the Workers' Party ideology, the migration thematic transcended political polarizations, even more acerbated at the Bolsonaro government. What explain this bipartisan convergence to advance a humanitarian migration agenda contrasting with other human rights agendas clearly impaired by a backlash, such as the environment, gender rights and LBTQ+, among others?

This proposal aims to present relevant aspects of the Brazilian legislative development on migration, presenting the legal norms and procedures applied to grant rights to different category of migrants. Further, it will inquire which reasons underpinned a pioneering advocacy to promote awareness to the adoption of a new migration law. The legacy of the Brazilian diplomatic activism, especially the human side-effects of the Haiti peacekeeping force resulted in *ad hoc* humanitarian visas to Haitians, unfolding the context associated to these avant-garde migratory policies. Moreover, the recent massive flow of Venezuelan migrants to South America, including Brazil, reveals the intersection between the 2017 Brazilian Migration Law and the 1997 Refugee Statute. Against this background, this proposal seeks to address gaps in the new Brazilian Migration Law, contextualizing with the phenomenon of the

Haitian and the Venezuela migration to Brazil. The role of the church, as first responders to the state inaction, suggests that these non-state actors, together with NGO's, are key stakeholders to understand why this exceptional legislation endured, so far, surviving ongoing turbulence in Brazilian politics.

848   How the global pandemic influenced asylum applications and the principle of free movement in the European Union? The EU an agent of collective securitization in becoming?!

Edina Lilla Meszaros

The year 2015 witnessed an unprecedented influx of third country nationals to the EU, creating deep dividing lines between the member states. This division culminated in fragmented rhetoric and antagonistic policies elaborated at Community and national level. While some member states (Germany, Austria, Portugal, Netherlands, France etc.) were willing to take in and integrate refugees, others were reluctant to share the burden, adopting a zero immigration policy (Hungary, Poland, Slovakia, Czech Republic etc.). The current coronavirus outbreak not only represents a challenge to the entire European and international order as we know it, but it also puts more obstacles in front of refugees' access to the EU and successful integration. We notice that even countries like Germany, which are considered as vivid defenders of the rights of refugees, are currently halting asylum interviews due to the pandemic, while the Hungarian leadership is using it as an excuse to suspend asylum rights and to close the transit zones. Consequently, in the present study we wish to shed light on the contrasting practices (declaring state of emergencies, halting *refugee* status hearings, quarantining rescue ships and migrant camps, sharpening of the political discourse adopted versus treating migrants as permanent residents) adopted in various Member States. Building on the insights of Webber and Sperling we argue that the process of securitization prompted by Covid-19 occurred in a collective setting, the European Community acting as an agent of collective securitization. However, the dilemma is whether the EU will act as an agent of collective securitization in relation to the migrants/refugees identifying them as potential threats to public health, or the securitization process will take place only at the level of Member States. Sperling and Webber argue that collective securitization is the result of a common perception of interstate threats, followed by an appropriate political response to that threat (Sperling, Webber, 2019). Furthermore, the assessment of the impact of the global pandemic on the Schengen regime and on the principle of free movement is also among the priorities set within the present research. We contend that the current health crisis has led to breaches of border control rules in the EU and undermined the Schengen acquis and thus the principle of free movement, calling for the implementation of immediate reforms in the Schengen Borders Code.

821 Challenges of the Immigration and Refugee Recognition Act Bill in Japan

Yukari Ando

The objective of this presentation is to examine legal protection of irregular migrations in Japan. The methodology is focused on the legal text of the Immigration and Refugee Recognition Act Bill and to analyse the state party obligation under the International Covenant on Civil and Political Rights.

The 204th session of the Parliament is currently in session, and Immigration and Refugee Recognition Act is proposed the reform. Two bills are at issue: the government bill approved by the Cabinet on 19th February 2021, and the opposition party bill submitted on 18th February 2021. The aim is said to be end long-term immigration detention of irregular migrants included refugee claimants. However, the government bill seems problematic from the point of international human rights law. It does not seem to be met international standard.

For instance, the government bill does not seem to resolve the prolonged detention, but criminalised those who denies the deportation order. The alternative protection does not meet "complementary protection" in international standard. The author strongly opposes to be called "complementary protection" as such.

Particularly, the problematic is the stipulation that limits the number of times a person can apply for refugee application. The Refugee Convention prohibits the repatriation of people who could be refugees, and under current Japanese law, people who are in the process of being assessed for refugee certification cannot be sent back to their countries of origin.

The refugee claimant under the refugee status determination process three or more times are subject to forced deportation unless the person has fresh evidence. The Immigration Services Agency of Japan explains that the system is being abused by people trying to avoid being sent back. However, many Turkish Kurds live in Saitama near Tokyo. None of them are recognised as refugee since 1982. Many Rohingyas live in Gunma near Tokyo, but most of them are not recognised as refugee. How the proposed bill can justify them as abusers and legally deport during the refugee status determination procedure?

Key References

-Adrienne Anderson, Michelle Foster, Helene Lambert, Jane McAdam 'Imminence in Refugee and Human Rights Law: A Misplaced Notion for International Protection', International Comparative Law Quarterly ,2019.

-Erika Feller et al.(eds) UNHCR "Refugee Protection in International Law: UNHCR's Global Consultations on International Protection" Cambridge University Press, 2003.

-安藤由香里「国際人権条約における入管収容とノン・ルフルマン原則」『法律時報』 1147号、2020年。

-平野雄吾『ルポ入管－絶望の外国人収容施設』ちくま新書、2020年。

-申惠丰「第1章「不法滞在の外国人」に人権はないのか」『国際人権入門-現場から考える』岩波新書、2020年。

652   Are transnational spouses more religious than movers and stayers? Spousal choice based on religiosity among Turkish migrants in Western Europe

Tolga Tezcan

This study investigates the extent to which the preference for a transnational spouse among Turkish migrants residing in Western Europe is related to the wish for a more religious spouse. The pertinent aims involved here are twofold. First, this study attempts to reveal if transnational spouses are more religious than movers and stayers. Second, it expands our knowledge on whether the religious spouse preference plays a stronger role for men than for women. Co-ethnic marriage is widespread among Turkish immigrants (Huschek, de Valk, and Liefbroer 2012) who generally marry a Turkish partner living in the host country (González-Ferrer 2006) or from Turkey by importing "spouses" (Timmerman 2006). Involving the potential "dangers" of being raised in the West, local co-ethnic community is often considered almost as unacceptable as outgroup. There is a bad reputation of young Turks among Turkish community; Turkish boys have gone astray and Turkish girls are too liberated (Timmerman, Lodewyckx, and Wets 2009). Therefore, a non-migrant spouse from Turkey may be more preferable, who are assumed to be "better behaved" and "more traditional" (Timmerman 2006). The transnational marriage has garnered substantial interest from social scientists; nevertheless, the effect of religiosity of the transnational spouses has not been studied quantitatively so far. Using a sample of families from five high-emigrant regions in Turkey derived from the survey "2,000 Families," this study conducted a series of multilevel multinominal logistic regression models. The results showed that transnational spouses are more religious than both movers and stayers. This effect remains strong even after controlling for parental religiosity. Furthermore, the models indicate that transnational brides are more religious than transnational grooms. This pattern suggests that, at least implicitly, the transnational marriage market is more open to brides who are more religious.

References

González-Ferrer, Amparo. 2006. "Who Do Immigrants Marry? Partner Choice among Single Immigrants in Germany." *European Sociological Review* 22(2): 171–85.

Huschek, Doreen, Helga A. G. de Valk, and Aart C. Liefbroer. 2012. "Partner Choice Patterns Among the Descendants of Turkish Immigrants in Europe." *European Journal of Population / Revue européenne de Démographie* 28(3): 241–68.

Timmerman, Christiane. 2006. "Gender Dynamics in the Context of Turkish Marriage Migration: The Case of Belgium." *Turkish Studies* 7(1): 125–43. http://www.tandfonline.com/doi/abs/10.1080/14683840500520642.

Timmerman, Christiane, Ina Lodewyckx, and Johan Wets. 2009. "Marriage at the Intersection between Tradition and Globalization. Turkish Marriage Migration between Emirdag and Belgium from 1989 to Present." *History of the Family* 14(2): 232–44.

725   Alevism as a Political-Theological Concept and Its Representation in Austria

Deniz Cosan Eke

Alevism is a faith that was shaped as a unique religious and cultural identity in the Anatolian geography but has spread to many countries through transnational migration processes. Alevis migrated to Europe as a part of the wave of immigration that had taken place in the 1960s from Turkey to Western Europe and were not seen as a separate group from the general Turkish immigrant group there for a long time. However, in recent years, Alevism, which has been used as a political and theological concept and Alevi movement, defined as a diaspora movement, have started to take place frequently in the agenda of European countries. This is because Alevism has been discussed as an exemplary phenomenon for the possibilities of religious and political pluralism and the integration of religious groups in Western Europe.

Religious groups differ in their rituals and their group dynamics due to political, legal, social, and cultural differences in each country where they are located. In the struggle for Alevi identity and its recognition, Alevism in Austria is one of the best examples to analyze the different definitions of Alevism that we often encounter in the literature at the organizational level. In the current study, the main research question is to investigate how Alevism is experienced and represented in Austria. The data collection is done through the news about Alevis and Alevism in the Austrian media channels and through the semi-structure questionnaire sent to the Alevi associations in different ways: by phone, by mail, and by computer-mediated communication (CMC) such as email, social media, etc.

This study aims to point out the importance of the representation of religion, which plays a central role in the transmission of religious knowledge and traditions from generation to generation. The Alevi associations were initially founded as a political organization and then had not only politics but also religious tradition in mind and then played an active role in the struggle for the recognition of Alevism. This study will use the example of Austria to answer the question of how Alevism came into use as a political and theological concept. In the light of this background, hopefully, this study will contribute to the debates between theology and politics that have been gaining attention in recent decades.

701 Religious consciousness in the context of the migration situation: case of Russia

Irina Alexandrovna Savchenko

The largest share of the immigrant community in the regions of central Russia is formed by immigrants from post-Soviet states where Islam is a traditional religion. The shared Soviet past facilitates the mutual integration of immigrants and members of the host community (Taran et al 2016). However, there are significant contradictions in the religious consciousness of migrants and one of the citizens of the host community. The author conducted a number of survey studies and found some trends that are typical not only for Russia, but also for many immigrant countries (Collins-Mayo 2012), (Horwath et al 2008), in the history of which Christianity played a leading role in previous eras.

Among Russian respondents aged 18 to 35 ($n = 947$) only 9% have a positive attitude to religious people (Orthodox), no more than 18% have a positive attitude to Christianity, and only 11% have a positive attitude to the Russian Orthodox Church. Finally, only 6% have a positive attitude to Islam. This is an unpleasant index when considering the religious affiliation of the majority of migrants. Russian respondents emphasize that one of the factors of their tolerance towards Muslim migrants is the lack of "obvious religiosity" among the latter.

Meanwhile, 100% of the respondents from Tajikistan stated a positive attitude to Islam; 92% of Uzbeks, 82% of Kyrgyz and 93% of Azerbaijanis gave a similar answer. However, this is not surprising. Among the people from the traditionally Islamic post-Soviet republics (173 people in total), 68% have a positive attitude to Christianity, 65% have a positive attitude to the Russian Orthodox Church, and 75% have a positive attitude to Orthodox religious people. We had to observe a situation when Georgy, the Metropolitan of Nizhny Novgorod and Arzamas spoke to students. The Metropolitan's speech was received with greater interest and comprehension by students from Muslim regions of Russia (Ingushetia, Dagestan and Karachay-Cherkessia) than by ethnic Russian students.

When a migrant from a Muslim country or region comes to central Russia, he sees an unusual picture. He sees a rather cool attitude of the host community towards their elderly people, their own culture and their own religion. When it comes to adaptation, the migrant faces a natural question: what exactly should he adapt to? What is acculturation, in addition to language acquisition? The immigrant gets the impression that the host society can not transfer anything to him, except for the workplace. It is no coincidence that many immigrants have told us that they feel an inner "spiritual" superiority over the locals, who "do not believe in anything", who "have forgotten who they are" and "where they come from".

Nevertheless, even among Muslim migrants, spiritual transformations are beginning. A certain part of them tries to match the way of life of local residents and is quickly marginalized.

References

Collins-Mayo, S 2012 'Youth and religion. An international perspective', *Theo-Web. Zeitschrädaift für Religionspgogik, no. 11, h.1*, pp. 80-94.

Horwath, J, Lees J, Sidebotham, P, Higgins, J & Imtiaz, A 2008 'Religion, beliefs and parenting practices. A descriptive study', *Sheffield: University of Sheffield*, 66 p.

Taran, PA., Neves de Lima, G, Kadysheva, O & Vardinoyannis, MV 2016 'Cities welcoming refugees and migrants: enhancing effective urban governance in an age of migration', *UNESCO. Director-General, 2009-2017 (Bokova, I.G.).* 87 p.

868   Construction of Collective Religious Memory in Migration Societies A Case Study from Austria

Evrim Ersan Akkilic

Recently, memory studies are gaining great popularity. However, the memories of migrants as a research subject is relatively new for memory studies, which has become an interdisciplinary field. The initial studies on collective memory mainly focus on national constructions of collective memory and its effects on the construction of cultural and national identities, which build a homogeneous identity. This is the crucial reason for the delay in engaging migrant memories, as they had no reference and access to these identities. Not only migrant memories, but also migration itself did not find a place in the collective memory in so-called host societies. Although collective memory is institutionalized in the host society and preserved in memory institutions such as museums and archives, regarding to Islam and the history of migration itself, such a development is either non-existent or its access to these institutions is a marginal phenomenon in Austria.

The central question of how the collective religious memory of Muslim youth develops in a migration society is analysed in this paper based on a group discussion conducted with two young Muslim women. In this study, group discussion is applied as the method for data collection and is evaluated with the documentary method. Group discussions allow access to the collective orientations and the framework of orientations by providing appropriate data for analysing "conjunctive spaces of experience" (in German "konjunktiver Erfahrungsraum"). The generation of descriptions or narrations of everyday life practices in group discussions enables a reconstruction of collective experience, that is, centres of collective memory and conjunctive spaces of experience of the group.

The aim of this study is to reveal the intersectional ongoing construction process of collective religious memory in the nexus of migration and to reveal the strategies of young Muslim migrants. Migration is among other social and political identities like gender, milieu or class one of the most significant aspects which has an impact on the construction of collective religious memory of Muslim youth in a migration society. The preliminary analysis of the data illustrates that young people's lives are formed in the intersection of hegemonic practices of majority, transnational affiliations, and on their own life experiences and expectations which in turn is felt in the construction of memory.

892 Transnational Muslim Humanitarianism: Syrian and other Arab Diaspora in Turkey

Yasemin Ipek

Ten years after the beginning of the civil war in Syria, there are currently more than 12 million displaced Syrians. Syrians are often portrayed in both policy-oriented and academic discourses as victims in need of help, especially from the "humanitarian" West. Rarely are they recognized as humanitarian actors even though thousands of Syrians have made concerted efforts to support other Syrians living in conditions even more dire than their own. Syrian diaspora set up hundreds of humanitarian NGOs in Turkey which brought together many Syrian and non-Syrian Arab diaspora from different parts of the MENA region such as Syria, Lebanon, Jordan, Kuwait, and Egypt, as well as from different parts of Europe and North America. My ethnographic research (2018-2021) focuses on several Syrian-led organizations in Istanbul, Ankara, and Gaziantep—three cities in Turkey that were central to Syrian refugee governance. In addition to in-depth interviews with managers, volunteers, and employees of these organizations, I draw on participant observation and discourse analysis of the published materials of the organizations.

This paper specifically asks what types of humanitarian discourses emerged in the context of the Arab diaspora's increased involvement in global refugee management as humanitarian actors. Turkey has recently become a flourishing center of humanitarian aid work in the MENA region. Arab diaspora based in Turkey and work in support of displaced Syrians through institutional means have a strong presence in both shaping the humanitarian field and policy-making towards Syrians. My discussion will explore this presence by attending to how Arab humanitarian actors blend global, nationalist, and Islamic discourses to articulate a different vision of humanitarianism. The findings and analyses will demonstrate that Arab diaspora's participation in Syrian-led organizations led to a growth of transnational Muslim humanitarianism. Syrian and other Arab actors were engaged in a complex negotiation of Western donors and international humanitarian norms on the one hand, and the Turkish state's growing authoritarian policies and nationalism on the other.

The findings and analyses of the paper will contribute to recently growing literature on Muslim humanitarianism. Scholarship on humanitarianism has mainly focused on secular organizations, discourses, and practices. Efforts by religious and in particular Muslim institutions have typically been studied as local initiatives of charity, efforts that are not "properly humanitarian," that is, "impartial." My findings will not assess whether Islam is compatible with universal humanitarian principles, which has been done previously. Instead, I will analyze the circulation and vernacularization of diverse humanitarian norms and practices among Arab humanitarian aid workers. My theoretical approach combines the anthropology of Islam, secularism, and nationalism with interdisciplinary studies on global inequality and transnational humanitarianism. Diverse groups of Arab actors have built complex transnational care networks that articulated a tapestry of secular, religious, and nationalist discourses. In examining these discourses, this paper will generate a conversation on how the Syrian war reconfigured global Muslim alliances and the existing discourses and practices of the humanitarian field more broadly.

8G   Analysing refuge and asylum process during the COVID age

Chair: Mª Jesús Cabezón Fernández, University of Almeria, Spain

1029 ""No time to lose": the quality standards of refugee reception conditions in European Union before and during the COVID age"
Encarnación La Spina

914 Challenges and work experiences in the Spanish assistance program for refugees during COVID-19 in a context of regulatory changes
Alexandra Rios-Marin, Beatriz Gonzalez-Martin, Clara Lopez Mora, Pablo Pumares

905 Interpreting with refugees in COVID times: increasing the vulnerability of beneficiaries and professionals
Daniela Herrera Rubalcaba, Maria Jesus Cabezon Fernandez, Pablo Pumares Fernandez, Ruben Rodriguez Puertas

1043 "Refugees in specific Mediterranean cases: what can we learn from grassroots fieldwork before and after the pandemic?"
Natalia Ribas-Mateos

1029   ""No time to lose": the quality standards of refugee reception conditions in European Union before and during the COVID age"

Encarnación La Spina, Alberto García Martín, Elena Martínez Goytre, Pierina Cáceres Arévalo

The article will focus on the data analysis from the action-research project FAMILIA. Due to the introduction of emergency and lockdown measures in response to COVID-19, in the first semester of 2020, there was an exceptional decrease in migration flows and asylum applications towards Europe. The intermittent evolution of pandemic crisis means new challenges for the EU migration and asylum management and the New Pact on Immigration and Asylum 2020 has just proposed an open-ended reform of the CEAS (Common European Asylum System). However, this set of common rules prioritises a new border procedure or an effective return system while the refugee reception conditions are an untouchable and discretional competence of Member States

(La Spina, 2020; Caponio et al. 2019; Glorious et al 2018). Consequently, the New Pact 2020 only urges a rapid adoption of an unfinished refugee reception regime despite its difficult legislative harmonisation.

Before the COVID age, a great part of the critical review of the Reception Directive 2013/33 and the 2016 reform proposal (Velutti, 2016; EASO 2020b) evidenced the inefficiency of asylum regime and the complex asymmetries of the national rules (Tsourdi 2015; EASO 2020b, FRA 2020, ERC 2020). Since the onset of the pandemic crisis, the European Union has intensified the adaptation of generic guidance's and special health measures but at national level, the practical implementation of reception living standards remains an unresolved limbo (García-Juan 2020; Tsourdi 2020: 375; Garcés-Mascareñas, Pasetti, 2019). Particularly, most of the new national measures proposed have focused largely on addressing the exceptional nature of the pandemic as if it were merely temporary but the pre-existing problems have collateral and structural effects more visible than ever. For instance, as noted European agencies, the higher incidence of occupation in the arrival of first reception centres, the overcrowded refugee centres, the deplorable situation of refugee camps in the Southern European territories or the obstacles for extraordinary or isolated living conditions in collective centres (UNCHR 2020, EASO 2020a, ECRE 2020).

Following the methodological SWOT technique and a critical- comparative perspective, the main aim of this paper is analysing how the pandemic has influenced the quality standards of refugee living conditions and if this new pandemic scenario will promote a structural change in refugee reception system. To this purpose, the first section pays attention at the weaknesses of the current Reception Directive and its reforms before the pandemic crisis. And, the second section will then compare and measure the quality of the living conditions in refugee reception systems in EU arena during the COVID age, taking into account the Member states legal strategy according to human rights and the European integration paradigm.

References

Caponio, T.; Ponzo, I.; Giannetto, L. Comparative report on the multilevel governance of the national asylum seekers reception system Chemniz: Ceseaval, 2019. ECRE. Housing out of reach? The reception of refugees and asylum seekers in Europe. Bruxelles:

ECRE, 2019. EASO. Covid-19 emergency measures in Asylum and reception systems. Public Issue n.3, 7 December 2020a. EASO. Judicial analysis. Reception of applicants for international protection. Recption conditions Directive 2013/33/EU. EASO Professional Development series for members of courts and tribunals Bruxelles: EASO, 2020b.

FRA. Fundamental rights of refugees asylum applicants and migrants at European borders. Bruxelles: FRA publications, 2020.

Garcés-Mascareñas, B. y Pasetti, F. "¿A más solicitudes de asilo igual recepción? El sistema de acogida en España desde 2015", Anuario CIDOB de la Inmigración 2019 (noviembre de 2019), p. 114-126.

Garcia-Juan, L. "Integration measures within the reform of the Common European

Asylum system. The unsolved limbo of asylum seekers". Migration letters, 4 (5), 2020, p. 597-608.

Glorius, B., Desch, L., Nienaber, B., Doomernik, J. "Refugee reception within a common European asylum system: looking at convergences and divergences through a local-to-local comparison". ERSJUNDE 73 (1), 2018, p. 19-29.

La Spina, E. La vulnerabilidad de las personas refugiadas ante el reto de la integración, Cizur: Aranzadi-Thomson Reuters, 2020.

Tsourdi, E. "Reception conditions for asylum seekers in the EU: towards the prevalence of human dignity". Journal of Immigration, Asylum and Nationality Law, 29 (1), 2015, p. 9-24.

Tsourdi, E. "Asylum in the EU and the Great expectations of Solidarity". International Journal of Refugee Law vol. 32 (2), p. 374-380.

UNCHR. Practical Recommendations and Good Practice to Address Protection Concerns in the Context of the COVID-19 Pandemic. UNHCR/Regional Bureau for Europe, 2020.

Velutti, S. "The revised reception conditions Directive and adequate and dignified material reception conditions for those seeking international protection. International Journal of Migration and Border Studies, vol. 2, nº 3, 2016, p-1-20.

914   Challenges and work experiences in the Spanish assistance program for refugees during COVID-19 in a context of regulatory changes

Alexandra Rios-Marin, Beatriz Gonzalez-Martin, Clara Lopez Mora, Pablo Pumares

Spain has abruptly changed from being a country with few asylum-seekers to be one of the top receiving countries in Europa during 2019, to this has been added the challenge posed by the expansion of COVID-19 and the limitations it has entailed. This has forced an accelerated adaptation to respond to a surge in demand that is far beyond the capacities of the system. This system has a minimal infrastructure that is mainly supported by specialised NGOs, which develop the Reception Programmes for asylum-seekers under the guidelines of the Spanish Ministry of Inclusion, Social Security and Migration. This Ministry has introduced many modifications in the procedures that govern the Reception Programme over the last few years. These alterations have forced NGOs to continually update the dynamics of intervention in the comprehensive care of the beneficiaries and to generate great uncertainty among workers and users. This situation has been compounded by the need to face the new challenges posed by the pandemic situation.

Specifically, this paper analyses the challenges encountered by reception programme professionals during COVID-19 and the problems they have had to face as a result of the State of Alarm decreed in March 2020 throughout the Spanish territory. Following a qualitative methodology, 19 in-depth interviews were conducted with key informants from the intervention teams of Cepaim Foundation and Red Cross in the province of Almeria.

The results obtained describe how before COVID-19 there was already a collapse in the first line of attention and referral of applicants due to the high level of bureaucracy and the delay in the processing of files with the relevant authorities, which during the confinement worsened, further prolonging the waiting times for a place in the programme. Besides, the mandatory use of teleworking in entities not prepared for this digital reality has increased the levels of stress and anxiety of the intervention teams as they are unable to communicate directly with the programme's users, communication which is already difficult due to language and cultural barriers.

Nowadays, there are new problems to which workers must respond among the most worrying of them are the 'express asylum refusals' that are emptying the reception centres, without the majority of seekers being able to complete their care itineraries and autonomy processes or even getting into the system. These massive refusals may be due to the detection of false refugees or it may be a strategy to stem the flow and drastically ease the burden on reception centres; nevertheless, intervention teams report feeling overwhelmed by having to manage so much uncertainty not only for themselves as individuals and professionals but also by the need to respond to and protect the rights of the individuals and families under the programme's responsibility.

905   Interpreting with refugees in COVID times: increasing the vulnerability of beneficiaries and professionals

Daniela Herrera Rubalcaba, Maria Jesus Cabezon Fernandez, Pablo Pumares Fernandez, Ruben Rodriguez Puertas

In the last decade, the international protection and asylum system in Spain has evolved within a context of precariousness, which has determined the resources allocated to the services associated with the asylum program. Such precariousness together with the "rigidity of the integration itineraries" (Garcés y Pasetti, 2019) increases the vulnerability of asylum seekers. Humanitarian interpretation is a key service on the refusal or acceptance of the asylum application due to the relevance of the interviews conducted during the asylum procedure. As a result, it could influence to some extent the well-being and the vulnerability of the asylum seekers (León-Padilla et al., 2016). The traditional weakness of the Spanish asylum system faces today new challenges due to the increase of the asylum applications received in 2019 and the pandemic context that emerged from the Covid-19 in 2020.

In this paper, from 25 in-depth interviews conducted with experts and humanitarian interpreters, we analyse to which extent the pandemic has influenced the situation of the interpreters and the asylum seekers, and which strategies have been implemented to guarantee asylum seekers' rights. First, the most common challenges on the humanitarian interpretation with refugees are the increase of the de-professionalisation on volunteers with no specific knowledge acquired on ethic codes, interpretation techniques, or sociocultural aspects regarding asylum seekers. The cause is the increase in the interpretation demand and the inadequacy of funding for this service. A usual strategy is to hire external companies to carry out interpretation and translation tasks that are not particularly trained to work in a humanitarian context and, in extent, to understand the beneficiaries' needs. As a result, a lack of congruence takes place between beneficiaries' narratives and interpreter reports.

Nevertheless, due to the pandemic context, these difficulties have been constrained. The narratives highlight that the face-to-face interpretation loses effectivity due to the requirement to wear the masks that make more difficult the interpretation of non-verbal language. One of the biggest obstacles was found in telephone interpreting because of the barriers in generating bonds and trust between interpreters and users. In this line, COVID-19 lockdown increased digital divide which is causing many difficulties in the interpretation and the access to the resources in general. Furthermore, the pandemic context has constrained other services associated to the assistance of the asylum seekers, for instance, Spanish courses were cancelled, delays on the the psychological and health assistance or the increase of domestic conflicts within the families sharing same housing spaces. These challenges compromise the accomplishment of the rights of asylum seekers.

References

Garcés-Mascareñas, Blanca y Pasetti, Francesco. ¿A más solicitudes de asilo igual recepción? El sistema de acogida en España desde 2015. *Anuario CIDOB de la Inmigración 2019* (noviembre de 2019), p. 114-126.

León-Padilla, J., Jordá-Mathiasen, E., & Prado-Gascó, V. (2016). La interpretación en el contexto de los refugiados: valoración por los agentes implicados. *Sendebar*, 27, 25-49.

1043   "Refugees in specific Mediterranean cases: what can we learn from grassroots fieldwork before and after the pandemic?"

Natalia Ribas-Mateos

What does "desertification" in the Mediterranean mean today? Why cases like the "Central Bekaa" in Lebanon or the Libya coast are paradigmatic cases to think about refugees and continuous displacement in the Mediterranean? How the construction of human vulnerability questions today the revival of the debate of the right to have rights and its humanitarian action? And, furthermore, How the responses to these questions must also face the consequences of the pandemic due to the COVID-19?

The arguments shown inside this paper transcend the limits on recent discussions on the proliferation of humanitarian spaces, suggesting instead that a focus on a specific setting makes easier the understanding of humanitarian responses to human vulnerability of refugees. The image of the desert as tyranny in Arendt's conception (1978, 1996) becomes the centre of the politics of the desertification for refugees. The information that is available to all says that the dispossession and forced migration of nearly 50 percent of Syria's population has produced the greatest refugee crisis since World War II. But can we see beyond this kind of headlines? In the heart of Bilad al-Sham, the Central Bekaa Valley located between the Lebanon Mountains and the Anti-Lebanon Mountains – paralleling the Mediterranean coast– represents a paradigmatic border region where the conditions of vulnerability and impositions of security in a border area can be analysed.

The starting point to end desertification is to ensure that Syrians fleeing conflict and persecution are properly recognized in Lebanon as refugees, that they can legally work and their children can go to school. Most reports work on this conception of vulnerability in mobilities: restrained mobilities in all senses (see, for example, the case of Rayak in 2017), from right holders to 'compassionate' people, by reviewing the impact of humanitarianism (see, for example, 'the humanitarian reason' in Shatila, Beirut, reviewed critically in Marron, 2016 or the case of sub-Saharan migrants-refugees in Libya in Ribas-Mateos 2021). Can this compassion also leave room for agency (see, for example, the case of Syrian refugees earning an income in new ways), which then also becomes problematic in such a desert area at a border site. However, there is also another side to the coin in this concept of the desert as a condition of human life.

However, this case is not unique. These examples presented here provides many clues about numerous processes which are also taking place in different ways around the world and can all be part of this desertification of the Mediterranean and the world and provide an overview of how we understand social vulnerability today according to generation and gender and particularly, with the social inequalities and constraints that the pandemic context is provoking in this desertic regions.

References

Arendt, H., & Feldman, R. H. (1978). The Pariah as Rebel: We Refugees. *The Jew as Pariah: Jewish Identity and Politics in the Modern Age.* New York: Grove Press: distributed by Random House, 55-67.

Arendt. H., (1996), *Entre el pasado y el futuro. Ocho ejercicios sobre reflexión política.*

Barcelona: Ediciones Península.

Marron, R. (2016). *Humanitarian Rackets and Their Moral Hazards: The Case of the*

Palestinian Refugee Camps in Lebanon. Routledge.

Ribas-Mateos, N. (2021). Transnational humanitarianism: blurring the boundaries of the Mediterranean in Libya. In *Handbook on Human Security, Borders and Migration.* Edward Elgar Publishing.

8H   COVID-19 Impact

Chair: Yaprak Civelek, Anadolu University, Turkey
583   Migration Physiology
      Tamoghni Manna
683   Migrants and Digestive Pathologies in a Pandemic Context: A comparison between the French and the Swedish healthcare systems and migration policies
      Fanny Christou and Niki Christou
738   Ethnic diversity in perinatal in Spain: the influence of family support
      Chiara Dello Iacono, Jesús García-Gomez, Mikolaj Stanek

1001 Understanding the Enablers and Barriers in Health Service Access
among COVID-19-Infected Refugees in Turkey
Turkish Red Crescent

583   Migration Physiology

Tamoghni Manna

Migration is   distinct from other movements. The endurance capacity of long-distance migrants has fascinated biologists for years, but recent work probing the physiological mechanisms that underlie their athletic performance has further strengthened this curiosity. Distinct mechanisms explaining their capacity for endurance exercise have now been uncovered, particularly with respect to energy storage, mobilization, transport and utilization. Using satellite technology, scientists have characterized the migration patterns of aquatic species such as the white shark using satellite technology.   (Carcharodon carcharias, L.) Specialized neuro-sensory systems involved in orientation and navigation also play important roles in energy economy of migration. (Alerstam, 2006; Lohmann et al., 2008).

Long migrations energetics

The longest migrations of land mammals barely reach a few thousand kilometers and can only be performed by large species such as wildebeest (Carcharodon carcharias, L.) .Soaring, rather than flapping flight, can significantly decrease the energy gap between flying and swimming, but this strategy is restricted to large birds   .

Mechanism of metabolism during migration

The metabolic rate that birds mostly maintain during migration is 10 to 15 times higher than in the resting state, or about twice the maximal oxygen consumption (mass-specific VO_2,max) of similarly sized mammals (Butler and Woakes, 1990). Maximum energy is provided to their working muscles from extra-muscular adipose reserves, and it is estimated that migrant birds can mobilize, transport and oxidize lipids at more than 10 times the maximal rates ever recorded in mammals (McWilliams et al., 2004).

The cost of Transport

The locomotory muscles of some species generate force with unusually high efficiency. (Klaassen et al., 2000; Kvist et al., 2001). This observation stems from the lower parts of body than expected whole-organism metabolic rate during flight, and the exact nature of this hypothetical muscle adaptation has never been characterized. To save energy, migrant birds also rely on morphological features such as pointed wings and low wing loading (Bowlin and Wikelski, 2008).

Mobilization of Lipid

At rest and under normothermic conditions, the ruff a wading bird, reveals its unique capacity to mobilize lipids by maintaining a higher lipolytic rate than any other animal measured to date.   In vivo measurements of lipid kinetics in migratory birds demonstrate that, in the resting state, they hydrolyse triacylglycerol at the remarkable rate of 55–60μmoles of glycerol Ikg–1min–1 (Vaillancourt and Weber, 2007).

Transportation of Lipid

The mammalian strategy of providing lipids to muscles as albumin-bound nonesterified fatty acids does not suit the needs of long-distance migrants.

Conclusions

The ability to rapidly process lipids emerges as a crucial component of the migrant phenotype, but remarkably few reports are available on fuel metabolism in these athletes. High lipid fluxes are made possible by lipoprotein shuttles, by high concentrations of FABP that accelerate lipid transport and by boosting the metabolic machinery for lipolysis in adipocytes and lipid oxidation in muscle mitochondria.

References

Corcoran, M. P., Lamon-Fava, S. and Fielding, R. A. (2007). Skeletal muscle lipid deposition and insulin resistance: effect of dietary fatty acids and exercise. Am. J. Clin. Nutr. 85, 662-677.

Alerstam, T. (2006). Conflicting evidence about long-distance animal navigation. Science 313, 791-794.

Butler, P. J. and Woakes, A. J. (1990). The physiology of bird flight. In Bird Migration (ed. E. Gwinner), pp. 300-318. Berlin: Springer-Verlag.

McWilliams, S. R. and Karasov, W. H. (2004). Migration takes guts: digestive physiology of migratory birds and its ecological significance. In Birds of Two Worlds (ed. P. Marra and R. Greenberg). Baltimore, MD: Johns Hopkins University Press.

Klaassen, M., kVist, A. and Lindström, Å. (2000). Flight costs and fuel composition of a bird migrating in a wind tunnel. Condor 102, 444-451.

Bowlin, M. S. and Wikelski, M. (2008). Pointed wings, low wingloading and calm air reduce migratory flight costs in songbirds. Plos One 3, e2154 1-8.

Vaillancourt, E., Prud'Homme, S., Haman, F., Guglielmo, C. G. and Weber, J.-M. (2005). Energetics of a long-distance migrant shorebird (Philomachus pugnax) during cold exposure and running. J. Exp. Biol. 208, 317-325.

683   Migrants and Digestive Pathologies in a Pandemic Context: A comparison between the French and the Swedish healthcare systems and migration policies

Fanny Christou and Niki Christou

This proposal stems from a current research project that has been submitted to get additional funding in order to strengthen multidisciplinary research when it comes to the articulation between migrants and health issues. Indeed, based on the comparison of two European regions in France and Sweden, this proposal aims to highlight the need for preventive measures linked to the covid-19 pandemic for vulnerable migrant populations, as well as to question the various inequalities in accessing health.

While the three symptoms of Covid-19 are currently well documented by the state of the art (fever, cough, respiratory distress), several studies report that half of patients who have been tested positive for the coronavirus also evoke digestive symptoms. On the other hand, since migrant populations are often already subject to chronic gastrointestinal illnesses, these digestive disorders seem to worsen with the Covid-19, thus reflecting the urgent need to scholarly question the articulation between the precarious situation of migrants and pathologies such as chronic diseases linked to the digestive system.

In addition, while France has adopted lockdown measures since the beginning of the pandemic, Sweden has favored a culture of trust, relying on the individual responsibility to deal with the Covid-19. With two opposite perspectives in managing the pandemic crisis, these two countries face a common issue highlighting extensive inequalities in accessing health and an excess mortality rate concentrated in the most economic precarious areas, where migrant populations often settle.

In this respect, based on an extensive literature review on the topic and preliminary data, this proposal aims to open for discussion and share knowledge. This presentation will introduce our research project that seek to implement health promotion measures towards migrant populations, preventing the development of new pathologies in the current pandemic context. To carry out this project, a multidisciplinary team already made up of health professionals and social science researchers is conducting a qualitative fieldwork and collecting quantitative data (based on the analysis of migratory and health backgrounds, spatial and social fragmentations) in two regions in France and in Sweden in order to compare the management of the Covid-19 crisis and access to healthcare in the wake of migratory journeys and chronic diseases linked to the digestive system. This presentation during the TMC Conference 2021 will thus give us the opportunity to introduce some of the preliminary results but also to discuss challenges with the audience and develop partnerships.

References

Dubost, C-L., Pollak, C. et Rey, S. (2020) Les inégalités sociales face à l'épidémie de Covid-19 - État des lieux et perspectives, *Les Dossiers de la DREES*, n°62, DREES

Brun, S., Simon, P., et al. (2020) Inégalités ethno-raciales et coronavirus, *Revue De Facto*, Institut Convergences Migrations

Rothschild, N. (2020) The Hidden Flaw in Sweden's Anti-Lockdown Strategy, *Foreign Policy*

Ungaro, RC., Sullivan, T., Colombel, JF. et al. (2020) What Should Gastroenterologists and Patients Know About COVID-19? *Clin Gastroenterol Hepatol*

Gu J., Han B., Wang J., (2020) COVID-19: Gastrointestinal Manifestations and Potential Fecal-Oral Transmission, *Gastroenterology*

Rampal, P., Piche, T., Collins, M. S. Rôle des infections digestives et de l'inflammation dans les troubles fonctionnels intestinaux, *Gastroentérologie clinique et biologique*, vol 26, n° 6-7, pp. 624-629

Greve, B. (2016) Migrants and health in the Nordic welfare states, *Public Health Reviews*

738 Ethnic diversity in perinatal in Spain: the influence of family support

Chiara Dello Iacono, Jesús García-Gomez, Mikolaj Stanek

In the last two decades, Spain has become a receiving country for immigrants from Latin America, Africa, Asia and high- and non-high income European countries and its immigrant population has grown from 1.6% in 1998 to 14.3% in 2019. International immigration mark is increasingly evident in the country's demographic and family dynamics, through the growing relative weight of immigrant households (González Ferrer 2006; González Ferrer 2011). It has been also observed that Immigrant in Spain have relatively complex household structures, (Requena 2011; Van Hook and Glick 2007). The size of immigrant households increases due to the phenomenon of family regrouping and the formation of new family units.

Massive inflows of woman in reproductive ages provide an excellent opportunity to analyse the reproductive and perinatal health outcomes of migrant subpopulations. Despite the increasing contribution of immigrant women to the total number of births and the higher fertility than Spanish couple (Requena and Sánchez-Domínguez 2011), there have not been many studies focused on the specific effect of family support on birth outcomes of immigrant's women.

The aim of our study is first to compare the birthweight outcomes among immigrant women of diverse origin. Second, to assess the role that family support plays in the association between the ethnic origin of the women and their reproductive outcomes.

This research takes advantage of the opportunity to use a new database linking the Natural Population Movement records from 2011 to 2015 with the 2011 Spanish Census, provided by the Spanish National Institute of Statistics. Categorising the family types recorded by the 2011 Spanish Census, we focused on native and immigrant women who have given birth and live alone with their children and those who live with their partner and children with or without family support.

We have used a logistic regression model to estimate the effect of family support on low-birth-weight outcomes and their differences between natives and immigrants' women.

References

González-Ferrer, A. (2006). Family and labor strategies in migration: Family reunification, marital choices and labor participation of immigrants in the host country. (Tesis doctoral), Universidad Autonoma de Madrid, Madrid.

González-Ferrer, A. (2011). Explaining the labour performance of immigrant women in Spain: The interplay between family, migration and legal trajectories. International Journal of Comparative Sociology, 52(1– 2), 63–78.

Reher, D. y M. Requena. 2009b. "Introducción: el impacto de la inmigración en la sociedad española". Pp. 7-19 en D. Reher y M. Requena (eds.), Las múltiples caras de la inmigración en España. Madrid: Alianza Editorial.

Requena, M., & Sánchez-Domínguez, M. (2011). Las familias inmigrantes en España. *Revista Internacional de Sociología, 69*(M1), 79-104.

Van Hook, J., Glick, J.E. Immigration and living arrangements: Moving beyond economic need versus acculturation. *Demography* **44,** 225–249 (2007).

1001   Understanding the Enablers and Barriers in Health Service Access among COVID-19-Infected Refugees in Turkey

Turkish Red Crescent

Turkish Red Crescent, Community Based Migration Programmes, SPSS Programme, Turkey

COVID-19 pandemic has been resulting in unprecedented economic and social consequences across the World. Where measures to prevent the disease and health service provision fell short in many countries during the pandemic, refugees became among the most vulnerable groups as they have preexisting adverse living conditions such as crowded households, poor living conditions, limited access to services and economic hardships (Brickhill-Atkinson, M., & Hauck, F. R., 2021). Yet, little is known about the constituents of health service access among refugees resettled in the Majority World Countries. Thus, this study aimed to understand the experiences of refugees in accessing health services in Turkey. Semi-structured interviews were conducted online with 17 adult refugees who were diagnosed with COVID-19 from three distinct of Turkey, i.e. İstanbul, Kahramanmaras, and Konya. Data were analysed through a thematic approach and results revealed two themes. The first theme, "the enablers in accessing health services" included high awareness of disease and transmission. Good level of knowledge about the disease and related symptoms, and having preexisting chronic disease prompted participants to apply to the hospitals. Most participants highlighted that they have no difficulty accessing health services, including having tests, medication, and in-patient care. They also reported that family practitioners made calls to check their health status after diagnosis. Moreover, participants with high awareness of transmission took precautionary measures before applying to hospitals, including wearing masks, applying hygiene practices and self-quarantine. Social media was reported as a source of knowledge, although the misinformation spread through the media regarding the disease caused anxiety in some participants. The second theme, 'the barriers', identify the difficulties in accessing health services. Fewer participants had difficulty in accessing health services because of registration issues. A participant stated that he had to apply private hospital as he was registered in another city. The language was another barrier for some participants as it causes communication problems with health workers and made it difficult for them to express related symptoms. Lastly, limited knowledge about service utilisation prevented some participants to apply hospitals. Understanding the refugees' experiences is essential in establishing their needs and increasing health service access. These findings suggest that the refugee population needs to be informed about the COVID-19, transmission and service usage, and language support should be provided by having interpreters presented at hospitals to increase the health service access.

References

Brickhill-Atkinson, M., & Hauck, F. R. (2021). Impact of COVID-19 on resettled refugees. *Primary Care: Clinics in Office Practice, 48*(1), 57-66. https://doi.org/10.1016/j.pop.2020.10.001

16:15-16:30 BREAK

Day Three 8 July 2021 - 16:30-18:00
Plenary Session III [Click here to Join] [in Spanish]
Moderator: **Dr** Ana Vila Freyer, **Universidad Latina de México, Mexico**
Keynote Speakers:
- Dr **Rodolfo Cruz Piñeiro**, Director, Departamento de Estudios de Población, El Colegio de la Frontera Norte, Mexico
- Hna. **Leticia Gutiérrez Valderrama**, General Director of Scalabrinianas Misión para Migrantes y Refugiados (SMR) sección México, México

END OF DAY THREE

833   Demographic (super-)diversity and metropolitanism: On inter-individual differences, untenably tidy categorisations and logics, and tousled urban realities

Lena Imeraj

Vertovec's (2007) *'super-diversity'* concept has been widely taken up by scholars from different research disciplines in a variety of ways. Initially intended to describe the arrival of more migrants from more places to more places in combination with long(er) established minority populations, the concept however often tends to be used at its face value. While there is much evidence enabling us to argue that super-diversity represents the emergence of a new demographic reality in Europe (and worldwide), the notion of super-diversity has perhaps refrained—or at least decelerated—scholars from critically thinking of and furthering conceptualisation, theorisation, methodologies and understanding of contemporary diversity (Beck, 2011). Without the pretence or ambition to develop more enhanced terms and frameworks covering all aspects of diversity, this paper explores two issues which continue to be underexposed; i.e., the diversity *in* (demographic drivers of) diversity *across* categories, groups and space, and the evolving nature of (the meaning of) diversity.

First, the idea that diversity can itself bring diversification—in an autocatalytic process—is very appealing but remains understudied. While international migration is the initial impetus for diversification, later sequences of immigration, natural change and internal migration, ethnic and socio-economic differences in (timing of) fertility and mortality patterns, ageing and second-generations growing into adulthood, as well as the ongoing de-standardisation of family-life and integration trajectories involve increasing diversity of timing and outcomes of demographic components (e.g., Falkingham et al. 2016 ; Kulu & Hanneman 2016 ; Sabater & Finney 2014). Depending on the differences in occurrence and timing of the demographic momentum, ethnic groups display different demographics which have a pivotal role in the local demographic diversification and redistribution of people across urban space.

Secondly, and perhaps more controversial, the notion of super-diversity itself entails the need to reflect more about the very meaning of super-diversity. Do super-diverse places and populations (again) become normalised and—if so—when? In other words, the temporal and spatial/contextual dimensions of super-diversity impact on whether and how the *new and unprecedented* variety of cultures, identities, faiths, languages and immigration statuses—which have emerged from greater speed, scale and spread of diversity then even before—stop being new and unprecedented.

Using individual-level longitudinal full population data, quantitative methods and a comparative empirical approach, this study contrasts and critically reflects upon a number of Belgian cases. In so doing, it unravels the complex demographic pictures of population groups and cities; it enhances our understanding of the potential mechanisms that promote and reflect inequalities; it allows for a more nuanced debate on migration and demographic diversification; and it encourages moving away from an 'applicable-to-all' framework for understanding ethnic population change towards a theoretical framing of intricate population dynamics at the intersection of people and places.

References

BECK (2011) Multiculturalism or cosmopolitanism: How can we describe and understand the diversity of the world? *Social Sciences in China* 32(4): 52-58

FALKINGHAM, SAGE, STONE, VLACHANTONI (2016) Residential mobility across the life course: continuity and change across three cohorts in Britain. *Advances in Life Course Research 30*: 111-123.

KULU, HANNEMAN (2016) Why does fertility remain high among certain UK- born ethnic minority women? *Demographic Research 35*: 1441-1488.

SABATER, FINNEY (2014) Demographic understanding of changes in ethnic residential segregation across the life course. In Lloyd, Shuttleworth & Wong (Eds.), *Social-spatial segregation: Concepts, processes and outcomes* (pp. 269-300). Bristol: Policy Press.

VERTOVEC (2007) Super-diversity and its implications. *Ethnic and Racial Studies* 30(6): 1024-1054.

1051 Ethnic diversity in perinatal in Spain: the influence of family support.

Chiara Dello Iacono, Jesús García Gómez, Mikolaj Stanek

In the last two decades, Spain has become a receiving country for immigrants from Latin America, Africa, Asia and high- and non-high income European countries and its immigrant population has grown from 1.6% in 1998 to 14.3% in 2019. International immigration mark is increasingly evident in the country's demographic and family dynamics, through the growing relative weight of immigrant households (González Ferrer 2006; González Ferrer 2011). It has been also observed that immigrants in Spain have relatively complex household structures, (Requena 2011; Van Hook and Glick 2007). The size of immigrant households increases due to the phenomenon of family regrouping and the formation of new family units.

Massive inflows of women in reproductive ages provide an excellent opportunity to analyse the reproductive and perinatal health outcomes of migrant subpopulations. Despite the increasing contribution of immigrant women to the total number of births and the higher fertility than Spanish couple (Requena and Sánchez-Domínguez 2011), there have not been many studies focused on the specific effect of family support on birth outcomes of immigrant women. The aim of our study is first to compare the birthweight outcomes among immigrant women of diverse origin. Second, to assess the role that family support plays in the association between the ethnic origin of the women and their reproductive outcomes.

This research takes advantage of the opportunity to use a new database linking the Natural Population Movement records from 2011 to 2015 with the 2011 Spanish Census, provided by the Spanish National Institute of Statistics. Categorising the family types recorded by the 2011 Spanish Census, we focused on native and immigrant women who have given birth and live alone with their children and those who live with their partner and children with or without family support. We have used a logistic regression model to estimate the effect of family support on low-birth-weight outcomes and their differences between natives and immigrants' women.

References

González-Ferrer, A. (2006). Family and labor strategies in migration: Family reunification, marital choices and labor participation of immigrants in the host country. (Tesis doctoral), Universidad Autonoma de Madrid, Madrid.

González-Ferrer, A. (2011). Explaining the labour performance of immigrant women in Spain: The interplay between family, migration and legal trajectories. International Journal of Comparative Sociology, 52(1– 2), 63–78.

Reher, D. y M. Requena. 2009b. "Introducción: el impacto de la inmigración en la sociedad española". Pp. 7-19 en D. Reher y M. Requena (eds.), Las múltiples caras de la inmigración en España. Madrid: Alianza Editorial.

Requena, M., & Sánchez-Domínguez, M. (2011). Las familias inmigrantes en España. Revista Internacional de Sociología, 69(M1), 79-104.

Van Hook, J., Glick, J.E. Immigration and living arrangements: Moving beyond economic need versus acculturation. Demography 44, 225–249 (2007).

1054   Integration, negotiation, interrogation: Climates of socialization for ethnic minority women in the academic workplace

Dounia Bourabain

This qualitative research investigates the interactional and contextual dynamics underlying the socialization of ethnic minority women (EMW) within the academic workplace. Based on 26 in-depth interviews with female ethnic minority early career researchers working in Belgian-Flemish academia, I identify three socialization climates: integration, negotiation and interrogation. Following a power perspective, results show that insiders play a crucial role in facilitating or hindering the socialization of EMW. Insiders' behaviour towards EMW newcomers are explained in light of racialized relations which are manifested through practices from perceived personal-professional identity mismatch, exoticization, tokenization, to exclusion. In addition, the organizational context sustains these racialised interactions. EMW are able to socialize rapidly only if they arrive in a context that is (radically) inclusive. Most of the times, EMW enter in a work environment with marginal awareness of diversity and (in)equality. In addition, first generation minority women experienced an additional integration barrier with regards to language. They indicate resistance from peers to use English as language of instruction in the workplace. This leads to feelings of exclusion and non-belonginess in participating to both social and academic life. This is one example in which first generation minority women experience socialization differently compared to second/third generation minority women. This paper is a stepping stone for future research on ethnic minorities' organizational socialization and development in the workplace taking into account inequality on individual and structural level.

1057   Who deserves more to be a refugee?

Duha Ceylan and Shagofah Ghafori

Under the Geneva convention, definitions on who gets to be a refugee can be found; the encompassing definition of a refugee includes any individuals who flee their home country and is afraid to return due to various reasons such as race, sexuality, political activism, and war that put them under the danger of persecution. At the European Union level, member states are in charge of deciding who to accept as refugees or not as long as they follow the Geneva Convention's criteria. Issues arise when considering such criteria, especially with the increased number of refugees arriving in Europe after 2014 and peaking in 2015 as a consequence of the Syrian conflict. Before the conflict, one of Europe's most prominent refugee groups had been from Afghanistan, but the figures had been consequently changing from 2014 onward, and Syrians became the most significant refugee group arriving in Europe. With the diverse and increased number of refugees arriving in the EU, member states aimed to limit their refugee intake by either refusing to welcome more refugees than a certain number. In contrast, other member states tightened their criteria on who gets accepted as a refugee.

Consequently, diverse groups of refugees responded to such tightening of regulation by creating conflicts within themselves while waiting in refugee camps. However, this competition and conflict between diverse refugee groups have not been fully reflected in the migration literature. Therefore, taking an entirely qualitative approach, this paper aims to evaluate how the criteria on eligibility for refuge are reflected on diverse refugee groups, namely Syrian and Afghan refugees. We also assess these perceptions' consequences on the interactions between them, especially during their asylum process. The paper evaluates the term 'refugee' as a relational category reflecting social negotiations set in national contexts. By that, we mean the national policies that determine who is granted refuge and who is not, function to set the classifications on refugee as a category that directly influences the image that circulates on refugees' definition. These classifications tend to strongly influence the experiences of refugees and their interaction with each other. As a concept characterized by its fluidity and constant adaptability to the national context, we evaluate what it means to be a refugee to Syrian and Afghan refugees by conducting semi-structured in-depth interviews with 20 respondents from each group, a total of 40 interviews. Additionally, policy content analysis on refugee criteria and acceptance within Belgium was conducted to understand refugees' perceptions further.

844   Understanding the Integration Process of Highly Skilled Migration from Turkey

Eda Ozdek and Tuba Bircan

Migration and skill mobility are among the most pressing topics on the agenda of governments and policymakers today. Turkish migrants are, with Moroccans, the largest migrant group in Europe. There are estimated to be 5.5 million Turkish citizens living abroad (including second and third generations born to Turkish parents outside Turkey), of whom around 4.6 million live in Western European countries[33]. In addition to the large Turkish community in Europe, in last decade, the number of highly skilled Turkish immigrants is on rise as of 2000s who might have diverse motivation factors (social, cultural, political etc.) other than economic factors to leave their home country. This brings in the question: How diverse the migration motivations of the recent Turkish immigrant community in Europe? Thus, there is a need of understanding the differentials within the recent Turkish migrant community and how this diversity serves to the integration process of different Turkish groups?

Having said that, it is important to understand how migrant capital serves as a resource created by migrants during the migration and integration process and are potentially available to their family and network members who will create social inclusion dynamics since there are diverse forms of capital in these

---

[33] De Bel Air, F. Migration Profile : Turkey, European University Institute, Issue 2016/09

populations.[34] The Bourdieusian understanding of different forms of capital together with the Network theory will provide the theoretical frame of this study to understanding how resources consisting of economic, social, political, and cultural transnational ties, practices and networks are utilised and further developed by Turkish high-skilled migrant communities. Thus, this study broadly engages with. two specific objectives of this study are (i) Elaborating the profile (lifestyle, occupation change, cultural activities etc.) of Turkish high-skilled immigrants, (ii) Understanding the perception of highly skilled migrants in their host country and the dynamics to stay or go or integrate in their host society. This perception on one hand will help us to understand their level of integration and on the other hand if they will stay or go back to their home countries. The qualitative data will be collected for this study. The semi-structured interviews will be conducted with highly skilled immigrants and refugees (40 respondents who left Turkey after 2000). For analysis, thematic and content analysis will be conducted through NVivo.

1055   How work-based social rights leave highly skilled migrants vulnerable

Damini Purkayastha, Tuba Bircan

This research paper challenges assumptions around skilled migration and integration policies, to question how and if 'skill' intersects with bordering mechanisms and patterns of inclusion and exclusion (Mezzadra & Nielson, 2013). Proliferating policies around skilled migration create stratifications among labour migrants, even among seemingly privileged highly skilled migrants. Looking at skill as a differential allows us to see how migrants are pushed into new and diverse subjective positions through policies (Iredale, 2000; Raghuram, 2020, Ruhs, 2013). Our study begins with the Single Permit Directive of 2011, which saw the European Union formally tie the "labour-citizen dyad" together into one identity card. It was designed to fast-track the application process for highly skilled migrants and grant them similar rights as intra-EU workers. However, the single permit cements employment as the central node for all points of access to the host society – from the legal right to residence to health insurance. This has its own pitfalls. For starters, the permit makes it even more difficult for workers to change jobs, thus forcing them to stay on even in unhealthy workspaces. While highly skilled migrants get access to healthcare, social security and longer contracts, they face higher thresholds of deliverables, report being asked to work longer hours or openly reminded about their 'dependence' on employers. Annual renewals of residence permits, linked to a certificate from the employer, are some of the ways in which the migrant worker is controlled on behalf of the state and the employer. Migrants are often locked into bad working conditions because changing jobs can mean months of paperwork and loss of residence rights in the interim. In some countries it can even mean losing the years accrued towards citizenship if the migrant arrived on a special employment category. This research paper explores the idea of 'precarious privilege' through policies and experiences, and

---

[34] Sanna Saksela-Bergholm *, Mari Toivanen and Östen Wahlbeck, Migrant Capital as a Resource for Migrant Communities

questions whether linking work and residence makes things better or worse for migrants in the long run. This paper will focus on highly skilled economic migrants to explore how the tension between access and opportunity created by the kind of access one has to the labour market is further compounded by other factors (Riano, 2012, Kofman, 2000) such as gender, nationality, ethnicity and category of skill.

References

Iredale, R. (2000). Migration Policies for the Highly Skilled in the Asia-Pacific Region. International Migration Review 34(3) p. 882.

Kofman, E. (2000). The Invisibility of Skilled Female Migrants and Gender Relations in Studies of Skilled Migration in Europe. International Journal of Population Geography 6, 45-59.

Mezzadra, S. , & Neilson, B. (2013). Border as method, or, the multiplication of labor . Duke University Press. https://doi.org/10.1215/9780822377542.

Raghuram P. (2021) Democratizing, Stretching, Entangling, Transversing: Four Moves for Reshaping Migration Categories, Journal of Immigrant & Refugee Studies, 19:1, 9-24, DOI: 10.1080/15562948.2020.1837325

Riano, Y. (2012) The Invisibility of Family in Studies of Skilled Migration and Brain Drain, Diversities 14(1), 25-44.

Ruhs, M., (2013). The Price of Rights: Regulating International Labour Migration. Princeton University Press, Oxford

9B   Space and Migration

Chair: Gökay Özerim, Yaşar University, Turkey

842   Rivers and Memories: Migration, Ecology and Landscape in the Narratives of India's Partition
Anuparna Mukherjee

882   Gender, agency, and the social imaginary in Japanese lifestyle migration to Europe
Yana Svezhenova Yovcheva

886   The Role of Lifestyle in Mexican Migration: Can Mexican Migration be defined as Lifestyle Migration?
Yolanda Lopez Garcia

881   LIFESTYLE MIGRATION IN TURKEY: THE CASE OF DATCA
Cemre Zekiroglu

842   Rivers and Memories: Migration, Ecology and Landscape in the Narratives of India's Partition

Anuparna Mukherjee

The literature on India's Partition, which uprooted nearly fifteen million people in the wake of the nation's political independence from the colonial rule, is deeply imbricated in spatial memories invested with meanings that are variously associated with violence, trauma or nostalgia. In Partition Dialogues, Alok Bhalla posits that the historical debacle of India's vivisection along religious lines into two nations not only deracinated the migrants from their homes but also plucked them from their lifeworlds suffused with "words like 'friendship', 'neighbourhood', 'peepul tree'" with which they had forged strong emotive bonds. The affective import of such "soft violence" whose outcome was more intangible is generally filtered through melancholia or nostalgia in the corpus on Partition literature. However, on occasions, it emerged as a cause for prolonged strife when the refugees were relocated to distant and inhospitable places. They missed the familiar surroundings, especially the riverine landscape of undivided Bengal around which the communities constructed their quotidian histories and identities. The rupture irrevocably altered their cultural, linguistic and economic environments, along with the essential food habits that were dominated by pescatarian diets.

Through a set of literary and cultural texts, this presentation, thus looks at the affective and social contours of the landscape in shaping the narratives of displacement in the context of India and Bangladesh. The paper will particularly focus on the rivers and their entanglements in migrant narratives by delving into the fluvial and riverine memories of deltaic Bengal in the inscriptions of space in Partition Literature.

It locates how the rivers imbue local, cultural and mythical values to the human sense of place that thickens in our 'everyday' experiences, and transmits as a memory when individuals negotiate with their manifold 'social relations' across time. Working through the predominance of rivers in the cultural imagination of the refugees, this presentation will subsequently move into the knotted problem of apportioning the geopolitical landscape to different countries in a manner that supports a discrete division, since the rivers constantly alter their borders with new sedimentations, flooding and the change of courses. Hence, from exploring the significance of rivers in the mnemonic register to the partitioning of the riverscape, the paper will culminate with a discussion on the ensuing water-problem between India and Bangladesh as a legacy of the Partition, and the environmental refugees as the new precariats whose lands are repeatedly swept away by the flooding of the embankments in the tidal basins.

882   Gender, agency, and the social imaginary in Japanese lifestyle migration to Europe

Yana Svezhenova Yovcheva

Gender has been shown to be not only an important variable in understanding motivation for migration, but a set of social relations that organize immigration patterns (Hondagneu-Sotelo 1994). For instance, while in the case of economic migration liberation from socially imposed gender constraints in the home country is typically assumed to be a secondary motivating factor, it appears to be one of the primary motivations for women lifestyle migrants (Croucher 2013). Here, the role of agency in its projective aspect (i.e., the one that has to do with imagination) is crucial in setting a plan into motion – to generate "possible future trajectories of action, in which received structures of thought and action may be creatively reconfigured in relation to actors' hopes, fears, and desires for the future" (Emirbayer & Mische 1998, p. 971). With regard to (lifestyle) migration, agency both shapes and is shaped by the social imaginary (O'Reilly 2014) – what is collectively imagined about destinations has a direct impact on individual imaginations and consequent actions and vice versa. The question is how gender intersects with the mutually-constitutive relationship between agency and the social imaginary.

Based on semi-structured interviews with Japanese migrants and experts, this paper looks at Japanese lifestyle migration to two European countries, and examines the impact gender has on the exercise of agency in engaging with the social imaginary about European destinations and how that affects subsequent migration decisions.

The research finds that Japanese women generally indulge in imagining a life abroad and act on the imagined much more freely and resolutely than men, as expectations for participation in Japanese society are gendered and women in fact have more liberty to opt out of Japanese society, as there is less to lose. The social constraints they (expect to) experience in Japan are a powerful push factor, while the imagined advantages of a life in the West are an equally powerful pull factor in migration decisions. It also becomes apparent that considering a life in (Western) Europe in particular is characteristic of Japanese women, rather than men, as cultural representations of European destinations resonate with gendered socialization practices in Japan.

In conclusion, gender clearly affects Japanese people's exercise of agency and engagement with the social imaginary, and that is likely a function of the state of gender relations within Japanese society.

Bibliography

Croucher, S. (2013). The gendered spatialities of lifestyle migration. In Contested spatialities, lifestyle migration and residential tourism (pp. 31-44). Routledge.

Emirbayer, M., & Mische, A. (1998). What is agency?. American journal of sociology, 103(4), 962-1023.

Hamano, T. (2011). Japanese women marriage migrants today: Negotiating gender, identity and community in search of a new lifestyle in western Sydney. (PhD dissertation.) University of Western Sydney.

Hondagneu-Sotelo, P. (1994). 2. The History Of Mexican Undocumented Settlement In The United States. In Gendered Transitions (pp. 19-33). University of California Press.

Kelsky, K. (2001). Women on the verge: Japanese women, Western dreams. Duke University Press.

Nagatomo, J. (2014). Migration as transnational leisure: The Japanese lifestyle migrants in Australia. Brill.

O'Reilly, K. (2014). The role of the social imaginary in lifestyle migration: employing the ontology of practice theory. In Understanding lifestyle migration (pp. 211-234). Palgrave Macmillan, London.

Pessar, P. R., & Mahler, S. J. (2003). Transnational migration: Bringing gender in. International migration review, 37(3), 812-846.

886 The Role of Lifestyle in Mexican Migration: Can Mexican Migration be defined as Lifestyle Migration?

Yolanda Lopez Garcia

Usually, research on lifestyle migration has focused on the movement of people from the global north to the global south, or from stronger economies to relatively weaker ones. Such is the case of research on North Americans in Latin America (Hayes, 2015; Hiernaux, 2011), or or Northern European pensioners in Spain (Schriewer & García Jiménez, 2005). Lifestyle migrants are understood to be "relatively affluent individuals, moving either part time or full-time, permanently or temporarily, to places which, for various reasons, signify for the migrants something loosely defined as quality of life" (Benson & O'Reilly, 2016, p. 22).

Mexico is often the destination for lifestyle migrants. However, this paper discusses whether the migration of Mexicans to Germany can be understood as a lifestyle migration and what role does lifestyle play in this migration? Through the method of life stories, this research focuses on the subjective dimension of people born and socialized in Mexico who decided to migrate in search of a better life. From their narratives it appears that they can be considered as relatively affluent people with economic and social capital. Parallels and differences in their mobility with respect to other studies on lifestyle migration are explored. The role of the social imaginary of privilege and the idealization of Europe as the imagined "first world" so different from Mexico is discussed. The participants of the study reflected upon the aspects in which their desires have been fulfilled and those in which they have not. In addition, they contrasted "the German dream" with the experience of being (treated as) migrants (López García, 2021).

This research opens a new panorama of discussion regarding the analysis of Mexican mobility from the perspective of lifestyle migration. It addresses the connections between skilled migration, status, privilege and/or a deeper need for security and "escape" from Mexico.

References

Benson, M., & O'Reilly, K. (2016). From lifestyle migration to lifestyle in migration: Categories, concepts and ways of thinking. Migration Studies, 4(1), 20–37. https://doi.org/10.1093/migration/mnv015

Hayes, M. (2015). 'It is hard being the different one all the time': Gringos and racialized identity in lifestyle migration to Ecuador. Ethnic and Racial Studies, 38(6), 943–958. https://doi.org/10.1080/01419870.2014.943778

Hiernaux, D. (2011, March). Migraciones por estilo de vida e imaginarios en México. 2nd International Workshop on Lifestyle and Residential Tourism, Madrid. Retrieved from https://www.yumpu.com/es/document/view/28461700/migraciones-por-estilo-de-vida-e-imaginarios-en-macxico

López García, Y. (September 2021, in press). Imaginaries of Migration: Life Stories of Mexican Migrants in Germany. Bielefeld: transcript.

Schriewer, K., & García Jiménez, M. (2005). Entre europeos: Acerca de una posible conciencia europea. El caso de residentes europeos en España. In J. Fernández-Rufete & M. García Jiménez (Eds.), Movimientos Migratorios Contemporáneos (pp. 181–204). Murcia: Quaderna Editorial.

881   LIFESTYLE MIGRATION IN TURKEY: THE CASE OF DATCA

Cemre Zekiroglu

Since 2013, Turkey has witnessed the emergence of a new internal migration trend: the post-80s generation leaving big cities such as Istanbul, Ankara and Izmir for coastal/seasonal villages located in the Aegean and Mediterranean regions of Turkey. In this paper, I aim to investigate the reasons behind this new trend of "leaving cities" for a coastal town located in the Aegean region, Datca. Based on 16 semi-structurated lifestory interviews in Datça conducted in July 2019, this research focuses on the following questions: How did these young people decide to the big cities to start a new life in Datça? Did they have a turning point in their life narratives? What were their reasons and motivations? In order to make sense of these lifestyle narratives, firstly, I define these youngsters as "lifestyle migrants" as defined by the Benson and O'Relly (2009). However, as the current literature on lifestyle migrations lacks a generational perspective, I deploy Mannheim's terminology of "generation unit" (1998) to contextualize the concept within the case of Datça and I argue that the decision to migrate from cities among post-80s generation is not a random choice but should be understood as a response to the modern in Turkey. Their response is constructed within time to establish a 'reflexive project of the self' as argued by Giddens (1991) and is closely intertwined with the environmental damage, earthquake risk, physical and mental health issues and eroded interpersonal relationships. As one of informants puts in: "One day we realized that this city got sick, everyone in this city got sick and this sickness arrived at our door. It was the day when we decided to leave."

References

Benson, Michaela, and Karen O'Reilly. 2009. "Migration and the search for a better way of life: a critical exploration of lifestyle migration." The sociological review 57(4): 608–625.

Giddens, Anthony. 1991. Self and society in the late modern age. Cambridge: Polity Press.

Mannheim, Karl. 1998. "The problem of generations." In Essays on the Sociology of Knowledge. Routledge& Kegan Paul.

9C   Economics of Migration

Chair *Ruchi Singh, Prin. L. N. Welingkar Institute of Management Development & Research, India*

694   Typologies of remittances and Transnational Ties: Study of Punjabi families in Netherlands, Gulf and Punjab (India)
Atinder Pal Kaur

695   The Impact of Albanian migration on their homeland in Tetovo, North Macedonia

Kujtim Ramadani

694 Typologies of remittances and Transnational Ties: Study of Punjabi families in Netherlands, Gulf and Punjab (India)

Atinder Pal Kaur

Objective

The present study explores the utilization of remittances in different settings that include flow of remittances from migrants to their home country. The context of sending remittances is in a particular time and situation. An attempt is made here to understand the hidden meaning of remittances from sociological approach in which sender/receiver's emotions are attached and seeks money as a medium of maintaining relationship, care and love in transnational settings.

Review of Literature: Majority of studies has given economic interpretations of remittances (Delgado et al., 2001; Semyonov& Gorodzeisky, 2005; Itzigsohn, 1995, D`emurger, 2015) in which major share of the remittances are used for household budgets (Canales, 2000; Adams & Cuecuecha, 2013; Adams, 2005; Balde,2011), children's education (Edward &Ureta, 2003, Kaur, 2016, Kaur 2019; Dharmadasa & Rathnayake, 2019), investment in agricultural land, property, health (Nguyen et al., 2007; Hefti, 1997, Heller & Kanshik, 2019; Green et al, 2019) and rebuilding of old houses (Hugo, 1995; Gulati ,1983, Roy et al, 2015). Singh (2010,) defined remittances are also used by migrant families as care economy.

Methodology

The study dealt with micro interpretation of remittances with special references to sender and receiver point of view that is missing in earlier studies. Keeping ethnography and sociological interpretation; the data was collected through longitudinal survey from 2016-2019 via open-ended interview and participant observation in different settings. 27 case studies were collected from Punjabis staying in Netherlands (via visiting gurudwara (Sikh Temple) conducting interviews and participatory observation; attending daily morning prayers and having lunger (afternoon meal)), 48 case studies were conducted with Punjabi left behind families staying in Doaba region of Punjab and lastly interviews were also conducted with 6 Gulf migrants during their holiday visit to their homeland Punjab.

Findings

The study finds that remittances are used in various ways to deal in family logistics and to maintain emotional bonds as(a) Shagun (money gifts during birth, death, marriage, festivals like Rakhi, Diwali, Lohri etc.) b) Economic remittances(for household budgets and constructions)c)Education d) development (for villages beautification and construction of roads, parks, religious places) e) Investments(purchase of commercial and agricultural land, entrepreneurial activities) f) Care money (use of money for care of parents, families and children) g) Migration (money invest for better future of their younger generation migration) h) lastly social remittances (transform ideas, culture , technology and goods via holidays visit of migrants).

Conclusion

The study concludes that the meaning attached to remittances by sender and receiver are not just economic money and currency of care rather an investment in social assets that does not includes only material wellbeing rather emotional bonds that are the foundations of these transactions. Remittances are also a way to maintain sense of belongingness with the families and at the same time also to show the identity of being money provider. With this the sender tried to show their presence and maintain strong relation with their families.

695   The Impact of Albanian migration on their homeland in Tetovo, North Macedonia

Kujtim Ramadani

Immigrants from the former Yugoslavia form the second largest group of immigrants in Switzerland. About 60,000 of these emigrants are Albanians from North Macedonia. For North Macedonia, respectively for the region of Tetovo, from which region a large part of immigrants come, this group of the population is of great importance, first of all, for the support of the region which they come from. The presented study examines the influence of Albanian emigrants from Switzerland, in their birthplace in Tetovo. To better understand and analyze the mutual impact of migration in Tetovo, interviews were conducted with members of the immigrants' families, with the immigrants returning to their homeland, as well as with key persons in the region. The subject of this study is oriented according to the relevant concepts of trans-nationality and remittances in migration research. Immigrants transfer to their homeland not only money but also other economic resources as well as other potential resources, key to development. These remittances can be classified into economic resources, professional knowledge and skills as well as socio-cultural resources. In accordance with this classification, this qualitative and exploratory study analyzes the flow of resources, and their impact on the Tetovo region in the field of economy, knowledge and professional expertise as well as in the socio-cultural field. In the economic sphere, migration has direct impact, especially on the household economy, on the transfer of money and provides these families in the region with an above-average standard of living. The regional economy selectively benefits from the economic resources of emigrants. A lot of capital flows into the construction sector and the establishment of new firms leads to the revival of the middle class economy. With the consumption driven by the financial flow, both the premises and the restaurants benefit to a certain extent. Immigrants generally invest little d.m.th. They invest unilaterally in the regional economy of Tetovo. For most, one of the safest investments of money is building a home, rather than investing in a private or foreign venture. In general, in the Tetovo region, transfers of resources in the field of professional knowledge are very rare. The transfer of professional knowledge is done only when the immigrants returning to their homeland start a business or when they find a job in a regional enterprise. The opposite flow and transfer of highly qualified professional knowledge from Switzerland to Tetovo is rare. In the socio-cultural field, the effects of migration processes are clearly visible - both on immigrants and their relatives. From the migratory experiences made in Switzerland, there is a noticeable change in the lifestyle, a change in the roles in the family as well as in the formation of new life preconceptions of an international character.

1061   Are Migrant Households better off than Non-Migrant Households: Insights from NSSO Unit-Level Data

Ruchi Singh, Uday Salunkhe, Vaishali Vivek Patil

Migration is way out of poverty for rural households in developing countries. Rural households often take migration decisions to diversify household income. In country like India where huge share of population resides in rural counterparts huge male exodus acts as substitute to non-farm income opportunities. Uttar Pradesh is state with highest male out-migration as per NSSO. Huge male exodus from the state can be attributed to predominance of agriculture and huge population pressure, underdevelopment and lack of income and non-farm employment opportunities. Despite the fact that Uttar Pradesh is huge reservoir of migrants and contributes lot in growth and development of destination state, the studies on analyzing and understanding the impact of migration is scarce in literature. Though few studies have been done to understand nature and determinants of the migration patterns from state of Uttar Pradesh but negligible attempt have been made to understand the impact of migration on migrant households. With this background the study will fill this void. The study aims to compare and analyse migrant and non-migrant households in rural Uttar Pradesh on the basis of monthly per capita expenditure. For better understanding of the migration impact in rural households in Uttar Pradesh monthly per capita expenditure (MPCE) analysis have been done on household type. NSSO unit level secondary data have been employed for the study. Study found that migrant households are better off than non-migrant households.

721   How Labour Market Needs Distort the Outcome of Prior Learning Assessment and Recognition of Immigrants: Insights of a Systematic Review

Britta Klages and Lea Mustafa

How Labour Market Needs Distort the Outcome of Prior Learning Assessment and Recognition of Immigrants – Insights of a Systematic Review

To incorporate immigrant professionals in a local labour market the assessment and recognition of their prior learning experiences is an important factor. Prior learning assessment and recognition (PLAR) is said to be a powerful tool for social inclusion, but at the same time it encourages a severe divisive practice that may build barriers rather than bridges. It is a conflicting process that gives affirmation, integration and recognition to a few, but means exclusion and dequalification for many others (Diedrich 2014; Andersson/Osman 2008; Guo/Shan 2013).

This article expands on a systematic review that examined the difficulties within current PLAR practices regarding immigrants. For this, four databases were systematically examined, using an explicit search string. A total of 1231 articles were retrieved in March 2020. Once the material was screened through established inclusion and exclusion criteria, 33 articles remained that were published between 1990 and 2020. For the extraction process the material was coded using thematic categories. In a next step the categorized text passages were evaluated and the results were discussed.

The focus of interest of the articles varies depending on the study. The systematic review summarizes what has been researched about the difficulties within the PLAR process. The analysis gives a new guideline for future innovative research. The present article focuses on one thematic result of this systematic review by examining aspects of PLAR of immigrants with regard to labour market needs.

A majority of the material reviewed addresses the issue that the PLAR process is often motivated by what skills are in demand in the local labour market (Bencivenga 2017; Andersson/Osman 2008; Andersson/Fejes 2010; Souto-Otero/Villalba-Garcia 2015). This creates a bias and complicates the assessment of learned skills of immigrants, shifting the focus of the process away from the competence of the individual to the needs of the labour market and accommodating the demanding system (Andersson/Osman 2008). Consequently, an excluding practice manifests in the fact that countries only validate what they recognize as useful within the context of their labour market. This results in a dichotomy for PLAR services regarding a neutral assessment and the adjustment to the labor market (Andersson/Osman 2008). The initial idea of PLAR gets lost within this process, as the application of PLAR strategies to satisfy a particular demand interrupts the full exploration of a person's skills and knowledge. To restore an accurate application of PLAR, a systemic change is required. It must become a new paradigm to support individuals to engage in their area of expertise rather than blocking interaction in advance. The focus of PLAR should be highlighting capabilities and skill sets. By doing so, the dynamics of PLAR in the case of immigrants evolve into a transformative practice, fundamentally encouraging equality by allowing deployment on same level positions rather than counting differences.

Publication bibliography

Andersson, Per; Fejes, Andreas (2010): Mobility of knowledge as a recognition challenge: experiences from Sweden. In International Journal of Lifelong Education 29 (2), pp. 201–218. DOI: 10.1080/02601371003616624.

Andersson, Per; Osman, Ali (2008): Recognition of Prior Learning as a Practice for Differential Inclusion and Exclusion of Immigrants in Sweden. In Adult Education

Quarterly 59 (1), pp. 42–60. DOI: 10.1177/0741713608325173.

Bencivenga, R. (2017): Translating the initial assessment of migrants' informal learning in practice. In Studies in the Education of Adults 49 (2), pp. 136–156. DOI: 10.1080/02660830.2018.1453321.

Diedrich, A. (2014): Classifying difference in organizing, or how to create monsters. In Equality, Diversity and Inclusion 33 (7), pp. 614–632. DOI: 10.1108/EDI-02-2012-0007.

Guo, Shibao; Shan, Hongxia (2013): The politics of recognition: critical discourse analysis of recent PLAR policies for immigrant professionals in Canada. In International Journal of Lifelong Education 32 (4), pp. 464–480. DOI: 10.1080/02601370.2013.778073.

Souto-Otero, Manuel; Villalba-Garcia, Ernesto (2015): Migration and validation of non-formal and informal learning in Europe: Inclusion, exclusion or polarisation in the recognition of skills? In International Review of Education / Internationale Zeitschrift für Erziehungswissenschaft 61 (5), pp. 585–607. DOI: 10.1007/s11159-015-9516-7.

9D   Migration and Identity
Chair: Emre Eren Korkmaz, Oxford University, UK

660   "My Grate in Migrate": Interrogating the Shades of Multi-- in Multiculturalism
Sukhpreet Kaur Bhatia
706   COVID-19 in the Rohingya refugee camps in Bangladesh: A litmus test of emerging agency among the refugee
Sodip Roy
723   Canadian Muslim Youth Identity Issues in Context of Global Conflicts
Aamir Jamal
Wasif Ali
747   Implications of Islam on minor girls in Europe; a gender identity crisis
Gireesh Bhatia

660   "My Grate in Migrate": Interrogating the Shades of Multi-- in Multiculturalism

Sukhpreet Kaur Bhatia

In the words of Bhikhu Parekh, a culturally self-contained life is virtually impossible for most human beings in the modern, mobile, interdependent post-human world. Cultural intercourse among diverse cultures has become more of an inevitability and it has forced the nations of the world, especially the Western Democracies on higher economic hierarchy, that have witnessed maximum immigration, to adopt policies that are ostensibly supportive of and liberally tolerant towards ethnic diversity. Multiculturalism was one such highly touted system, advocated and recommended since the 1970s to offer legal and political accommodation, to migrants from foreign cultures. Beginning on a very celebratory note it encouraged the people both native and those belonging to outside cultures to mutually espouse the variegated social aspects of multiethnic cultures in the direction of elimination of earlier racialist ideologies. Post the 1990s, however, the balloon seems to have burst leading to a kind of debacle of the experiment in many European countries. The paper hypothetically explores the journey of a migrant, from isolation and alienation in a multicultural society, to his maniacal quest for his true identity and its culmination in his ideological radicalization dissecting threadbare the proclaimed notion of multiculturalism and exposing its harsh realities which are a far cry from its avowed objectives and the fissures that exist between policy and practice, and public domain and private domain.

Key words: Immigrant, assimilationism, ethnocultural diversity, multiculturalism, religious fundamentalism, racialization

706   COVID-19 in the Rohingya refugee camps in Bangladesh: A litmus test of emerging agency among the refugee

Sodip Roy

No health crisis, as well as COVID-19, can have a positive impact on a community and public health. But it can be said in the case of Rohingya refugee and overall Bangladeshi people that they are saved from devastating causalities of this pandemic unlike in many other parts of the globe. Instead of what impacted is that the exposure of COVID-19 had challenged for a demonstration of community engagement among the Rohingya people (Islam & Yunus, 2020). The obvious concerns of the Corona virus caused 'massive and rapid' aid staff reduction in the camps. The limited number of essential staff operated the emergency services there. Resultantly, the refugee community themselves were obliged to maintain their protection in the face of unknown precarity of the disease and the crisis aroused from lockdown. More than 200,000 Rohingya people participated in the community awareness build-up and prevention program (ISCG, 2020). Considering the limited scope of participation in the camp activities in Bangladesh, this study unfolds the emerging agency among the Rohingya people in the camps. To that end, it has explored relevant reports, academic studies, news and particularly the Inter Sector Coordination Group's (ISCG) week reports in a qualitative setting. After an exploration of the secondary data, it finds that Rohingya people have exercised their forgotten spirit of agency for their well being during the COVID-19 epidemic. Thus, the study comprehends that there is no scope to consider refugees as 'bare lives' (Agamben, 1998), 'bogus' and in more labeling (Zetter, 2007) instead there should have scope to utilize their agencies (Omata, 2017; Turner, 2016) in leading their life as human being.

Key literature

Agamben, G. (1998). *Homo sacer: Sovereign power and bare life*. Stanford University Press.

Inter Sector Coordination Group (ISCG), (2020). COVID-19: Preparedness and response for the Rohingya refugee camps and host communities in Cox's Bazar District Retrieved from: https://reliefweb.int/report/bangladesh/covid-19-preparedness-and-response-rohingya-refugee-camps-and-host-communities-0.

Islam, M. M., & Yunus, M. Y. (2020). Rohingya refugees at high risk of COVID-19 in Bangladesh. *The Lancet Global Health*, 8(8), e993-e994.

Omata, N. (2017). Unwelcome participation, undesirable agency? Paradoxes of de-politicisation in a refugee camp. *Refugee Survey Quarterly, 36*(3), 108-131.

Turner, S. (2016). What is a refugee camp? Explorations of the limits and effects of the camp. *Journal of Refugee Studies, 29*(2), 139-148.

Zetter, R. (2007). More labels, fewer refugees: Remaking the refugee label in an era of globalization. *Journal of refugee studies, 20*(2), 172-192.

723   Canadian Muslim Youth Identity Issues in Context of Global Conflicts

Aamir Jamal; Wasif Ali

The Muslim population of Canada is over one million people. They belong to diverse ethnic backgrounds and speak different languages. Canadian Muslims (CM) also represent the youngest Canadian population with a median age of 28.9 years (National Household Survey, 2011). With the recent influx of Syrian refugees, the number of Muslim population has significantly increased.

Despite growing public interest in understanding challenges and issues of Muslim youth identity construction amongst Muslims living in Canada has received relatively limited attention in the literature. Several studies have targeted particular issues, still little is known about the construction of multiple identities or the dialogical construction of identity as they pertain to the wider and diverse Muslim community's perspective on youth identity. In spite of strong research on how extremist narratives find fertile soil around the world, we are no closer to understanding why those narratives appeal to certain youth and to crafting effective counter narratives to reduce the risk of religious extremism and promote a resilient and positive youth identity.

We are filling this gap through a two phase qualitative research project. We seek to address the following questions: 1) What are the varieties of identity found amongst CM youth? 2) How do CM youth construct, negotiate and maintain their individual, communal, religious and transnational identities? 3) What are the factors (e.g. gender, religion, experiences of discrimination etc.) impacting upon CM identity development? 4) What features of the narrative sense-making environment attract, justify and support some CM youth moving to extremism? 5) What avenues of prevention and disengagement are seen as most promising in countering violent extremism? 6) What avenues and strategies of prevention and disengagement do Muslim community see as most promising in positive youth development?

We have began interviewing immigrant Muslim youth (aged 18–32, the UN Habitat Youth Fund definition of youth) that is recruited from ethnically diverse Muslim communities (Arab, African, Turkish, Pakistani, Syrian, Iranian etc.) through contacts with mosques, social networks, community organizations, schools and universities located in Toronto, Calgary, Montreal, and Vancouver.

Through individual interviews with CM youth across Canada, we have developed a framework to evaluate how and where self, others and the conflict in between is negotiated and transformed. In second phase of research, through a qualitative Delphi study, we seek the insight, experience and collective wisdom of the Muslim community to develop viable counter narratives to extremist ideologies. We explore avenues and strategies of prevention and disengagement do stakeholders (such as Muslim community and Islamic scholars) see as most promising in building resiliency, and promoting positive youth development.

A second intellectual outcome, we are developing a model for a counter narrative for Muslim youth that signifies a collective identity, collaborative civic participation and peaceful co-existences, leading, we expect, to social benefits involving citizenship, multiculturalism, and integration.

747 Implications of Islam on minor girls in Europe; a gender identity crisis

Gireesh Bhatia

This paper explains the problems related to social and cultural implication on Minor girls that are from Muslim background upon their arrival in Europe Union countries. The paper explains the problem based on religion and not the destination of the subject in question. Based on the literature review and interviews undertaken, the author explains the perception of the minor girls and the problems faced in their day to day life while living in the Western world. The data collected as an interview from these respondents, that are originally from Syria, Afghanistan, Somalia and parts of Central Africa. The respondents interviewed were in the age group of 15-16 and were interviewed as part of a family group.

There are different stages in this paper that are limited to Personal, Social and Cultural and the implications their religion of origin causes them to go on with their normal daily lives. Their education ability is compromised and so are the skills related to physical education and sporting activities, that are considered banned or illegal in some Islmac countries. Based on the interview, the author is able to construct the most likelihood of problems faced by minor females. As the ongoing problem with integration, these children face Profiling and Day to day harassment when it comes to calling their new country a home.

They have two fundamental problems to face, dealing with a home culture and a host culture. Somehow, parents of these minors are not fully integrated and are limited on what they can (are allowed) or they can't (are not allowed) to give freedom to these minor children. As a result, these children face gender identity crisis on a regular basis and are not able to be transparent to seek help through counselling facilities as there is a social stigmatization that is built in it. The host countries have done their part by inviting and giving residence to these families, but done very little to integrate their offsprings into the mainstream culture.

The problem starts with issues on how to integrate entire families into the culture and just issuing them a permit to reside does not solves much of the problem. There are Personal problems; mail order groom and female genital mutilation, Societal; Racism and Social Profiling, Cultural; honour killings and Submissive to male society. Some issues discussed are illegal in European Union while others fall under the grey area if legislation is to be applied. As a result, the host countries try to Socially condition these children and although there is a success in some cases but over all as these children grow into adulthood being a victim of gender identity crisis.

This paper is a presentation of original research conducted with Primary Data collection using Interviews and will be presented using Quantitative Data Analysis.

References

Nannestad, P. (2004) Immigration as a challenge to the Danish welfare state? European Journal of Political Economy

Agergaard, S., la Cour, A.M., and Gregersen, M.T., (2015). Politicisation of migrant leisure. A public and civil intervention involving organised sports. Leisure studies.

Benn, T., Dagkas, S., and Jawad, H., (2011). Embodied faith: Islam, religious freedom and educational practices in physical education. Sport, education and society, 16 (1), 17–34.

Malik, M. (2008) 'Complex equality: Muslim women and the "headscarf"', Droit et Societé, 68(1).

Nielsen, G., (2013). The usual suspects. Daglig fysisk aktivitet og idrætsdeltagelse blandt børn med anden etnisk baggrund end dansk [The usual suspects. Daily physical activity and sports participation among youngsters with another ethnic background than Danish]. In: S. Agergaard and H. Bonde, eds. Integration gennem kroppen. København: Museun Tusculanums Forlag, 131–160.

9E   Migration, Politics and Law

Chair: K. Onur Unutulmaz, Ankara Social Sciences University, Turkey

780   Complementary Protection Between Human Rights Obligations and Humanitarian Motives: Italian Case Study
Gabriella Morrone, Maria Teresa Rovitto, Mariella Crisci

783   Interaction of Law, Culture, and Political Attitudes in Integration: Comparison of Four Countries Hosting Syrian Refugees
Ayşegül Balta Özgen

894   The "DREAMers" social movement in the context of hostile anti-immigration policies in the United States.
Jorge G. Arenas

812   Selfish States and Global Challenges of Human Mobility: COVID-19 Crisis as an Opportunity for States?
Kadir Onur Unutulmaz

780   Complementary Protection Between Human Rights Obligations and Humanitarian Motives: Italian Case Study

Gabriella Morrone, Maria Teresa Rovitto, Mariella Crisci

Complementary protection has emerged over the last decades as a generic label including all such forms of protection used by States to avoid the return of asylum seekers who have failed their claim under the 1951 Geneva Convention but cannot be returned to their countries of origin for various reasons, and in order to comply with their *non-refoulement* obligation under international law. Although the term is not specifically defined in any international instrument, it nevertheless arises from international human rights obligations that are based not only on article 33 of the Geneva Convention, but also more widely on various international human rights instrument – to name a few, art. 3 of CAT, art. 66 of ICCPR, art. 3 of ECHR. In the CEAS, such possibility is set out in Considerandum 15 of the Qualification Directive 2011/95, that establishes the possibility for member states to allow third country nationals to remain in their territories on a "discretionary basis on compassionate or humanitarian grounds", therefore falling outside of the scope of the Directive.

This paper seeks to explore the scope of complementary protection, and its connection to human rights law, with a specific outlook towards the Italian protection system; the aim being to investigate how such form of residual protection has translated into Italian law and has been interpreted by Courts and implemented by asylum officials over the last decade, and lastly to inquire its compliance with international and European standards, as well as to analyze its potentialities and shortfalls.

As for the methodology, the first part of this paper explores the international and European legal frameworks on complementary protection and then focuses on the evolution of relevant national legislation. The challenges in the implementation of such legislation are also examined, by analyzing both the evolution of national caselaw on humanitarian protection and the work of the administrative authorities responsible for refugee status determination at the national level. Last, the paper will explore what indicators of vulnerability and human rights violations usually emerge from asylum interviews – in order to draw an overview of the categories that fall into this type of protection. The paper also offers an overview on the main statistical trends related to the application of complementary protection over the last years – when the main legislative changes have occurred – using available data from the Ministry of Interior.

As a result, this work provides a broad picture of the beneficiaries of complementary protection in Italy as well as of the main grounds for its application, measuring its impact on the actual needs of the Country's migrant population. In conclusion, it shows how the interpretation effort made by Italian administrative authorities and Courts has pushed complementary protection even beyond the principle of *non-refoulement* and the main human rights obligations mentioned above, thus creating an instrument that is able to cover the wider principle of human dignity, and at the same time a powerful political tool for States' discretionary policies.

References

Ineli-Ciger, M., Bauloz, C., Singer, S., & Stoyanova, V. (Eds.) (2015). Seeking Asylum in the European Union: Selected Protection Issues Raised by the Second Phase of the Common Asylum System. Brill Academic Publishers.

Feijen, L. (2021). The Evolution of Humanitarian Protection in European Law and Practice. Cambridge University Press.

Foster, M. (2009). Non-Refoulement on the basis of socio-economic deprivation: the scope of complementary protection in international human rights law. New Zealand Law Review, (2), 57-310.

Hathaway, J.C. (2005). *The Rights of Refugees under International Law*. Cambridge University Press.

McAdam, J. (2007). Complementary Protection in International Refugee Law. Oxford University Press.

Sadowski, P. (2019). A Safe Harbour or a Sinking Ship? On the Protection of Fundamental Rights of Asylum Seekers in Recent CJEU Judgments. European Journal of Legal Studies, 11(2), 29-64.

783   Interaction of Law, Culture, and Political Attitudes in Integration: Comparison of Four Countries Hosting Syrian Refugees

Ayşegül Balta Özgen

In this paper, I discuss the impact of perceived temporariness on the experiences of integration of Syrian refugees in Canada, Germany, Turkey, and the United States. I ask: What are the structural conditions under which the perception of temporariness takes shape? How does the perception of temporariness influence the possibilities of integration? What can we learn about integration from the comparison of the policies and practices in different countries? Based on 130 in-depth interviews (98 with refugees and 32 with key informants) in four countries, I argue that refugees do not experience the permanent versus temporary legal status dichotomy as rigid and inflexible; rather, their experiences involve cultural and political elements that complicate and problematize the conventional dichotomous understanding. Eventually, their perception of temporariness impacts their integration in distinct ways. This paper aims to contribute to discussions that try to understand the meaning and implications of temporariness beyond the dichotomy of temporary versus permanent. We do not often see how refugees themselves perceive this dichotomy from their own perspective, and I aim to fill this gap. I add to the debates that unsettle "the taken-for-granted links between status, belonging, and inclusion in a single nation state" (Latham et al. 2014:6).

Reference

Latham, Robert, Leah F. Vosko, Valerie Preston, and Melisa Bréton. 2014. "Introduction: Liberating Temporariness? Imagining Alternatives to Permanence as a Pathway for Social Inclusion." Pp. 3-31 in *Liberating Temporariness? Migration, Work, and Citizenship in an Age of Insecurity*, edited by L. Vosko, V. Preston, and R. Latham. Montreal and Kingston: McGill-Queen's University Press.

894   The "DREAMers" social movement in the context of hostile anti-immigration policies in the United States.

Jorge G. Arenas

The presidential period of Donald Trump (2017-2021) gave way to a profound change in the national and international policy of U.S.A., due to the radical nature of the content of his actions, which reflected a distancing from the former presidents, and polarized opinion even within the members of the Republican

Party that elevated him. This was the case of his policy regarding immigration issues, which, under the categorical statement of "Zero Tolerance", justified actions such as the separation of minors from undocumented parents captured in that country; a measure refrained by the same government in the face of national and international repulse. Several international organizations and important sectors of U.S. society itself expressed their rejection of such punitive measures against undocumented immigrants, to the point of pointing out that they have caused a humanitarian crisis.

It is not surprising then that the intolerance that Trump showed for immigration policy issues was also applied to the specific sector of young immigrants known as the "DREAMers", which is the matter of this study. The designation of DREAMers includes a particular type of young undocumented immigrants who entered U.S. territory as children in the company of their parents (or of relatives or close friends who took them under their guardianship during their journey). However, for this sector of young people, the American dream suddenly became a nightmare, as they realized that the country where they have developed their roots and social experiences, where they have built their daily lives and forged their expectations according to the values of American society, was the entity that denied them recognition as citizens.

The DREAM Act proposes to grant legal status to certain undocumented immigrants who entered to the United States as children, who have lived and gone to school in this country, and who assume their identity as Americans. The DREAMers owe their nickname to this law, but it also lends itself to the double interpretation of undocumented youth with hopes and dreams for a better future. For some young people belonging to this movement, the term DREAMers, although attractive to the mass media (as it aligns with the ideal of the "American Dream"), does not reflect the aspect of resilience in the face of adversity and discrimination, so they would actually prefer another appellation such as "DOers".

This study draw from relevant literature (Nicholls and Fiorito 2015, Peréz 2016, Truax 2015, Nicholls 2013, Cruz 2016) to track the rise and development of such important social movement in the contemporary history of the EE.UU. The social movement of the DREAMers illustrates the situation of almost one million Mexican and Latin-American immigrants, which suddenly faced such adverse conditions and persecution on part of American authorities that almost pushed them to the verge of massive deportation. In order to offset their adverse situation, the DREAMers put into practice a broad range of strategies and mobilization resources, which combined a clever capacity of organization with attractive symbols that strengthened the image of the DREAMers as worthy citizens that deserved those opportunities conferred in the past to similar immigrants.

References

Cruz, Estefanía. 2016. "Young Immigrants' Association and the Future Latino Leadership in the U.S.: Dreamers' Social Capital and Political Engagement." *Norteamérica* (Año 11, 2):165-191.

Nicholls, Walter J. 2013. *The DREAMers: how the undocumented youth movement transformed the immigrants rights debate*. Standford, California: Stanford University.

Nicholls, Walter J., and Tara Fiorito. 2015. "Dreamers Unbound: Immigrant Youth Mobilizing." *New Labor Forum* 24 (1):86-92.

Peréz, Zenén Jaimes. 2016. "A force to be reckoned with." *The Sur File on Migration and Human Rights* 13 (23):85-95.

Truax, Eileen. 2015. *Dreamers: an immigrant generation´s fight for their American dream*. Boston, USA: Beacon Press.

812 Selfish States and Global Challenges of Human Mobility: COVID-19 Crisis as an Opportunity for States?

Kadir Onur Unutulmaz

Most widespread theoretical approaches to international relations tend to revolve around concepts such as international anarchy, self-relying and competitive states, a lot of wars. While there have been various failed attempts previously, since 1945, a renewed faith is visible in the ability of states to create sustainable cooperation mechanisms, through regimes and institutions to deal with common/mutual issues, and thereby replacing the anarchy in the international system with the eventual formation of an international society. With globalization, increasing interdependencies of various states to one another, and the unprecedented growth in the pace and volume of flows of information, capital, goods and people, a new concept of global governance started to become popular.

Global governance, i.e. polycentric, multi-level, dynamic processes of interactive decision-making and coordination by multiple actors through norm-based and often informal international regimes, has been an important point of discussion in recent decades. Does it effectively work? Will it be sustainable? Is it going to make (nation-) states redundant in time? The actual discussion, however, appears to come down to 'intergovernmentalism'- the argument that states cooperate with international actors and abide by international regimes only when and in so far as it is in their interests. When such cooperation is significantly in conflict with such national interests, most states appear to look for ways to bail out, and the most powerful of them usually find such ways.

This study reviews the actions and discourses of a diverse set of states during the COVID-19 pandemic in this context. By its very nature, this crisis made the necessity of international coordination and global cooperation abundantly clear, highlighting the importance of institutions like World Health Organization. By contrast, however, the way various states handled the Pandemic could be seen very self-centered and even selfish. In no other issue area was this point so clearly demonstrated than it was regarding migration and asylum.

Relying on a comprehensive review of media sources, official reports, and academic literature, this study aims to discuss the significant implications of states' behavior during a global pandemic regarding human mobility and particularly asylum-seekers.

Chair: Inci Aksu Kargin, Usak University, Turkey

838   Food security of temporary foreign farm workers under the seasonal agricultural worker program in Canada and the United States: a scoping review
Samer Al-Bazz

829   Between Insecurity and Agency: (Im)Mobility in Una-Sana Canton, Bosnia & Herzegovina
Philipp Themann

855   The Role of Capitals in Migrants' Onward Migration Aspirations: The Syrian refugees in Turkey as a case study
Ibrahim Sirkeci and İnci Aksu Kargin

883   Gender-Based Violence in the Line of Transition: Stories From Nigerian Female Migrant Survivors
Avwerosuoghene Hope Golah-Ebue

838   Food security of temporary foreign farm workers under the seasonal agricultural worker program in Canada and the United States: a scoping review

Samer Al-Bazz

Background

Temporary foreign farm workers (TFWs) working under the temporary foreign worker programs (TFWP) in Canada and the United States are among the most vulnerable and exploitable groups. Recent research has shown alarming rates of food insecurity among this group.

Objectives

This study undertakes a scoping review of the literature to explore the extent research has addressed food security of TFWs in Canada and the United States, what geographic areas are represented, summarize findings, determine current status of knowledge, and identify research gaps.

Design

Online databases and government and non-government websites were searched for peer reviewed and non-peer reviewed papers and reports published between 1966-2020 on food security of TFWs for review. Identified papers were quantitatively analyzed to determine publication type, country, year, target population, and main findings. Content analysis was performed to identify major themes.

Results

Of the 291 citations identified, 11 citations were relevant and met selection criteria and were selected for the final review. All articles were peer-reviewed; all citations referred to the U.S. SAWP only; none addressed the Canadian SAWP. six publications (55%) reported quantitative cross-sectional studies, one quasi-experimental study, and 4 (36%) did not provide the study design. The study population in most of the articles (91%) comprised Latino/Mexican/Hispanic TFWs. From the content analysis, 11 themes emerged which were collated under 4 overarching categories.

Conclusion

Research on the food security of TFWs working under the Canadian and American SAWP is scarce. There is a need to advance research to address this vulnerable group particularly within Canadian context. There is also a need to transition future research agenda from pure quantitative to qualitative studies that explore lived experiences of TFWs and key informants about factors contributing to the high food insecurity prevalence among TFWs in Canada.

829   Between Insecurity and Agency: (Im)Mobility in Una-Sana Canton, Bosnia & Herzegovina

Philipp Themann

Una-Sana Canton is situated in the north-west of Bosnia and Herzegovina, in direct proximity to the Croatian border. The geographical closeness to the EU's external border and the infrastructural connections make it an ideal starting point for the onward journey of many displaced people to the European Union. This is why the cities of Bihać and Velica Kladuša have been major transit points for refugees on their way to the European Union for several years. Due to the intensified border protection and the illegal push-backs of the Croatian border police, Una-Sana has also become a place where displaced people are forced to stay on. In this way, they are deprived of their chance and right to apply for asylum once they have crossed the border.

In the Canton, forced migrants can be found (1) in central, state-recognised camps, (2) in the periphery of the towns in larger mutually solidarity communities in empty houses, collapsed industrial buildings, so-called squats or in wooded surroundings of the towns, so-called jungle camps, (3) in various localities in smaller mutually solidarity communities in the immediate vicinity to the Croatian border (for instance just before they cross the border) or in some few cases (4) hidden in private houses by Bosnian citizens.

The freedom of movement of these forced migrants is extremely limited as a result of police repression by Bosnian authorities and their being moved to official and informal shelters. Increasing control mechanisms and multiscalar migration and border regimes create specific spaces of immobility (CRESSWELL & MERRIMAN 2011, SCHEWEL 2019). Besides police repression, lacking resources to meet (basic) needs and the numerous push-backs by Croatian border officials exacerbate this space of immobility. The findings from this field research indicate that the immobilisation of refugees and their precarious socio-economic living conditions in predominantly informal housing infrastructures is mainly caused by the EU border regime and respective state-organised orders of violence (BEZNEC et al 2016).

For this reason, I am concerned in this research with the questions of what strategies refugees develop to deal with protracted displacement, marginalization, and immobility (ETZOLD et al. 2019). Furthermore, I will examine the interrelations between official and informal shelter infrastructure (see above) and how they are connected through social interaction and translocal connectivity (WALTERS 2015). From this perspective, refugees do not act independently, but organize themselves in social relations and networks in which they are embedded. Translocal connectivity is considered to be of high importance in this context, for example, to be connected to close family members, relatives, and friends in a wide variety of locations, thereby enabling individual mobility phases (SCHAPENDONK 2015). In the context of this article, these connections will be analyzed under the aspect of the individual or collective agency of refugees. Finally, the question will be addressed to what extent the observations in Una-Sana are reflected in current scientific-geographical debates and at which points they should be complemented or combined.

The paper is based on a two-week research in Bosnia and Herzegovina between December 28, 2020 and January 10, 2021 in which mixed qualitative and ethnographic research methods were applied.

References

BEZNEC, B.; SPEER, M.; MITROVIĆ, M. (2016): Governing the Balkan route: Macedonia, serbia and the european Border regime. Belgrade: Research Paper Series of Rosa Luxemburg Stiftung South East Europe. (5).

CRESSWELL, T.; MERRIMAN, P. (Eds.) (2011): Geographies of Mobilities: Practices, Spaces, Subjects. Farnham / Burlington: Ashgate.

ETZOLD, B.; BELLONI, M.; KING, R.; KRALER; A.; PASTORE, F. (2019): Transnational Figurations of DisplacementConceptualising protracted displacement andtranslocal connectivity through a process-oriented perspective. TRAFIG working paper, No. 1.

SCHAPENDONK, J. (2015): What if Networks Move? Dynamic Social Networking in the Context of African Migration to Europe. Population, Space and Place, 21(8), 809–819. https://doi.org/10.1002/psp.1860

SCHEWEL, K. (2019): Understanding Immobility: Moving Beyond the Mobility Bias in Migration Studies. International Migration Review, 1(1), https://doi.org/10.1177/0197918319831952

WALTERS, W. (2015): Migration, vehicles, and politics: Three theses on viapolitics. European Journal of Social Theory, 18(4), 469–488. https://doi.org/10.1177/1368431014554859

855   The Role of Capitals in Migrants' Onward Migration Aspirations: The Syrian refugees in Turkey as a case study

Ibrahim Sirkeci and İnci Aksu Kargin

The motivations behind the migration act have been some of the main interests of several scholars and the focus of a wide range of theoretical discussions. The Conflict Model of Migration, which is one of the novel approaches on human mobility, claims that the main dynamic behind the human mobility is the individuals' 'perception of insecurity.' Thus, the model avoids making a classification of voluntary and involuntary migration, since in either case the individuals decide to migrate in response to their high perception of insecurity. The model also sets forth that, even though the would-be refugees have the aspiration to engage in international migration, they can only do so if they have sufficient capitals, which are stated as financial, social, human, and physical capitals. Finally, the model asserts that, if the individuals' perception of insecurity continues in the first country of asylum, they might engage in onward migration, either as a return to their homeland or migration to a third country. By employing in-depth interviews with Syrian refugees in Gaziantep, Turkey and using the Conflict Model of Migration as a theoretical framework, this study aims to analyze what kind of capitals the refugees own, how the amount of capitals they own influence their perception of insecurity in Turkey, and their aspirations for onward migration. Although the model essentially claims that the capitals play a role mainly during the flight period, this research contributes to the literature by displaying that the role of capitals is not limited to the flight period; it also shapes the refugees' perception of insecurity in the host society and their aspirations for onward migration. Based on the narratives of Syrian refugees, we suggest in this study that the more capitals the refugees own in their host country, the lower their perception of insecurity, and thus have a greater tendency to become permanent in the host country and have less aspiration to engage in onward migration, either as a return to their homeland or migration to a third country.

883 Gender-Based Violence in the Line of Transition: Stories From Nigerian Female Migrant Survivors

Avwerosuoghene Hope Golah-Ebue

(883) Avwerosuoghene Hope Golah-EbueEvery year several women and girls leave their countries in the hope of finding a better place and country to live in, while some of these migratory women use legal means to relocate, others use illegal routes to flee their country. According to some scholars some of these women flee their counties where they are exposed to violence in an uncertain journey in the hope of finding safety in a new country[1]. In recent times, it has been revealed that young Nigerians make up the largest population of migrants from Africa to developed countries, in 2016 alone, over 20,000 Nigerians crossed the Mediterranean sea including young girls and women[2]. Many of which were done to escape the dire economic situations in Nigeria, unemployment, discrimination, and exploitation as well as the insecurity in the nation ranging from the Boko Haram crisis, Fulani-Herders clash, kidnapping, arm robbery among others, which all contribute to amplifying violence in Nigeria.

This paper explores the various forms of Gender-based violence-GBV- Nigerian females face as they seek for better livelihood, social upliftment, and economic stability before, during and after their migration journeys, to other parts of the world especially to Europe and America. Extant literatures have revolved majorly on the aspect of Human trafficking of Nigerian women and girls, whereas other vital aspects of GBV which encompasses Human Trafficking such as rape, domestic violence, assault, psychological and emotional abuse as well as physical abuse of Nigerian females have remained highly undertheorized. Hence the need for this study as it provides a shift from human trafficking especially for sex to other forms of violence pertaining to Nigerian female migrants. The paper also outline why Nigerian females continue to embark on such torturous journeys across borders. For instance, between 2014 - 2019, Nigerian females who arrived in Europe increased from 1,454 to 11, 009 respectively, accounting for more than 50% increase in female migration[3].

This work made use of stories and reviews from literature, to extract information on Nigerian females who survived various forms of violence, mainly from those that embarked on irregular migration. The paper comprised of secondary data drafts gotten from Human Right Watch, International Organization for Migration, newspapers, articles, reports and the local Nigerian newspapers to analyse the data gotten from qualitative literature review. One major aspect revealed from the analysis indicated that over half of Nigerian women and girls reported sexual violence and abuse on their journeys which are done multiple times simultaneously[4]. The paper further advocate for the Nigerian government to fully implement across all states in Nigeria, the laws to protect violence against women as well as Gender-based violence. Also, more opportunities should be created for young people in government and other aspects of the economy, which will drive the upward growth of the Nigerian economy as it will in turn foster reduction of irregular migration from Nigeria to other parts of the world.

References

Parish, A. (2017). Gender-Based Violence against Women: Both Cause for Migration and Risk along the Journey. Migration Policy [Online]. September 7. Available at: https://www.migrationpolicy.org/article/gender-based-violence-against-women-both-cause-migration-and-risk-along-journey [Accessed February 20, 2021].

Ikuteyijo, L. (2020). **Why young Nigerians risk illegal migration to find their 'Eldorado'.** *The Conversation* **[Online]. January 21. Available @** https://theconversation.com/why-young-nigerians-risk-illegal-migration-to-find-their-eldorado-129996 [Accessed January 30, 2021].

Odhiambo, A. (2019). *"You Pray for Death" Trafficking of Women and Girls in Nigeria.* Human Rights Watch, United State. 1-98.

United Nations International Children's Emergency Fund [UNICEF] (2017). *A Deadly Journey for Children: The Central Mediterranean Migration Route.* New York: UNICEF. 1-20.

9H   COVID-19 Impact

588   Impact of the COVID-19 pandemic on migration processes in the Russian Far East and in the countries of Northeast Asia

Evgenii Gamerman

The purpose of this scientific work: to analyze the impact of the global coronavirus pandemic on migration processes, on existing trends in this area, in the region of Northeast Asia, as well as in the Far East of Russia, which is directly adjacent to the region.

Methods

Within the framework of this article, an extrapolation method was used, which made it possible to compare the situation in the field of migration before the onset of the pandemic, as well as one year after its onset. In addition, a comparative method was used, which made it possible to compare, identify common trends and differences between different countries of the region, as well as between the countries of NEA and the Russian Far East. In addition, a statistical method was used that made it possible to analyze and compare the digital indicators of migration in different countries and in the region as a whole.

Literature review

There is a fairly large layer of scientific literature on migration processes in the Russian Far East. These are the works of Academician L. Rybakovsky, Far Eastern scientists E. Motrich, S. Mishchuk. The works of the Siberian scientist E. Anokhina are devoted to the migration processes in modern China, as well as in the scientific works and dissertation of E, Trakova. Similar processes in modern Japan are considered in the works of E. Shevtsova and L. Avetisyan. Migration of the Korean Peninsula is considered in the works of Y. Minkhairova. As for the current state of migration processes in the Russian Far East and in the countries of Northeast Asia, and the impact of the coronavirus pandemic on them, these issues are currently unexplored

Research results

In the course of the conducted research, it was possible to establish serious changes in the migration processes that are taking place in the region. And this is not surprising, given the pandemic, the closure of partial or complete borders, and the tightening of quarantine measures. One of the first to experience serious changes was the Russian Far East. First, labor migration has dropped significantly. There were practically no Chinese workers left who drove the border enterprises in large quantities. Because of this, the construction industry has suffered a lot, residential buildings are not being built, infrastructure facilities are not being erected. This led to higher prices, lower living standards. The situation with internal migration has also changed. The rate of population outflow from the Russian Far East has significantly decreased, which has been the main trend over the past 30 years in the life of these territories. Residents of the region's countries have also felt the shortage of migrants in a number of sectors of the national economy.

Conclusions

Thus, despite the fact that Northeast Asia is not perceived as a traditional region with a high level of migration flows, this phenomenon has covered all countries in the region. And the coronavirus pandemic could not help but hit most NEA countries, seriously transforming migration flows and trends.

Literature

Anokhina E, "New" Chinese Migration and the PRC's Policy on Its Regulation. - Tomsk, 2012 - 248 p.

Minhairova J. Migration in the Republic of Korea // Kazan Bulletin of Young Scientists. 2018.Vol. 2.No. 1 (4). S. 45 -54

Mischuk S. Internal and international migration in the Russian Far East in the middle of the XIX - early XXI century. // News of the Russian Academy of Sciences. Geographic series. 2013. No. 6. P. 33-42

Motrich E. Population of the Russian Far East. Vladivostok. 2006.224 s.

Rybakovsky L. Population of the Far East for 100 years (monograph). - Moscow, "Science", 1969.180 p.

Trakova E. Internal migration of the population in the PRC in the course of economic reforms (2000-2016). Abstract of the dissertation for the degree of candidate of economic sciences. Moscow. 2018 - 29 p.

Shevtsova E. Japan's migration policy: lessons for improving the federal and regional migration policy of Russia // Bulletin of NSUEU. 2009. No. 2. P. 61 -67

590   Closing the border for Chinese migration in the Russian Far East due to the COVID-19 pandemic: kill coronavirus or kill cross-border interaction?

Olga Zalesskaia

By the beginning of the 21st century, the Chinese migration has become an integral part of the Russian Far East (RFE) socio-economic life. The economic activity of the Chinese migration has a direct impact on the development of Sino-Russian cooperation at all levels. Sino-Russian cross-border interaction in the RFE are important to consider, as well as last year it was interrupted: the Sino-Russian border in the RFE was closed to prevent the spread of a new type of coronavirus.

Nowadays, ethnic and migration studies remain "a rag-tag field," defined by one scholar as "a ragged field of study, not an intellectually unified discipline". [35] Scholars have mainly studied the socio-economic aspects of the Chinese migration to the RFE, as well as the peculiarities of the Chinese migrants' legal status. [36] Yet the daily Sino-Russian interaction, including cross-border interaction has not yet sufficiently been analyzed.

The purpose of this study is to analyze the role of Chinese migration in the RFE border area as an integral part of cross-border Sino-Russian cooperation and to consider the changes in the situation of Chinese migration after border closures due to the COVID pandemic last year. This article explores this interaction, as it is most obvious in the RFE border, where, due to the geographical proximity of Russian and China, maximum rapprochement occurs.

This article argued that Chinese migration has functioned as an actor in the cross-border cooperation in the RFE. The COVID pandemic has halted a significant part of Sino-Russian cross-border cooperation. The Chinese stopped coming to the RFE, they lost interest in investing these territories, and it is already obvious that such extraordinary circumstances will seriously hinder the development of cross-border cooperation in the future. Killing the coronavirus, the cross-border Sino-Russian interaction was practically killed.

617   From offline to online: how the Lockdown challenged the refugee services in Italy

Claudia Lintner

This article focuses on the dimension identified in the IOM study (Guadagno, 2020) of accessing appropriate care services, through study of the experiences of social services in Italy during the two-month Lockdown – from March 2020 to May 2020 – by asking social workers, volunteers and other professionals involved to evaluate the accessibility of services for refugee groups during this period.

To lay the groundwork for analysing the complexities experienced by social services in Italy during the two-month Lockdown in reaching refugees and

[35] DeTona, C., Frisina, A., & Ganga, D. (2019). Research methods in Ethnic and Migration Studies. In Sirkeci, I., Iosifides, T., DeTona, C., & Frisina, A. (Eds.), Reader in Qualitative Methods in Migration Research (pp. 7–9). London, Transnational Press London.
[36] Larin, V. (2020). "Chinese expansion" in the eastern regions of Russia at the beginning of the XXI century through the prism of comparative analysis. In Comparative politics. Vol. 11, No. 2, pp. 9-27; Luzyanin, S. G., Zhao, H. (Eds.). (2020). Rossijsko-kitajskij dialog: model' 2020 [Russian-Chinese Dialogue: Model 2020]. Moscow, NP RSMD, No. 58, 254 p; Song, Chenghua & Ouyang, Lingyao. (2020). Analysis of modernizing countermeasures of economic and trade cooperation of Heilongjiang province with Russia against the background of the construction of a free trade zone. In Shangye jingji. No. 6, pp. 11-12. (In Chin.); Tong Yifu. (2020). Study of Cross-Border Port Trade between Heilongjiang Province and Russia]. In Shangye jingji. No. 3, pp. 11-13. (In Chin.); Zalesskaia, O. (2019). The entrepreneurial activity of Chinese migrants on the border areas of Russia and China at the turn of the centuries: the features of "shuttle" migration in the context of state and regional policy. In Journal of Economy Culture and Society. Vol. 60, pp. 27-44., etc.

asylum seekers, the research adopted a qualitative approach to understand the complex settings through semi-structured interviews.

This article shed light on how social and digital inequalities are experienced by refugees and highlights the consequences of this intersection in times of crisis. Three causes of the digital divide amongst refugees during the Covid-19 pandemic emerged from the interview data: affordability, which distinguished between refugees with access to digital devices and those without. The second factor which emerged from the data related to accessibility in terms of electricity and connectivity. The third factor influencing access to technology related to digital literacy. To use services that have been transferred online and to participate in home school activities, for example, advanced digital literacy skills are necessary.

621   The COVID-19: Bringing the notion of "nation-state citizenship" back in?

Deniz Eroğlu Utku

The Covid-19 pandemic brought the many concepts under criticism of scholars. Capitalism, the power of international organisations, the argument of globalisation, cosmopolitan values and even the concept of global citizenship have been re-thought. Quarantine days pave the way for questioning significant concepts with respect to citizenship as well, namely the ability to guarantee rights, performing duties and participation, feeling secure, and who belongs and who is excluded. Against the argument of citizenship beyond states, the paper will explore that Covid-19 demonstrated nation state citizenship is still important; lack of it makes immigrants quiet vulnerable. In this paper, it is argued that although international organisations and norms promise to broad the range of rights people can enjoy, immigrants without the legal status of citizenship could not enjoy these rights as nation-states relied upon Covid-19 measures. That process showed that neo-liberal countries failed to provide citizenship rights to those who do not have formal citizenship status, although they are part of prominent international organisations and treaties.

This study begins with explaining the meaning of citizenship. Here, two competing notions of citizenship are highlighted: the national citizenship and post-national citizenship. Since 18th century nation states are key institutions to decide who can access and be the member of their political community (Staeheli, 1999: 62). They are indicated as main provider for citizenship rights, including economic, political and social ones (Marshall, 1950). However, scholars started to consider a wider understanding of citizenship as the role of international organisations and human rights norms increased in the international arena. According to them, the process of globalisation has paved the way for eroding centrality of nation-state (Soysal 1994). Relying on this theoretical discussion, the paper next moves onto the role of the key international organisations in the Covid-19 process. As post-national citizenship arguments attribute high importance to the development of international organisations and treaties, its important to take a look the role of the key organisations during the pandemic. Later on the paper discusses non-citizens', particularly refugees', positions in the pandemic and indicates their limited access to basic rights with respect to the health and security.

All in all the paper shows that lack of national citizenship jeopardies even basic human rights of immigrants and puts their life in danger in the process of Covid-19 pandemic. In that sense, despite post-national claims, international organizations and treaties are inefficient to provide rights as nation states justify their treatment by relying on Covid-19 threat.

12:15-12:45 BREAK

Day Four 9 July 2021 - 12:45-14:45
Plenary Session IV [Click here to Join]
Moderator: **Dr Bahar Baser Ozturk, Coventry University, UK**
Keynote Speakers:
- Dr **Élise Féron**, Tampere Peace Research Institute, Tampere University, Finland: "**Diasporas, new generations, and homeland conflicts: between transmission and rearticulation of the conflict heritage**"
- **Camilla Orjuela**, Professor, School of Global Studies, University of Gothenburg, Sweden: "**Diaspora struggles for memory and justice: opportunities and limitations**"

14:45-15:00 BREAK

Day Four 9 July 2021 - 15:00-16:30
10A   Environment and Migration
530   Examining millennia of climate migration to understand climate change migration
Ilan Kelman
664   Potential implications of changing climate for human sustainability and migration across Asian Russia
Amber J. Soja, Elena I. Parfenova, Nadezhda M. Tchebakova, Susan G. Conard
799   Global Warming and Climate Refugees of 21st Century: A Threat Assessment of Sea Level Rise for the Looming Humanitarian Crisis
Ismail Utku Canturk
820   Reservoir-induced displacement and social participation: Evidence from the Spanish dictatorship
Laura Munoz Blanco
898   Catalyzing decision making for migration and sustainable water-energy-food systems - The Texas case study
Konstantinos Pappas

530   Examining millennia of climate migration to understand climate change migration

Ilan Kelman

Objectives

Many locations are being told that they must prepare to migrate due to climate change, with several initiatives currently ongoing or being planned. This paper places these discussions of, and actions on, climate change migration—which are often based on assumptions that cannot be fully supported (Hartmann, 2010; Nicholson, 2014)—within the context of humanity's millennia of climate migration.

Methods

Starting from foundational conceptual literature alongside basic definitions within international frameworks, this research sought to:

(i)   Define and identify refugees and migrants due to climate and due to climate change from any time period.

(ii)   Develop a method for counting these people, to indicate who is moving now due to climate and due to climate change as well as considering models for future movement scenarios.

Results

Significant problems were shown in defining, identifying, counting, and projecting movement and lack of movement (immobility) due to climate and due to climate change. Discourses can centre around "climate refugees" or "climate change refugees" without factoring in the legal aspects of refugee status (Lister, 2014). Considering "climate migrants" and "climate change migrants", wider and deeper understandings of migration and immobility are frequently subsumed by dominating assumptions which are based in neither basic science nor key policy documents (Hartmann, 2010; Nicholson, 2014). History, especially, is not fully considered, to recognise how patterns of human migration over millennia are sometimes influenced by climate and changes in it (Pei et al., 2018). Today, immobility due to human-caused climate change within wider contexts is particularly neglected (Ayeb-Karlsson et al., 2018).

For labelling, calculating, and counting people migrating or immobile due to climate and due to climate change, subjective choices are required from the beginning. Consequently, numbers tallied are easily challenged from a scientific basis. Ultimately, it appears to not be possible to develop and apply a repeatable, robust, and verifiable method for calculating, counting, or projecting the number of people migrating or not migrating due to climate change. Meanwhile, examples from history indicate that people migrating due to climate can be tabulated in specific instances (e.g. Pei et al., 2018).

Overall, nuances, subtleties, provisos, and historical contexts raised by theoretical, empirical, and policy research are often bypassed in contemporary work, despite them pervading choices and lack of choices for people's migration and immobility due to human-caused climate change (Ayeb-Karlsson *et al.,* 2018; Hartmann, 2010; Nicholson, 2014). To ensure a scientific foundation based on history, combined with contemporary challenges and opportunities, it might be counterproductive for migration and immobility to:

(i)   Seek causality from human-caused climate change, whereas causality from climate can be much clearer.

(ii)   Focus on actual or projected numbers.

Conclusions

The keys for understanding the intersection (or lack thereof) between each of (i) climate and climate change and (ii) migration and immobility tend to be resources and choices to act. Most commonly, climate can heavily influence those resources and choices, as has happened throughout history, but human-caused climate change should not be characterised as either an inevitable or sole forcer of migration or immobility.

References

Ayeb-Karlsson, S., C.D. Smith, and D. Kniveton. 2018. A discursive review of the textual use of 'trapped' in environmental migration studies: The conceptual birth and troubled teenage years of trapped populations. *Ambio,* 47, 557–573.

Hartmann, B. 2010. Rethinking Climate Refugees and Climate Conflict: Rhetoric, Reality and the Politics of Policy Discourse. *Journal of International Development,* 22, 233–246.

Lister, M. 2014. Climate change refugees. *Critical Review of International Social and Political Philosophy,* 17, 618–634.

Nicholson, C. 2014. Climate Change and the Politics of Causal Reasoning: The Case of Climate Change and Migration. *The Geographical Journal,* 180, 151–160.

Pei, Q., H.F. Lee, and D.D. Zhang. 2018. Long-term association between climate change and agriculturalists' migration in historical China. *The Holocene,* 28, 208–216.

664   Potential implications of changing climate for human sustainability and migration across Asian Russia

Amber J. Soja, Elena I. Parfenova, Nadezhda M. Tchebakova, Susan G. Conard

Past human migrations have been associated with climate change. As our civilizations and infrastructure developed, humans depended less on the external environment. Asian Russia is currently sparsely populated, with most of the population in southern regions of forest-steppe where fertile soils support agriculture and climate is reasonably temperate. We used current and predicted climate scenarios from 20 CMIP5 general circulation models to evaluate the potential comfort of climate for human settlement in various landscapes throughout the 21st century. We applied two CO_2 Representative Concentration Pathway scenarios, RCP 2.6 representing mild climate change and RCP 8.5 representing more extreme changes, across Asian Russia. We used three climate indices that relate to human well-being: Ecological Landscape Potential, winter severity, and permafrost coverage. Climates predicted by the 2080s over Asian Russia would be warmer and milder without excessive aridity. The permafrost zone is projected to shift to the northeast. Ecological Landscape Potential in the current permafrost zone would increase from 'low' to 'relatively high' with a resulting higher capacity for human populations across Asian Russia. Understanding ecological landscape potential is crucial information for developing viable strategies for long-term economic and social adaptation to changing climate. We also conducted a GIS analysis of population density with climatic layers of warmth, water resources and climate severity. The resulting bioclimatic model Russia explained 38% of current variation in population density. We applied this population model to the RCP 8.5 scenario. Over most of the country, the potential population density would increase, but it would remain low in permafrost regions in Siberia and the Far East by 2080. This contrasts with demographic projections that the population in Russia may decrease by the mid-century from the present 146 million to 92-120 million people. Thus there will be much more suitable habitat than the expected population. This leaves open the possibility for migration from more southern areas where climate has become less tolerable.

The reported study was supported by RFBR, project number 19-45-240004 («Predictions of the ecological-economic potential for possible "climatic" migrations in the Angara-Yenisei macroregion in a changing climate of the 21st century») funded by Russian Foundation for Basic Research, Government of Krasnoyarsk Territory, Krasnoyarsk Regional Fund of Science.

799   Global Warming and Climate Refugees of 21st Century: A Threat Assessment of Sea Level Rise for the Looming Humanitarian Crisis

Ismail Utku Canturk

As one of the most complex issues that threaten the international security in the 21st century, global warming stems from the anthropogenic deterioration in the structure of the athmosphere. The depletion of ozone layer in the athmosphere is caused by the excessive industrial production (fossil fuels, industrial agriculture and husbandry) and consumption during the Anthropocene; due to the exponential increase in greenhouse gas density within the athmosphere, global temperature levels have increased by approximately 1°C relative to the pre-industrial levels. According to the Intergovernmental Panel on Climate Change (IPCC), this increase is going to be exacerbated to 1,5°C between 2030-2052.[37] Many newer simulations using advanced AI suggest far worse outcomes, asserting that IPCC's predictions are quite optimistic. This brings with it the possibility of one of the worst humanitarian crises in human history: environmental refugees of 21st century. According to Myers, there were at least 25 million environmental refugees globally in 1997; the total number of recorded conventional refugees in the same year is only 22 million. The majority of the environmental refugees reside in sub-Saharran Africa, Indian subcontinent,

---

37 Intergovernmental Panel on Climate Change (IPCC), "Global Warming of 1.5°: Summary for Policymakers", Geneva: IPCC, 2018, 4-10.

China, Mexico and Central America. Myers' famous prediction suggests that rising global sea levels, draughts and disruption of rain patterns is likely to cause existential and agricultural migrations that will increase the number of climate refugees up to 200 million within 21st century.[38]

This work aims to focus specifically on the rising global sea levels and its consequences for coastal and island communities, using various data acquired from contemporary research and simulations that are based off of various scenarios in global temperature rise. Currently, over 60 million people living in China, Bangladesh, India, Vietnam, Indonesia, Thailand, Phillipines and Japan are facing the destructive consequences of the rising sea levels. Thus, not only providing information regarding the volume of humanitarian destruction the sea level rise will cause throughout the 21st century and promoting collective consciousness about the issue, the work focuses on its state-ending aspect. A recent simulation suggests that even in a scenario in which the greenhouse gas emissions are radically reduced, the rising sea levels will result in coastal areas that consist 19%, 26% and %17 of the populations of Bangladesh, Vietnam and Thailand respectively to be completely submerged underwater.[39] Furthermore, the work discusses many questions regarding national sovereignty and historical responsibility over the environmental crisis and connecting them with the phenomenon of global sea level rise; many island states completely vanishing out of existence will create threats in the international relations that are both humanitarian and systemic in conception[40].

820   Reservoir-induced displacement and social participation: Evidence from the Spanish dictatorship

Laura Munoz Blanco

By 2018, 70.8 million people worldwide had been forced to flee from their home (UNHCR, 2019). This paper explores how variation in exposure to internally displaced population that happened in the past affect social participation in host municipalities during the last 40 years. To measure forced displacement, I exploit the displacement associated with the construction of reservoirs during the Spanish dictatorship (1936-1975). And I rely on a newly collected historical dataset on forced displacement and social participation

Empirically, I look at municipalities which received internally displaced persons. I call them host municipalities. To uncover the mechanisms, I also study the effects on the modern municipalities of those municipalities of origin. I call them sending municipalities. To estimate the effects of reservoir-induced displacement, municipalities with at least one reservoir (but, non-generating displacement) and their adjacent municipalities function as my control groups.

---

[38] Myers, Norman, "Environmental Refugees", *Population and Environment: A Journal of Interdisciplinary Studies*, 19(2), November 1997, 167-182.
[39] Kulp, Scott A. and Strauss, Benjamin H., "New elevation data triple estimates of global vulnerability to sea-level rise and coastal flooding", *Nature Communications*, 10(4844), December 2019, 3-4.
[40] Yamamoto, Lilian and Esteban, Miguel, "Vanishing Island States and sovereignty", *Ocean & Coastal Management*, 53(1), January 2010, 1-9.

Importantly, the presence of these control groups allows me to isolate my estimates from reservoir effects on social participation (Duflo and Pande, 2007). Clearly, being exposed to displaced population may be correlated with unobservable variables that may affect social participation. These omitted variables may be endogenous to my outcome variable, which is social participation. To overcome potential endogeneity, I instrument displaced population inflows with reservoir size and distance to closest sending municipality.

The main results point out that exposure to internally displaced persons inflows has long-term and sizable benefits on social participation. Interestingly, the effects occurred right after the arrival of displaced population and persisted for more than 50 years.

In particular, I find that host municipalities exhibit a statistically significant increase in presidential voter turnout of 26 percentage points with respect to the bordering municipalities to those municipalities with a reservoir but never displaced. The effect is significant at the 5\% level and economically important, corresponding to 35\% of the outcome mean in 1976-2015. Total number of agrarian cooperatives is also positively affected by displaced population inflow. The positive effects on agrarian cooperatives persisted during the dictatorship (1936-1975), and the entire democracy (1976-2015). Non-profit associations are statistically non-significant.

I propose two mechanisms for these results: social ties moving together with the population displaced and an upward shift in trust. Results are robust to potential cofounding effects of violence during the dictatorship and to a battery of robustness checks.
Internal displacement as a result of water infrastructures is a reality that affects a significant number of communities worldwide (e.g. Son La Dam (Vietnam), Gilgel Gibe III Dam (Ethiopia-Kenya), or Ituango Dam (Colombia)).

This paper contributes to three strands of the literature. First, it belongs to the growing literature of the economics of forced displacement studying the long-term effects of hosting forced displaced (Alix-Garcia et al., 2018; Murard and Sakalli, 2018; Morales, 2018). Second, it contributes to the literature focusing on the long-term determinants of social participation (Levy, 2018; Cagé and Rueda, 2016). Finally, this paper adds to the literature studying the consequences of infrastructure projects. Among the earlier attempts are the work from Duflo and Pande (2007) and Bao (2012).

References

Alix-Garcia.J and et.al (2018). "Do refugee camps help or hurt hosts? The case of Kakuma, Kenya". In: Journal of Development Economics. 130,66-83.

Bao.X (2012). "Dams and Intergovernmental Transfer: Are Dam Projects Pareto Improving in China". In: Working paper.

Cage´e.J and Rueda.V (2016). "The Long-Term Effects of the Printing Press in sub-Saharan Africa". In: American Economic Journal: Applied Economics 2016, 8(3): 69–99.

Duflo.E and Pande.R (2007). "Dams". In: The Quarterly Journal of Economics, Volume 122, Issue 2, May 2007, Pages 601–646.

Levy.M (2018). "The Effect of Immigration from Mexico on Social Capital in the United States". In: International Migration Review.

Morales.J.S (2018). "The impact of internal displacement on destination communities: evidence from the Colombian conflict". In: Journal of Development Economics Volume 131, March 2018, Pages 132-150.

Murard.E and Sakalli.S.O (2018). "Mass refugee inflow and long-run Prosperity: Lessons from the Greek Population Resettlement". In: IZA Working Paper No. 11613.

UNHCR (2019). "Global Trends. Forced Displacement in 2018". In: United Nations.

898   Catalyzing decision making for migration and sustainable water-energy-food systems - The Texas case study

Konstantinos Pappas

Introduction

Population growth, climate change, resource depletion and consequent rising of water, energy, food prices, and changing disease patterns, are likely to result in increased migration patterns over the next few decades, which requires better understanding and planning. The water, energy and food system, interconnected with migration and economic systems, is under growing pressure to deliver its services both reliably and sustainably to growing demands across multiple sectors. Resource stress can both trigger migration or be triggered by migration and lead to the causation or worsening of associated events.

Objectives

Migration to Texas (internal and international) accounts for half of the state's total population growth, and creates a significant impact on its labor markets (US Census Bureau, 2020; American Immigration Council, 2020). As Texas' population continues to increase, the state's resources may be under pressure. Immigrants will have a difficult time adapting to a WEF resources' strain, on top of existing socio-economic impacts and difficulties accessing services. Multi-sectoral decision-makers lack the tools for quantifying the impact of anticipated migration flows on these interconnected resource systems. This paper, focusing on Texas as a case study, introduces an objective framework to: quantify the impact of different migration scenarios on water-energy-food systems; examine migrants' contribution to Texan economy; evaluate the impact on WEF resources under different migration scenarios in Texas; and develop policy recommendations.

Methodology

The proposed conceptual framework starts with simple population projection which accounts for the gradual increase in population as well as the net inflow of migrants in the projected year. Next, the key interactions in basic and shared resources are identified and an integrated water-energy-food system is developed. Based on different scenarios of net migration inflow, identified food, water and energy portfolios, the feasibility and performance of any proposed scenarios can be assessed while respecting resource system interconnections with local characteristics.

Figure 1. The proposed conceptual scenario-based framework for the case study.

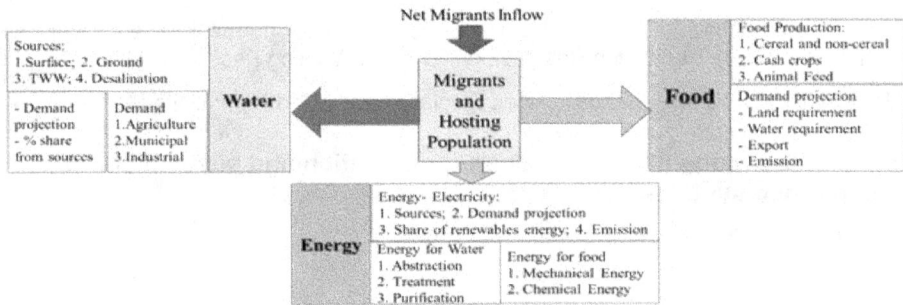

Results

Five different scenarios were developed by changing the production quantities for different types of crops, sources of water, sources of energy and the number of migrants Texas is projected to host and assess the impacts in a future year. The scenarios include migrants' inflows experienced in the past years by Texas, along with selecting a share of sources for water and energy. The lists of food products were chosen in groups which represents the state's food portfolio. The reference year is year 2018, and the resource demand is projected for year 2030 and 2050 under net zero migration condition and assumptions were made for assessing scenarios (TWDB 2017). Figure 2 shows the results for the proposed scenarios.

Conclusions

Understanding how migrants will impact the future size and composition of a country's population and its water, energy, food resources is important for public and private sector decision-makers. This understanding is crucial now when the world seeks facts and expertise for political lobbying on migration related challenges and stimulating discussions for managing synergies between its different dimensions.

References

American Immigration Council. (2020). *Immigrants in Texas.* https://www.americanimmigrationcouncil.org/sites/default/files/research/immigrants_in_texas.pdf

Texas Water Development Board. (2017). *2017 State Water Plan | Texas Water Development Board.* http://www.twdb.texas.gov/waterplanning/swp/2017/

US Census Bureau. (2020, January 2). *Population Estimates Continue to Show the Nation's Growth Is Slowing.* The United States Census Bureau. https://www.census.gov/newsroom/press-releases/2019/popest-nation.html

Figure 2. Assessments for the listed scenarios

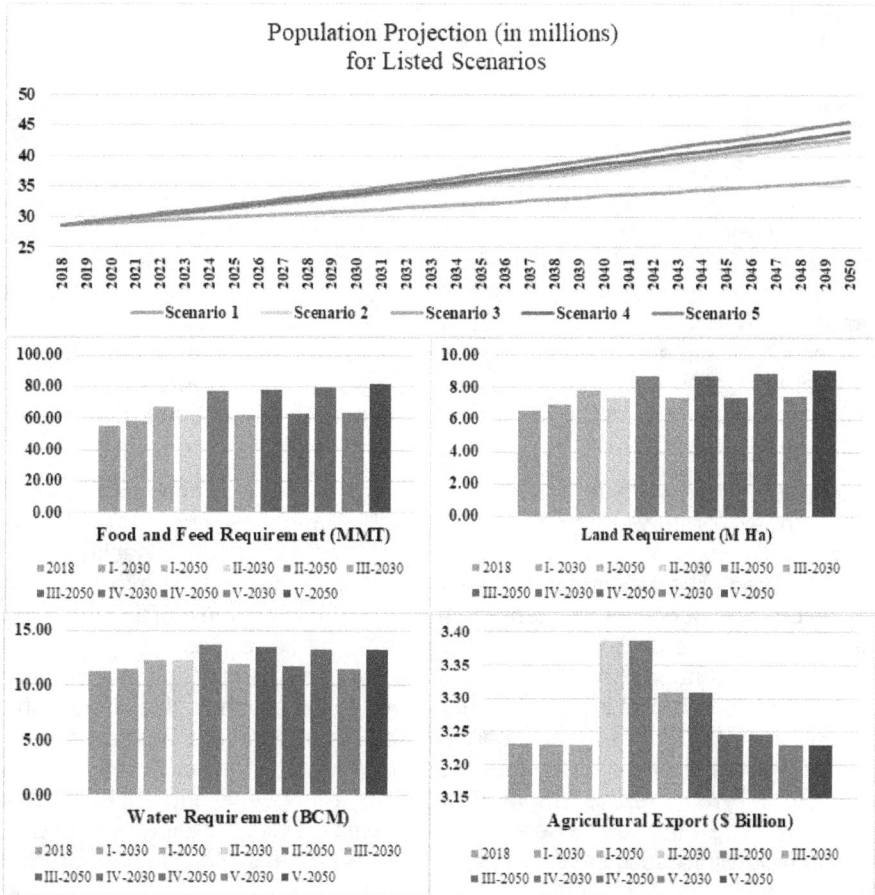

Population Projection (in millions) for Listed Scenarios

——Scenario 1 ——Scenario 2 ——Scenario 3 ——Scenario 4 ——Scenario 5

Food and Feed Requirement (MMT)

Land Requirement (M Ha)

Water Requirement (BCM)

Agricultural Export ($ Billion)

10B Education and Skilled Migration

Chair: Inci Aksu Kargin, Usak University, Turkey

806 The integration of international faculty at Japanese universities: A qualitative approach
Lilan Chen

672 "We are known as aliens": experiences of regional student migration to South Africa
Veera Tagliabue

823 Alternative Politics for Skilled Refugees: a comparative study of Syrians in Canada and Venezuelans in Mexico
Camelia Tigau

824 ***** This presentation has been removed at the request of authors.*****
****

806　The integration of international faculty at Japanese universities: A qualitative approach

Lilan Chen

With the development of economic globalization and the internationalization of higher education, the international mobility of highly skilled talents, such as international faculty, has been an intense concern for policymakers and researchers in recent decades. Despite the perceived value of international faculty, the overall environment in Japan has been criticized as a negative case to migrants (Bartram 2000; Liang 2018). International faculty at Japanese universities have even been criticized as the tokenized symbol of internationalization (Brown, 2019; Brotherhood et al., 2019). To tackle this issue, scholars' attention needs to be directed to not only the recruitment but the integration of this population in Japan (Ota 2018) since integration is the most critical challenge and significant indicator when considering their career experiences (Oishi 2020).

The purpose of this study is to explore the integration of international faculty in Japan. An exploratory study of semi-structural interviews with 40 full-time international faculty hired in Japanese universities with various backgrounds was conducted. The key findings drawn from this study suggest explicitly that from the emic perspectives of international faculty, in the context of their working aspects, equality and acceptance have been perceived as integration. In addition, in the context of their social-cultural aspects, equality and involvement have been considered as integration. Moreover, in the psychological aspect, the attachment to Japan has been characterized as integration. Based on their integration in different aspects, four types of international faculty have been categorized. Type 1 represents those who have low work and socio-cultural integration. Type 2 implies those who have integrated well in their work, but with low integration into social-cultural aspects. Type 3 refers to those who have integrated well in the social-cultural aspects, but with low work integration. Type 4 is those who have integrated well both in work and social-cultural dimensions, and feel at home in Japan. This study also suggests that only when Work integration and Social-cultural integration have achieved at the same time will they feel integrated psychologically. Theoretical and practical implications drawn from the key findings are provided to not only better understand the integration of international faculty at Japanese universities, but also to better serve and support them in practice.

672　"We are known as aliens": experiences of regional student migration to South Africa

Veera Tagliabue

South African universities have received a lot of attention due to their central role in highlighting the shortcomings of the post-apartheid political system and demanding transformation of higher education. The student protests across South African university campuses in 2015-2016 were especially visible, calling attention to persistent inequalities based on race, class, and gender (Steyn

Kotze, 2018). However, a notable minority of students on South African campuses – particularly migrant students from the Southern African (SADC) region – were not active in the protests. Drawing from qualitative interviews with SADC student at Rhodes University in Grahamstown, South Africa, this paper explores the reasons and implications of SADC students' disengagement. It offers a fresh perspective on the topical subject of transformation in South African universities by highlighting the intersections of transnational and class identities, which have not hitherto received such attention.

Migration has been a prominent issue in post-apartheid South Africa due to high levels of in-migration from the SADC region and because of the country's contested immigration policy (see Crush and Dodson, 2007). This discussion has often concentrated on unskilled and undocumented migrants, whilst the experience of university students is less understood, even though they share some similar concerns. Indeed, many SADC students did not participate in the protests of 2015-2016 because they were concerned about the lack of protection provided for immigrants in South Africa. They were also experiencing xenophobia and Afrophobia both on and off campus, and therefore reported feelings of non-belonging.

This paper argues that migrant students in South Africa have been excluded from participating in the transformation of higher education due to their transnational identities, which intersect with their experiences of social class. Migrating for educational purposes has created expectations of upward social mobility back home. Furthermore, due to different understandings of social class in their home countries, many SADC students on South African campuses felt that they were wrongly ascribed as 'privileged' during the 2015-2016 protests. This was, however, contradicted by their experiences of precarious middle-classness in Southern Africa. This paper concludes that SADC students have been excluded from the transformation processes in South African higher education due to *identity misrecognition*, which has been theorised by Taylor (1994) and discussed in the African context by Englund and Nyamnjoh (2004). This identity misrecognition has implications for the transformation project.

References

Crush, J. and Dodson, B. (2007) 'Another lost decade: the failures of South Africa's post-apartheid migration policy', *Tijdschrift voor Economische en Sociale Geografie* 98 (4), pp. 436-454.

Englund, H. and Nyamnjoh, F. B. (eds.) (2004) *Rights and the politics of recognition in Africa.* London: Zed Books.

Steyn Kotze, J. (2018) 'On decolonisation and revolution: a Kristevan reading on the Hashtags student movements and *Fallism'*, Politikon 45 (1), pp. 112-127.

Taylor, C. (1994) The politics of recognition. In: Gutman, A. (Ed.) (1994) *Multiculturalism. Examining the Politics of Recognition.* Princeton: Princeton University Press, pp. 25-73.

823 Alternative Politics for Skilled Refugees: a comparative study of Syrians in Canada and Venezuelans in Mexico

Camelia Tigau

Skilled mobility has been pictured as a best scenario of emigration, in which individuals actually get to choose the place where they want to live, and they even prepare their leave through education in foreign languages. However, there are cases when skilled migrants are forced to migrate in the same way as the unskilled ones; wars, poverty and violence may cause sudden or half planned decisions to migrate. Alternative hybrid actors, such as Talent Beyond Boundaries and Refugee Point have emerged to complement the activities of traditional institutions in displacement diplomacy, such as ACNUR. Their role is to match the skills of refugees with employment needs in some OECD countries.

This paper explores political and economic approaches to deskilling and skills mismatch in skilled professionals, based on the experience of Syrians in Canada and Venezuelans in Mexico. These two countries may be considered as second options of resettlement in North America, at a time when the US image as a historical asylum receiver was damaged by the populist anti-migrant discourse. The role of hospitality in the Canadian identity has been widely studied including its outcome on the integration of new migrants (Roberts 2015). At the same time, Mexico has shown an ambiguous position towards refugees and asylum seekers. With Central American transit migration taking the lion´s share in the media discourse on refugees, Venezuelans are less discussed and studied, with some exceptions (Gandini, Prieto, and Ascencio, 2020).

In Canada more than in Mexico, skilled refugees were shown to have difficulties in their integration to the job market (Enns, 2017; Nichles and Nyce, 2018). Many displaced professionals do not carry their diplomas and even when they do, they lack local experience and knowledge of the culture of reception; furthermore, the definition for certain skills in their country of origin is not the same as in their country of destination. As a matter of fact, these differences in skills definition are quite common among various knowledge economies (Lo, Li and Yo, 2019)

This paper adopts a comparative methodology to analyze the alternative actors that complement official public policies meant to integrate skilled refugees in Canada and Mexico in the last five years. I consider various levels of intervention on the international, national and local levels. My work proves that skilled displacement may be an opportunity to rethink the classical separation between economic and forced migration, when economic pathways are created to integrate certain refugees.

824 **** This presentation has been removed at the request of authors.****

689   Movilidad humana. Experiencia con las caravanas migrante en Centroamérica, México y los Estados Unidos de América

Diana Zambrano

Challenges and reconfigurations on Global South initiatives for Higher Education: Habesha Project, a Mexican project for displaced Syrian youth.

By the end of 2018, 70.9 million individuals were forcibly displaced worldwide due to conflict, persecution and human rights violation: 41.3 million internally displaced people, followed by 25.9 million refugees and 3.5 million asylum seekers (UNHCR 2018, 2). As one of the main consequences these massive forced movements is the limitation for host countries to provide basic humanitarian rights to displaced population. In addition to food, shelter and health, there has been a noticeable increase from governments and civil organizations to recognize education as part of a crucial humanitarian right (Sinclair 2001, 2; Zeus 2011, 257). However, the main efforts and projects for education are focused in primary and secondary levels (Rahseed & Munoz 2016, 174).

Concerning higher education, only 3% of the refugee sector around the world are registered in university programs, an alarming gap contrasted with the 36% of the global population enrolled (UNHCR, 2019), not including the number of displaced and asylum seekers who are also left out from higher education access. Due to the continuous loss of several young generations and the latest focus on the Syrian conflict, diverse initiatives have been created with the aim to provide higher education for refugees and asylum seekers. Most of these international organizations, governments and civil associations are positioned in the Global North, thus there is few academic discussion concerning Global South initiatives.

In 2015, the Mexican civil organization Habesha Project started providing scholarships for young Syrians to continue or start their tertiary education in private universities across the country. Habesha Project is run by a young and small team that so far has been able to bring up to 17 Syrian students to Mexico. The initiative includes a full university scholarship, a monthly stipend and ensure Spanish classes. This is the first project of its type in the country and in the Latin American region. Therefore, in depth research about the functioning, accomplishments and failures through the lenses of the Syrian beneficiaries and staff are necessary to analyze the challenges higher education projects through civil organizations in the Global South. This research is based on thematic analysis with recollection of interviews and fieldwork in 2019 in Mexico, as well as an online continuation in 2021. This proposal intends to demonstrate the power relations between beneficiaries (Syrian students) and its consequences on the improvements and challenges for Syrians to continue their educational journey.

893   Familias transnacionales mexicanas frente a condiciones de adversidad en Estados Unidos y Mexico: una perspectiva desde la resiliencia sociocultural

Jose Salvador Cueto-Calderon

Las condiciones políticas en Estados Unidos, traducidas en la implementación de acciones represivas hacia las comunidades de inmigrantes no autorizados, de parte de la administración federal y de algunos gobiernos locales del vecino país, han generado que las comunidades migrantes de origen mexicano estén enfrentando condiciones de adversidad. Estos escenarios se han traducido en acciones y políticas de corte xenofóbico y restrictivas, que trasgreden su estabilidad y bienestar económico y social, colocándoles en situación de vulnerabilidad (Durand, 2013; Márquez, 2013; Abrego, Coleman, Martinez, Menjivar y Slack, 2017; García, 2018; Kerwin, 2018; Farina, 2018). Dichos escenarios se presentan no sólo en los Estados Unidos, sino también en México debido al incremento del flujo de migrantes retornados a sus comunidades de origen (Durand, 2013; Márquez, 2013; Moctezuma, 2013, Montoya-Ortiz y González-Becerril, 2015; Moctezuma y Martínez, 2016; Burgueño y García, 2017; Cueto-Calderón, García y Burgueño, 2019).

La presente propuesta de investigación es una iniciativa de un grupo interdisciplinario de investigadores de la migración México-Estados Unidos, que ha venido trabajando sobre las condiciones de las familias migrantes mexicanas, enfocándose en el desarrollo de actitudes resilientes y estrategias de adaptación y cambio, presentes entre sus miembros y la comunidad. Dichas actitudes se muestran como una respuesta para enfrentar los escenarios de hostilidad y vulnerabilidad, a través recursos socio-culturales y acciones que se diseñan como herramientas que les permite sobreponerse ante dichos escenarios.

Estos recursos socio-culturales favorecen el diseño de estrategias que permiten dar respuesta a los procesos de inserción-reinserción en los diversos ámbitos sociales, económicos y culturales como producto de sus experiencias migratorias. El estudio se lleva a cabo en el estado de Arizona por su peculiaridad en la implementación de leyes y políticas de carácter antinmigrante y, en el caso de México, el estudio se desarrolla en el estado de Sinaloa, dado el flujo de familias retornadas a las comunidades de origen en dicho estado.

References

Abrego, L., Coleman, M., Martinez, D. E., Menjivar, C. y Slack. J. (2017). "Making Immigrants into Criminals: Legal Processes of Criminalization in the Post-IIRIRA Era." Journal on Migration and Human Security 5(3):694–715. Recuperado de: https://doi.org/10.1177/233150241700500308

Burgueño, N. y García, I. (2017). Procesos de incorporación socioeconómica de familias transnacionales de retorno en la comunidad de Cosalá, Sinaloa. En J. Soto y M. Verdugo (Coords.), Sinaloa en el siglo XXI: temas globales y políticas públicas (pp. 183-208). México: Juan Pablos Editor, Universidad Autónoma de Sinaloa.

Cueto-Calderón, J., García, I. y Burgueño, N. (2019). Retorno actual como estrategia resiliente de sobrevivencia de familias mexicanas establecidas en Arizona. Revista nuestrAmérica, 7(13), 241-263.

Duran, J. (2013). Nueva fase migratoria. Papeles de Población 19 (77): 83-113.

Farina, M. (2018). White Nativism, Ethnic Identity and US Immigration Policy Reforms: American Citizenship and Children in Mixed Status, Hispanic Families (Routledge Advances in Health and Social Policy). Taylor and Francis. Kindle Edition.

García, I. (2018). Perspectivas de una reforma migratoria que regularice a indocumentados mexicanos, en el contexto político actual de Estados Unidos. Nóesis. Volumen 27. No. 53 Enero-Junio 2018 www.revistanoesis.mx 62 Revista de Ciencias Sociales y Humanidades. En: http://dx.doi.org/10.20983/noesis.2018.1.3 (ingresada en febrero 2019).

Kerwin, D. (2018). From IIRIRA to Trump: Connecting the Dots to the Current US Immigration Policy Crisis. Journal on Migration and Human Security, 6 (3), 192-204.

Márquez, H. (2013). El redoble de la migración forzada: inseguridad, criminalización y destierro, en Migración y Desarrollo, vol 11, no. 21, pp.159-175. En: http://www.scielo.org.mx/scielo.php?script=sci_arttext&pid=S1870-75992013000200007 (ingresada en enero 2017).

Moctezuma, M. (2013). Retorno de migrantes a México. Su reformulación conceptual. Papeles de Población, 19(77), 149-175.

Moctezuma, M. y D. Martínez (2016). "El retorno de migrantes mexicanos con acento en Michoacán", en Levine, Elaine; Núñez, Silvia y Verea, Mónica (coords.) Nuevas experiencias de la migración de retorno, UNAM, Instituto Matías Romero, pp. 135-158.

Montoya-Ortiz, M. y González-Becerril, J. (2015). Evolución de la migración de retorno en México: migrantes procedentes de Estados Unidos en 1995 y de 1999 a 2014. Papeles de población, 21(85), 47-78. Recuperado en 29 de octubre de 2019, de: http://www.scielo.org.mx/scielo.php?script=sci_arttext&pid=S1405-74252015000300003&lng=es&tlng=es.

899   Remesas Sociales en tiempos de Pandemia

Lisseth Alexandra Gordillo

La investigación planteada se basa en la importancia y relevancia de las remesas sociales en tiempos de pandemia, que son realizadas por familias migrantes originarias de Ecuador. Inicialmente busca desarrollar una línea de tiempo estratégica para entender en qué fechas específicamente existía mayor contacto con su país natal mediante estas remesas o por el contrario cuando estas disminuían, seguido se presenta un análisis de cómo estas remesas ayudaron a las familias migrantes ecuatorianas a sobrellevar estos tiempos difíciles alejados de sus hogares natales, y de cómo las mismas se involucraron con sus familias que viven en el lugar de origen a pesar de la distancia. El presente trabajo tiene un enfoque cualitativo, para el cual utilizamos los conceptos claves; remesas y redes sociales, prácticas transnacionales y globalización. Se realizo mediante un diseño de investigación etnográfico, el cual estudia a los individuos en su propio espacio y dimensión temporal alcanzando una íntima y cercana familiaridad con ellos y con sus prácticas, mediante las entrevistas semiestructuradas hacía cuatro familias de migrantes transnacionales se logró la obtención de las prácticas que ellos realizan. De acuerdo con los resultados se identificaron y luego se clasificaron varias de las prácticas que mantenían las familias transnacionales con su país de origen. En conclusión, de acuerdo con la línea temporal planteada existieron cambios a lo largo de la misma, existiendo variaciones mínimas de las prácticas transnacionales entre las familias.

1000 "MIGRACIÓN, ACCESO A LA SALUD Y TICS - Aprendizajes frente al Covid-19 México"

Pascual Garcia Zamaro

Resumen

La migración ha sido compañera de la especie humana desde el momento en que el Homo erectus salió de África e inició su expansión por otros continentes en busca de recursos alimentarios (McKeown, 2006). La sobrevivencia desde entonces ha sido el principal expulsor de humanos desde su lugar origen a otros contextos. Con el paso del tiempo, los motivos incrementaron y el proceso migratorio se ha convertido en un fenómeno complejo y de mucho riesgo para la integridad y salud de las personas que lo realizan (Silva et al., 2020) (CEPAL, 2019)

Abstract

Migration has been the human species comrade since the moment Homo erectus left Africa and began his expansion across the continents in search of food resources (McKeown, 2006). Since then, survival has been the main reason why humans have been expelled from their place of origin to other contexts. Over time, the reasons for people to migrate increased and the migratory process became a complex phenomenon and of great risk, both for the integrity and for the people health who carry it out. (Silva et al., 2020) (CEPAL, 2019)

Introducción

Actualmente puede hablarse de dos tipos de migrantes: a) Los forzados por falta de opciones laborales, condiciones de vida dignas, problemas políticos, violencia e inseguridad en sus lugares de origen b) Por elección, son personas con mejores condiciones socioeconómicas pero insatisfechas con las expectativas de vida y desarrollo personal que ofrecen sus lugares de origen (OIM, 2020).

Se aborda la primera opción por presentar condiciones más complejas y de mayor vulnerabilidad a sus protagonistas. El objetivo de este trabajo es identificar los procesos que pueden coadyuvar al empoderamiento de las personas migrantes en el ejercicio de sus Derechos Universales, principalmente la salud, plasmados desde 1948, y su relación con las Tecnologías de la información y comunicación (TICS) de los países de tránsito que le ayuden a realizar este proceso con mayor seguridad y dignidad, con la nueva normalidad post Covid-19 (ONU 1948). Se utilizó la metodología de Revisión bibliográfica sistematizada.

El contexto migratorio, la salud y TIC

Hoy, un mundo globalizado en crisis económica, ambiental y sanitaria, la migración se ha exacerbado en algunas regiones, desplazando aproximadamente 244 millones de personas entre diversos países y 740 millones como migrantes internos (OIM 2015), la magnitud del problema ha crecido y los elementos que vulneran la integridad física, psíquica y social de los desplazados; además se vuelven más complejas y multifactoriales; entre ellos, el más acuciante, junto con la alimentación y la inseguridad es la accesibilidad a los Servicios de salud integrales (OIM, 2018).

Estudios realizados en Chile en migrantes internacionales, 66% de los encuestados manifestó no estar preparado para afrontar la pandemia y asocian esa inseguridad con la información recibida sobre ella, si es de calidad o no; hacen referencia a padecimientos como angustia y depresión cuando la información es reducida y de mala calidad (Cabieses & Oyarte, 2020). Las utilizaciones de las TIC alcanzaron una notoria distinción por parte de los colectivos migrantes por su valor en cada etapa del proceso migratorio (Jaramillo-Dent & Contreras-Pulido, 2020) (Lerma, 2015).

Por lo anterior se concluyó que el contacto con las TICS de los colectivos migrantes, grupos en Facebook y/o WhatsApp, donde la información proporcionada tanto en albergues como en diversas ONG y los medios masivos de comunicación coadyuvaron en cierta medida para que el proceso migratorio se realice con mayor certeza y seguridad (Torre Cantalapiedra et al., 2020).

Referencias

Cabieses, B., & Oyarte, M. (2020). Acceso a salud en inmigrantes: Identificando brechas para la protección social en salud. *Revista de Saúde Pública*, 54, 20. https://doi.org/10.11606/s1518-8787.2020054001501

CEPAL, O. (2019). *Desarrollo y migración: Desafíos y oportunidades en los países del norte de Centroamérica*. 301.

Jaramillo-Dent, D., & Contreras-Pulido, P. (2020). *Migrantes y redes sociales: Entrevista semi-estructurada para explorar usos y apoyos*. https://www.researchgate.net/profile/Daniela-Jaramillo-

Dent/publication/345342590_Migrantes_y_redes_sociales_Entrevista_semi-estructurada_para_explorar_usos_y_apoyos/links/5fa43d21458515157bec9381/Migrantes-y-redes-sociales-Entrevista-semi-estructurada-para-explorar-usos-y-apoyos.pdf.
https://www.researchgate.net/publication/345342590_Migrantes_y_redes_sociales_Entrevista_semi-estructurada_para_explorar_usos_y_apoyos

Lerma, A. (2015, septiembre 3). *El uso de las Redes Sociales en las migraciones – Adra*. https://adra-es.org/el-uso-de-las-redes-sociales-en-las-migraciones/

McKeown, T. (2006). *Los orígenes de las enfermedades humanas |*. Editorial Triacastela;
http://www.trabajosocial.unlp.edu.ar/uploads/docs/mc_keown__el_origen_de_las_enfermedades_humanas.pdf. http://www.marcialpons.es/libros/los-origenes-de-las-enfermedades-humanas/9788495840257/

OIM, O. (2018, mayo 25). *Migración y Salud*. Organización Internacional para las Migraciones. https://www.iom.int/es/migracion-y-salud

OIM, O. (2020, enero 14). Tipos de migraciones y cómo diferenciarlas. *OIM*. https://oim.org.mx/tipos-de-migraciones/

ONU, I. (1948). *La Declaración Universal de Derechos Humanos | Naciones Unida. Adoptada y proclamada por la Asamblea General en su resolución 217 A (III), de 10 de diciembre de 1948*. United Nations; United Nations. https://www.un.org/es/about-us/universal-declaration-of-human-rights

Silva, J. M. G., Borré, J. R., Montero, S. R. A., & Mendoza, X. F. B. (2020). Migración: Contexto, impacto y desafío. Una reflexión teórica. *Revista de Ciencias Sociales (Ve), XXVI*(2), 299–313.

Torre Cantalapiedra, E., Mariscal Nava, D. M., Torre Cantalapiedra, E., & Mariscal Nava, D. M. (2020). Batallando con fronteras: Estrategias migratorias en tránsito de participantes en caravanas de migrantes. *Estudios fronterizos*, *21*. https://doi.org/10.21670/ref.2005047

10D Migration and Identity
Chair Emre Eren Korkmaz, Oxford University, UK
734 "I never ever give up, I just continue my effort" individual-level narratives of resilience in forced migrants
769 Promoting LGBTQ Forced Migrants' Integration in Mexico City's Labor Market: Perspectives From Mexican Government Agencies & Civil Society
Rolando Diaz
860 Migrant identity, a mindset that comes with migrating. Narratives of tertiary educated middle class Mexican migrants in the United States
Monica Laura Vazquez Maggio

734 "I never ever give up, I just continue my effort" individual-level narratives of resilience in forced migrants

Introduction

Resilience is often described as the ability to adapt well in the face of adversity (Sleijpen et al, 2017). Categorised as internal and external factors, pre-defined criteria have been centre-stage to analyse refugees' resilience processes. Resilience is also often interpreted as a neoliberal form of governmentality, in which individuals are expected to take responsibility for their own social and economic wellbeing, thus legitimising a withdrawal of state support (Joseph, 2013).

In contrast to either of these understandings, this paper takes a perspective on resilience in which individual-level circumstances, including experiences and narratives from the past and present, as well as imaginations about the future are centre-stage, without ignoring structural issues which impact on refugees' lives and their choices. This paper wishes to focus on refugees' agency and the process of negotiating in their resilience processes, thereby moving away from focusing on resilience outcomes which are often subject to normative judgements.

Objectives

1) To explore the resilience processes of forced migrants and develop an understanding of what it looks like if someone is resilient and shows agency.
2) To highlight the role of past and present experiences and imaginations about their futures in refugees' resilience processes.
3) To develop an understanding of resilience which pays attention to individual-level circumstances and meaning making but is cognizant of structural inequalities, thereby criticising the neoliberal interpretation of resilience.

Methods

Data was collected in a photo-elicitation study conducted with refugees and asylum seekers in Newcastle upon Tyne, making this one of few studies conducted with forced migrants in the North East of England. In total, 14 interviews were conducted, of which three will be analysed in detail.

Results

Individual memories of the past, experiences in the present, and imaginations of the future play a central role in forced migrants' resilience processes. Personal interests and self-identifications facilitate overcoming personal adversities, such as feelings of depression. However, bureaucratic and systemic adversities are harder to overcome, as structural impediments remain and restrict individual behaviour.

Refugees' agency is manifested in different ways, and it does not always materialise in concrete actions. Waiting for example can be considered a from agency (Thomson, 2013; Krause and Schmidt, 2019): individuals strategically choose to delay employment due to a lack of language skills.

Conclusions

There is no one-size-fits-all approach to resilience; instead, we need to be mindful of the role of individualised processes of meaning-making, and navigating past and future experiences in refugees' resilience processes. While resilience is often conceptualised as a 'positive outcome after adversity', this paper highlights that outcomes play a less important role. However, we need to be careful not to mistake an outcome such as waiting for a lack of choices.

It is therefore important not to depoliticise issues such as poverty or barriers to enter the job market, and expect individuals to take full responsibility for their own wellbeing when the adversities they face require action at a macro-level.

Key references

Joseph, J, (2013) 'Resilience as embedded neoliberalism: a governmentality approach,' *Resilience,* 1(1), pp. 38-52.

Krause, U. and Schmidt, H. (2019) 'Refugees as Actors? Critical reflections on global refugee policies on self-reliance and resilience', *Journal of Refugee Studies,* 33(1), pp. 22-4.

Sleijpen, M. et al (2017) 'Lives on hold: A qualitative study of young refugees' resilience strategies', *Childhood,* 24(3), pp. 348-365.

Thomson, S. (2013) 'Agency as silence and muted voice: the problem-solving networks of unaccompanied young Somali refugee women in Eastleigh, Nairobi', *Conflict, Security and Development,* 13(5), pp. 589-609.

769   Promoting LGBTQ Forced Migrants' Integration in Mexico City's Labor Market: Perspectives From Mexican Government Agencies & Civil Society

Rolando Diaz

Mexico has long been a country of immigration, emigration, refuge, transit, and return migration. These phenomena compound migration policy for the Mexican government, which grapples with a highly securitized northern border and a southern border that continues to see troubling patterns of mass migration from the Northern Triangle of Central America (NTCA). High levels of violence rooted in social inequities, political instability, and armed conflict across the region have driven many to flee and seek safety in North America. Images of a "Rainbow caravan" appeared in US media in 2017, underscoring how NTCA asylum-seekers belonging to the LGBTQ community face particular hardships and conditions exacerbated by inadequate government protection and interest in strengthening LGBTQ rights. While the "Rainbow caravan" moved to seek asylum in the US, many LGBTQ forced migrants stay in Mexico, particularly in the capital. Mexico City, seen as an LGBTQ Mecca, coupled with the city's sanctuary city policy protecting migrants, offers suitable conditions for studying LGBTQ migrants' inclusion and integration in the city's labor market.

In using queer theorists' scholarship, chiefly in the realm of queer migration studies, this study gives rise to the emerging understandings of Mexico as a migrant-receiving state within an LGBTQ context. Through a qualitative research study, this paper includes the results of 17 in-depth semi-structured interviews with individuals representing 11 entities ranging from Mexican government agencies, international organizations, and civil society stakeholders with roles in labor market integration in Mexico City. Themes collected include insights into LGBTQ rights awareness, budget requisition, active integration efforts, and emerging economic sectors/ regions for future government-civil society cooperation. As migration flows into Mexico continue to be studied, the diversity within those flows offers an opportunity to visibilize the uniqueness of certain groups, especially those pertaining to sexual and gender diversity, in order to test how stakeholders in migration respond to migrants' particularities.

860 Migrant identity, a mindset that comes with migrating. Narratives of tertiary educated middle class Mexican migrants in the United States

Monica Laura Vazquez Maggio

This paper explores the ways, both positive and negative, in which the lived experience of migration has a transforming impact on migrants' identities, their concept of self and their modes of belonging. Drawing on findings from a mixed-methods research project (which employed an online survey and semi-structured interviews) with middle-class tertiary educated Mexican migrants living in the US, the paper explores how three phenomena associated to the impact of the process of migration on identity: migration lived as a new dimension that adds to the migrants' identity, recognition of a group identity (being migrants from a similar social class) and being torn between two cultures. We argue that these migrants experience a great ambivalence in the way the lived experience of migration is perceived. Further, we also found that they continuously turn challenging experiences into positive experiences, something that could be interpreted as exercises of empowerment and agency.

10E Migration, Politics and Law

Chair: Ülkü Sezgi Sözen, University of Hamburg, Germany

748 Prolonged Liminality in the Transition from Asylum Seeker to Newly Recognised Refugee: A Temporal Exploration of Britain's Asylum System
Hannah Underwood

755 What strategy to choose if it is impossible to obtain refugee status? The Case of Syrian Circassian Refugees in Russia
Alfiya Lyapina

761 University students' preferences for restrictionist or lenient immigration policies
Jana Sladkova, Kristin Cook, Seokbeom Kim

774 Control as a nexus of the migration governance patterns (The case of the United States).
Jonathan Palatz

748   Prolonged Liminality in the Transition from Asylum Seeker to Newly Recognised Refugee: A Temporal Exploration of Britain's Asylum System

Hannah Underwood

This paper explores temporal dimensions to policies that affect people who seek and obtain asylum in the UK. The Home Office has no obligation to deal with asylum claims within a particular timeframe and are not held accountable for their inadequacies. In contrast, individuals going through the asylum system have to wait for inexplicably long periods and are asked to complete things within unrealistic timeframes. The paper aims to unmask the imbalance of power between the British state and asylum seekers and refugees.

Anthropologists have examined enforced waiting as an aspect of migration control by European states (Anderrsson 2014; Tsianos 2010; O'Reilly 2020), forging spaces, such as camps, reception centres and detention centres, where movement is 'decelerated' (Tsianos 2010: 384), and lives are put on hold (O'Reilly 2020: 3). Systematic waiting has been identified to contribute to a sense of 'sticky' and 'suspended' time, where asylum seekers are forced into idleness and cannot attain personal, professional or social progression (Griffiths 2014: 1996). This experience of time is bound up with a state of 'liminality', inherent to the experience of being an asylum seeker (O'Reilly 2020: 81).

Prior studies acknowledge the 'temporal ruptures' and 'frenzied time' (Griffiths 2014: Anderson et al. 2013) experienced when a negative decision leads to people being speedily removed and deported from the UK (Gibney 2008). However, there does not appear to be research on the 'temporal rupture' that occurs when asylum seekers are granted leave to remain, and the consequent frenzied time that unfurls as they are given 28 days to find accommodation and become financially independent before state support is taken away. As this approach remains briefly addressed in the literature, this paper explores the temporality of transitioning from an asylum seeker to a refugee in the UK.

Britain's 'move-on' policy is presented as a liminal phase, where newly recognised refugees are expected to transition from 'state-dependent' to 'self-sufficient' in 28 days. This paper includes ethnographic reflections from interviews with five participants who have sought and obtained asylum in the UK. Their accounts expose this length of time as inadequate, especially when considered alongside the temporal uncertainty and exclusionary policies imposed upon them before they were granted leave to remain. Consequently, hostile asylum policies are seen to protract into life as a newly recognised refugee and the frenzy of time enforced by the 28-day move-on period restricts their choices.

References

Anderson, B., Griffiths, M., & Rogers, A. (2013). *Migration, Time and Temporalities: Review and Prospect.* Oxford: Centre On Migration, Policy and Society. Available at:

https://www.compas.ox.ac.uk/2013/migration-time-and-temporalities-review-and-prospect/ (Accessed: 10th May 2020)

Andersson, R. (2014). "Time and the Migrant Other: European Border Controls and the Temporal Economics of Illegality". *American Anthropologist.* 116 (4), 795-809.

Gibney, M.J. (2008). "Asylum and the Expansion of Deportation in the United Kingdom." *Government and Opposition.* 43 (2), 146-167.

Griffiths, M. (2014). "Out of Time: The Temporal Uncertainties of Refused Asylum Seekers and Immigration Detainees". *Journal of Ethnic and Migration Studies.* 40 (12), 1991-2009.

O'Reilly, Z. (2020). *The In-Between Spaces of Asylum and Migration: A Participatory Visual Approach.* Switzerland: Palgrave Macmillan.

Tsianos, V. (2010). "Transnational Migration and the Emergence of the European Border Regime: An Ethnographic Analysis". *European Journal of Social Theory.* 13 (3), 373-387.

755   What strategy to choose if it is impossible to obtain refugee status? The Case of Syrian Circassian Refugees in Russia

Alfiya Lyapina

With the start of the civil war in Syria in 2011, the number of refugees from Syria increased around the world, however, slightly affected the numbers of asylum seekers and people with refugee status in Russian Federation. From 2012 to 2018, there were only 2 people from Syria with refugee status. Nevertheless, more often refugees from Syria were turned to the help of human rights defenders and received temporary asylum, particularly for a one-year period. By comparing the drastic increase of Syrian refugees' number, there were 13 people seeking temporary asylum in 2012; increased to 1,158 in 2014, and finally to 1,924 people in 2015 (Rosstat 2019).

However, the author's research noted a non-standard category of refugees: about 3,000 Syrian Circassians arrived in Russia in different years and about 1,000 of them left Russia to go to the European Union countries. These Syrian Circassians used the so-called repatriation technique [which is the process of returning an asset or homeland] to legalize in their historical homeland, where is in the modern Republics of Adygea and Kabardino-Balkaria in the North Caucasus in Russia. These territories in the historical context, the Circassian people inhabited the territories of these republics until the 19th century, and after more than a 50-year long war [The Caucasian War between 1817–1864 and the capture of the North Caucasus by the Russian Empire, they were forced to flee to the Ottoman Empire. Then part of the Circassian diaspora entered the population of modern Turkey, Syria, Jordan. Nowadays some of them are moving to live in their historical homeland. Syrians make up the majority in this stream due to the war that pushed them to repatriate.

This research is based on the methods of observation included in the Republic of Adygea in Russia, in-depth interviews and descriptive statistics. This paper demonstrates how the social solidarity of the small Circassian population in the Republic with respect to Syrian Circassians who fled from the war. The social solidarity among Circassians happens at different levels, such as the help of local NGOs, the creation of a State Commission in the Republic for assistance to the Syrians, cooperation with the federal authorities of Russia, humanitarian assistance from wealthy countries, neighboring republics of the North Caucasus. This paper introduces the social cooperation, solidarity and assistance take place between Circassian in the Republic of Adygea in Russia and Syrian Circassians who fled from the war and seek refuge in their historical homeland.

761 University students' preferences for restrictionist or lenient immigration policies

Jana Sladkova, Kristin Cook, Seokbeom Kim

Few attempts have been made to examine the effects of perceived threats that immigrants pose to host society on young people's preferences for restrictionist or lenient immigration policies. Moreover, the existing literature is scarce on whether such perceived threats mediate the relationship between previously identified demographic antecedents such as gender, race or age and preferences for certain immigration policies. To address these gaps, this study examines direct and mediating effects of perceived economic, cultural and security threats on preferences for lenient or restrictionist immigration policies. Using a sample college students' survey data (N=604) on their attitudes towards immigration, our findings of logistic regression analysis show that the three dimensions of perceived threat were all positively associated with preference for hardline immigration policies. In addition, regardless of inclusion of perceived threats in the logistic model, being Republican was a consistent positive predictor of the hardline immigration agenda, while female was a consistent negative one. Finally, the results of path analysis of Structural Equation Modeling indicate mediating effects of cultural threat on the relationships between political affiliation (Republican and Independent) and race (Latinx) and support for hardline immigration policies.

774 Control as a nexus of the migration governance patterns (The case of the United States).

Jonathan Palatz

The emergence of a global economy has contributed both to the creation of potential emigrants abroad and to the formation of economic, cultural and ideological links between industrialized and developing countries, turning these links into bridges for international migration, which has supplied the specific needs of capital at different stages of its development.

The high mobility of human beings as migrants, as seen in the report "World Migration Report 2020" of the International Organization for Migration (IOM), shows how since 2000 the number of migrants increased by 81% and reached 272 million worldwide in 2020. It is important to note that the proportion of migrants, as a percentage of the world population, went from 2.3% in 1970 to 3.5% in 2020[41].

These figures have generated new dynamics of human mobility that have been translated into policies that go beyond a simple control of people on the move, implying the consolidation of a medium-term trend that has sought to discipline human mobility since the 1980s. Through the establishment of an ideal mobility regime of control based on the conjunctural needs of the global capitalist system, the new emerging mobility regime unfolds and morphs into a variety of practices that lead people to believe that such practices are disconnected from control and, more importantly, that they oppose control.

Therefore, controlling (or managing) migration is not just about inspecting people on the move; it is also about creating the conditions for human mobility to take place without what Nikos Papastergiadis calls "turbulence"[42], that is, without disturbing the "national order of things"[43], without challenging state sovereignty, without damaging the socio-economic interests of dominant groups, etc.

Starting from the idea that international migration is a key feature of globalization, we decided to rely theoretically on this study by Antoine Pécoud, who in his article "Philosophies of migration governance in a globalizing world" highlights that there are currently five different patterns of migration governance, which are as follows: 1) national / sovereign migration governance, according to which migration is a matter of strict state sovereignty; 2) global anti-migrant governance, which postulates that cooperation exists, either to control migration (global governance of forced immobility) or to exploit migrant labor (global governance of labor exploitation); 3) governance of migration based on global and human rights, based on human rights and international standards; 4) governance of global migration management / development, which aims to direct migration flows to optimize their usefulness; and 5) the free (non) governance of migration, based on ethical and utilitarian arguments in favor of free movement[44].

The objective of this article is to show with the American example how these patterns work simultaneously at different levels, overlapping in their actions to establish new barriers or controls, the purpose of which is to discipline migration flows under the establishment of different immigration mobility regimes, without being able to consolidate as a contradiction to the system itself. These changes in migration governance, far from being an isolated event, are part of a global process that, due to the pandemic caused by Covid-19, has had an

---

[41] International Organization for Migration (IOM), *World Migration Report 2020* (Ginebra: OIM, 2019),
https://publications.iom.int/books/world-migration-report-2020
[42] Nikos Papastergiadis, *The Turbulence of Migration: Globalization, Deterritorialization and Hybridity*
(Oxford: Polity Press, 1999).
[43] Liisa H. Malkki, "Refugees and Exile: from Refugee Studies to the National Order of Things", *Annual Review Anthropology* 24 (1995).
[44] Antoine Pécoud, "Philosophies of migration governance in a globalizing world", *Globalizations* 18, n° 61 (2020).

unprecedented momentum because of the increasing securitization of migration.

References

International Organization for Migration (IOM), *World Migration Report 2020.* Ginebra: OIM, 2019.

https://publications.iom.int/books/world-migration-report-2020

Malkki, Liisa H. "Refugees and Exile: from Refugee Studies to the National Order of Things".

Annual Review Anthropology 24 (1995): 495-523.

Papastergiadis, Nikos. *The Turbulence of Migration: Globalization, Deterritorialization and Hybridity.*

Oxford: Polity Press, 1999.

Pécoud, Antoine. "Philosophies of migration governance in a globalizing world". *Globalizations* 18, n° 61 (2020): 1-17.

10F   Gender, Sexuality and Migration

Chair *Şebnem Koşer Akçapar, Ankara Social Sciences University, Turkey*
658   Gendered Dynamics of Labour Migration in Turkey: Migrant Women in Professional Sectors
Eleonore Kofman, Ezgi Tuncer, Zeynep Eren-Benlisoy
531   Women Refugees and Covid-19: The case of Greece
Foteini Marmani
651   Gender and Deskilling in Forced Migration: A Study of the Experiences of Refugee Women in Turkey
Aysima Çalışan and Şebnem Koşer Akçapar
891   Pashtun Diaspora in Canada: Bringing a culturally relevant model (Hujra) for a transformative learning approach to promote healthy masculinity and well-being
Aamir Jamal, Liza Lorenzetti, Omer Jamal, Sarah Thomas

658   Gendered Dynamics of Labour Migration in Turkey: Migrant Women in Professional Sectors

Eleonore Kofman, Ezgi Tuncer, Zeynep Eren-Benlisoy

Turkey has been a significant hub for female migrant workers since the 1990s. The first of the two groups of irregular migrants are those who practice continuous circular migration from Eastern European countries and former Soviet republics to Turkey. The second are from South-eastern Asian and North African countries. Turkey also has a population of regular migrants who have residence and work permits, which includes female professionals.

This presentation discusses the gendered dynamics of labour migration of women working in professional sectors in Turkey. It is based on research funded by the UKRI GCRF Gender, Justice & Security Hub, which contributes to the slowly growing analysis of South-to-South and North-to-South migration, as well as a wider range of sectors other than domestic and care work. Although these are significant, they are not the only ones that employ female migrants. Professional female migration has been largely ignored in the Global South has expanded especially in upper middle-income countries such as Turkey. This presentation includes our results from 15 in-depth interviews with migrant women working in professional sectors in Istanbul. We shall discuss our preliminary results based on four themes: dynamics of migration, experiences in the country of origin, process of migration experiences in Turkey and public access and spatial mobility before Covid-19 outbreak. The impacts of Covid-19 outbreak in Turkey on the high skilled migrant women will also be analysed.

There are numerous reasons behind these women's migration, including having precarious conditions and family issues in their home countries, the possibility of getting a better education and well-paid jobs in Turkey, marriage, life-style changes, as well as political pressure and war. The majority are from Europe or North America, some hold dual citizenship, and many speak English as their native language. Many become highly-paid English teachers or upper-middle income editors, academics, translators and NGO workers. They attain a higher standard of living than they might be able to in their countries of origin, even though some do not have a bachelor's degree. Others, however, experience de-skilling. Despite having privileged backgrounds, many faces physical and/or sexual harassment in public spaces in Istanbul, although the city itself is often one of the main reasons they stay in Turkey. In addition, Turks often stigmatize foreign women saying that they are stupid, easily taken advantage of and hypersexual, which has led women to avoid local people in their social relations and rather stay in international circles. The cultural differences and lack of inclusivity in Turkey often makes these women feel unwelcome. Others, however, are affected by their partner's families which follow their every movement and limit their daily lives. Although they are socially active and mobile in the city, most live in limited, secular environments and prefer not to go to conservative neighbourhoods due to the likelihood they will be ogled and harassed by men there in addition to the need to adhere to conservative dress codes to prevent possible harassment.

531   Women Refugees and Covid-19: The case of Greece

Foteini Marmani

Purpose

Refugees face thousands of problems around the world, but women and children face individual issues, especially in the context of a coronavirus pandemic. In this announcement we will focus on the conditions that prevail today during the pandemic compared to the corresponding conditions that prevailed in the period 2011-2012 when the research was conducted on the accommodation structures of Attica in Greece. The purpose of the present paper is to highlight living conditions from the perspective of gender on the grounds that such groups as single women or mothers still remain shrouded in obscurity to some extent and their survival is hugely dependent on individual initiatives and occasional assistance received

Design/methodology/approach

A combination of quantitative and qualitative methods, fieldwork and carrying out structured interviews involving questionnaire completion by women and men asylum seekers.

Findings

The gender differences among asylum seekers cannot be clearly verified due to great social and economic problems, although in the past the contradictions were intense. Today women and men living in refugee camps are especially vulnerable to Covid-19 and other diseases as a result of living in overcrowded conditions, lack of sanitation, and lack of access to decent healthcare or vaccination programmes. Physical distancing and permanent hand washing are simply impossible.

Migrant women and men not living in camps are also vulnerable. They can face barriers to accessing healthcare, such as language, financial costs, legal restrictions and lack of awareness of available services. Pregnant refugees and migrants in Europe face a higher maternal mortality rate than non-migrant women, which may be exacerbated when healthcare services are stretched due to the Covid-19 pandemic.

Research limitations

The research refers to the specific accomodation centers and the people living there and should be taken into account that a simple random sampling has not been plausible but the data collected is fairly enlightening.

Originality/value

Due to the lack of data from similar studies, it was necessary to carry out this comparative study of the living conditions of refugee women in organized temporary accommodation structures. The gender dimension has led us to conclusions and proposals that need to be heard and taken into account in policy-making.

References

Douglas M, Katikireddi SV, Taulbut M, McKee M, McCartney G. Mitigating the wider health effects of covid-19 pandemic response. BMJ 2020;369:m1557.10.1136/bmj.m1557 32341002

EIGE, Health,covid-19 and gender equality.16/01/2021 available at: https://eige.europa.eu/topics/health/covid-19-and-gender-equality

Hargreaves S, Kumar BN, McKee M, Jones L, Veizis A. Europe's migrant containment policies threaten the response to covid-19. BMJ 2020;368:m1213. 10.1136/bmj.m1213 32217531

Kondilis E, Pantoularis I, Makridou E, Rotulo A, Seretis S, Benos A. Critical assessment of preparedness and policy responses to SARS-CoV2 pandemic: international and Greek experience. CEHP Report 2020.2. 2020. available at :https://www.healthpolicycenter.gr

Tsovili, Theodora D., Eftihia Voutira. *Practical reception of asylum seekers in Greece with special emphasis on mothers alone, single women and children who have been separated from their families* . (UNHCR, Athens: 2004).

UNHCR, Q&A: Access to health services is key to halting COVID-19 and saving refugee lives.16/01/2021 available at: https://www.unhcr.org/news/latest/2020/3/5e7dab2c4/qa-access-health-services-key-halting-covid-19-saving-refugee-lives.html

UNHCR and Office of the High Commissioner for Human Rights (OHCHR). Global Roundtable on Alternatives to Detention of Asylum-Seekers, Refugees, Migrants and Stateless Persons: Summary Conclusions, July 2011, para. 10, available at:http://www.unhcr.org/refworld/docid/4e315b882.html

United Nations Women. (2014) available at https://www.unwomen.org/en/news/in-focus/end-violence-against-women/2014/poverty

World Health Organization. Interim guidance: preparedness, prevention and control of coronavirus disease (Covid-19) for refugees and migrants in non-camp settings. 17 April 2020. https://www.who.int/publications-detail/preparedness-prevention-and-control-of-coronavirus-disease-(covid-19)-for-refugees-and-migrants-in-non-camp-settings

651   Gender and Deskilling in Forced Migration: A Study of the Experiences of Refugee Women in Turkey

Aysima Çalışan and Şebnem Koşer Akçapar

Despite its evident challenges, international migration brings countless advantages to both origin and destination countries' economic development by providing a diverse workforce and extending the available skill pool that can respond to the labor market needs timely and effectively. From the integration-based perspective, refugees and migrants with higher formal skills and qualifications are seen as those who can easily be integrated into society and the labour markets. However, many skilled and highly skilled refugees often work in jobs for which their skills and qualifications are under-utilized. This issue is conceptualized as deskilling and occurs when their skills and qualifications are not recognized in the countries of destination (Bauder, 2003). Deskilling is associated with brain waste and may hinder the full utilization of refugees' skills and integration processes.

There are almost 4 million registered refugees living in Turkey including 3.6 million Syrian nationals under temporary protection. Of the non-Syrian refugee population in Turkey, approximately 44 percent are from Afghanistan, 42 percent from Iraq, and 10 percent from Iran (UNCHR Turkey, 2021). According to DGMM (2021), women comprise over 46.2% of all refugees and asylum seekers in Turkey. In Turkey's case, many female refugees received less formal education and/or never experienced working outside the home due to the patriarchal and cultural norms of their home country. In addition to less skilled female refugees in Turkey, there are also those with higher human capital and even though they are almost equally educated and qualified as their male counterparts, they still make less money. This gendered and skilled aspect of forced migration is yet to be studied at length. Anecdotal evidence and participant observation suggest that regardless of their skills, prior work experience, and higher education level, many highly skilled refugee women often work in jobs they are overqualified for. It shows that these refugee women are being deskilled in Turkey, and this deskilling is complicated by the intersectionality of gender, ethnicity, class, and citizenship in the neo-liberal order.

The aim of this paper is to analyze the gendered dimension of deskilling and its negative effects on economic development and social cohesion by focusing on the lived experiences of highly educated refugee women in Turkey coming from Syria, Afghanistan, Iraq, and Iran. Therefore, theoretical framework of this paper is based on intersectionality and neo-liberalism in an effort to unearth what kind of patriarchal and neo-liberal social structures lead to deskilling in forced migration. The data is collected through in-depth and focus group interviews with 50 selected refugee women aged between 25 to 55 and having at least a bachelor's degree and work experience. In order to get a more detailed perspective, the interviews take place in different provinces, such as Ankara, Bursa, Istanbul, Mersin, and Gaziantep.

References

Bauder, H. (2003). 'Brain Abuse,' or the Devaluation of Immigrant Labour in Canada.

Antipode 35(4), 699–717.

DGMM. (2021). Temporary Protection. Retrieved from Republic of Turkey Ministry of Interior Directorate General of Migration Management: https://en.goc.gov.tr/temporary-protection27

UNCHR Turkey. (2021). UNCHR Turkey Stats. Retrieved from UNHCR Turkey: https://www.unhcr.org/tr/en/unhcr-turkey-stats

891　Pashtun Diaspora in Canada:　Bringing a culturally relevant model (Hujra) for a transformative learning approach to promote healthy masculinity and well-being

Aamir Jamal, Liza Lorenzetti, Omer Jamal, Sarah Thomas

Developing a culturally relevant and accessible approach for social change among diverse communities is a challenge for social work policy and practice. Keeping in view the urgent need and significance of culturally relevant social justice approaches and its application to diverse cultural realities of the Canadian landscape, we developed a community-oriented, culturally relevant model that makes use of an established cultural institution (Hujra) for personal reflections and transformative learning. 'Hujra' is a deep rooted and established informal traditional institution within the Pashtun community where men come together to socialize and discuss sociocultural issues in the manner of an indigenous talking circle. However, increasing urbanization, modernization, and migration has weakened the Hujra culture among Pashtun communities, both at home and among the Pashtun diaspora. With the support of Calgary Pashtun Association, Alberta Men's Network, and action researchers at the University of Calgary, Faculty of Social Work, a series of 'Hujra nights' were organized. This approach built on the traditional aspects of Hujra, a male only gathering, traditional food and dress, seating on the floor, and included intentional questions and storytelling by a facilitator from the same community, to introduce topics regarding healthy masculinity and well-being. Pashtun men were invited to bring forward their constructions of masculinity and reflect on them in a multicultural Canadian context. This meaningful approach successfully opened up key conversations on well-being, healthy families, and stronger communities. A Pashtun "Hujra night" experience in Canada demonstrated the significance of co-construction of practice knowledge for social workers and community development practitioners as they work on the sensitive issues of gender justice and domestic violence within immigrant communities. The main learning objectives from this presentation include the importance of cultural relevancy in mainstream social work practice; development of culturally relevant and community-oriented transformative approaches and the implications of their holistic integration within the broader global context.

10H COVID-19 Impact

Chair: Liudmila Konstants, American University in Central Asia, Kyrgyzstan

737   Emergency COVID-19 and migrants: tips and comments related to retrospective study from February to July 2020.in a RC RC MondoMigliore of Rocca di Papa
      Beatrice Casella
739   The pandemic Covid vax plan: the migrants and the citizens, two different sides of the same question
      Beatrice Casella
763   How the COVID-19 pandemic has affected Syrian government-assisted refugees in Canada
      Abe Oudshoorn, Cindy Brown, Eman Arnout, Fawziah Rabiah-Mohammed, Leah Hamilton, Luc Theriault, Mohammad Zaid Bakhash, Mohammed El Hazzouri, Rima Tarraf, Sagida Elnihum, Sarah Benbow, Victoria Esses
845   Labor Migration and Pandemic Paradox
      Liudmila Konstants

737   Emergency COVID-19 and migrants: tips and comments related to retrospective study from February to July 2020.in a RC RC MondoMigliore of Rocca di Papa

Beatrice Casella

Unfortunately Italy, one of the Mediterranean countries most affected by migratory flows, was the first European area hit by the severe acute respiratory syndrome coronavirus 2 (SARS-CoV2) epidemic.

The situation has been really difficult but more in the group of migrants. To inform and answer the doubts of Italian citizens, the ministry of health immediately activated a number of public utility (number 1500). Number active 24 hours a day; the calls were answered by experienced doctors with the possibility of simultaneous translation into English, Spanish and Chinese.

The number was particularly useful for migrants and tourists who did not understand the information in Italian on how to behave in using the mask, quarantine, what to do if you have COVID-like symptoms, etc.

In this unusual time of the COVID-19 pandemic, there is concern about the risk of public responder contracting COVID-19 from a person when providing CPR or using an AED.

The vast majority of cardiac arrests (over 80%) will be in the home setting and responders are likely to be friends or family.

The general recommendations, have been to reduce the risk of the public responder getting the virus from the person when providing CPR and using an AED during cardiac arrest, to do the Hands-Only CPR (without breaths) and so only chest compression without breathing.

Through this simple system not expensive , the migrant communities have correctly received the Moh messages and no specific problems were encountered

In the RC 'MondoMigliore' of Rocca di Papa the main critical issue of strategies adopted for epidemic control was the difficulty in making Italian population aware and actively involved in respect for quarantine, social distancing and the use of facial masks to prevent transmission of the disease. The issue was particularly relevant in the management of the reception centres (RCs) due to the linguistic, cultural and social differences linked to the heterogeneity of the migrants hosted.

The RC hosts an average of 300 migrants largely from Africa and Asia with a prevalence of . Residents have no restriction for entry and exit. Double or multiple rooms, outdoor/indoor common areas, canteen and a medical centre are available. Due to the pandemic risk, the RC has developed a surveillance programme with the aim of intercepting and managing an eventually SARS-CoV-2 outbreak.

Some simple precautions have been implemented. A health promotion intervention was carried out to provide information on correct behaviours to avoid contagion. The division into small groups, homogeneous by cultural context, represented an effective resource to target the intervention. Cultural mediators reinforced the message in the next time.

Despite the general idea "more migrants= more problems" this retrospective study aims at underlining as in Covid times even more It is important to use clear, simple and straightforward communications which enable in particular migrants to feel less isolated and responsible for their own health and that of the Community.

Reference

Department of Public Health and Infectious Diseases, Sapienza University of Rome, Rome, Italy,

Azienda Ospedaliero-Universitaria Policlinico Umberto I, Rome, Italy, [3]Migrants and Global Health Organization (Mi-HeRo), Rome, Italy,

Anesthesiology and Intensive Care Unit University "Campus Bio-Medico" Rome, Italy,

Director International Traing Center American Heart Association "Centro Formazione Medica",

Medical assistant Ministry of Health

Professor of Health Sociology, International University UniCamillus, Rome, Italy

Director of CIRS (Center for social studies in health), International University UniCamillus, Rome, Italy

Professor of Moral Philosophy, International University UniCamillus, Rome, Italy

Press Office & Master Online Coordinator, International University UniCamillus, Rome, Italy

739   The pandemic Covid vax plan: the migrants and the citizens, two different sides of the same question

Beatrice Casella

The purpose of this paper is to investigate the sensitive intersection between migrants and Covid vaccination.

No demonstration looks to be shown concerning the fact that Europe goes on different speeds. This is a fact. It is of course a multiple question. On a side there are all the legal aspects. They concern the regulation of migration and all the questions concerning the so called Dubliners. On the other side, there is a question of primary importance and it resounds from the today tv news until the columns of the first pages of the today's newspaper, the Covid pandemia.

The two elements looks both to be of a certain consistency.

They do not only remind all of us to the needs of having common standards, but even more to read a common point of view.

Health is maybe the problem number one related to emigration. Sociology of health is one of the possible tools which can be used as to read the different elements.

In fact, to speak about health means to speak about a complicated and intricated net of questions that can be resumed in this way.

Health is not to be considered just as a benefit exclusively reserved to a class of privileged people.

Health of emigrants is not a question separated and to be considered apart. Health is as a unique core multicell.

Health and Migration go hand in hand. This is not only valid for what concerns a formal way of interpretation but even a substantial one.

To speak of health cannot mean to avoid speaking of politics.

When we speak on Covid vaccination where is the line of separation between public and private?

And which are the limits the state and the single have not to trespass?

How the freedom of the single can be said not violated when the power of the state looks to be so strong not to permit an individual choice?

Interrogations similar are on the other side made from the institutions on the front of the vaccinal plan as well.

How difficult looks to choose without trespassing the thin line of separation between personal choice and freedom compulsory acts?

Of course these questions are more important if we are considering migrants in general and Dubliners in particular. The weakness of these positions makes these questions/ issues very sensitive.

References

Professor of Health Sociology, International University UniCamillus, Rome, Italy and Director of CIRS (Center for social studies in health), International University UniCamillus, Rome, Italy

Professor of Moral Philosophy, International University UniCamillus, Rome, Italy

Press Office & Master Online Coordinator, International University UniCamillus, Rome, Italy

763   How the COVID-19 pandemic has affected Syrian government-assisted refugees in Canada

Abe Oudshoorn, Cindy Brown, Eman Arnout, Fawziah Rabiah-Mohammed, Leah Hamilton, Luc Theriault, Mohammad Zaid Bakhash, Mohammed El Hazzouri, Rima Tarraf, Sagida Elnihum, Sarah Benbow, Victoria Esses

Background

Previous research finds that Government-Assisted Refugees (GARs) achieve the poorest settlement outcomes among other groups of refugees in Canada (Dhital, 2015; IRCC 2016; Rose & Charette 2017). The one-year government support timeline does not align with the length of time GARs need to adjust to their new life in the receiving country (Oudshoorn, Benbow & Meyer, 2019). COVID-19 has exacerbated GARs' vulnerabilities and intensified their precarious economic and housing situations.

Aim

The current study explored the experiences of Syrian GARs living in Canada during COVID-19 and addressed two overarching questions: 1) How are Syrian refugee families in Canada experiencing housing stability during the pandemic? 2) What barriers to integration has the pandemic created for Syrian GARs?

Methodology and Methods

To explore Syrian GARs' experiences during COVID-19, 37 families were interviewed during Summer 2020. Critical Social Theory guided the analysis, which involves focusing attention on the social inequalities that resulted from the pandemic. Using a qualitative descriptive methodology (Thorne, Kirkham, & MacDonald-Emes, 1997), three themes emerged.

Findings

The three themes that emerged from the analyses were: Social Isolation, Financial Challenges, and Housing Instability. The Social Isolation theme told the story of the thin social fabric that this group has experienced during the pandemic. The Financial Challenges theme involved the unique challenges this group has faced during the pandemic regarding employment, budgeting, and expenses. The Housing Instability theme subsumes two narratives of housing instability for this group. The first narrative focused on the inadequate housing conditions this group experienced during the lockdown, and the second narrative was related to the limited resources to achieve housing stability.

Conclusion

Employment precarity compounded with social isolation and insufficient housing has amplified GARs' struggles during the lockdowns and Stay at Home Orders. To address these challenges, policy and practice recommendations are recommended to reduce the negative effects of COVID-19 on refugees in Canada.

Keywords: Government-assisted refugees, COVID-19 pandemic, social inequalities, housing, Syrian refugees

References

Dhital, D. (2015). The Economic Outcomes of Government Assisted Refugees, Privately Sponsored Refugees and Asylum Seekers in Canada. Retrieved Feb 22, 2021 from https://ruor.uottawa.ca/bitstream/10393/32311/1/DIKSHYA,%20Dikshya%2020151.pdf

IRCC. (2016). Evaluation of the Resettlement Programs (GAR, PSR, BVOR and RAP). Retrieved Feb 17, 2021 from Evaluation of the Resettlement Programs (canada.ca)

Oudshoorn, A., Benbow, S., & Meyer, M. (2019). Resettlement of Syrian refugees in Canada. *Journal of International Migration and Integration*, 1-16.

Rose, D., & Charette, A. (2017). *Finding housing for the Syrian refugee newcomers in Canadian cities: challenges, initiatives and policy implications. Synthesis report.* INRS Centre-Urbanisation Culture Société.

Thorne, S., Kirkham, S. R., & MacDonald-Emes, J. (1997). Interpretive description: a noncategorical qualitative alternative for developing nursing knowledge. *Research in nursing & health, 20*(2), 169-177.

845   Labor Migration and Pandemic Paradox

Liudmila Konstants

Kyrgyzstan is one of the leading pushing labor migrants and remittances-dependent countries of the World. Shares of remittances in country's GDP is around one-third.[45] Over the past ten years, labor migrants transferred over $19 billion. Over the same time, the country earned $18 billion from the export. Without remittances more than 30% of the population would live in extreme poverty because even now 1.3 million - from around six million of citizens of Kyrgyzstanis - live on less than $ 1.50 a day. 46

The main objective of the research is to analyze the effect of pandemic lockdown in Russia on labor migrants from Kyrgyzstan.

To analyze the situation, the available data and literature were examined (the finding and collection of them is under process). We are looking for the additional data for 2020 and an appropriate model to analysis. At the same time, the first analysis revealed the following:

Due to serious plunge of the demand on labor migrants in Russia around 180 thousand labor migrants returned to Kyrgyzstan in 2020.

Labor market of Kyrgyzstan has replenished with almost 150 thousand young people and another 150,000 new employees are expected this year. (Thus, about 500 thousand "go without work". Ministry of Internal Affairs said about the increase of number of thefts.) 47

Some Russian's politicians (populists) saluted the returns of labor migrants in their countries proposing to replace them by local unemployed. When it became clear that Russians would not replace migrants, panic arose among employers in the labor market. Large business began of exporting migrants using charter flights, bus transportation within the framework of an organized selection. Since there is a struggle for legal migrants, their wages have been raised in all sectors.48

The results of the latest sociological research have revealed that due to the "shadow activity" of labor migrants when employers don't pay any taxes, employers pay significantly higher salaries. As a result – local potential employees are forcing out from some labor markets. 49

The shortage of labor migrants, whom residents of large Russian cities are used to hiring to perform hard physical work, led to a paradoxical effect - they began

[45] Share of remittances of the Kyrgyzstan in GDP: 37.1% (2017), 32.5 (2018), and 28.5% (2019): Sources:https://www.knomad.org/data/remittances?tid%5B160%5D=160
https://data.worldbank.org/indicator/BX.TRF.PWKR.DT.GD.ZS?locations=KG&view=chart
Most of remittances (More than 90%) are sent from Russia - http://www.cetrn.org/ru/post/perevody-migrantov-v-kyrgyzstan-sokratilis-za-god-pochti-na-200-millionov Decline in 2019 could be explained, mostly, by the Russian's economy slowdown and decrease of the oil prices. But – this is not the issue of this topic.
[46] https://www.bbc.com/russian/features-53167907
[47] https://kloop.kg/blog/2021/01/20/dissonans-zhaparovyh-deputat-predlagaet-otpravlyat-kyrgyzstantsev-v-rossiyu-eshelonami-hotya-pobedivshij-na-vyborah-obeshhal-ih-vozvrashhat/
[48] https://novayagazeta.ru/articles/2020/11/26/88138-operatsiya-chi-nibud-ruki?fbclid=IwAR0mrFAIFW-osg-ZKRBWeV4JOJxNNtiSSpjlDPH6zJ-orDWECxea3i1waGw
[49] http://stanradar.kz/news/full/43004-pochemu-migrantam-v-rossii-platjat-na-tret-bolshe-chem-mestnomu-naseleniju.html?fbclid=IwAR2e-QfrXFPP1KqV_NGfzuVszzaOynDsNgwdXAK8cu3ynezpu5v7gAio76A
https://www.ritmeurasia.org/news--2021-01-15--pochemu-migrantam-v-rossii-platjat-na-tret-bolshe-chem-mestnomu-naseleniju-52784

to ask for more for their services in the context of the coronavirus than local residents - sometimes in two or three times.50 This is the pandemic paradox.

Nobody can claim that such a situation could be preserved for any significant period of time. Experts admit that this "balance" could be upset at any moment with unexpected results. That's why a consecutive analysis of the situation should be continued.

Paper could be of interest of students of Economic and Business departments, of the officials of the Migration entities of the Kyrgyz Republic and Russia, of researchers in the field.

Paper with preliminary results is planning to be published in English and Russian languages.

Day Four 9 July 2021 - 16:45-18:30
Special Panel: Syrian refugees in Canada, safe but worry about food [Click here to Join]
Moderator: Ginny Lane, Adjunct Professor, School of Public Health, University of Saskatchewan, Canada
Panellists:
* **Hassanali Vatanparast**, Professor of Nutrition, University of Saskatchewan, Canada
* **Mustafa Koc**, Professor of Sociology, Ryerson University, Canada

END OF DAY FOUR

---

50 https://www.ritmeurasia.org/news--2020-12-22--kem-zamenit-trudovyh-migrantov-52487

11A   Technology and Migration
Chair Emre Eren Korkmaz, Oxford University, UK
796   Knowledge Base Sphere of AI for Migration studies
      Almila Alkim Akdag Salah and Tuba Bircan
574   Uses and Gratifications of Digital Diasporic Media Amongst Same-
      Language Minorities: A Qualitative Case Study on the Venezuelan
      Immigrant Communities in Chile and in Colombia After the Refugee
      Crisis (215 - onwards)
      Matthias Erlandsen
880   The Identification Trap for Refugees Digital Identity Solutions for the
      Financial Inclusion of Refugees: Empowerment or Denial of Their
      Agency?
      Emre Eren Korkmaz

796   Knowledge Base Sphere of AI for Migration studies

Almila Alkim Akdag Salah and Tuba Bircan

The concept of Big Data and application of Artificial Intelligence (AI) is gaining popularity at many scientific disciplines and migration and mobility studies is not an exception. The potential of Big Data and application of AI techniques to fill some of the gaps in traditional data sources and methods feeds to the advantages of using new data sources for the analysis of migration-related elements. Using AI technologies to analyse Big Data for migration and mobility research recently attracts notable attention of scholars from different disciplines. There have been several studies within disciplines assessing AI applications for migration and mobility related questions. Nevertheless, given the multidisciplinarity of the concepts, the common impact of these articles is not straightforward. This study aims at conducting an elaborate bibliometric study on publications of human mobility and Big Data analytics. Bibliometrics is a research line that studies the evaluation of sciences, by especially focusing on the citations between papers and journals. The resulting citation networks showcase not only how a new concept diffuses into the scientific literature, but also renders the disciplines, and subject areas that are most influenced by it. The bibliometric data for indexed scientific publications in this study is drawn from the Web of Science for the years 2015 and 2020. For analyses, bibliometrics methodology is adopted to map the time trend, the disciplinary/subject distribution, the high-frequency keywords, the topic evolutions, funding institutes, most influential journals and citation impact of the related academic articles.

574 Uses and Gratifications of Digital Diasporic Media Amongst Same-Language Minorities: A Qualitative Case Study on the Venezuelan Immigrant Communities in Chile and in Colombia After the Refugee Crisis (215 - onwards)

Matthias Erlandsen

According to the literature, mass media are an essential institution in the migration process (Park, 1920, 1922, 1925). Several studies, particularly those in sociology and social psychology, demonstrate that along with other institutions, mass media are one of the first to emerge every time a new group of migrants settles (Hickerson & Gustafson, 2016).

However, these studies mostly focus on societies that do not share the same language. Therefore, their conclusions are apparent when they state that "ethnic media" helps navigate the hosting society and learn the local language for the newly-arrived immigrants.

Drawing on Park's ideas on "Ethnic and Foreign Media," and considering the new patterns in South-South human migration, especially in Latin America and the former colonies, this study aims to, on the one hand, to distinguish the concept "Ethnic Media" from "Diasporic Media" regarding digital media created by and for migrant communities—particularly those sharing the same language;

On the other hand, this research aims to analyze and document new Uses and Gratifications (Katz, Blumler, & Gurevitch, 1973) that Venezuelan migrants in Chile and Colombia report over their experiences after consuming two different local news outlets of this kind: "El Vinotinto" in Chile, and "El Venezolano Colombia" in Colombia.

This research is based on an exploratory qualitative research (Creswell & Plano Clark, 2018), which involves online one-on-one interviews with migrants in both Chile and Colombia to detect new categories of uses and gratifications.

Preliminary conclusions demonstrate that there are new uses and gratifications. In the first category, audiences report using this type of media to promote entrepreneurship and professional services, access to censored news in Venezuela, and as a channel of humanitarian aid. They report legal compliance in the migration process in the gratifications category, stronger bonds with Venezuela's daily life, and an ethnonationalism without community-building.

References

Creswell, J. W., & Plano Clark, V. L. (2018). *Designing and Conducting Mixed Methods Research* (3rd ed.). Thousand Oaks, CA: SAGE.

Hickerson, A., & Gustafson, K. L. (2016). Revisiting the immigrant press. *Journalism, 17*(8), 943-960. doi:10.1177/1464884914542742

Katz, E., Blumler, J. G., & Gurevitch, B. (1973). Uses and gratifications research. *Public Opinion Quarterly, 37*, 509-523.

Park, R. E. (1920). *Foreign language press and social progress.* Paper presented at the National Conference of Social Work, Chicago, IL.

Park, R. E. (1922). *The immigrant press and its control.* New York; London: Harper & Brothers.

Park, R. E. (1925). The immigrant community and the immigrant press. *American Review, 3,* 18-24.

880   The Identification Trap for Refugees Digital Identity Solutions for the Financial Inclusion of Refugees: Empowerment or Denial of Their Agency?

Emre Eren Korkmaz

The year 2020 marks the beginning of the 'decade of action,' the 10-year global push to move each country closer towards attaining the United Nations Sustainable Development Goals (SDGs) by 2030. Chief among these goals is **the target 16.9, "providing legal identity for all."** (UN, 2015; Brown, 2018) The commitment to leave no one behind is crucial at a time when the number of peoples forced to flee their homes either as refugees or internally displaced persons (IDP) is the highest since World War II (79.5 million). The UN High Commissioner for Refugees, Filippo Grandi states that "displacement nowadays is not only vastly more widespread but is simply no longer a short-term and temporary phenomenon." (UNHCR, 2020).

Economic inclusion is integral to helping refugees sustain themselves. A precondition to even the most basic forms of financial inclusion is the provision of identity. A recognised identity determines the social transactions in which someone can participate and it is needed to access the formal financial sector and retain a sense of dignity and agency so profoundly connected to an individual's ability to fully participate in society. A lack of documentation presents a critical barrier to financial inclusion and threatens continued marginalisation (Appaya and Varghese, 2019; Accentura, 2019; Caribou, 2019; Castells, 1997; Fiege et.al, 1988; Goodwin et.al, 2007; IFC, 2017).

The methods used to register and manage identities as well as the possible number of services and transactions that depend on identification are changing as states, humanitarian organisations, and financial institutions embrace digital identity (Shoemaker, Currion and Pon, 2018; Jacobovitz, 2016; Ko and Verity, 2016; Natarajan et.al, 2018). A digital identity created by or used on, with, or through digital technologies makes it possible for individuals and institutions to manage a collection of digital identifiers, stored as bits and bytes of data, that describe attributes or transactions (Bostrom and Sandberg, 2011; Gelb and Metz, 2018).

The shift in technologies and processes used by issuing agencies has the potential to streamline and accelerate the financial inclusion of refugees, but also presents new risks and exacerbates existing challenges. This research argues that the power of governments and corporations to deploy surveillance technologies to control, manage, manipulate and indeed halt migratory movements is far greater than the benefits provided to refugees. **The research offers a comparison between how new technologies are used to surveil migratory movements and how they are used to support the identification**

for the financial inclusion of refugees as two aims that interact, overlap and sometimes come into conflict with one another. The project will examine whether the tech-backed identification ecosystem empower or deny the agency of refugees and shed light on whose interests are served, examining the mainstream model of identification and surveillance of refugees carried out by governments, supra/international organisations and corporations.

The research will investigate the tension that emerge with the dual faces of technology, e.g. technology-for-good and technological threat. On one hand, technology can be the key to empowering individuals around the world and particularly those kept outside the formal institutions of power. On the other hand technologies can be appropriated by a small number of corporations and states, leading to a concentration of power benefitting certain firms or sectors or indeed certain countries to the exclusion of others (Floridi, 2007; Agamben, 2005; Brayne, 2014).

A number of scandals, such as Cambridge Analytica, have recently revealed the extent of the dangers underlying these new technologies (Solon, 2018). Tech criticism ranges from misgivings about censorship and ever more sophisticated manipulation techniques ushering a world replete of attempts at *hijacking the mind* or *the mining of our lives* as documented by Zuboff (2019) in Surveillance Capitalism. This leads to the loss of individual sovereignty as we witness an increasing concentration of power, be it corporate or political, created by technological advances (Zuboff, 2019).

The resarch will benefit from Naomi Klein's (2007) *disaster capitalism* and s*hock doctrine* approach when analysing the digital ID initiatives for refugees in the global South and examining the interests and motivations of tech corporations to invest in humanitarian emergencies. Klein (2017) describes *shock doctrine* as a tactic for neo-liberal politics and corporations to exploit the public's disorientation following a collective shock, such as wars and disasters, to push through radical pro-corporate measures. The ongoing digital ID projects are not sourced from the demands of refugees, they are introduced and promoted by corporations to **expand their markets, reach new clients, solve the *Know Your Customer* requirement of financial transactions, experiment their technologies and mining more data without any legal restrictions like GDPR.** As refugees are sharing a collective shock, they are not in a position to judge these projects and provide voluntary consent (Bigo, 2012; Duffield, 2012; Ellerman, 2010; IFC, 2018). Therefore, the project will contribute to this approach by analysing digital ID initiatives at the intersection point of data management, privacy, agency, financial inclusion and surveillance (Hosein and Nyst, 2013; Latonero and Kift, 2018; Madianou, 2019).

The research question is "What is the role of digital ID initiatives on the financial inclusion of refugees and their impact on the issues related to privacy and agency of refugees?"

The research has following objectives

1- Digital ID initiatives provide solutions to collect and store refugee data that would allow states, financial institutions, NGOs and companies to evaluate these sets of data to provide service. The research will explore the tension between refugees wanting more control over their data (decentralizing data storage and control for the beneficiary); organizations desire to use individuals data for coordination purposes (to avoid duplication and fraud) and to be accountable to donors (demonstrate real people received the assistance) and discuss what the trade-offs are.

2- Legal identity for all is one of the main targets of the UN's Sustainable Development Goals (SDG) that will pave the way for the financial inclusion. The research will analyse the relationship between the UN SDGs for identification and corporate-state surveillance as a byproduct of these solutions. Corporate surveillance to check out the credit history and evaluate the refugee data collected and stored in these digital identities is a requirement for providing financial services. The research will discuss the limits and potential challenges of such surveillance of a vulnerable population. Therefore, the practicality and the future of the humanitarian standarts such as "do no harm", voluntary consent, and privacy rights will be elaborated.

3- The research will debate the quest for innovation for refugees which needs to avoid the trap of experimentation with vulnerable populations

We selected **four case studies** from Turkey, Jordan and Kenya to discuss and compare the deployment of digital ID solutions for different displaced communities. These are

- Turkey: European Bank of Reconstruction and Development-funded digital ID for the financial inclusion of Syrian refugee entrepreneurs in Turkey project and

- Turkey: the European Union-funded Kızılay (Red Crescent) Card for aid distribution

- Jordan: Zardari camp. World Food Programme blockchain-based cash transfer programme

- Kenya: IF Red Cross Dignified ID (DIGID) project which is a self-sovereign digital ID initiative. As this project will be concluded until September 2021, this will be mainly based on document review.

11B Education and Skilled Migration
Chair: Merita Zulfiu Alili, South East European University, N. Macedonia
731   Academic Brain Drain: The Case of North Macedonia
        Merita Zulfiu Alili, Memet Memeti, Blerta Ahmedi Arifi, Pranvera Kasami
736   Education and skilled migration: UniCamillus' educational offer
        Beatrice Casella
827   High-skilled female labour migration from India in an age of
        Globalisation
        Mia Maria Haugen Feuh

731   Academic Brain Drain: The Case of North Macedonia

Merita Zulfiu Alili, Memet Memeti, Blerta Ahmedi Arifi, Pranvera Kasami

Skilled labour is an important asset for any country in the development process
and the emigration of skilled individuals presents a threat of a 'brain drain' which
can affect growth, development and the quality of education. Brain drain in this
research represents the loss of academic staff and researchers from a source
country to a recipient country. Using survey data this study investigates the
factors affecting academic staff's decision on migration. It critically examines
brain drain in higher education institutions in North Macedonia and its
implications. Most of the academic staff intends to migrate to more developed
countries mainly because of low standards of living and wages, political
influence in universities and lack of promotion possibilities based on merit. The
recent pandemic opened new possibilities of academic staff and researchers to
work or emigrate 'virtually' without the need to be physically present there.
These possibilities should be explored and could be attractive as well for the
skilled emigrants to transfer their knowledge to their colleagues and institutions
in the home country, i.e. 'virtual return'. Based on the finding this paper proposes
policy recommendations for institutions to explore strategies on how to best use
the skills of academic and research staff for improving socio-economic benefits,
and most importantly commitment to implementing these strategies.

736   Education and skilled migration: UniCamillus' educational offer

Beatrice Casella

Introduction

The Universal Declaration of Human Rights (1948) in art. 2 states that: "Each
individual is entitled to all the rights and freedoms set forth her ein Declaration,
without distinction for reasons of race, color, sex, language, of political or other
opinion, of national or social origin, of wealth, of birth or of another condition. "
Education is an essential right with wich even fight the stereotype of migration.
Students with a migrant background often face difficulties in adjusting to a new
learning environment. Education and training practitioners can benefit from
guidance and the sharing of good practices to be able to address the learning
needs of students in increasingly diverse and multilingual classrooms.
UniCamillus – International Medical University in Rome - it is precisely the
reflection of the education as a migration opportunity

In a world increasingly globalized, education is synonymous with acceptance
and integration. The open meeting with others cultures and models of life, the
guarantee for all citizens to acquire in the universities a real learning experience
and social inclusion, are essential objectives to which educational institutions
must aim with the strong collaboration of the national and international
institutions. The phenomenon of immigration is considered a constitutive

element of ours societies in which individuals belonging to different cultures are increasingly numerous. Full integration of immigrants into the host society is a fundamental goal and, in this process, the role of the University is primary.

Goals

Internationalization and humanitarian mission are the distinctive values of UniCamillus, an Italian University dedicated exclusively to Medical Sciences. It is a "foreign policy through health" initiative made possible through an educational program aimed at preparing doctors and health professionals capable of operating even in countries less developed. Over 30% of students come from 36 non-EU countries and the percentage is destined to increase. UniCamillus, indeed, has the ambitious mission of bringing health to the center of dialogue between nations, given that health is an absolute value to which the North and the South of the world must work tirelessly.

Work method

In accordance with the international characteristic of the University, the six-year Degree Course in Medicine and Surgery and the Bachelor's Degree Courses in Physiotherapy, Nursing and Radiology, Diagnostic Images and Radiotherapy Techniques are taught entirely in English. The University constantly guarantees the use of various didactic tools and support programs to help students of different cultures and languages to improve their scientific English fluency to reached the desired level to take advantage of their degree in most countries of the world, without any linguistic difficulties. Moreover, UniCamillus grants an important number of scholarships, that partially or totally covering the university tuition fee, to non-EU students who do not have sufficient economic resources and who show themselves deserving and motivated. There is not a specific number of scholarships because the aim is to provide an unlimited support to all brilliant students from developing countries who need to be financially helped.

One of the tools: "loan of honour"

In particular, the formula used by the University is the "loan of honour" which is completely extinguished if after graduation the young health professional returns to work in his country of origin for a period of at least three years. It was introduced with Law no.390 of 2 December 1991, as a form of support from the State to guarantee the right to education enshrined in the Constitution. With a loan of honour we mean a form of financing that provides for facilitated repayment conditions and easier access to credit than other solutions. In fact, the applicant does not necessarily have to prove an income, nor present a guarantor or a co-obligator. This type of loan allows university students to have a sum of money in a current account, disbursed in several installments for the entire duration of their studies.UniCamillus accepts the most deserving students who really express their interest in undertaking a healthcare path. Last year teenagers from 46 countries took the admission test to study at UniCamillus. New nationalities from Saudi Arabia, Brazil, Burkina Faso, Costa Rica, Republic of Congo, Egypt, El Salvador, Iraq and so on were added. Just why The University is secular and open to young people who practise the most varied

352

religions. At the moment, there are Christian, Muslim, Jewish, Hindu, Shinto and even animist students. This diversity enriches the University's culture, because health is its only belief. UniCamillus, through an excellent teaching staff that adheres to these values of brotherhood and compassion, trains its students to pursue health as an absolute value, a science for the benefit af all without discrimination or differences of any kind. UniCamillus graduates will always keep in mind the humanitarian values acquired during their study path.

827   High-skilled female labour migration from India in an age of Globalisation

Mia Maria Haugen Feuh

Research question: How has the process of globalisation affected the movement of high-skilled female labour migrants from India?

India has seen unprecedented economic growth for the last three decades. With the implementation of neoliberal economic- and political policies since the early 1990s, the country has risen from being on the brink of collapse, to become a major economic superpower. It has revolutionized its Information and Communication Technology (ICT) accordingly with the current high global demand and dependency from an industry that insists on never ending expansion and growth. As a result, the country has become a mass exporter of ICT professionals. And Norway, with its commitment to technology and development has become one of the countries in the world who through the implementation of lenient high skilled migration laws are experiencing a rapidly growing flow of high skilled ICT professionals from India.

With the demand for high-skilled labour migrants increasing, India's process of globalisation has facilitated the rise in the number of ICT professionals who chose to travel abroad for work opportunities.

This study aims to examine how India's process of globalisation has facilitated the rise in high-skilled female labour migrants from India to Norway. Analysing the rise in ICT

professionals through a gendered lens, within an Indian context, gives insight into a number of obstacles that obstruct Indian women's opportunity to be a part of the Indian labour force, as well as limiting their ability to partake in the global market as high skilled labour migrants.

To be able to analyse my research question my own data set consists of digital semi-structured interviews conducted with fourteen Indian women, who had either worked or were currently working as ICT professionals in Norway. They were chosen through the use of convenience sampling. Additionally, to be able to substantiate my analysis I am relying on data from secondary sources, both qualitative (previous research on the topic of India and high skilled migration) and quantitative studies (statistics, graphs etc.).

What I found was that India's process of globalisation has to a large extent only benefitted a very small percentage of the population, notably those who have the ability and opportunity to acquire a degree through tertiary education. It became clear that to be able to partake in the global labour market as a skilled migrant from India, especially as an Indian woman, you need to be a part of the Indian upper classes. Additionally, to be able to grow up in an Indian household where the parents see the importance of educating their girls proved paramount.

Finally, my findings emphasize that given the immense inequalities within the Indian society, the access to education, rights, information, and formal work is a good reserved mostly for the privileged. The inequality of opportunity is especially notable in India as caste belonging, class affiliation and sex is all intertwined in a halted hierarchy where the probability for upwards social mobility is arduous.

852   International Migration of Highly Educated, Stay-at-home Mothers: The case of the United Kingdom

Arzu Kırcal Sahin

The purpose of this study was to explore about the experiences of highly educated mothers with at least one child who have left their jobs and have immigrated to the UK because of their spouse's job. The study investigates the barriers that these Turkish women may face in the UK. Research on immigrants has been mostly restricted to quantitative methods which rely on statistical data sets. A search of the literature revealed that qualitative studies are rarely used within the field. In order to examine this issue, in-depth interviews were held with 20 Turkish participants who met the research criteria. Integrating these findings with relevant international migration theories, this doctoral research reveals that those highly educated Turkish women with advanced career success who took part in this research have not managed to break the cycle of traditional gender roles. It also shows that these women have, not only taken care of their children, but also have established a harmonious family environment in order to assist their husbands' career. The findings of this study show that moving to the UK with their spouses inevitably has resulted in a decline in the career success, financial and social status for the participants.

11C   COVID-19 Impact on Migration Governance
Chair: Afzalur Rahman, University of Chittagong, Bangladesh
897   The Covid-19 pandemic and its impacts on migration governance in Greece
Dimitra Manou, Anastasia Blouchoutzi and Jason Papathanasiou
637   COVID-19, Rohingya Refugees in Bangladesh and the Uncertain future
Afzalur Rahman
678   Insecure Immigration Status and Covid-19
Nicole Dubus

897   The Covid-19 pandemic and its impacts on migration governance in Greece

Dimitra Manou, Anastasia Blouchoutzi and Jason Papathanasiou

The Covid-19 pandemic seems to have disproportionate effect on refugee and migration populations (OECD, 2020) and the undocumented migrants may be the most vulnerable (Wickramage K. et al, 2018). The profound impacts on migrants/refugees may be observed either at newly arrived populations, or populations at reception centres, or even settled refugees. The pandemic has affected migrants/refugees's livelihoods in many ways; it has affected their basic rights (i.e. access to health and education), their efforts to re-unite with their families in other countries, their personal pursuits. Overall the pandemic has certainly brought disruption in migrants' and refugees' lives.

Meanwhile, governments face new challenges in managing and coordinating this new situation, which has widespread implications on migration governance. State responses have focused mostly on safety and security. Other actors, especially International Organizations and NGOs, have in many cases been faster than the state in their responses. COVID-19 requires endorsement of new governance approaches, more migrant-inclusive (Guadagno 2020).

This paper has a two-folded goal: a) to identify the impacts of Covid-19 pandemic on migrants/refugees' livelihoods who are located in Greece, especially with regard to their basic rights, their access to education, labor market and health services and b) to explore the impacts of the pandemic on migration governance in Greece focusing on state and local policy responses.

The authors have contacted both desk research and fieldwork in the framework of the H2020 project "Migration Governance and Asylum Crises – MAGYC" with semi-structured interviews of relevant government authorities, NGOs and other state and non-state actors. The authors first present migrants' and refugees' locations in Greece and discuss the differentiated conditions of their livelihoods depending on the region they are located. In addition, they examine the specific vulnerabilities regarding access to basic rights. They then provide an analysis of migration governance during the pandemic as exercised by state and non-state actors at both state and local levels. Finally, the authors discuss the challenges faced by the Greek government regarding migration management and governance and highlight any migrant-inclusive measures.

References

OECD, What is the impact of the Covid-19 pandemic on immigrants and their children?, 19.10.2020

Guadagno L., Migrants and the COVID-19 pandemic: An initial analysis, IOM 2020

Wickramage K. et al, Missing: Where Are the Migrants in Pandemic Influenza Preparedness Plans? Health and Human Rights Journal 20:1, 251-258, 2018

637 COVID-19, Rohingya Refugees in Bangladesh and the Uncertain future

Afzalur Rahman

COVID-19 has triggered unprecedented challenges in all over the globe. Bangladesh has been encountering with some tough problems from the very beginning. The scales and scopes of the impact of this pandemic are severe which might alter the social relations of Bangladeshi society for the long term. However, it had a different scale of impact on the 8.6 stateless Rohingya refugees in Bangladesh who have displaced after the persecution in Myanmar at 2017. Thus, this paper sheds light on the socio-economic and political-conflict dynamics of the COVID-19 in mainly Rohingya refugee camps with focusing the uncertain repatriation process of the Rohingya refugees from Bangladesh to Myanmar. Bangladesh Government Refugee Commissioner's office reported, as of 7 August 2020, the number of confirmed cases is 78 and the number of deaths to six among Rohingyas. But the number of affected refugees is higher than the government statistic. This paper also focuses on the challenges faced by the Rohingya refugees living in Bangladesh after the outbreak of COVID-19. These are mainly the shortage of testing facilities for diagnosing the corona virus, bar in the communication with the refugees, lifting the restriction of movement to emergency service partner workers and foreigner's in the camps areas etc. In addition, there is also uncertainty of getting Covid-19 vaccine from Bangladesh and international donor agencies. Nonetheless, the cases of Rohingya refugee's involvement in human trafficking and drug smuggling have been increased after the outbreak of COVID-19 pandemic. Finally, the uncertainties of repatriation will be assessed linking with the impact of this pandemic.

678 Insecure Immigration Status and Covid-19

Nicole Dubus

Research Problem

The immigration policy known as Deferred Action for Childhood Arrivals (DACA) was developed to address the needs of children brought to the United States when they were young and have no clear path toward citizenship. This study examines the experiences of DACA eligible and recipient college students from one public university in California.

Theory

Critical Relations Theory is used to understand the experiences of the participants.

Methods

This was a mixed method study using a survey of DACA students (n=107) that focused on their experiences, and in-person interviews from key informants (n=4) who provide resources for DACA students, and from interviews of DACA students (n=7).

Findings

The qualitative data complemented the quantitative data in showing the additional stressors DACA students experience that impact their graduation and career outcomes, such as family obligations, work obligations, financial strain, mental health, academic strain, and fear.

Conclusions

To be helpful to this population, educators, policy makers, social support agencies, and immigration advocates need to be involved. It is important to understand the layered barriers that make it difficult for DACA students to succeed.

11D Arts, Literature and Migration

Chair: Ali Tilbe, Tekirdag Namik Kemal University, Turkey

851   Street art and migrations. The Ultrabandiere project
       Anna Di Giusto
536   Welsh Italian Literary Accounts of Internment in World War II: Les
       Servini's A Boy from Bardi and Hector Emanuelli's A Sense of
       Belonging
       Manuela D'Amore
854   The migration crisis as a crisis of European civilisation in Terremoto by
       Jarosław Mikołajewski and Ewelina Barbara Śliwa
913   Narrative and Migrant's Identity: Searching for the Meaningful Self
       Through Telling Stories from the Past in Kapka Kassabova's Street
       Without a Name: Childhood and Other Misadventures in Bulgaria
       Alina Ielisieieva

851   Street art and migrations. The Ultrabandiere project

Anna Di Giusto

The *Ultrabandiere* project was born in November 2017 in Turin within the Neruda People's Space, a school long abandoned and recently occupied by a group of migrants. One hundred fifty people live there, especially families with children, in a few cases young adults. According to several studies, immigrant populations are undergoing severe stresses associated with immigration and acculturation. The consequences could cause significant psychological or somatic symptoms. To prevent this risk, the street artist group *Guerrilla Spam* has worked with these migrants to imagine, design, and finally sew fourteen fabric flags. Their project aims to use art as an instrument to tell, transfigure, and sublimate stories, thoughts, dreams, and memories of their authors, both adults and children. These artefacts are called ultra-flags (*Ultrabandiere*) because they carry an excess of meaning. They are no longer just flags of identity, but open narratives, which everyone can read and interpret in his way. These tools are the gateway that permits them to transform their condition of illegality and human inequality in a shared insight into their story.

Guerrilla Spam's work aims to open Neruda's place to the neighbourhood, thus creating a bridge between the Italian inhabitants and the school's illegal occupants.

The migrants took over public space to reopen it, on the exhibition's occasion, to the community that had abandoned it. The re-signification of the place transforms the school from a protected environment for kids to a place of cultural exchange. The sewing machine's use by all the protagonists involved refers to the ancient feminine art of weaving as a collection of stories and an imaginary thread capable of linking a community through the invention of a new tradition. In 2019, the exhibition of flags took place in Rome, at the Macro Contemporary Art Museum, and in March 2020 in Bologna, at the MAMbo, the Museum of Modern Art. In this project, art serves as a rereading of the individual and family story, of origin and arrival, out of the process of refugee-maker organized by the Western institutions and voluntary activities. However, it is above all used as a language of an encounter of diverse experiences and maturation.

References

Blusseau, Y. (2017). *Portraits Urbains. De visage en visage.* Grenoble: Critères Editions.

Dal Lago, A., Giordano, S. (2018). *Sporcare i muri. Graffiti, decoro, proprietà privata.* Roma: Derive e Approdi.

De Finis, G. (2015). *Exploit. Come rovesciare il mondo ad arte.* Roma: Bordeaux Edizioni.

De Innocentis, I. (2017). *Urban Lives. Viaggio alla scoperta della street art in Italia.* Palermo: Dario Flaccovio Editore.

Dogheria, D. (2015). *Street Art, Storia e Controstoria, tecniche e protagonisti.* Milano: Giunti.

Dogramaci, B., Mersmann, B. (2019). *Handbook of Art and Global Migration. Theories, Practices, and Challenges.* Berlin: De Gruyter.

Grasso, M. (2013). *Rassismi, discriminazioni e confinamenti.* Roma: Ediesse.

Guerrilla Spam (2016). *Alla mia nazione.* Self-production.

Guerrilla Spam (2017). *Bizzarrio.* Lodi: Perpetua Edizioni

Guerrilla Spam (2018). *Compiti per casa.* Self-production.

Guerrilla Spam (2020). *Il Bestiario di Guerrilla Spam.* Self-production.

Ianniciello, C. (2018). *Migrations, Arts and Postcoloniality in the Mediterranean.* London: Routledge.

536   Welsh Italian Literary Accounts of Internment in World War II: Les Servini's A Boy from Bardi and Hector Emanuelli's A Sense of Belonging

Manuela D'Amore

Forgotten by academic criticism, Welsh Italian literary narratives are little known to the public, yet, they are rich in precious documentary evidence of the condition of the Italian immigrant community in major cities like Cardiff and Swansea during World War II. The aim of this paper is to show how authors such as Les Servini (1914-1999) and Hector Emanuelli (1920-2018) recounted their long and painful internment experiences in their memoirs.

In point of fact, after briefly introducing the distinctive features of Welsh Italian literary narratives – also Les Servini and Hector Emanuelli – our focus will be on *A Boy from Bardi: My Life and Times* (1994) and *A Sense of Belonging. From the Rhondda to the Potteries: Memories of a Welsh-Italian Englishman* (2010): they recount the two authors' condition as "enemy aliens" and internees in 1940-1942.

The first memoir in Anglo-Italian migration literature, *A Boy from Bardi* dedicates part of the narration – especially Chapters Three, *War*, and Four, *The Ile of Man* – to the outbreak of World War II and to Servini's detention in one of the British POW camp on the Ile of Man. His long journey to the little island and the description of his new routine there also parallel with a special account of the Arandora Star tragedy, which occurred on 2nd July 1940 and caused the death of 446 members of the Italian immigrant community in the UK. Most importantly, however, there is room for positive qualities such as courage, hope and resilience.

A similar type of approach can be found in Emanuelli's *A Sense of Belonging*. Published in the same year as Anita Arcari's *The Hockey Pockey Man*, this memoir also includes an attack against Mussolini, as well as the author's sudden and painful transition to the condition of Italian "enemy alien" after Churchill ordered to "collar the lot" on 10th June 1940. The detailed narration of his confinement in Camp M, again, on he Isle of Man complements that of Servini as it shows not only the hardships that the immigrants-internees had to face, but also the solidarity that they developed and kept them alive.

Part of a larger project of study on Anglo-Italian literary narratives of World War II, this paper will finally compare the distinctive features of these two memoirs with one of the iconic works in Scottish Italian migration literature, Joe Pieri's *Isle of the Displaced: An Italian-Scot's Memoirs of Internment in the Second World War* (1997). Aside from the wider political considerations which are at the heart of this latter, we shall demonstrate that Servini and Emanuelli experienced the same sense of estrangement and isolation that Pieri felt before and after he was released and savoured freedom. In post Brexit times these authors' works need to be rediscovered and researched on for the future generations in Italy and in the UK.

Select Bibliography

Primary Sources

Emanuelli, Hector (2010). A Sense of Belonging. From Rhondda to the Potteries: Memories of a Welsh-Italian Englishman. Langenfeld: Six Towns Books.

Pieri, Joe (1997). Isle of the Displaced: An Italian Scot's Memoirs of Internment in the Second World War, Castle Douglas: Neil Wilson Publishing.

Servini, Les (1994). A Boy from Bardi. My Life and Times. Cardiff: Hazeltree Press.

Secondary Sources

Ceserani, David and Tony Kushner (eds.) (1993). The Internment of Aliens in Twentieth Century Britain. London and New York. Routledge.

Chezzi, Bruna (2015). Italians in Wales and Its representations, 1920s-2010s. Newcastle upon Tyne: Cambridge Scholars Publishing.

D'Amore, Manuela (2020). "Identità, straniamento e resilienza in Joe Pieri, Isle of the Displaced: An Italian Scot's Memoirs of Internment in the Second World War, in Valentina Calì (ed.), Isolitudine, Confine, Identità. Messina: Lippoli, pp. 83-98.

Hughes, Colin (1991). Lime, Lemon, & Salsaparilla: The Italian Community in Wales, 1881-1945. Bridgend: Seren Books.

Sponza, Lucio (2006). "Italian Immigrants in Britain: Perceptions and Self Perceptions", in Kathy Burrell, Panikos Panayi (eds), Histories and Memories: Migrants and Their History in Britain. London: Bloomsbury, pp. 57-74.

Paolini Stefano (2015). Missing Presumed Drowned: A True Story of the Internment of Italians Resident in Britain During the Second World War, Published by Stefano Paolini [sic].

Sprio, Margherita (2013). Cultural History, Cinema and the Italian Post-War Diaspora in Britain. Oxford and New York: Peter Lang.

854 The migration crisis as a crisis of European civilisation in Terremoto

by Jarosław Mikołajewski and Ewelina Barbara Śliwa

In the reportage *Terremoto* (2017) the migration crisis is not in the foreground. It is, as on the Peter Bruegel's painting *Daedalus and Icarus* – somewhere aside. The author takes us on a journey through Italy after the earthquake which took place few years ago. The broken church of saint Benedict (the patron of Europe) becomes the symbol of the metaphorical end of our continent. Migrants and the migration crisis occur in the background as flashbacks and allusions. However, the catastrophic climate of this hybrid non-fiction book strongly refers to refugees. The migration crisis is understood here as a crisis of Europe. Dobrosław Kot, polish contemporary philosopher and novelist writes that the word "crisis" is more connected with Old Continent than with the refugees. The great growth of immigration becomes a chance to redefine European identity, values and also institutions. The refugee damages connections between country-nation and territory. What question does a refugee ask us? What can he/she teach us? In my presentation I would like to analyse the poetic reportage *Terremoto* in the connection of Dobrosław Kot's essay *Ulysses raft* (in which the author is inspired by the thought of Giorgio Agamben, Emmanuel Lévinas, Hannah Arendt and more philosophers and thinkers). I would also define the poetic reportage and point out that the hybridity of the book as an interesting choice of speaking about contemporary times and migration problem.

913   Narrative and Migrant's Identity: Searching for the Meaningful Self Through Telling Stories from the Past in Kapka Kassabova's Street Without a Name: Childhood and Other Misadventures in Bulgaria

Alina Ielisieieva

Telling stories, an innate mode of verbalizing and passing on the experience, is one of the oldest media of communication through which people not only share the knowledge but also understand the world and ultimately themselves. Whether it's a novel, an essay or a biography, distinct events built into one coherent story make any literary form a narrative which brings the meaning to experiences which account for human life. Unusual or common, happy or painful, they all embody emotions, which lie in the core of the basic needs to love, to be loved, and to be accepted. Through integrating one's reconstructed past, perceived present, imagined future into one coherent story of the self, a narrative gives a chance for emotions to be expressed and for a person to reconstruct the setbacks, upsetting experiences or even family and ethnic traumas in order to find the meaning and reimagine an identity through telling, writing or composing a story.

In migrant literature a narrative is an essential tool of the construction of individual and collective identities and a means to make place in one's (life)story for both. Kapka Kassabova in her *Street Without a Name: Childhood and Other Misadventures in Bulgaria* literary travels in time and space in order to find the answer to the ultimate question "Who am I?" and through the reevaluation of her Bulgarian past manages to find and collect the missing fragments of her present Self. A narrative, words and sentences, in this case are paints in a painter's hands who can only see the unity and the meaning when the whole picture is finished on canvas.

11H   COVID-19 Impact on Refugee Communities
Chair: Deniz Eroglu Utku, Trakya University, Turkey
636   The impact of COVID-19 on asylum seekers and migrants in Belgium
        Julia Zomignani Barboza
        Lisa Feirabend
650   The Impact of Covid-19 on different migrant groups in Turkey
        Şebnem Koşer Akçapar
729   Combating Covid-19 Pandemic in 2020 Views and Experiences of the
        Pakistani Migrant Workers in Saudi Arabia
        Muhammad Saeed
730   A Crisis within a Crisis: The Impacts of the COVID-19 Pandemic on
        Syrian and Palestinian Refugees in Jordan
        Cevdet Acu

636   The impact of COVID-19 on asylum seekers and migrants in Belgium

Julia Zomignani Barboza and Lisa Feirabend

Asylum seekers and migrants in Belgium have seen important rights severely limited or even temporarily suspended by measures imposed to contain the spread of COVID-19. This contribution looks at two developments that had a significant impact on these two groups – the change of the system to request international protection; and restrictions on visits to immigrations detention centres.

Between 17 March and 3 April 2020, the arrival centre for asylum seekers was closed.[51] Consequently, no one was allowed to request asylum in Belgium for almost three weeks. On 3 April, application for international protection became possible again, though the in-person system was replaced by a new online appointment one.[52] Everyone wishing to request international protection had to fill in an online form, available only in French and Dutch, and wait to receive an email for an appointment, sometimes days or even weeks later. Only after the appointment would asylum seekers be housed in reception centres and start receiving material assistance. This system presented many challenges (e.g. related to language barrier, digital literacy and access to the internet) but mainly it prevented asylum seekers from entering the reception network from the moment they expressed their desire to obtain protection (i.e. upon completion of the form). A group of non-profit organisations challenged this system in Court. On 5 October, the francophone tribunal of first instance of Brussels ruled that the fact that asylum seekers could not request material assistance the moment they present their request online was *prima facie* illegal.[53] Consequently, the in-person system was reinstated with the necessary sanitary restrictions.

Sanitary measures also affected migrants in closed detention centres. While multiple detainees were released as returns and expulsions were mostly halted due to travel restrictions, those who remained in detention were not allowed to receive visitors, both personal and from organisations providing oversight.[54] Indeed, even a member of parliament was prevented from visiting the closed centre in Vottem.[55] Oversight of detention centres is of the upmost importance,

---

[51] Fedasil (17 March 2020), Le centre d'arrivée ferme ses portes. Available at: https://www.fedasil.be/fr/actualites/accueil-des-demandeurs-dasile/le-centre-darrivee-ferme-ses-portes

[52] Fedasil (3 April 2020), Reprise des demandes d'asile. Available at: https://www.fedasil.be/fr/actualites/accueil-des-demandeurs-dasile/reprise-des-demandes-dasile

[53] Ordonnance 2020/105/C, 5 October 2020, Tribunal de première instance francophone de Bruxelles.

[54] In normal times, NGO members of the so-called Transit Group conduct regular visits to closed detention centres in the country. See CIRÉ (17 August 2011), Groupe Transit: le réseau des visiteurs ONG en centres fermés. Available at: https://www.cire.be/groupe-transit-le-reseau-des-visiteurs-ong-en-centres-fermes/

[55] Sarah Schlitz (26 March 2020), Coronavirus : l'office des étrangers refuse une visite parlementaire au centre fermé de Vottem. Available at: https://sarahschlitz.be/coronavirus-loffice-des-etrangers-refuse-une-visite-parlementaire-au-centre-ferme-de-vottem/?fbclid=IwAR3rtM7sXoRpdVxhdya74C-VVRsOQI2qEnjYUuZ0xuH0-Los-AlmxrPugZl

especially as in early April media sources expressed concern over the situation in closed centres, reporting that expired food had been served and that sanitary measures were insufficient and inadequate.[56] While both personal and NGO visits were restored in July, with the increase in COVID cases at the last quarter of 2020, new restrictions were put in place, once again limiting the extent of independent oversight.

With the benefit of hindsight, the authors argue that these examples should constitute lessons learned that should guide the implementation of future measures in the continuation of this crisis or of possible new ones.

650   The Impact of Covid-19 on different migrant groups in Turkey

Şebnem Koşer Akçapar

Turkey has been a country of origin, transit, and destination for mixed migration flows that includes refugees, asylum seekers, irregular migrants and migrant workers. Mixed migration flows are defined as complex population movements of different migrant and refugee groups due to the various purposes, motives, means, and consequences (Nimkar, 2018). A mixed migration approach emphasizes three issues: 1) Motives for migrations are various; however, they can converge, 2) Means of travel or use of smuggling services might overlap, 3) An individual might change one category (e.g., a labor migrant) to another (e.g., refugee) in his/her life course (Vullnetari, 2012). As of 2021, Turkey hosts over 3.6 million Syrians under temporary protection along with approximately 330.000 under international protection mainly from Afghanistan, Iraq, and Iran (UNHCR, 2021). Due to its geographical proximity to the European Union, Turkey has also been affected by irregular migration flows. According to DGMM (2021), 454.662 irregular migrants were apprehended in 2019 while their numbers went down to 122.302 in 2020 due to the pandemic-related travel restrictions and strict border controls. In addition, migrant workers from diverse countries, especially from Eastern Europe and Central Asia, choose Turkey as a destination country due to wage differentials. In 2019, the total number of work permits given to foreigners reached to 145.232 whereas 27.448 of them came from the Turkic Republics including Uzbekistan (4480) (Yabancıların Çalışma İzinleri, 2019). However, many migrant workers in Turkey find employment in gendered informal sectors.

Against this background, this paper aims to give insights into the impact of COVID-19 on mixed migration flows in Turkey. Available evidence in the world indicate that the pandemic has created a multidimensional crisis for different categories of migrants by affecting their fundamental rights such as protection, employment, health, education, and shelter (Guadagno, 2020). It is crucial for the purposes of this study to assess such impact on different groups of migrants and refugees in Turkey since the legal frameworks and their status predetermine certain privileges and challenges while accessing basic yet life-

---

[56] RTBF (16 April 2020), Situation au centre fermé de Merksplas : Myria demande que des mesures soient prises. Available at: https://www.rtbf.be/info/societe/detail_situation-au-centre-ferme-de-merksplas-myria-demande-que-des-mesures-soient-prises?id=10483832

saving services. Adapting a qualitative method, online and face-to-face in-depth interviews were conducted with Syrians under temporary protection, followed by Afghans a) under international protection, b) irregular migrants; and Uzbek migrant workers. Main research questions were formulated to understand the change in motivations to continue their onward migration journey, resettlement, voluntary return, access to employment, fundamental rights and services, survival strategies and coping mechanisms during the height of the pandemic and under lockdowns. The data collected was then analyzed by thematic analysis through MaxQDA. Referring to mega-risks (Beck, 1992) under the conditions of 'pandemic' uncertainty (Bauman, 2007), we found out – as expected – that the impacts of COVID-19 are dire on the already vulnerable social groups such as refugees and migrants. But it has even more devastating effects on women and irregular migrants, exacerbating existing inequalities not only due to gender, but also due to migrant status. These findings point out that COVID-19 has indirect consequences on social cohesion, mobility and migration management in Turkey.

References

Bauman, Z. (2007). Liquid Times: Living in an Age of Uncertainty. Cambridge: Polity Press.

Beck, U. (1986). Risikogesellschaft: Auf dem Weg in einer andere Moderne. Frankfurt am Main: Subrkamp Verlag.

DGMM. (2021). Irregular Migration. Retrieved from Göç İdaresi Genel Müdürlüğü: https://en.goc.gov.tr/irregular-migration

Guadagno, L. (2020). Migrants and the COVID-19 pandemic: An initial analysis. International Organization for Migration, Migration Research Series, (60).

Nimkar, R. (2018). Split Loyalties: Mixed Migration and the Diaspora Connection. https://mixedmigration.org/wp-content/uploads/2018/05/023_split-loyalties.pdf

T.C. Aile, Çalışma ve Sosyal Hizmetler Bakanlığı, 2020. Yabancıların Çalışma İzinleri. https://ailevecalisma.gov.tr/media/63117/yabanciizin2019.pdf

UNCHR Turkey Stats. (2021). Retrieved from UNHCR Turkey: https://www.unhcr.org/tr/en/unhcr-turkey-stats

Vullnetari, J. (2012). Beyond 'Choice or Force': Roma Mobility in Albania and the Mixed Migration Paradigm. Journal of Ethnic and Migration Studies, 38(8), 1305-1321.

729   Combating Covid-19 Pandemic in 2020 Views and Experiences of the Pakistani Migrant Workers in Saudi Arabia

Muhammad Saeed

Approximately 2.5 million Pakistani migrant workers live on temporary basis in the Kingdom of Saudi Arabia. Nearly 80 percent of these migrant workers hail from the rural areas of Pakistan, semi-skilled with less or no education. Further, their concentration is high in the big cities like the capital city of Riyadh followed by Dammam, Jeddah, Khobar, Jubail, Makkah and Madinah. These migrant workers work in the hard laboring fields such as construction sites and abode in combined housings with 5 to 10 members in a room with shared kitchen and laundry. It has been observed that Pakistani migrant workers in Saudi Arabia least comply with the health and safety regulations of the work. Their non-complying attitude were also observed during the initial period of Covid-19 pandemic in 2020. For example, in the beginning of the Covid-19 pandemic majority of these workers took it less serious and believed in the fake social media propaganda spreading from Pakistan considering Covid-19 as fake news, a conspiracy, less effective and can do nothing to them and therefore ignored the precautionary measures of the health authorities. Consequently, Covid-19 pandemic hit them the most compared to other groups. This article reflects on the views and experiences of the Pakistani workers in their combating of Covid-19 in Saudi Arabia. Data for this article were gathered from 300 workers through FGD and telephonic interviewing. The results show that migrant workers adopted different survival and combating strategies during the Covid-19 pandemic such as restricting the visiting of housing units of other laborers, adhering to the precautionary measures and reducing the number of persons in rooms avoiding sharing of meal, mobilizing the local doctors for raising awareness among the workers and providing online counselling services for the depressed patients, the use of informal laborers' organizations in KSA, voicing to corridors of powers back home, and the use of different social media platforms for the help of needy and suffering workers in term of expatriation, food and reprisal with contractors.

730   A Crisis within a Crisis: The Impacts of the COVID-19 Pandemic on Syrian and Palestinian Refugees in Jordan

Cevdet Acu

The coronavirus 2019 (COVID-19) pandemic, which began in Wuhan, China, in late 2019, has influenced the lives of millions of people, reaching almost every part of the world. Many countries have tightened borders and imposed travel restrictions to reduce the spread of COVID-19. During the coronavirus pandemic, the pithy tagline "we are all in this together", indicating that everyone was equally threatened by the virus and implying that the disease would be defeated through social solidarity, was repeatedly emphasised by governments around the world, international organisations, and the mass media. However, this sentiment has meant nothing to refugees, who were already suffering poor conditions before the coronavirus crisis. Structural inequalities in society have meant that the virus does not threaten everyone equally. The COVID-19 outbreak has affected the lives of huge numbers of people worldwide; personal experiences of the disease have differed drastically. The COVID-19 crisis exacerbates refugees' existing vulnerabilities because they are one of the most marginalised groups in society. Based on ethnographic observations and twenty semi-structured interviews with Syrian and Palestinian refugees in Jordan, the paper discusses to what extent "we are all in this together." The piece explores how the coronavirus restrictions impact Syrian and Palestinian refugees' lives in Jordan and contributes to ongoing debates in the context of structural vulnerability. The research findings show that displaced populations, those living in high-density settlements with reduced access to water, sanitation and limited health services, are especially vulnerable during the coronavirus crisis.

Finally, this piece aims to contribute to the ongoing debates by providing recommendations to response to the current global health crisis for the sake of learning for future health emergencies.

Migration as Art Museum

Stephen Copland

Orhan Pamuk, the Nobel Prize-winning Turkish author, who founded the Museum of Innocence in Istanbul, was a keynote speaker at the 2016 International Council of Museums (ICOM) conference in Milan. He said that in the future we need "small and economical museums that address our humanity". Pamuk suggested that the great national museums "construct a historical narrative of our community as a narrative of faction, nation and state."

He argues that, "In museums we have History, but what we need is stories. In museums we have nations, but what we need is people. We had groups and factions in museums, but what we need is individuals. Concluding that, "We need are small and economical museums that address our humanity."

Migration as Art Museum is an archive of artworks over three decades that aims to "promote social and aesthetic education through art" and provide links with art and the sciences. The Museum programs of migration and heritage education are interdisciplinary with an emphasis of the study of works of art in relation all aspects of all areas of human activity that create society. The innovative social justice education programs are designed around an archive of sculptures, painting, drawing, artist's books, installations, photography, video and prints by artist Australian Stephen Copland.

After decades of conducting international exhibitions and the workshop, Landscape of Heritage and speaking at conferences, I found a location in the village of Conzano, Italy in 2019. The town became famous for having been declared, in 1992, as the symbol of the massive emigration of the people to the northern Queensland, Australia, about 1890-1935. The ancient town square, named Piazza d'Armi (Weapons Square), was renamed Piazza Australia.

The Mayor of Conzano. Emanuele Demaria and local artist Albina Dealessi assisted me to find a suitable building for the Museum given the Immigration context and Australian connections. We purchased the building and despite the pandemic we are continuing our plan to establish the Museum and create heritage links with Ingham, Queensland and internationally.

The film I am presenting made by Italian filmmaker David Celoria visualizes the story of the journey.

Migration as Art Museum aim is to enhance social connectedness and foster connections, which develop links within new and existing global community members. In this way it seeks to encourage personal understandings between new migrants, not so new migrants and members of mainstream communities internationally.

1 First published by the Italian newspaper La Repubblica

Day Five 10 July 2021 14:30-16:00

Special Panel: Türkiye Sınırötesi Kentlerde Göç Hareketliliği ve Kentsel Yaşanabilirlik: Afrin ve İdlib [Turkish]

Chair: Prof. Dr. M. Murat Erdoğan, Türk-Alman Üniversitesi, Turkey

- Doç. Dr. Serhat Erkmen (Jandarma ve Sahil Güvenlik Akademisi, Uluslararası Güvenlik ve Terörizm Ana Bilim Dalı Öğretim Üyesi) **"Güvenlik Perspektifinden İdlib'te Toplumsal Sorunlar"**
- Dr. Öğr. Üyesi Zeynep Banu Dalaman (İstanbul Ayvansaray Üniversitesi Göç Politikaları Araştırma ve Uygulama Merkezi Başkanı) **"Göç Kaynak Ülkesinde IDP (yerinden edilmiş kişiler) Hareketliliği ve Geri Dönüş Koşulları: Afrin"**
- H. Murat Lehimler (Kentsel Gelişim ve Sosyal Araştırmalar Derneği Başkan Yardımcısı, Rumeli Üniversitesi Küresel Politikalar Uygulama ve Araştırma Merkezi Koordinatörü) **"Suriye İç Savaşının Kitlesel Göç Hareketlilikleri Kaynağı Alan Analizi: Kuzey Suriye Analizi"**
- Dr. Gökçe Ok (T.C. İç İşleri Bakanlığı Göç İdaresi Genel Müdür Yardımcısı) **"Göç İdaresi Genel Müdürlüğü'nün Gönüllü Geri Dönüş Politikaları ve Süreçlerine Katkısı"**

END OF THE PROGRAMME

www.migrationconference.net

www.ingramcontent.com/pod-product-compliance
Lightning Source LLC
Chambersburg PA
CBHW070758280326
41934CB00012B/2967